PERSUASIONS
AND
PERFORMANCES

PERSUASIONS AND PERFORMANCES

The Play of Tropes
in Culture

JAMES W. FERNANDEZ

INDIANA UNIVERSITY PRESS • BLOOMINGTON

For Lisa Oyana from the Tinman

No part of this book may be reproduced or utilized in any form or by any means, electronic or mechanical, including photocopying and recording, or by any information storage and retrieval system, without permission in writing from the publisher. The Association of American University Presses' Resolution on Permissions constitutes the only exception to this prohibition.

Manufactured in the United States of America

Library of Congress Cataloging-in-Publication Data

Fernandez, James W.
Persuasions and performances.

Bibliography: p.
1. Symbolism. 2. Rites and ceremonies. 3. Ethnology—Philosophy. 4. Ethnology—Spain. 5. Spain—Social life and customs. I. Title.
GN452.5.F48 1985   306   85-45311
ISBN 0-253-34399-2
ISBN 0-253-20374-0 (pbk.)
1 2 3 4 5 90 89 88 87 86

CONTENTS

INTRODUCTION

> Finally a few examples may be given of cases
> in which the use of descriptive terms for
> certain concepts or the metaphorical use of
> terms has led to peculiar views or
> customs. . . . More convincing are examples
> taken from the use of metaphorical terms in
> poetry, which in rituals are taken literally, and
> are made the basis of certain rites. I am
> inclined to believe, for example, that the
> frequently occurring image of *the devouring of
> wealth* has a close relation to the detailed form
> of the winter ritual among the Indians of the
> North Pacific Coast.
>
> Franz Boas (1911)

Over the last decade and half—since 1970—I have been trying to do an anthropology that is alert to the arguments that lie at the heart of our human experience in culture. In my view, whatever humans are, they are certainly argumentative animals . . . not always shrilly or aggressively so, but surely fundamentally so. It may be the consequence of being a very generalized animal with very little in specific adaptations to specific milieus wired into our brains. As a consequence we are required to invent ways of being—from rules and plans to world views and cosmologies— more or less appropriate to any of the diverse milieus in which we have in- stalled ourselves. We endlessly argue over the appropriateness of those rules, plans, and world views. It may be a consequence of the self-conscious unrequitement implicit in the melancholy fact that, with great frequency, we fail to realize our rules and plans in the world . . . our reach so often exceeds our grasp. We are bound to wonder why this is so and to argue about the reason for this failure. We are a primate that makes promises to ourselves and to others and so often fails or is unable to keep these promises and this generates argument as well:[1] This argument may be what the virtually infinite rationalizing powers of human language have added to the primordial solipsism of our creaturehood . . . which is to say our tendency as social animals to try and maintain ourselves at the center of, or in the right position in, the social world to which we belong and whose roles we have learned to perform with satisfaction. We want to continue performing such roles or, if we are adventurous or disgruntled, finding new roles to perform that will be even more gratifying. This maintenance of satisfying role performance by argumentative means seems to be a fundamental mission in human life—to use the metaphor of the main theoretical piece in this collection (Chapter 2). It is the mission of our argumentative powers, I argue, to preserve our place and our gratifying performances and hence the world in which these things are lodged and to persuade others to recognize that place, that performance, and that world.

Now arguments can be conducted in various ways. In the academy we are most concerned with—indeed, are practitioners of—formal argument . . . argument that follows logical constraints and is syllogistic in its progressions. It is an argument that is most often about how domains are organized within themselves, as it were. But there is another more fundamental argument in my view and that is figurative argument—or the argument of images, as we call it here. This is a popular style of argument in which quite differing domains are brought together in unexpected and creative ways. The assertion of a metaphoric comparison is a prime form of that argument. But it is not the only one. For the predication of one domain of experience upon another is of many kinds. It is diversified by all the variety in the play of tropes. This collection of articles is really about that kind of argument and that kind of play as I have experienced it in fieldwork. That is, each of these essays addresses itself to such problems, each from rather different perspectives.

It is appropriate that this collection begin with the article—published in *Daedalus*—in which I first argued the position that I have briefly outlined above. It is appropriate that that article also give its title to this collection. This *Daedalus* piece was very shortly followed by an attempt at fuller and more persuasive theoretical treatment of the subject matter. It took two closely related forms: an article in *Current Anthropology* on the "Mission of Metaphor in Expressive Culture" and a subsequent article on "The Performance of Ritual Metaphors" published in a book edited by my colleagues David Sapir and Christopher Crocker and called *The Social Use of Metaphor.* I have placed the first version of this theoretical statement as the second chapter here (in Section One, *Persuasions*) despite its rather technical nature. All the subsequent articles in the second section *(Per-*

formances) of this collection are expository and not technical attempts to examine and clarify the various ideas put forth in these first two articles. These subsequent articles, therefore, *are* performances not only in the sense that they examine instances of human performance in terms of the play of tropes but that they are themselves performances . . . they take the set of ideas involved in the perspective being argued here as guides to that most challenging performance which confronts anthropology, the interpretation of field data. Anthropologists, too, are performers in their *sotto voce* way. At the same time the series of articles taken together constitute a more comprehensive and expanded statement of my position on these issues of the place of figurative argument in human interaction—as they provide, perhaps, a more illuminating and comprehensible statement than concentrated technical discussion.

Let me emphasize that I, as a participant observer in and upon dynamic human situations, am more interested in what tropes do than in what they are in any formal analytic sense. Here also lies the primacy of the series of essays as against the technical statement, for they all contain and seek to be grounded in "revelatory incidents," events where tropes are actually at play and where images are actually argued by, I hope, recognizable human agents, and where the figurative actually does something to these human agents, to their relationship with others, and to their relation to their world as the figurative helps them define that relationship and that world.

To argue that I am more interested in what the tropes do in human situations than in what they are in a formal analytic sense may be to say nothing more than that I am an anthropologist and not a philosopher—a student of behavior and not a logician. The emphasis in anthropology, after all is upon "being there" and not upon ultimate being. In my view anthropology is essentially a pragmatic and not a platonic or idealist enterprise. It is the kind of study primarily concerned with how humans in real situations get things done such as living together with some sense of fulfillment and satisfaction; mastering an environment, providing food, clothing, and shelter; creating some sense of ultimate meaning to life as well as some sense of humor; bringing up the next generation. My own particular concern here has been in how humans—those I have lived with over extended periods—construct, given their problems, identities through the argument of images and the play of tropes. Constructing identities is something that humans get done all the time. To be human is to have, to one degree or another, a problem of identity for it is to have, sooner or later, a gnawing sense of uncertainty—what I call here "the inchoate"—which lies at the heart of the human condition and which energizes the search for identity through predications. "Dubito ergo sum!"

It should not be argued, however, that formal argument is irrelevant to our considerations here. First, there is a certain amount of formal argument in this collection of essays and especially in the first section. It is important for anthropologists interested in the role of the tropes in behavioral dynamics to have some sense of the long history of discussion on this issue in philosophy from the Sophists and Aristotle through Quintilian to the present. Such a sense is given to us, for example, by Samuel Levin in a book[2] otherwise devoted to formal analysis of the feature transfers that take place between the poles of metaphoric predication. Such historical perspective and such formal analysis can give us a better sense of our problems if only that be a sense of the distance that separates the multiplex world of ethnography from the carefully delimited world of formal analysis. Most recently Lakoff and Johnson[3] have given us a cognitive analysis of the system of metaphoric predications that underlie not only everyday experience but philosophy itself. Their quite formal approach is important to anthropology because it is—as is anthropology—experiential in orientation. That is, these authors seek to show us how our experience of the world, including our experience of formal argument, rests upon choices of metaphor. And they seek to show how these choices are integrated into a system by the logic of implication. They thus suggest ways to understand our experience of cultures and of the integration of cultures. One employs the plural here because what is most anthropologically interesting in their argument is the possibility for comparative research into the variation in systems of integration that it implies. Comparative research, to be sure, is central to anthropological inquiry and it is to be noted that the essays collected here assume interesting and important differences as regards central tropes and trope inventories as we move from culture to culture.

One main difference between the philosophic and anthropological approach, perhaps, lies in the examples chosen for discussion . . . the kind of experiences that animate discussion. Almost always philosophic discussion is based on a very limited corpus of illustrative items such as, in respect to tropes; "the stone died," "the lily smiled," "that is a shallow argument," or "you are wasting my time." These items are then subject to intense formal analysis. In fact they are chosen for their aptness to the

analytic task at hand. While inevitably there is some of this in anthropology as well, I would argue that anthropology begins with those
"revelatory incidents" which we have mentioned . . . those especially
charged moments in human relationships which are pregnant with meaning. As a consequence of long-term participant observation, of "being
there," an anthropologist is likely to be present at a number of these very
real events. It is our task to describe them as accurately as possible and
then, placing them in their multiple contexts, to tease out their multiple
meanings. One emphasizes and repeats the word "multiple" because such
events are inevitably multi-vocal and over-determined. That is what gives
them their force and salience. Thus the reader will discover that the
discussion in these various chapters arises out of such events (sometimes
involving the ethnographer directly): an exchange of insults between
government officials, a children's game and associated comment in a
village plaza, a song sung in a bar, a verse recited by one group of miners
to another, an amusing bus ride, a frustrating visit to the Prado Museum,
a challenge to the use of a research protocol by young villagers, directions
given to young mountaineers on a high ridge in a snowstorm, a shift into
dialect at a street corner bus stop, ironic comments directed at a socialist
mayor just before a street parade.

On the one hand, these "revelatory incidents" are not such highly
charged moments as, let us say, a bar fight or someone being run over in
the road, much less a riot. On the other hand, they are not so frequent in
the flow of everyday life as to be easily noted by any tourist. And in any
event the awareness of them and their significance is the fruit of participation over the long term in a culture. It is only such participation that
enables us to give these moments of a sudden constellation of significances
an adequate reading. I regard these moments as a prime source of insight
in fieldwork . . . an opportunity to relate events to the structures we
otherwise spend much of our time studying in the field. And it also ought
to be said that being present at a "revelatory incident" is one of the
attractive aspects of fieldwork . . . something that makes it, despite the
discomforts that often enough accompany it, and its many other challenges, ultimately rewarding.

The "revelatory incidents" are most often colloquial in at least two
senses of that word. First, they involve dialogue between members of a
culture who differ from each other in generation or sex or class or
occupation. Second, they often contain colloquialisms, which is to say the
kind of pithy figurative expression which is the restricted code[4] but

evocative speech of everyday life. This figurative expression—these colloquialisms—are full of images. They argue with images and they play with
tropes, and that accounts in important part for their revelatory character.
Such speech will be a main object of our interest here. But to make the
colloquial the object of our interest, it ought to be further remarked, is not
to create a special interest within anthropology. Indeed I would argue that
colloquy—referring first to the dialogue between anthropologist and informant and subsequently to all the other revelatory dialogues that are going
on around us in the field and to which our participation makes us attentive—lies at the center of our practice in this discipline.

While the succession of articles must argue in their way and in more
detail the perspective on our human nature and comportment here taken,
let me bring one more point to the reader's attention. This collection of
essays presumes, although the point will not be argued in detail, that
humans organize their social worlds into domains of belonging and that a
great deal of human life is spent in maintaining, arranging, or rearranging
these domains. In one sense this is to say nothing more than that we are
conceptualizing animals constantly engaged in concept formation and
reformation. For concept formation is the formation of "domains of belonging." Much fruitful effort has been expended in that branch of our
discipline known as cognitive anthropology in explaining the way that
these domains of knowledge, say of the plant world or of diseases, are
organized. We have had many good studies of cultural systems of classification.

The idea of "domains of belonging," however, has another Durkheimian
sense of more relevance to us here. It is a concept having to do not so
much with our intellectual organization of the world as with social dynamics and the aggregation and disaggregation of groups. As Durkheim argued, behind some of our most august intellectual achievements—our
most persuasive concepts—lies the reality of human social life. That
reality we argue here is the dynamic of "domains of belonging." One
emphasizes further the word "dynamic" because of the constant flux in
human social life vis-à-vis "domains of belonging." It is my view that the
study of the "play of tropes" is one important way to help us to understand
that dynamic. For the "play of tropes" is essentially a play of mind within
domains (by metonym principally) and between domains (by metaphor
principally). It is a play of mind that emerges out of our sense of the
world's predominant classifications and collections of significant beings—
the predominant "domains of belonging"—while it also affects these

classifications and collections. Likewise, it is a play of mind that is energized by social situations even as it is influential in shaping them.

Because I sought for coherence in the developing argument these articles make, I have followed the sequence of their publication. I was first of all interested in figurative predication as accomplishing the "movements" of social subjects in culture conceived of as a quality space. It is an elementary way of conceiving of "domains of belonging," as it is an elementary image of argument. The three chapters that appear after the opening section on "Persuasions and Performances" and "The Mission of Metaphor" are all concerned with this figurative movement: "Poetry in Motion," "Syllogisms of Association," and "Lexical Fields." On the face of it the argument that metaphoric predication moves social subjects around in a figurative quality space seems simple enough. But it will be seen in reading through these three chapters that the notion of quality space is in itself too simple and that the problem of imagistic argument—the predication of identity—faces a number of complexities, which is to say the paradoxes that lie at the heart of the human condition. Chapters 6, 7, and 8—"Reflections on Looking into Mirrors," "Edification by Puzzlement," and "The Dark at the Bottom of the Stairs"—focus upon these complexities and paradoxes in our behavior which yet, however, can have edifying consequences. We try in these chapters to get a look at, if not to grasp, the inchoate—the dark at the bottom of the stairs—which lies at the center of human experience. It is a source of so many impulses, above all, the impulse to find identity in domains other than those we actually occupy. For, however inchoate our condition, we are bound to try and transcend it. It is that transcendence, that "return to the whole," that I examine in the final three chapters of this collection: "Returning to the Whole," "Moving up in the World," and "Convivial Attitudes."

All this may seem sui generis to a fault, preoccupied as I am here with the progression of this decade-long argument. Let me hasten to say that though I bring together ideas in my particular way I cannot claim any ultimate originality. The importance of the figurative imagination in behavior has been long argued in the kind of cultural anthropology I practice—in the work of Paul Radin, A. L. Kroeber, and Ruth Benedict in particular—and I put this old quote from Boas in the epigraph to remind us of this precedence. Kenneth Burke, who argued many of these points in his precocious and tantalizing oeuvre, was an important influence in my undergraduate days, as were G. H. Mead and Claude Lévi-Strauss in graduate school. No one working the anthropology of the last two decades can have failed to benefit from the work—the social symbology—of the late Victor Turner and the virtuoso cultural interpretations of Clifford Geertz. It was by the invitation of the latter that the first article in this book and the first article of this argument was published. I have also had the good luck of colleagues with similar interests whose work has stimulated my own: the late Robert Plant Armstrong, Keith Basso, T. O. Beidelman, Carmelo Lisón, Ivan Karp, Shelly and Renato Rosaldo, David Sapir, and Peter Seitel. I am grateful to the various institutions that sponsored the talks or papers that resulted in most of these chapters: the Advisory Committee on Myth. Symbol, and Culture of the American Academy of Arts and Sciences; the departments of anthropology at Indiana, Illinois, Pennsylvania, Madrid, McGill, Minnesota, Cornell, and UCLA; the New York Academy of Sciences (anthropology section); the American Anthropology Association; and the American Ethnological Society. The Institute of Advanced Study at Princeton in its two year-long seminars of 1975–76 and 1981–82 oriented to symbolic anthropology provided a challenging arena for the presentation of some of these ideas. My fellowship year, 1982–83, at the Center for Advanced Study in the Behavioral Sciences, Stanford, was a particular boon. Whatever identity these articles may seem to predicate upon me, since I authored and signed them, cannot ignore the collegial and institutional milieus in which they arose and which made them, insofar as is possible for this pro-tem author of more enduring ideas, more useful and clear-headed. I am grateful.

Let me make one final set of anthropological observations as to the ground from which these articles have arisen, the field locales from which these arguments derive. I started my career in anthropology as an Africanist working on revitalization movements in Africa in which peoples were in such ultimate circumstances as to desperately need to predicate new identities upon themselves. I have worked in several parts of Africa, but principally in western Equatorial Africa (Gabon, among the Fang), southeast Africa (Natal, among the Zulu), and West Africa (Ghana, Togo and Dahomey among Ewe and Fon). In recent years I have worked in the Cantabrian mountains and the Peaks of Europe among Asturian cattle keepers and miners. I am still interested in problems of vitalization and devitalization, and how these mountain peoples maintain and energize their identities as the first of these lifeways gives way to the second.

Materials from the various parts of Africa and from the mountains of northern Spain, in any event, are the ground upon which these chapters are based. In practically all this work my wife, Renate Lellep, has been a collegial and sustaining presence. If I had not worked these many years among these various peoples I would surely not have written any of these articles. For they are all attempts on my part to puzzle out what I came to believe was fundamentally at play in these societies. My an-trope-ology would not exist without their kindness and tolerance and patience in admitting me among them. To them also I am grateful.

Notes

1. See the general argument about the conditions of human evolution in Peter J. Wilson, *Man: The Promising Primate,* 2nd. ed. (New Haven: Yale University Press, 1983).

2. Samuel R. Levin, *The Semantics of Metaphor* (Baltimore: The Johns Hopkins University Press, 1977).

3. George Lakoff and Mark Johnson, "Conceptual Metaphors in Everyday Language", *The Journal of Philosophy* Vol. LXVII, No. 8, August 1980, pp. 453–486.

4. The term is Basil Bernstein's; Chapter 7, "A Socio-linguistic approach to social learning", in *Class, Codes and Control* Vol. 1, Theoretical Studies Towards a Sociology of Language (London: Routledge and Kegan Paul, 1978).

ACKNOWLEDGMENTS

PERMISSION TO REPRINT THE ARTICLES BELOW WAS GRANTED BY THEIR ORIGINAL PUBLISHERS:

"Persuasions and Performances: Of the Beast in Every Body and the Metaphors of Everyman," *Daedalus*, Vol. 101, No. 1, winter 1972, pp. 39–60. Reprinted by permission of *Daedalus*, Journal of the American Academy of Arts and Sciences, Boston.

"The Mission of Metaphor in Expressive Culture," *Current Anthropology*, Vol. 15, No. 2, June 1974, pp. 119–145.

"Poetry in Motion: Being Moved by Amusement, Mockery, and Mortality in the Asturian Mountains," New Literary History, Vol. VIII, 1976–77, pp. 459–483.

"Syllogisms of Association: Some Modern Extensions of Asturian Deepsong," in *Folklore in the Modern World*, R. Dorson, ed., pp. 183–206. The Hague: Mouton, 1979.

"Some Reflections on Looking into Mirrors," *Semiotica*, Vol. 30, Nos. 1 and 2 (1980), pp. 27–39.

"Edification by Puzzlement," in *Explorations in African Systems of Thought*, Ivan Karp and Charles S. Bird, eds., pp. 44–59. Bloomington: Indiana University Press, 1980.

"Returning to the Whole," *The Anthropology of Experience*, Victor Turner and Edward Bruner, eds., Urbana-Champaign: University of Illinois Press, 1985.

"The Dark at the Bottom of the Stairs: The Inchoate in Symbolic Inquiry and Some Strategies for Coping with It," in *On Symbols in Anthropology: Essays in Honor of Harry Hoijer—1980*. Malibu, Calif.: Udena, 1982.

"Moving up in the World: Transcendence in Symbolic Anthropology," *Stanford Literature Review* 1, no. 2 (Saratoga, Calif.: Anma Libri, 1984), pp. 201–226.

"Convivial Attitudes: A Northern Spanish Kayak Festival in Its Historical Moment," reprinted from *Text, Play, and Story: 1983 Proceedings of the American Ethnological Society*, pp. 199–229. Washington, D.C., 1984.

I would like to acknowledge the support of the National Science Foundation, the Fulbright Commission, and the Spanish-North American Joint Committee in this research.

Part I
PERSUASIONS

1

PERSUASIONS AND PERFORMANCES

OF THE BEAST IN EVERY BODY AND
THE METAPHORS OF EVERYMAN

He who only cricket knows,
knows not cricket.

C. L. R. James, *Beyond a Boundary*

Anybody who learns to become a crow can
see it . . . it is possible to become a lion or
a bear but that is rather dangerous . . . it
takes too much energy to become one.

Don Juan in Castaneda, *The Teachings
of Don Juan*

A Cattle Complex

I am situated as I write this between cows and rodents. At night the
rodents rustle and gnaw in the attic while the cows and calves periodically
shift their weight, stomp, and sigh heavily in the stable below. During the
day the cattle are driven out and up to the pastures and the rats descend to
their nests in the stable. The house is left to us and occasionally, to a
donkey who brays at being left in the stable during the day.

These animals have become very much a part of our world, although I
cannot pretend they mean as much to me as to the Asturian mountain
countrymen with whom we are living. We have been in these green
mountains a bare two months and little yet can be said with confidence.
Asturias is another part of Spain, green and lush, covered most often with
celtic mists and clouds off the Cantabrian sea. It has scarcely a month of

3

sunny weather a year. These mists evaporate on the high passes and divides—*los puertos*—that open out upon the Castilian plateau, brown and sere already with its summer burnt look under the Sahara sun.

The cattle in the summer are driven up to those *puertos* and hence they and those that go and live with them up in the *caseríos* have more of the benefit of the sun. Men turn brown up in the *puertos* but the immaculate tan cow of Asturias, the *casina*, grazing back and forth between *sol* and *sombra*, retains her placid and reflective character. There is nothing in these cows of the *vaca brava*—the brave black bulls of Salamanca or Andalusia. In fact one sees very few bulls at all. Heifers are carefully tended and brought to maturity for milk and progeny but *novillos* are butchered early for veal. Artificial insemination has been accepted everywhere.

Cows and calves have an enormous weight in village life. They are a constant topic of conversation. When one is shown the family pictures, photos of cows and calves are as likely to tumble out amidst the shuffle. And a family given a picture taken five years earlier of the father and baby posing before a cow team pulling a hay cart spent most of an excited half hour remembering those cows with nostalagia. I don't know all there is to walking cows from the stable through the streets and up to the pastures. But there is a satisfaction in it for men and women that makes them highly resistant to government efforts to consolidate their scattered meadows— their stubborn *minifundia*. For if they were consolidated one would no longer walk one's cows about one's wide world. In part, of course, one is parading one's fortune. A good milk cow is worth several months' wages and a herd of fifteen is a sizable nest egg—to mix our metaphors.

The love of calves equals the *cariño* for young children. Both loves are very great and volubly expressed and in the closest association. The urban middle class deplores the villagers' attitude toward education. "They raise them like calves that they should be strong and fecund, capable of climbing to the *puertos* in the summer and with enough fat to survive the winter." As for boys beyond five they are more likely to be treated as *quajes, rapaces*—fractious, superfluous elements in the society who serve principally to get into trouble, break things, soil clothes, interrupt their sisters who are working hard at various tasks. Girls grow up usefully to produce in their time more of the milk of human kindness and the babies upon which it can be lavished. This cattle complex has something to do with the quite central place of women in this society, and perhaps even with the cult of the Virgin.

Asturian mountain character, formed by mists and the encirclement of the sierra and the following-after of cows, is unhurried, contemplative. it is austere, even dour, when compared with the ebullience of the Andaluz or the briskness of the Castilian. But if one is tempted to say that it is cowed by this round of life and the celtic twilight in which it develops, then one forgets that this is the only part of Spain never fully under Roman control, never conquered by the Moors—a rebellious outpost of Carlism in the last century and, in this century—in the militant collectivity of its miners—a turbulent challenge to many succeeding regimes including the present one.

One remembers that there are other animals men study to situate themselves. There are the bears in the forests whose demise in hand-to-hand conflict with the many folk heroes is celebrated in tale after tale. Of the donkey there is not much to be said. Other parts of Spain seem to be in greater communion with its qualities as was Jiménez with Platero. Donkeys carry no names here—only wood, hay, manure, and blows. But of course, there are the rats whose furtive life is contrary to right nature. They come up at night and go down in the day and they are never to be seen. Women say to children, "If you don't eat your food or keep yourself clean we will put you into the attic tonight and the rats will eat you," as they eat anything that is carelessly left around and not well formed, well disciplined, or well seen. And when one is very hungry one says, "The rats are running around in the drawer," in chagrin that the stomach should have gotten so empty and oneself so careless as to be taken over by that furtive animal nature. It is not well formed or well seen to admit to hunger or to accept food, like rats, in any house other than one's own.

A cow in short is everything a rat is not, and men are wise to draw the appropriate lessons that each nature has to teach. Men can be and are, through the diverse powers of culture, many things. Their choices are manifold. If they can look around and find some lesson in cows and calves, bears and rats, their choices are made easier.

The Study of Metaphor

This is as far as I can presently take the reader into the preoccupation with animals in the Asturian mountains—a paleolithic preoccupation, after all, throughout Franco-Cantabrian country. It seems apparent to me that the intimate contact these villagers have with these animals has an impact upon them. In a sense, those we domesticate have domesticated us and those we have not domesticated are still useful in measuring the achievement or excesses of our domestication. If life becomes too much a following about of cows, men may be excused for turning a bit bearish.

What all this points to, it seems to me, is the importance of the analysis of metaphors in anthropological inquiry. In fact, the analysis of metaphor seems to me to be the very nature of that inquiry. One always feels a bit sheepish of course about bringing the metaphor concept into the social sciences and perhaps this is because one always feels there is something soft and woolly about it. Yet one recognizes that the finest anthropological field studies[1] have been highly sensitive to figures of speech of all kinds and surely to metaphor. As one of our epigraphs reminds us, the anthropological literature on religion and folklore is full of those shape shiftings and possessions which constitute in most dramatic form the assumption of a metaphoric identity. And even behaviorists recognize that metaphor is one of the few devices we have for leaping beyond the essential privacy of the experiential process.[2]

Indeed, metaphors jump out at us from every side in human behavior. As S. E. Asch has said, if we but reflect on it we find like Molière's character "we have been speaking metaphor all of our lives!"[3] In November of 1970 the American press gave front-page coverage to the director of the Federal Bureau of Investigation. He called the former Attorney General a jellyfish. The Attorney General had criticized the director for imposing upon the bureau a preoccupation with the director's own image and for giving the bureau an ideological character.

Perhaps this was mere petulance. If so, the somber work of Herman Kahn may be more telling. In a book entitled *On Escalation: Metaphors and Scenarios* (1965), Kahn takes two metaphors as models of international relations: that of the strike, on the one hand, in which both parties though antagonistic recognize mutual need, and that of the teenage game of chicken, on the other, in which both parties are concerned to establish their manly (or at least nonchicken) identity. In part Kahn takes these metaphors as analytic models to aid his understanding, but at the same time these metaphors can be adopted by actors. They can lead to performance and create a scenario. I will argue here that the metaphoric assertions men make about themselves or about others influence their behavior. Such assertions make manageable objects of the self or of others and facilitate performance. In respect to behavior such assertions—you are a chicken, I am not a chicken, you are a hawk or a dove or a rat or a donkey—provide images in relation to which the organization of behavior can take place. We can call them organizing or performative metaphors. I am going to define the uses of several kinds of metaphor, persuasive or colocative metaphor in the first place, and performative or organizing metaphor in the second. I am then going to ask how these metaphors operate in respect to culture conceived of as a "quality space."

Resistance to the study of metaphor arises for several reasons. One reason is that structural analysis in linguistics has made so important an impact on anthropological analysis. The burden of this influence rests upon the study of the discriminations and contrasts by means of which intellectual structures (paradigms and taxonomies) are built up. But a good reason for studying metaphoric assertion is that it is a way of avoiding building up precise intellectual structures. It is so congenial a thought style to many of the third world peoples anthropologists have studied because it has the profundity of a concrete immediacy. Many of these people incline to rhetorical devices of representation—iconic and enactive rather than symbolic forms of representation.[4] They incline toward assessment by analogy. Our subtle analyses of the discriminations they make within various domains of their experience is matched by their subtlety in linking these domains in unexpected and creative ways.

If we have much to learn from painstaking dissections of our informants' kinship terminology, diseases, or firewood lexicon, we can also learn from their powers of extension and synthesis. More is involved in the games people play than the rules and boundaries by which they play them. Our epigraphs from the Trinidadian, James, and the Yaqui, Juan, remind us of that. We have only to consider the popularity of proverbs and riddles in many parts of the world—a genre which rests in large measure upon leaping to metaphoric similarities between two distinct domains of experience.

Another reason for resistance to the study of metaphor arises from the fact that metaphor has so much to do with feelings. Such obscure matters have quite naturally provoked the distrust of social scientists. J. Piaget in his essay on structuralism[5] strongly supports C. Lévi-Strauss's "penetrating critique of explanations in terms of affectivity," and lauds his axiom[6] that that which is refractory to explanation cannot ipso facto serve as explanation.

One may well wish to create explanations by preventing what is refractory from intruding, but to deny its existence and importance is another matter. Emotions in human affairs may easily, and regrettably, outweigh the influence of logical structures. And those who want to write their ethnologies where they conceive the action to be, in the midst of affectivity and the conditioning of the emotions, are entitled to our attention. It is too easy to say that they are soft. In any case a false dichotomy can too easily prevail. Might not there be a structure to sentiment?

In respect to affectivity Robert P. Armstrong[7] has recently given us a revelatory anthropological essay which seeks to dwell in the very center of what he calls "the affecting presence." He uses metaphor as a central term of analysis. His discussion of metaphor is essentially contemplative, as one would expect in an essay written from the aesthetic point of view. That is to say, Armstrong assumes the enduring status of the objects and events he studies as expressions of existing (universal or cultural) feeling states. But the student of behavior wants to know what metaphors do, where they come from, and how they emerge. How do they work in human affairs? To use Armstrong's own vocabulary: in the "affecting transaction" what emotions are transferred and how is this done? Perhaps metaphors are not alone arresting repositories of feelings. Perhaps they can be strategies taken in respect to feelings.

Metaphoric Strategies

Though I cannot do justice to all these questions I should like to approach them by defining metaphor simply as "a strategic predication upon an inchoate pronoun (an I, a you, a we, a they) which makes a movement and leads to performance." More can be said about metaphor than that, but it should carry us a little distance. There is nothing new in regarding a metaphor as a strategy. The notion is present throughout the work of Kenneth Burke[8] and is expressed in his well-known definition of a proverb as a "strategy for dealing with a situation."[9] Since a proverb, as we have said, rests upon a metaphoric sense of similarity between two domains of experience, Burke's definition applies equally to metaphor. A proverb in its way is, like the metaphors I will discuss, a predication upon an inchoate situation. It says that something much more concrete and graspable—a rolling stone, a bird in the hand—is equivalent to the essential elements in another situation we have difficulty in grasping.

The strategic element in metaphor glares at us from this contretemps we have reviewed between the Attorney General and the director of the FBI. Obviously the director intended a put-down. It became the Attorney General's lot to put up or shut up. Already the reader will see that the language we both speak shows us a continuum: a continuum of ups and downs. As it happened, the Attorney General responded in balanced prose about the ideological conformity imposed upon the FBI and the director's preoccupation with his self-image. It is difficult to remember what he said, though the director's salty metaphor still sticks.

The Attorney General had various options. He could put up by staying in the same metaphoric domain. He might have responded, in turn, that the director was a walrus, or more sharply a shark, or a Portuguese man-of-war, or an octopus—"a thousand tentacled octopus releasing the ink of ideological obfuscation over the land." Or the Attorney General might have shifted to another domain, the familiar gastrointestinal one. Here the opportunities are rich. Perhaps the director thought of himself as a man of heart or real guts. The Attorney General could put him down by referring to him as an old flatus. That would have deflated him!

Of course people do not simply jump into a strategic posture willy-nilly. They do occupy positions, by force of their social condition and the fate of physiology, both in their own estimation and the estimation of others. Everyone knows where the director stands and has stood foursquare for fifty years. If we had not followed his pronouncements over that time as he has admirably constructed his agency brick by brick we might gather it from his concentrated boxer's gaze—his bulldog jaw. As for the Attorney General, who built nothing but occupied an existing edifice of office with compassion and intelligence, we see something of his position in his long bloodhound's face, his aristocratic nose, his troubled eyes. These are prepossessing men and to some extent are prepositioned—prepostured as are we all. We see that the bulldog who knows throughout his fiber the mass and power of his opponent must be impatient with the bloodhound who does not really know his opponent except as traces in the air to be followed with uncertainty amidst a multititude of other stimuli. The bloodhound lives in a much more complicated world than the bulldog, but the bulldog has reason to believe that his is the more real.

We will assume that metaphoric strategies involve the placing of self and other pronouns on continua. The salient continuum here chosen by the director to confirm his position is the hard-soft one which is omnipresent in American life, as far as men are concerned. The first strategy of

anyone who puts forth a metaphor in predication about a pronoun is to
pick a domain of equivalence whose members have some apt shock value
when applied to a pronoun and give perspective by incongruity. Almost
any domain will do if people know enough about it and the strategist is
ingenious.

The strategy is to make it appear that the incumbent occupies a desirable or undesirable place in the continuum of whatever domain has been
chosen. As Aristotle says, "To adorn, borrow metaphor from things superior, to disparage, borrow from things inferior." And while metaphors may
be put forth in an honest attempt to assess the position the pronoun
actually occupies as a consequence of its physical and social condition, we
are generally inspired to metaphor for purposes of adornment or disparagement. If a pronoun inspires predication we generally want to move
it about on the continuum. We want to put down or put up.

The second strategy belongs to the subject upon whom a metaphor has
been predicated. If he does not accept the way he has been moved, he
may choose to reorient the continuum. Reorientation is obtained first by
finding members of the domain relatively less desirable and more op-
probrious than the metaphor with which you are saddled: for jellyfish
return octopus. Better a jellyfish than an octopus if one must dwell in the
sea. For the one floats blithely upon its surface and the other is sinister
and sunk in its tangled depths. We see here, incidentally, a complexity in
metaphor which we should not deny though we will for the main part
ignore it. A number of continua may be involved in any metaphoric
predication. In the above example we have hard and soft, light and dark,
above and below, grasping and relaxing. The continua may be so melded
as to be indistinguishable, or they may be in an interesting state of
tension.

Reorientation is obtained secondly by suggesting an alternative metaphor better placed on the continuum or continua. If a hawk calls you a
dove, you suggest rather owl. Reorientation is obtained thirdly not by
finding even more undesirable members of the domain or by offering an
alternative metaphor but by giving a positive interpretation to what is
ostensibly undesirable. If you are made out to be a bleeding heart on the
corporeal continuum you return numbskull. For there is, after all, nothing
intrinsically good about the end of any continuum. No culture is so
unambiguous about its choices that a clever man cannot turn a continuum
to his advantage. In a culture that lauds whiteness there is yet an attrac-

tion and an energy to blackness. In a competitive culture the last shall yet be first.

The final strategy in this enterprise of metaphoric placement is to change the venue. One simply chooses to pass beyond a boundary and as a consequence, it is another ball game. If one is disadvantaged in the domain of sea creatures, one shifts to the domain of corporeality and a desirable position in the gastrointestinal continuum.

The Quality of Cultural Space

In the intellectual sense the movement accomplished by these metaphors is from the inchoate in the pronomial subject to the concrete in the predicate. These are basic if not kernel predications in social life which enable us to escape the privacy of experience. For what is more inchoate and in need of a concrete predication than a pronoun! Personal experience and social life cries out to us, to me, to you, to predicate some identity upon "others" and "selves." We need to become objects to ourselves, and others need to become objects to us as well. At the earliest moment our infants receive metaphoric attributions: they become sweet peas, tigers, little bears, kittens, little fish. How often those earliest objects are animals. And how inclined we are to comb the world for cunning animals to surround our children with. Is it that without them we feel helpless to give definition to the infantile inchoate? For millennia of course we have been in the most intimate contact with animals who have provided us with just such reference points in our quest for identity. But intellectual concretization is not the movement we are really interested in.

Let us say of George that he is a lobster. Men, faced with the inchoate pronoun, always have hard alternatives. Most reasonably we can appeal for clarification to the customary domains to which the subject belongs and offer a predication by superordination or subordination within that domain. Of George we say: he is a teller, he is a banker, he is a businessman, he is a Harvard alumnus, he is a father, he is an adult, he is a *Homo sapiens*, he is anthropoid, he is a vertebrate, and so on. Of course men belong to a number of domains and hence in qualifying the inchoate pronoun we must choose one domain or another: the domain of business activity, of educational activity, of domestic activity, of phylogenetic classification. We can combine domains but that always makes for problems—if not for us, surely for George. He is an ivy league anthropoid, or a businesslike father.

But to say of George that he is a lobster is to learn something very different about him. For it is to follow a different kind of logic in defining George than the logic of superordination or subordination within customary domains. George is not really an arthropod. He really has, logically, more backbone than that. But in a deeper sense perhaps he does not. Perhaps he is a scuttling, snappish, popeyed, soft-centered, rigidly defensive creature. It is true that the mind by abstractions can integrate all its experiences. Thus, at a very high level of abstraction both George and lobster are members of the same domain. They are both metazoans. But for all practical purposes we see how metaphor accomplishes an unaccustomed linking of domains.

The shift in feeling tone—of adornment and disparagement—is also most always present and may be the dominant impulse to metaphor. Every metaphor has its mood which has motivated its employment and is perhaps a major part of the satisfaction of having employed it. Metaphor is, like synesthesia, the translation of experience from one domain into another by virtue of a common factor which can be generalized between the experiences in the two domains. These generalizable factors can be of a variety, but there are two main kinds: structural and textual.[10] In the case of structural metaphor the translation between realms is based on some isomorphism of structure or similarity of relationship of parts. By textual metaphor we mean an assimilation made on the basis of similarity in feeling tone. Thus in synesthesia when we speak of music being hot we are moving from one domain of experience, that of sound, to another, that of temperature. The Law of Parallel Alignment prevails. That is, in the domain of sound the rapid beat of jazz music has a parallel intensity on the scale of fast to slow to that on the temperature scale of hot to cold. Somehow that which is hot feels like that which is rapid in tempo.

The metaphors in which we are interested make a movement. They take their subjects and move them along a dimension or a set of dimensions. They are not satisfied with parallel alignment, if indeed that were possible, given the inchoate nature of the pronominal subject. The Attorney General is really not as soft as a jellyfish, but the strategist hopes that saying it will move him and make it so in the eyes of others. On the continuum of purposiveness in the domain of sea creatures, the Attorney General is, perhaps, *really* a porpoise. The strategy is to make him out a jellyfish.

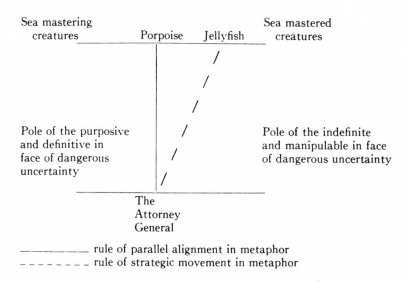

Sea mastering   Sea mastered
   creatures   Porpoise Jellyfish   creatures

Pole of the purposive   Pole of the indefinite
and definitive in   and manipulable in face
face of dangerous   of dangerous uncertainty
uncertainty

              The
              Attorney
              General

——————— rule of parallel alignment in metaphor
– – – – – – – rule of strategic movement in metaphor

Behind this discussion, as the reader will have perceived, lies a top-ographic model of society and culture. I am inordinately attracted to it, but it may be useful. Culture from this view is a quality space of "n" dimensions or continua, and society is a movement about of pronouns within this space. Of course, pronouns move about by many means of locomotion, but the metaphoric assertion of identity by the linking of domains is one important way.

Since it is so difficult to think of a space as defined by "n" dimensions, we may have a Euclidean space by taking, for illustrative purposes, Charles E. Osgood's semantic space.[11] This space is defined by the three dimensions of goodness, potency, and activity. The meaning that Osgood's method explores and plots in semantic space is connotation—the feelings held about various concepts. Similarly, the topographic model proposed here would suggest that in cultural life pronouns come to possess appro-priate or inappropriate feelings of potency, activity, and goodness attached to them. Language has devices of representation at its disposal, mainly metaphor, by which pronouns can be moved about—into better or worse position—in quality space. Social life from the perspective of this model is the set of those transactions by which pronouns, the foci of identity, change their feeling tone—the sense of potency, activity, and goodness attached to them.

Lest our discussion evolve into an *idée fixe* we had best remind our-selves that metaphors can serve a variety of functions: informative, expressive, declarative, directive, and so forth. I do not pretend that what I want to say about metaphor here encompasses all these uses. The point is that there is an important social use of metaphor involving the occupancy of various continua which in sum constitute a cultural quality space. Persuasive metaphors situate us and others with whom we interact in that space.

Some Fang Metaphors of Debate and Supplication

If we have spent some time here among cattle and rodents and with the implications of an acrimonious exchange that arose between two government officials, it is only because what that husbandry and that politics teaches us is an everyday lesson and a commonplace of the idiom of interaction in many cultures known to anthropologists. I learned a good deal about the skillful use of metaphor some years ago sitting day in and day out in the "palabra house" of the Fang people of western equatorial Africa. The Fang are a neo-Bantu culture practicing slash-and-burn agriculture in the equatorial forest. They rewarded me for paying such unrelenting attention to things that had no obvious personal implications with the sobriquet "the dyspeptic one" *(nkwan minsili)*—that is, he who is sick by reason of the many questions he has on his stomach. In some quarters I was at first known as *nsinga,* the cat, probably because I was obliged to insinuate myself a bit too much. In any case having laid out our definitions and our model, I would like to discuss some metaphors characteristic of the Fang and say something about the continua upon which these metaphors operate.

The Fang institution of the palabra or council house *(aba)* is the most salient in the lives of men. Activity in the *aba* is almost constant, whether it be the manufacture of various crafts, folkloric performances of an evening, or the daily discussions, debates, and moots involving marriage, divorce, brideprice, fraternal rights and debts, territorial claims, and inheritance. The Fang are a very open, unstructured, and egalitarian society and men are not appointed nor do they gain permanent positions as judges *(nkik mesang)* in village moots and litigation. But men are selected to hear and make judgments in the conflicts of others by virtue of a reputation they have achieved. And though selections are made on an ad hoc basis according to the affair at hand, the same set of men tend to appear as judges in repeated instances.

In general these men are called upon because they have a reputation, *ewôga,* that is a kind of authority granted to them because they are listened to (*wôk,* to listen, understand) and can make themselves understood. To say that they have this authority because they are eloquent, or persuasive, or intelligent, or wise is to deal in abstract descriptions which, though used by the Fang themselves, do not capture the metaphoric predications upon these people on the basis of which their reputation is established. One does not start out in any convincing way saying of a man he is wise, or eloquent. One starts by saying that he breaks palabra *(a buk adzô)* or he slices them *(a kik adzô).* For if you are so clumsy, however powerful, as to break apart a palabra you leave jagged ends which are hard to fit back together again. You do not resolve it; you simply put it off to another day when it shall surge forth again in perhaps more festered condition. But if you cut or slice it, the two parts may be easily put back together again.

In an egalitarian society where there is no effective hierarchy to enforce judgments, the slicing of a palabra demands careful ambiguity of statement. Aphorisms and proverbial statements, various kinds of metaphor in short, are very suitable for such purposes for they provide ways of commenting upon the essentials of experience in one domain by extending these essentials to analogous experiences in another domain. The essential wisdom of the comment may be preserved in the extension while a painful and indeed unenforceable precision is obscured.

But the point I wish to make is that the metaphoric description of juridic techniques—he is a slicer or he is a breaker of palabras—refers the listener to the domain of what we may call forest work. In Western culture we can easily understand the difference between breaking and cutting. But the distinction is much more loaded with meaning in Fang culture, were everyman, if he was to provide successfully for himself and his family, had to work the forest skillfully. He had to be a craftsman carefully cutting and not breaking raffia palm wands, lianes and other fibers, and all the various woods of the forest. Out of the equatorial forest Fang men make their shelters, their essential tools, their comforts, and their admirable carvings. For a people heavily involved in forest exploitation and forest crafts, the linking of this realm to techniques of argument and judgment is particularly convincing. Men cannot well survive nor be esteemed if they break rather than carefully cut in either arena.

Nkikmesang a kui elik—"The judge has arrived at the *elik,*" the site of the former village deep in the forest. The implication is that the judge has found the old clearing in the forest where the resentments which have given rise to the present conflict lie. By casting light on these resentments he has clarified them, if not cleared them up. He has made his way skillfully through the forest (the affair). He has also—this is implied in returning to the *elik*—encouraged in the parties in conflict the sentiment of their common origins. One basic use of the variety of metaphor we have under view here is to encourage social sentiments—the primordial sentiments of a community and a common belonging or, on the other hand, of a lack of community and an exclusion. The apt judge is he whose verbal powers are able to encourage in the disputants a sentiment of common belonging.

Let me mention a final metaphor in this domain—there are so many—which is predicated upon participants. Not only is the palabra an obstruction which must be carefully sliced, it is also, as we have seen, a forest that one must wend one's way through. The clumsy disputant or judge chops down the forest, but that only leads to a conflagration. The able judge leads the parties in this judgment carefully through the forest to the discovery of the *elik*. And the able litigant as well should be capable of wending his way through the forest. In the process of argument a litigant *(nteamadzô)* may be complimented or may compliment himself on being an *nyamoro nsôm adzô*, "a mature man and a hunter in the affair." He is proceeding carefully and skillfully through the "forest." He breaks no twigs. By his verbal powers he reaches the "game" and makes it his own. Should he wish to disparage his opponent, he may refer to him as *nyamoro ôyem*—"a man mature as the bearded monkey" *(Cercopithecus talapoin)*. With his beard he may appear as a full man but he is a chatterer not a debater. He does not dominate the "forest" by making his way skillfully through it, but simply plays around within it failing, as we would say, to know the forest for the trees. Moreover, rather than the hunter he is the hunted—in short, the dominated in the palabra situation. Here is another continuum, hunter-hunted or more abstractly dominating-dominated.

There are then a variety of continua upon which these palabra metaphors operate: slicing/breaking (chopping), skillful hunting/clumsy hunting (pathfinding), hunting/being hunted. By examination of this variety of continua we may come to the conclusion that we are dealing with one factor only, competence-incompetence. But such an abstraction does not capture a rich domain of Fang experience—the domain of forest and woods working—to which the events of the palabra house are referred by metaphoric extension. Because of the complexity of the palabra situation, it seems, it is difficult to see what makes a good litigant or judge.

Metaphor extends that inchoate experience to more concrete domains of Fang experience where comparisons in performance are more easily recognized. Everyone knows the difference between a good and a bad hunter. The evidence comes home in his bag. In the adversarial situation of the palabra house the strategy is to situate oneself advantageously and one's opponent undesirably in respect to the continua which characterize the relevant domains of metaphoric reference. The sum of the relevant domains and the set of respective continua constitute the quality space of Fang litigation. In that quality space, reputation is not first a matter of wisdom or eloquence. It is a matter of cutting or slicing, pathfinding, hunting. By such metaphoric predications do the Fang come to know their judges.

The adversary nature of life in the palabra house may perhaps give a special quality to the use of metaphor that we find there. Let us submit this proposition—that metaphors operate in respect to quality space—in another situation. Let us examine the metaphors put forth in supplications to divine powers *(evangiles)* in a Fang syncretist cult called Bwiti.[12] This cult has been active among the Fang since the First World War. Originally it was a reworking of various western equatorial ancestor cults, but recently it has been incorporating many Christian elements. One might say, of course, that the members of Bwiti do exist in an adversary relationship with the condition of the African in the colonial world. And they are using metaphor to situate themselves more desirably in respect to that condition.

The packing of meaning is typical of Bwiti sermons, but it happens that the particular branch of this cult from which the *evangiles* are taken (*Asumege Ening*—New Life) puts exceptional value on recondite speech and regards it as a sign of power in the cult leader. This packing of imagery and the illusive and often determinedly arcane manner in which sermons are put forth has led me elsewhere to discuss them as "unbelievably subtle words." As subtle as they may be, we may note a resonance with those metaphors of the palabra house which extend to the domain of forest work. The following text is taken from the *Evangile Fete Kumba*, the September 1959 Bwiti festival held before planting and preparation of the earth. It was given by the cult leader at Kougouleu chapel (Kango District, Gabon Republic), Ekang Engono, called *Akikos Zambi Avanga*.

> Eboka tells us that the afterbirth of the spirit is the blood. Women must close the backdoor of the cookhouse before the setting of the sun. The member of Bwiti is buried in a white robe with ashes on his face for it is by

means of fire that the Fang can chop down the trees to heaven. The spirit
flees the body because of the noise of the body but when the body sleeps the
spirit wanders fitfully. The Fang have come to divine that vibrating string on
which music is made between heaven and earth—between God above and
God below. That string is played sweetly. God below is the bath of the soul,
the seat of the soul. For a child in being born falls to earth and must be
cleaned of dirt that he may arise to the wind which is God above. Man can be
tied as a package with that string—as his afterbirth is tied and buried in the
earth—as the umbilical cord is tied and buried in the earth—as leftover food
is tied in a leaf package to be eaten later. We are all of us leaf packages of
leftover food—the food of God above—we should not rot in that package for
our brothers to eat us in witchcraft—we should open up that package so that
God above may eat us—we should untie that string that leads us from God
below to God above.[13]

Let us begin with the Bwiti name of the leader of the cult—*Akikos
Zambi Avanga*. He is the "parrot's egg—god who creates." We also note
the general name for the cult members—*Banzie* (angels, or those who fly).
Both of these are metaphors of height, of loftiness, of heavenly connotation. The African gray parrot nests in the tallest trees of the equatorial
forest and frequently in the *Adzap (Minusops djave)*, the sacred tree of the
Banzie. The parrot has the power to speak. His red tail feathers have
always been important in Fang ritual and folklore and are highly significant in Bwiti ritual which is organized around something they call the red
"path of life and death" *(zen abiale ye awu)*. The parrot is surely a liminal
creature and difficult to categorize. But what I would emphasize is his
occupancy of the high realms of the forest, his capacity to communicate,
his characteristically purposeful, rapid, and unambiguous flight.

Now these metaphors are both very apt—that is, they make a proper
movement—in respect to the situation of the Fang. For the Fang have in
recent decades found themselves badly situated. As they would put it,
they are too much of the ground—of things of dirt and earth and thickets.
Figuratively, they find themselves meandering through dense undergrowth. Images of the ground and undergrowth abound in Bwiti *evangiles*. Clay and swamps and fens appear and men lost in the leaves of the
underbrush who wander unable to see each other, let alone their tutelary
supernaturals. There are powers of the below of course. These were the
powers cultivated by the old religion—the ancestor cult and the witchcraft
societies—powers of the dead, powers of the forest, secret powers of the
living. Many of the Fang have come to adopt the generic term *Zame Asi*,

God of the below, for these powers and their rituals. In Bwiti, Fang recognize the inescapable attraction of the evangelical God of the above, and in Bwiti they seek to establish by syncretism a communication between these two gods—a communication that is represented in this *evangile* by the vibrating cord of the one string harp, *béng*, seen as binding God below and God above together.

The metaphors of Bwiti *evangiles*—this should not surprise us—move the membership toward higher things—towards realms of the above. They do this by treating the members as *Banzie*—spirits of the wind. They do this by giving the leader his name—"the egg of the parrot"—the essence of the potential of superior knowledge. For the leader, like the parrot with his arresting cry and unambiguous flight, calls out to men below struggling and wandering in the suffocating thickets of the forest and gives them direction upwards.

Because this *evangile* does in fact give us a continuum of gods below and above joined by a vibrating cord, it supports my point that metaphors operate upon continua—in this case belowness and aboveness—moving people and things aptly about on the continua. I think this understanding is essential if we are to see how the *evangile* works, though admittedly the matter is not so simple. Rare is the communication between men and surely rare is the *evangile* that moves us only in one direction on one continuum. In the *evangile* given, something is surely said for belowness. Men are born to it. It gives them stability. They can stand on it though it dirties their feet and obscures their vision and, in the end, they stand on belowness, really, the better to launch themselves to aboveness. The Bwitist does not abandon *Zame Asi* in moving upwards. It is a rich source of creative tension in this cult to try to keep *Zame* below in mind as they search for the above. It is the tension between *Zame* above and *Zame* below that keeps the cord vibrating.

To reduce any of these *evangiles* to movement on a continuum or a set of continua violates a deep richness they possess, a richness contained in some of their most apt metaphors. Consider the metaphor of man as a leaf package of leftover food tied by a string that should be connecting the below and the above. How aptly this image captures the notion of forest-bound man closed in by leaves. How aptly it captures the feeling of bodily decay, so widespread a feeling in the colonial period. How aptly it summarizes the anxiety Fang felt about the increase in witchcraft and the consumption of brother by brother. "Men are as food to each other." At the same time there is a positive element in the image, for these leaf packets of leftover food are a great delight and solace to hunters and gatherers in the deep forest at noontime.

Who can deny that there are many subtle things to be said about the work of metaphor and symbol? Strategies may so often end in poetry, perhaps the ultimate strategy, where instead of being moved anywhere we are accommodated in many subtle ways to our condition in all its contrarieties and complexities.

At the same time we should avoid making a mystery of these subtleties—making séance out of science—if we can find a relatively reduced number of dimensions upon which we can follow essentials of movement in metaphoric predication. Despite all the things that can and must be said about the package metaphor, its object in the end is to convince the *Banzie* to disentangle themselves and become properly attached to the above.

The Performance of Metaphors

The metaphors which have interested us to this point have been mainly rhetorical. They have been put forth for reasons of persuading feelings in certain directions. Still there are always the implications for action in them. The metaphoric predication can be self-fulfilling. The king can be told so often that he is a lion that he comes to believe it. He roars at his subjects and stealthily stalks those he thinks are enemies to his interest. He finally springs upon them in fell and summary justice. In the privacy of our experience we are usually not sure who we really are. A metaphor thrust upon us often enough as a model can become compelling.

Such persistence in the application of metaphors does not often occur, so that persuasion does not usually pass over into performance. But at a deeper level of fantasy men may hold to predications which cause them irresistibly to organize their world, insofar as they can, so as to facilitate or make inevitable certain scenarios. It has been frequently remarked that the American entanglement in Southeast Asia, complete with air cavalry, ranger battalions, and native scouts, was a scenario based upon a deep definition of our national pronouns as frontiersman or Indian fighter extending enlightenment and civilization over against the "hostiles" on the dark side of the frontier. Whether fantasies are lived out or not, they may still be defined as scenarios arising from metaphoric predication on pronouns.

In Bwiti we have a particular opportunity to witness metaphors arise in fantasy and be put into action. For the cult is especially atune to fantasies and even promotes them through dependence upon the alkaloid narcotic *Tabernanthe eboka*. The members of Bwiti feel that they obtain knowledge useful to ritual elaborations from their dreams and visions. In a syncretist religious movement undergoing, before our eyes, its rapid evolution, we can readily discover what it is tempting to call the kernel metaphoric statements: the deep-lying metaphoric subject (pronouns) and metaphoric predicate out of which by a series of transformations we see arise the complex surface structure of cult ritual. In my study of some six of these movements in Africa I have attempted to give an account of the organizing metaphors that appear time and again in ritual performance. These metaphors include the militant metaphor of Christian soldiering in the Apostle's Revelation Society in Ghana, the pastoral metaphor of the bull who crashes in the kraal in the Church of God in Christ in Natal, South Africa, the atmospheric metaphor of the circumambient Holy Wind (or Ghost) in Zulu Zionism, the linguistic metaphor of the voices of God in Christianisme Celeste in Dahomey, and the sylvan metaphor of the lost hunters and the parrot's egg in the Bwiti cult.[14] These metaphors and their performative implications may be listed.

Metaphoric assertion	*Performative consequence*
We are Christian soldiers.	Our church activities must show our militance in fighting against the forces of the devil.
I (the pastor) am the bull who maintains order in the cattle kraal. You the members are the cattle I protect and invest with my substance.	In my sermons I must show my powers and I must lay on hands in the healing circles with such force that my power will shoot into the membership and they will be disciplined and directed. We must open ourselves up to the power of the pastor.
We are vessels of the Holy Wind.	Our actions must build up the presence of the wind around us and open us up so that we may incorporate it. We must fly.

We are the voices of God.	We must study the Bible so that we can learn God's language. We must concentrate our attention on sermons and seek speaking in tongues.
We are lost hunters in the forest searching for its secrets. I (the leader of this cult) am the parrot's egg holding a secret for which the membership must search.	Our liturgy and our leader must guide us through the forest and lead us to the secrets that the forest holds—principally communication with the wandering shades of the dead.

It should not be presumed that these are the only metaphors that appear in each of these cults though, I believe, they are the ones which set the dominant feeling tone of the cults and most do something for the members in a strategic sense.

Let us take just one metaphor from the Bwiti cult. It is a metaphor subsidiary to the one we have given above but it is in the same domain. It is the metaphor of the rituals of entrance into the cult house—*minkin*. The members say at this time *bi ne esamba* (we are a trading team). Historically the main association of this metaphor is with that adventurous team of young men that collected rubber and ivory at the turn of the century and took it to the coast to exchange for trade goods. These groups were characterized by high solidarity, the euphoria of hunting and gathering, and the satisfaction of a rewarding trading relation with the colonial world. It was a group with a sense of purpose which led to significant fulfillment. The aptness of this metaphor is readily understood when the goallessness, the lack of solidarity in village and kinship, and the high degree of ambivalence about the larger colonial world is grasped. For these conditions make for feelings to which the metaphor is a compensatory representation. If metaphors are a compensatory representation in themselves, they are even more so when they are acted upon, when they are images in the sense of plans of behavior.[15] In the case of the *esamba* metaphor, we see that it is an organizing force in the performance of the rituals of entrance and exit. These rituals, of course, are an accretion of many elements. But when we see narrow paths being cut through the underbrush on the margins of the village so that the membership at the midnight exit from the chapel can wend their way through the forest and then return, we have reason to assume a metaphor is being put into action as a plan of ritual behavior. And when we see the members begin the rituals of entrance at the margins of the forest and dance as a tightly packed mass across the village plaza into the chapel, we have reason to assume we are seeing the realization of a metaphoric assertion. It is an old question as to how rituals arise. We may avoid the fruitless debate on the primacy of myth or ritual by stating simply: rituals are the acting out of metaphoric predications upon inchoate pronouns which are in need of movement.

People undertake religious experiences because they desire to change the way they feel about themselves and the world in which they live. They come into their particular cult with some constellation of feelings—isolation, disengagement, powerlessness, enervation, debasement, contamination—from which they need to move away. Metaphors put forth in these movements accomplish that. By persuasion and performance they operate upon the member allowing him eventually to exit from the ritual incorporated, empowered, activated, euphoric. They allow him eventually to exit better situated in quality space. Of course these are just psychological abstractions. My point here is that we come to understand these operations only if we study metaphoric predications upon pronouns as they appear in persuasion and performance. The strategy of emotional movement in religion lies in them.

Conclusion: What It Means to be Moved

The materials we have examined bear first on the way that appropriate impressions of persons are formed, but further they cast light upon the important question of the images of the ideal personality and how these images are generated. Boulding called our attention to the importance of this problem and to our persisting ignorance of how these images arise, compete, change, and decline. "Like the gods and goddesses of ancient mythology one almost gets the impression of ideal types battling above the clouds for the minds and allegiances of men. It is the fall of the ideal image that leads to the collapse of empires and the decay of cultures. Yet how little we know about the forces which support or destroy these powerful beings."[16]

I may not have accounted for the collapse of empires, but what I have said may relate to processes of decay in acculturation. It has been my view that the images of social beings are generated by metaphoric predications upon pronouns which are themselves the primary—if not primordial—ideal types. These metaphoric extensions generate qualities in pronouns.

They invest pronouns with emotional meaningfulness if the domains into which extension takes place are important arenas of activity for the culture involved. If the forest, for example, becomes a less preoccupying arena of life for the Fang—as, in fact, because of their increasing activity along the arteries of commerce, it is—then it becomes harder and harder for the Fang to form meaningful images of the peoples involved in the palabra house except by employing vitiated abstractions (wise, eloquent, forceful) or old metaphors dead or dying because they extend into moribund aspects of their lives. The vitiation of metaphor through drastic change in the domains of activity of a people is an aspect of acculturation that has not been fully enough explored. This vitiation makes it difficult for a people to have satisfactory feelings about their pronouns.

I have not been content, however, with examining the ways in which by use of metaphor we learn to have feelings about the qualities of people. I have suggested that there is a strategy involved in the adversarial condition of social life and that strategy involves placement of self or other on the various continua of the important domains of experience of a culture. The set of these continua define the quality space of that culture—the quality space within which the pronouns of that culture operate, or are operated upon.

It is my argument, therefore, that the systematic study of those most meaningful forms in human intercommunication—metaphors—involves among many other approaches the study of the movement they make in semantic space. A sensitive ethnography must obtain the metaphors that men predicate upon themselves so as to locate the movements they desire to make in the culture they occupy.

But we should not overestimate the applicability of this model. Though it indicates the method by which we must discover a structure of sentiment, it remains essentially topographic. To be a structural model [17] it should specify the transformations to which the parts of the model are susceptible. Systematic description must show how the state of the space, that is the nature of the culture, imposes or inspires certain characteristic kinds of shifts in pronouns—toward, for example, greater potency or activity or goodness.[18]

In any event it is my view that these complicated and, so often, opaque structural matters must begin with a topographic model of quality space and with some idea of the movement that kernel metaphoric predications make in that space. And though this model may be problematic there is precedent in believing that our minds organize our perceptualized experiences by reference to their relative distances from each other on some prelinguistic quality space which arises out of the very nature of life in a world defined by gravitational forces.[19] Metaphoric predication would be the dynamic element in such a space. There may even be reason for believing, if we can learn from frogs in this regard, that what our ears, eyes, mouths are really telling our brains—or what the brain finally undertands from what it is told—about the bloom and buzz of experience is the essential qualitative pattern of potency, activity, and goodness (edibility) of the things which catch our attention. [20]

It will be enough if anthropologists pay attention in the field to the ways in which men are aided in conveying inchoate psychological experiences by appealing to a range of more easily observable and concrete events in other domains of their lives. There must surely be some universals involved. It is likely that the domain of corporeal experience is used everywhere to clarify the heart and the head of many inchoate matters or the warmth or coolness of any personality. And it is likely, since the succession of bodily sensations is also a sequence of social experiences which arise to accommodate and control them as men mature, that the extension of social experience into the domain of corporeality and vice versa is also a universal.

While I first felt sheepish about taking up the problem of metaphor in the social sciences, I now feel more bullish. At the least we should have been tossed on the horns of the following dilemma which I believe fundamental to the understanding of culture. However men may analyze their experiences within any domain, they inevitably know and understand them best by referring them to other domains for elucidation. It is in that metaphoric cross-referencing of domains, perhaps, that culture is integrated, providing us with the sensation of wholeness. And perhaps the best index of cultural integration or disintegration, or of genuineness or spuriousness in culture for that matter, is the degree to which men can feel the aptness of each other's metaphors.

La Casona, El Pino, Alto Aller, Asturias

Notes

My thinking on the problem of "representations" and upon metaphor specifically has been aided by discussions with Robert Kleck, John Lanzetta, and Edward Yonan. I am grateful to the Ford Foundation for their support and to the Social Science Research Council and American Council of Learned Societies for support of the African field work. The National Science Foundation is supporting the Asturian field work.

1. Bronislaw Malinowski, *Coral Gardens and Their Magic*, 2 vols. (London: Allen and Unwin, 1935); E. E. Evans-Pritchard, *Witchcraft, Oracles and Magic Among the Azanda* (Oxford: Clarendon Press, 1937), and *Nuer Religion* (Oxford: Clarendon Press, 1956).

2. B. F. Skinner, "The Operational Analysis of Psychological Terms," *Cumulative Record* (Boston, 1945), pp. 272–286.

3. S. E. Asch, "On the Use of Metaphors in the Descriptions of Persons," in Heinz Werner, ed., *On Expressive Language* (Worcester, Mass.: Clark University Press, 1955), p. 30.

4. Jerome Bruner, "The Course of Cognitive Growth," *American Psychologist*, 19 (1963), 1–27.

5. J. Piaget, *Structuralism* (New York: Basic Books, 1970).

6. C. Lévi-Strauss, *The Savage Mind* (Chicago: University of Chicago Press, 1962), p. 69.

7. Robert P. Armstrong, *The Affecting Presence: An Essay in Humanistic Anthropology* (Urbana: University of Illinois Press, 1971).

8. Kenneth Burke, *Permanence and Change*, 2d rev. ed. (Los Altos: Hermes Publications, 1954), and *The Philosophy of Literary Form*, rev. ed. (New York: Vintage Books, 1957).

9. Burke, *Philosophy of Literary Form*, p. 256.

10. D. Berggren, "The Use and Abuse of Metaphor," *The Review of Metaphysics*, 16 (1962–1963), 238–258.

11. Charles E. Osgood and others, *The Measurement of Meaning* (Urbana: University of Illinois Press, 1957).

12. James W. Fernandez, "Symbolic Consensus in a Fang Reformative Cult," *American Anthropologist*, 67 (1965), 902–929.

13. The Fang from which this is a running translation is the following, a little over half of the full text: Ebôka a zô na: ku nsisim a ne meki. Nyi na nkawla mewala mesaman ye etun ôngoase mininga ye ayong nyingwan mebege a yian dzip nda mbi atarega. Môt a dzebe ye mfum étô ening mon Fang é dzô alé. Nsisim wa mara ékôkôm akale a ne engôngôm. Edô a ne oyô. Mwan Fang a nga sô a zu a sok beng nye na; Zame esi Zame ôyô. Nya na beng é ne nkôl, nya na e ne fe etuge nzum, nya na Nzame esi enye éne etok nsisim, Nzame oyo a ne mfonga. Minkol mite emyo Nyingwan Mebege a nga eka mwan . . . bininga bi kak ekôp. Bia bise bi ne nyim Zame. Edô nyim a nga sô sô etôm. Bôbedzang be dzi nyim . . . ô ta dzi nyim, nyim Nzame. Aki Kos Zambi Avanga enye a nga kôbô. Me mana dzô. Bi nga van tsi beng nyim Zame.

14. References to each of these cults and their organizing metaphors may be found in the following: Fernandez, "Revitalized Words from the Parrot's Egg and the Bull Who Crashes in the Kraal: African Cult Sermons," *Proceedings of the American Ethnological Society for 1966: Essays on the Verbal and Visual Arts* (1967), pp. 45–63; *Microcosmogeny and Modernization*, Occasional Papers, Centre for Developing Area Studies, McGill University (1969), pp. 1–34; "Rededication and Prophetism in Ghana," *Cahiers d'Etudes Africaines*, no. 38, VII (1970), 228–305.

15. George A. Miller, E. Galenter, and K. H. Pribram, *Plans and the Structure of Behavior* (New York: Holt, 1960).

16. K. Boulding, *The Image: Knowledge in Life and Society* (Ann Arbor: University of Michigan Press, 1956), pp. 144–145.

17. Piaget, *Structuralism*.

18. Some of these things can be worked out with the model as it stands, where all we need to investigate are predications across domains of the form; P is A [I (a man) am a hawk]. Of greater interest are complex associations within and across domains of the form, still derived from these basic predications; P1 : P2 :: A : B [I (a man) am to you (a woman) as hawk is to dove]. For in these formulae we begin to get a sense of order in culture—a sense of congruences in sets of associations within and across domains. And beyond that and still of greater interest are the characteristic transformations that metaphoric associations undergo in various bodies of expressive culture, such as ritual. These are purportedly summed up for us in the sibylline Lévi-Strauss formula over which so much blood has been shed.

$$f_x(a) : f_y(b) :: f_x(b) : f_{a\text{-}1}(y)$$

This may be read in terms of our argument here as: The emotional movement or function (x) accomplished by some metaphor (a) is to the movement (y) accomplished by some metaphor (b) as the appropriation by metaphor (b) of its complementary movement (x) is to the transformation of a previous metaphor (a) into a significantly new movement (a-1) of a new metaphor (y) itself transformed from a previous movement. The only thing this can mean in terms of our discussion here is that movement can be transformed into metaphor and metaphor into movement within a given quality space.

An article on "The Performance of Ritual Metaphors," which attempts to give an account of metaphoric transformations in ritual, will appear in a collection of articles on *The Social Use of Metaphor*, edited by David Sapir for Cornell University Press.

19. W. V. O. Quine, *Word and Object* (Cambridge, Mass.: MIT Press, 1963), pp. 83ff. *Proceedings of the Institute of Radio Electronics*, 47 (November 1959), 1940–1959.

2

THE MISSION OF METAPHOR
IN EXPRESSIVE CULTURE

> Thanks to a total reorganization of the real and
> the imaginary . . . metaphors take over the
> mission of metonyms and vice versa.
>
> CLAUDE LÉVI-STRAUSS, *The Savage Mind*

The relevance to inquiry of the metaphor concept has recently been given renewed recognition. Nisbet (1968) has devoted a book to the development metaphor by which Western man has sought to grasp the essentials of change. He finds this metaphor of genesis and decay in the most systematic thinkers. Edmonson (1971) has called the scientific study of metaphor of elemental importance in the analysis of folklore, and Armstrong (1971) has used the metaphor concept as a basic tool in the comparative analysis of cultural materials from the aesthetic point of view. The influence of Lévi-Strauss (1962) is, without doubt, very strong in these developments, though he may not be specifically recognized and though he himself is influenced by Boas (1911), Evans-Pritchard (1956), and especially Jakobson and Halle (1956). In *The Savage Mind* (Lévi-Strauss 1966) and the succeeding *Mythologiques*, metaphor and metonym are central terms of analysis. This distinction was recognized very early in anthropology by Tylor, who distinguished between metaphor and syntax in cultural process, and by Frazer in his discussion of sympathetic or similarity magic and contagious or contiguity magic. These are distinctions otherwise discussed by Plato, Locke, Hobbes, Hume, and others, and the death of metaphor was fundamental to the rise of religion in Müller's theories. Current interest in metaphor and metonym, diseases of language in the eyes of many, is a return to an old focus of inquiry.

Every anthropologist knows that the really fine ethnographies are sensitive to local figures of speech, the chief of which is metaphor. That metaphors have been organizing principles in inquiry itself has been less apparent, except when put forth in too unrestrained a fashion as in the Kroeberian Superorganic. Literary anthropologists have been well aware of this, however (Hyman 1959), and Polanyi's (1964:10) argument that every interpretation of nature is based on some intuitive conception of the general nature of things relates to the view that these intuitions are expressed in metaphors (as intuitions of inchoate matters must be). Present throughout the work of Burke (e.g., 1957) is the notion that every perspective requires a metaphor to organize it. Metaphors, therefore, lie at the base of inquiry and animate it.

When one looks around in such a mood, one becomes aware of the growth metaphor of evolutionism, the Frazerian metaphor of the struggle over succession, the pebble-in-the-pool metaphor of diffusionism, and the recent dramatistic metaphor—life is a play and men performers. Lévi-Strauss's structuralism has been assessed as itself artistic metaphor by which a vast conglomerate of materials can be brought together for purposes of presentation, not prediction (Simonis 1968:301). Behaviorists have recognized that metaphor is the device men possess for leaping beyond the essential privacy of the experiential process (Skinner 1945).

I do not wish to develop these ultimate and virtually metaphysical matters concerning the organizing metaphors of human endeavor or "world hypothesis" (Pepper 1942). Almost eveything the mind puts forth may well be metaphor from a certain view, but this does not necessarily make all students of behavior poets (though they may be able to learn from literary critics). Some metaphors are better models of perceived actualities than others (Black 1962). Some metaphors conform more closely to the shape of experience (structural metaphor) and others to the feelings of experience (textual metaphor). Some metaphors work better than others in enabling men to confront given situations, according as they face problems of shape or feeling.

I wish to examine the metaphor concept as it can be of use to anthropologists in respect to materials that confront us from the expressive aspect of culture. I am going to ask not alone what metaphors are, but how they work, since our interest, fundamentally, is in behavior. This inquiry, if it can be clearly pursued, is useful because, as so often happens on the frontier of the sciences and the humanities, where two logics meet, much that has been written on metaphor has preferred to be (or by necessity has been) obscurely right rather than clearly wrong. Shands (1971) has identified in such "social science" a kind of obscurantism that seems to assume that the chief attribute of greatness is vagueness, since it assumes a host of deciphering followers. In any case, I will try to say some simple but possibly useful things about metaphor and then suggest (1) some complications that show the extent to which such things may be limited in their applications to behavior—simplicities this side of the complexity— and (2) some methodological guidelines for such an-trope-ology.

Metaphor and Symbol

As anthropologists have moved to accept the Lévi-Strauss notion of their discipline as a "semiological science," the symbol concept has taken precedence in inquiry. The justification for introducing a concern with metaphor lies in the primacy of metaphor among the devices of representation of experience, and the advantage lies in the greater clarity with which it can be defined. From very early on, as Sapir (1934:492) complained, the term *symbol* has been used to cover a great variety of apparently dissimilar modes of behavior. The problem of definition may well arise because symbolic analysis is primarily a humanistic enterprise in the social sciences, attracted to the insights which are contained in the language and logic of the humanities and not really congenial to propositional statements and their submission to testing. Failure to provide testable definitions can lead to rounds of exercises ceaselessly devoted to clarifying the implications of central terms without clarifying the terms themselves. Great terms such as *symbol* beckon on to succeeding conferences but ever recede before us—luminous but not really illuminated. Science borders on séance, and obscurantism is bound to obtain currency in professional transactions.

Most of the symbols to which our attention is called in symbolic analyses condense so many and often incompatible meanings as to, in fact, make them difficult to discuss except in the language of the humanities, attuned as it is to complex ambiguities. Such symbols as are manipulated in the religious life, for example, do not have easily discoverable subjects. That is to say, it is not easy to discover what they represent to whom. Unlike signs and signals, symbols are dissociated from specific social contexts and can work in many (Sapir 1934:494; Morris 1955:23–27). They pick up meanings from the many contexts in which their generalization allows them to appear. They come to represent many things about which it is difficult to establish consensus. If we are to discuss devices of representation, we had best begin at that point in their appearance in interaction and discourse at which we can be most sure of what they represent to whom.

Signals, signs, and symbols exist in dynamic and evolutionary relation both within culture and within individual experience (Fernandez 1965). The same item or token of communication can be, according to the situation, a sign-image, pregnant with felt but unconceptualized meanings; a symbol, possessed of fully conceptualized and often articulated meanings; or a signal, whose meaning lies in the orientation it gives to interaction. For example, a cross on a hill, simply a signal to some citizens of Jerusalem that a public event is to take place, is to others a sign-image which they take up and preserve within a religious tradition. To the clergy within this tradition, the cross becomes a symbol. To laity and clergy alike, however, the cross in many moments of their lives is neither affectively pregnant nor replete with articulated meanings, but simply a signal useful to orient action in worship or to identify membership in an in-group. Behind the shifting back and forth of the same token from signal to symbol lies the arresting sign-image, which, because of its power, its attractiveness, its vitality, is sorted out from the bloom and buzz of experience and preserved in memory, rising again and again in dream or mythopoeic performance.[1]

Over time, the affectivity bound up in these sign-images is pared down as they become part of the syntax of behavior, either as signals in social interaction or as symbols in cultural interaction. An adequate discussion of these signals, signs, and symbols rests, however, upon scrutiny of sign-images and the relationship they bear to human subjects who have sorted them out from experience. That relationship is one of predication. Symbols are abstracted sign-images which have lost their direct link with the subjects on which they were first predicated in specific contexts, developing thereby plausible links with multitudinous subjects in multitudinous contexts. As Wheelwright (1962) has argued, symbols begin in metaphoric statement and can be translated back into such statement. The view taken here is that associational processes in symbolic behavior can be more clearly understood if we examine underlying metaphors and the subjects upon which, as sign-images, they were first predicated. The elementary definition of metaphor (and metonym) from which one should work is the predication of a sign-image upon an inchoate subject.[2] The first mission of metaphor is to provide identity for such subjects.

Primordial Metaphors

The relevance of this elementary definition can readily be grasped by
examining materials that anthropologists in the nature of their work are
especially aware of: mankind's ancient, virtually universal, and inveterate
interest in animals. Lévi-Strauss has been especially concerned with
myths in which animals take human attributes. In this concern he follows
the Rousseauian thesis that a distinction between Humanity and Animality, or between Culture and Nature, is one of the primary preoccupations of human thought. However, Lévi-Strauss is mainly interested in the
intellectual exploitation of natural objects for purposes of social categorization and differentiation. He focuses on form rather than content, the
system rather than the substance, transformations and inversions rather
than objective or intrinsic properties. Given the great diversity of ways in
which the same natural objects can be employed, there is no doubt a
virtue to this approach, yet it does not begin at the beginning. The various
animals and objects of the natural world are, after all, sensible images
which can be predicated upon inchoate subjects, not simply "counters in a
game of combinations."[3] Is it not arguable that primordially animals are
predicates by which subjects obtain an identity and are thus objects of
affinity and participation? If so, the first problem is not how animals take
human shape, but how humans take animal shape and enact nature. In
fact, there is plentiful evidence that animals have been such primordial
points de repère in the pronouns' (the essential inchoate subjects') quest
for identity.

Mankind's ancient interest in assuming animal identities may be in-
ferred from Paleolithic art. While we must for the most part infer the
imitation of animals in the rites which accompanied the art, the actual
assumption of an animal identity may perhaps be seen in the dancing
sorcerer of Trois Frères. More animal than human, he may constitute the
earliest evidence of the shape-shifting of shamans and culture heroes the
world over. There is no need to develop this point through Paleolithic
speculations, however, for these primordial predications may be confirmed in many contemporary societies in the culture of infancy and
childhood. Examples may be drawn from my field experience in Africa
and Western Europe.

Among the Fang people of western equatorial Africa, one watches
young children day in and day out play a variety of animal games, among
these a kind of Run Sheep Run (*mwan kubn*) in which one child takes the

part of a leopard and another the part of the sheep. The rest of the children, holding hands in a circle, attempt to protect the sheep from the leopard without. A younger boy or girl plays the sheep, an older boy the leopard. In *ndong-mba* ceremonies in mid-childhood, a shaman is brought from another clan to purify the village from the repercussions of brother-sister incest. He is represented as a large bird flying in from the east. In the forest precincts, the boys are thrown on their stomachs and to the sound of flapping of palm leaves the shaman rushes out from the bush, catches the initiate on the shoulder with a "claw," and with the other hand cuts him three times on the back of the neck. Among a neighboring people, the Mitsogo, the ancestral cult of *bwiti* climaxes at a vertiginous moment in which the men, having danced for hours at an increasing pace, begin to exit one by one from the cult house. They dance out in the forest and shortly return bedecked with skins, feathers, and fronds representing various animals: pythons, leopards, elephants, and various birds. While it is said that the powers of *bwiti* are demonstrated in its capacity to charm the animals (who have an identification with the dead) out of the woods so that they can take part in cult life—take up human attributes—the essential fact is that cult members have taken the role of animals. Throughout equatorial Africa, leopard societies showed men taking that role.

In a village in the Asturian mountains of northern Spain, I have been watching, daily, the activities of boys six to twelve years old in the schoolyard as they gather in the morning, at recess, and after school. In the spring, when the social structure of the schoolyard is well established and everyone knows each other, they play soccer. While there are winners and losers, the games are so brief, so oriented to individuals, and so constantly shifting in respect to team membership that no comment is made on the social structure. The older and dominant boys play the advanced scoring positions and the younger subordinates the defense positions and goal. In the early fall, in contrast, there is hardly any soccer. The boys play *a caballos* or *lobos, el xugo,* and *a la morena.* In *a caballos* one boy ties a cord around another and drives him through the village streets as a mounted hunter hunting wolves. At first every boy volunteers as horse or as wolf, but gradually it is the older and more dominant boys who become the hunters and the younger and less dominant who are most often horses or members of the wolf pack. Much practice and alternate pairing off of horse and rider goes on before the actual chase. *El xugo* (the yoke) is very similar. Here the boys are linked up as a cow team and attached to a leafy branch that they drag behind them. They are then driven through the dry autumn streets, where the branch raises great clouds of dust. Here, too, it is the younger and the subordinate who are more often the yoked and driven.

Though one way to regard these games is as a struggle for dominance in the schoolyard social order, one should not overlook the eagerness with which the children take the part of the animals. The younger boys, most of whom do not pretend to be drivers or riders, charge off with a will as horses or wolves, and the older boys readily undergo role reversal from time to time, showing that as horses, cows, or wolves nobody can hold them.

In the game of *a la morena* one boy plays the role of a female donkey *(burra)*, bending over while the others leapfrog over him in a series of challenging ways until someone touches him with a foot and must then assume the position. Here there is struggle to avoid taking the position and to prove physical skill. But one notes as well that the younger boys assume the position readily, and very young children bend over happily for long periods while others practice leaping over them. Perhaps they do not fully realize they are taking the position of a *burra*. Yet two- and three-year-olds passing the summer months in the *caserío* in the mountains will spend hours playing at *xetu* (calf), swinging and nodding their heads as if they were cropping grass or collared with a ball. When they are a bit older, they will play at cow and milker with their older brothers, one assuming the position of a cow and the other milking him and then reversing roles. This animal play easily translates later into the horse, cow, and wolf play of the schoolyard.

Since children in twentieth-century urban America and Europe spend so much of their time identifying with machinery—themselves assuming the dynamics and making the power sounds as they push car and truck or plane around—it may be hard to convince a reader from such a culture of the importance of these animal metaphors and of the primordial nature of horse play. Since we are surrounded not by animals but by machinery, we may have forgotten man's close relation for millennia to animals, with which he has identified and from which he has learned. But the sense of this powerful source of identity and learning survives. We have only to think of how we surround our infants with stuffed animals and tell them animal stories; how we give them animal nicknames (tiger, kitten, little bear); how, in rough-and-tumble with young children, we play at eating them up or carrying them piggyback. The primordial metaphors are still there. We are still in some part being taught by the animals through identification with them. An acquaintance was very disturbed by his two-year-old's habit of climbing up on the back of a sofa or the piano and leaping off like the family cat. Other than the danger to bones, there should have been little cause for concern. The child, although in a machine culture, had fallen back upon a primordial procedure for the gaining of identity. Compared with the Asturian mountain people, he simply had an impoverished range of animals with which to identify; no one in these mountains would identify with a cat when horses, wolves, cows, and *burras* are present.

The proposition behind these examples is a simple one. In the growth of human identity, the inchoate pronouns of social life—the "I," "you," "he," "it"—gain identity by predicating some sign-image, some metaphor upon themselves. These pronouns must, in Mead's (1934) terms, become objects to themselves, by taking the point of view of "the other," before they can become subjects to themselves.[4]This becoming an object, this taking the other, this predication upon the pronoun, is a process that has for millennia turned to the animal world.

The ontogeny of this metaphoric recapitulation is seen in the childhood dramas we have reviewed, as children who have identified with animals come to act out their mastery over them. They fully become subjects, that is, themselves, by becoming masters of animals.[5] The identity process by which the youth becomes first an object and then a subject is seen in the games of *a caballos* and *el xugo* as over time cows become drivers and horses and wolves become riders. It is seen as an enduring dialectic in *a la morena* as the boys become the *burra* and then the master and then the *burra* agian. I do not wish to deny that much of child play and identity search in anthropological literature involves the reproduction in small of adult work and family life, as children play house, make mud pies, take roles like the mother, the father, the child, make hay with grass, or stable toy animals. I do not wish to deny the complexity of infantile processes of subject-object differentiation or the complexity of the process of identity formation in general. I do not wish to deny the deep emotional currents of the "family romance." I wish, in these examples, to draw attention to the primordial and underlying predication upon the pronoun. I argue that the understanding of metaphor begins with these initial predications, and the understanding of identity processes involves basically an understanding of how we master these predications—how we move, that is, from the preoccupation with the predicate back across the copula to an understanding of the subject and its difference from the natural world. This movement from the sense of similarity between animals and men to the sense of difference is accomplished by changing the sign-images we predicate upon the subject.

We never become so confident of the identity of the inchoate subject, however, as to escape such metaphoric predications. Even in supposedly sophisticated societies, men in situations of ambiguity or conflict return to likening each other and themselves to hawks, doves, or owls, dogs or their offspring, donkeys. In one such society, machine-oriented and highly literate, one public figure has referred to another as a jellyfish.[6] In uncertain social circumstances, subjects return to primordial predications in search of a more concrete object upon which the subject can be fixed. There is an interplay, not only in mythology, but in life, between metaphoric predicates and subjects whose identity they illuminate but who must come to master them. Human social life has long demanded not only that we be hawks and doves or leopards, but that we be masters of hawks or doves. Periodically our mastery slips and we return to primordial predications.

In archaic societies living very close to nature—whether as hunters and gatherers, pastoralists, or agriculturalist—primordial predications often persist in totemism. While totemism must be studied as an intellectual structure which achieves social classifications, as Lévi-Strauss has demonstrated, fundamentally it represents a mastery by the subject (or the society of subjects) over the plurality of its possible natural predicates (not always animals or plants, though predominantly so). The power in totemism is that it at once preserves a sense of these primordial identification processes and achieves a sense of separation both from nature and from other social subjects. As it is so often put in totemic myths, "We once married animals (or were born from them)," or "We once were animals, but now we know better." Totemism is one of a variety of tropic structures—apt in the archaic world because of the proximity of that world to nature—arising out of the earliest experience of inchoate subjects attempting through various concrete predications upon themselves to escape the anxiety of inchoateness. The theory of the development—the juvenile ontology (Weinreich 1963:141)—of such metaphoric structure as totemism or mythology would be, like the following, one that shows us movement from subjective utility to objective analogy in respect to men's predications of the object world upon themselves: Phase 1 involves individual identification with salient sign-images (primarily animals) in the object world through the predication of such objects upon the inchoate subject. In Phase 2, multiple predication of such objects upon the subject leads to the sense of a self—of an identity—as different from the multitude of its possible predicates. Mastery is thus achieved through multiple predication. Phase 3 is the employment by the masterful self (or society of selves) of natural objects in a structure of metaphoric predications in order to achieve, by analogy, social movement or social order. Movement is obtained by the use of metaphor for purposes of persuasion and perform-ance (see Fernandez 1972) and order by the use of metaphor for purposes of classification. Wheelwright (1962) has pointed out, by reference to the Greek roots of the term, that metaphor means "change in motion." Indeed, the term "vehicle" employed in the humanities to refer to the metaphoric predicate emphasizes that dynamic. It is a dynamic otherwise found in the lifelong search for identity, in the interplay between subject and object as the latter gives identity to the former and the former seeks to master it in turn through a new predicate[7] But this interplay, or dialectic, does not explain or help predict the particular choice of sign-image or the particular transformations to which sign-images are suscepti-ble in respect to particular subjects.

How are we to conceptualize this dynamic and these transformations? Metaphor, after all, is not the only kind of predication that can be made upon an inchoate subject. We may prefer to be literal-minded and attempt to define a subject by reference to the domains to which it "really" belongs. We do this by taxonomic intellectual operations. Suppose we have called George, metaphorically, a muffin. George may object, in any case, but certainly will if he is literal-minded. He may want to be identified according to the characteristics (the distinctive features) he gives evidence of at some level of the semantic domains to which he really belongs. He is an animal, a man, an adult, a father; he is a businessman, a banker, a teller, etc.[8]

A subject or set of subjects is assigned a metaphoric predicate, however, according to a set of characteristics which may overlap with, but is not the same as, that set which literally characterizes it (except at a very high level of abstraction, for the mind is, after all, one entity which can unify all its experiences). A metaphor is a predication upon a subject of an object from a domain to which the subject belongs only by a stretch of the imagina-tion. In that sense metaphor makes a false attribution, and in that sense Aristotle defined metaphor as the extension of a name from that to which it usually belongs to some other object.

It is sometimes said that literal predication singles out the essential or important features of the subject while metaphoric predication singles out striking but not essential or important features (McCloskey 1964:219; Morris 1955:136). This may be the case by reference to literal membership in certain domains or to logical rules of classification and contrast, but it does not hold when we have affective matters in mind. Though Locke, from the logical point of view (in *The Essay on Human Understanding*), criticizes such eloquent and artificial invention as metaphor obtains for "insinuating wrong ideas and moving the passions," it is precisely this insinuation and this movement which is behaviorally of greatest interest. The mind, as has been frequently enough pointed out (La Barre 1970), is not only an instrument for grinding out rational truths, but also a homeostatic organ. And society is not only a system of interlocking categories, but an ebb and flow of emotion. The scrutiny of metaphor illuminates that homeostasis and that ebb and flow in the subjects upon which it is predicated, for the second mission of metaphor is to accomplish affective movement in inchoate pronouns.

If we follow Aristotle, metaphoric movement may be conceived of as adornment or disparagement of a subject: "To adorn borrow metaphor from things superior, to disparage borrow from things inferior." The adorning or disparaging metaphors we have in mind are primarily prescinding rather than perspective (in Van Steenburgh's [1965] terms) and textual (Berggren 1962–63) rather than structural (Black 1962:222).

The first distinction refers to the fact that metaphors vary in their effects according to the clarity with which the subjects upon which they are predicated are held in mind. In perspective metaphor, my arm, clearly conceived, is a lever; in prescinding metaphor, hate, obscurely conceived, is a smoldering fire. In general, the semantic movement accomplished by metaphor is from the abstract and inchoate in the subject to the more concrete, ostensive, and easily graspable in the metaphoric predicate. Thus, in "mercy . . . droppeth as the gentle rain from heaven," the "gentle rain" gives to the abstract and vaguely conceived "mercy" a concreteness that literal definition is hopeless to achieve. Metaphor obtains in such cases what has been well called by T. S. Eliot an "objective correlative" of what is subjectively inchoate in perception and reflection.

The second distinction hinges upon the principle of association, the rule by which the metaphor is predicated upon its subject.[9] In structural or analogic metaphor, the predication is made on the basis of some isomorphism in structure or pattern. Thus one says the "branch" of the stream or one uses "tree" diagrams in logic or one speaks of the "mechanical" relationship of self-sufficient parts in traditional societies and the "organic" relationship of mutually dependent cells in bureaucratic societies. Black (1962:223) warns us with good reason that "identity of structure is compatible with the widest variety of content—hence the possibilities for construction of analogic models are endless . . . [and] the risks of fallacious inference from inevitable irrelevancies and distortions in the model are present in aggravated measure." In textual metaphor, the predication is made on the basis of similarity in feeling tone—"glowering" clouds, a "brooding" landscape, a "dyspeptic" bureaucracy.

It is, of course, the intent of science to eradicate mere textual or emotional association and capitalize as much as possible on the analogic mode of metaphor, attempting to develop more systematic precision in the analogy, but this does not make structural metaphors any less subject to caution as "speculative instruments." Black's warning is well heeded, for in the analogic mode of metaphoric reasoning there may often be emotional (textual) reasons behind the predication. For example, the Durkheimian mechanical and organic metaphors seem to have different emotional weights—the former an objectivity, an exteriority, a detachment, the latter a subjectivity, an interiority, an attachment. These metaphors move by a kind of "principle of compensation." One can speculate that the assignment of the mechanical metaphor to traditional society objectifies societies of which the emotional subjectivity of kinship is characteristic, while the assignment of the organic metaphor to the impersonal and rational bureaucratic societies subjectifies them and gives them an interiority they do not, in fact, possess. As in every case of the analysis of metaphoric usage, one must be alert to the emotional movement accomplished by the use of the assigned metaphor, whether textual or analogic in emphasis.

In any case, it is primarily the textual metaphors of social life in which we are interested, for not only do they give identity to inchoate subjects, they move them about affectively by adornments and disparagements. To say of a pronoun that he is a rat is to move him quite differently than to say that he is a lion.

Metaphoric Movement in Quality Space

One may usefully conceive of the movement accomplished by metaphors as taking place in quality space. The third mission of metaphor is to move inchoate subjects into an optimum position in quality space. There are many problems with such a topographic model of human experience, but there is some precedent for assuming that our minds organize our experiences by reference to some prelinguistic quality space which arises out of the very nature of life in a world defined by gravitational forces (Quine 1963:83). This may seem too simple and empirical a notion, particularly when compared with the rationalist approach of the transformational grammarians and their affirmation of innate ideas determining the form of acquired knowledge (Chomsky 1965:203–4). But we are already presuming here the innateness of the subject-object predication, based on the sense of discontinuities in experience, and the innate tendency of the subject to form itself by imitating apt attention-getting objects in its milieu. It seems inescapable that even the most empirical theories of the acquisition of experience must assume innate ideas (Stemmer 1971).

In the Asturian mountain world to which I have referred, children come to quickly perceive a difference between a cow and a cat, chicken, dog, donkey, etc., and one can assume they innately assign these objects distances from each other. In their earliest search for identity, these children tend towards the imitation (i.e., the predication upon the inchoate pronoun) of some animals rather than others, choosing the animals that occupy the more desirable positions in the quality space of their culture.

The quality space of any culture can be defined by n dimensions or continua, which must be discovered by anthropological inquiry in the particular case. It is doubtful whether the discipline would be well served by the advocacy of any particular set of dimensions, but to illustrate how metaphoric predication operates in respect to quality space we may take for these dimensions either the seven axes of bias of Jones (1961), a scheme which itself owes something to Morris (1955), or the three dimensions of Osgood's (Osgood, Tannenbaum, and Suci 1957) semantic space. Jones proposes that various cultural products (intellectual and material) can be understood as expressing positions taken in respect to these axes: static-dynamic, order-disorder, discreteness-continuity, spontaneity-process, soft-sharp, inner-outer, this world-other world. Every culture can be defined by the positions its expressive and material products characteristically take on these dimensions. Osgood's method assumes that the affective meaning of all verbal concepts (including pronouns) can be scaled by reference to qualitative continua, all eventually factorable to the three dimensions of potency, activity, and goodness.[10]

This point, as well as the unaccustomed linking of domains of experience accomplished by metaphor, is perhaps best understood by appealing to the phenomenon of synesthesia. In synesthesia we translate experience from one sense modality, say sound, to another, say touch. We speak of hot music. The "law of parallel alignment" is said to prevail. On the sound continuum of fast to slow, a certain kind of music, jazz, occupies a position parallel to that occupied by hot objects on the continuum of hot to cold. Metaphoric predication is the same sort of translation, in our case of an inchoate subject from one domain to another,[11] and it can be conceptualized in relation to continua.

However, in metaphoric predication we are generally not interested in mere parallel alignment, but in adornment or disparagement. The intention is to move the "I," the "he," the "we" around. If an inchoate Asturian pronoun, for example, predicates upon itself that it is a cow, it probably, in respect to the Jones axes, is moved to greater stasis, order, continuity, process, softness, and innerness. (Movement doesn't have to take place on all the dimensions of the culture's quality space.) Certainly it is moved to greater goodness and lesser activity in Osgood's terminology. When the Director of the F.B.I. calls the Attorney General a jellyfish, he is trying to present him as less potent, active, and good than he probably really is. Metaphorical strategies are rhetorical devices whose sophistic potentiality has long been recognized (see Chapter 1). But whether we are inspired to metaphor for purposes of disparagement or adornment or to obtain a concrete parallel in another domain for an inchoate experience, metaphors accomplish a kind of synesthesia in respect to continua in different domains. The items belonging to any domain can be arranged (if we know enough about them) on various scales. (Compare, for the domain of trees, "I am an oak" with "I am a willow," or for the domain of weeds, "I am a dandelion" with "I am a groundwort.") The sum total of these continua defines the quality space of a culture. Metaphor is the chief means by which pronouns take their places and move about in that quality space. Society, in simple, is the movement of pronouns about within quality space. Of course, pronouns move about by many means, but metaphoric assertion of identity by the linking of domains is an important way. Insofar as the metaphoric predication is of a simple and straightforward kind—a pronoun A is a B—common sense tells us the shifts in quality space that the assertion intends. The semantic-differential technique is always available if we wish to measure these in a more precise way.[12] There are, however, more complex metaphoric persuasions and performances. Religious ritual, for example, is a particular challenge to our understanding of the missions of metaphor, for, as Boas recognized, metaphorical terms can be taken literally in ritual and made the basis of the rites. That is, metaphors are not only rhetorical devices of persuasion; they can also lead to performance.

The liturgy of any ritual is composed of a series of ceremonial scenes which may be regarded as putting into effect metaphoric predications upon the pronouns participating in the ritual. There is greater or lesser variation in the distribution of scenes within the total scenario, particularly as we descend to the inspection of smaller segments of scenes (Pike 1967). Nevertheless, this distribution is not probabilistic and dependent solely upon the outcome of the accumulating series of scenes. In acting as well as in speaking, persons have an image of the pattern to be completed and make plans accordingly.[13] The essential type of such images is the sign-image I have been discussing. Their analysis is crucial to the understanding of ritual performance. These images, predicated upon the pronouns of cult life, are put into effect by a series of scenes. It is by means of the performance of these scenes that the ritual brings about those transformations of the experience of the member pronouns which are or should be the prime accomplishment of religion. While some men may undertake worship with a specific and articulated purpose in mind, most men, suspending disbelief, do so because it transforms their experience: it moves them. The essentials of this movement must be traced to the acting out of metaphoric predications. The fourth mission of metaphor is to act as a plan for ritual behavior.

It is axiomatic to such an argument that people undertake religious experience because they desire to change the way they think about themselves and the world in which they live. One frequently hears that men enter into ceremonial processes in such psychological states as anomie, individuation, comparative deprivation, status denial, etc. In terms of this argument, these are instances of an inappropriate location in quality space, which gives rise to feelings of isolation, disengagement, powerlessness, enervation, dysphoria, debasement, contamination, transgression, etc. One can speak at length about such feelings and what ritual does for them. Interest in metaphoric movement focuses our attention upon shifts within quality space. When one says that men exit from ritual incorporated, empowered, activated, and euphoric, one essentially means that they have shifted the inchoate pronoun to greater potency and activity and less goodness in quality space. Or perhaps it is more appropriate for a given culture to talk in terms of greater stasis, order, continuity, process, softness, and innerness. A basic organizing metaphor of the Christian religion, for example, to which sign-image a number of ceremonial scenes (the Eucharist especially) are devoted, is "We are the living body of Christ." Insofar as the ritual scenes operate to make this image a reality, the member leaves the ritual better located in respect to his goodness and his sense of potency and, perhaps, less active. He may otherwise be seen to exit more other-world, more inner, softer, more orderly, and with greater sense of continuity and process. This more satisfactory situation in quality space can only be discussed, in any case, in terms of the value dimensions of a particular culture.

A ritual is to be analyzed, then, as a series of organizing images or metaphors put into operation by a series of superordinate and subordinate ceremonial scenes.[14] Each of these scenes plays its part in realizing the implications of the image-plan. If one is to be the mystical body of Christ, one must first purify that body through confession, discipline it through genuflection, hear of the life of that actual Christ through scripture, and finally, through Eucharist and Communion, achieve a state conforming to the image-plan. Through such ceremonial scenes, men become the metaphor predicated upon them. It follows from this view that no successful ritual can permit the exit of its participants until the set of ceremonial scenes has achieved the approximation of the subject to the metaphor—until the subject has achieved the movement in quality space implied by that metaphor. Though we speak here of only one familiar metaphor, every religion is made up of a number of metaphors, and it is the analysis of the relationship between them and the transformation from one to the other that is challenging.

The Transformation of Metaphors

While the phenomenological account of a religious experience or any expressive event remains uncertain in nature and perhaps as densely metaphoric as the experience itself, understanding may be sharpened by scrutinizing the network of associations brought into play in metaphoric predications and performances. Association may be by contiguity or by similarity. Metonym is commonly understood as resting on contiguity in the same frame of experience as the subject and metaphor as resting on similarity, perceived or felt (structural or textual), of experiences in different domains. The complexity of expressive experience lies in the interplay of contiguity and similarity associations in the predications upon the pronouns participating in this experience. To metaphoric predication, in any case, we must now add the notion of metonymic predication.

The scientific approach to behavior is more persuaded by metonymic predication, since it is context-bound and more susceptible to part-to-whole and cause-and-effect analysis (part-whole and cause-effect associations being basic metonyms). Science is metonymic in method although metaphoric in theory. Nevertheless, it is generally recognized in associationist theory that the contiguity principle fails to explain much of the phenomena: "We must be willing to admit the possibility that obtained associations may never have occurred together in the experience of the person who yields them—they may instead be the result of schemata which serve the function of bringing together structurally related elements from diverse experience" (Deese 1965:20). The nature of these schemata has become the object of intense research in psychology and linguistics and need not be pursued here except to emphasize that the sign-images of metaphoric predications are a kind of schema that dictates certain associations and denies others. As Deese says (1965:159), "Our cognitive structures are the outcome of the operation of hypothesis upon our experience." The pronominal metaphors we have identified are surely hypotheses (cf. Pepper 1942) brought to bear upon our experience.

But in what manner are diverse experiences brought together under the aegis of metaphor? What is the nature of the interplay of contiguity and similarity associations? In language study, associations of these two kinds are labeled syntagmatic and paradigmatic. Syntagmatic associations are those which occur by reason of grammatical contiguity—the association of "good" with "boy," "kindly" with "neighbor," or "reasonable" with "doubt." Paradigmatic associations rest upon equivalence of function—the capacity to occupy the same frame in the chain of experience. Objects, actions, and events, however diverse and causally unrelated, which can occupy the same frame in experience are associated by that fact. What linguists call form classes or function classes constitute a very large and weak set of associations. Nevertheless, the extension of the grammatical notion of behavior as a sequence of frames each of which contains a set of appropriate actions or objects is fruitful (Pike 1967). From such a perspective, what has been discussed here is the filling of frames and the role of metaphor in this fulfillment. In the largest sense, men are framed between the remembered past and the imagined future, with a need not only to predicate an identity upon their inchoate selves but to fill the present with activity. We are, indeed, "time binders" concerned to find the kind of identity and activity that will concretize the inchoate, fill the frame in which we find ourselves, and bind the past and the future together.[15]

Microcosmogony, then—this filling of frames including the space framed by our own bodies at various levels of our experience—can be seen as the product of the interplay of paradigmatic and syntagmatic association, the interaction of metaphors and metonyms. This is a relationship that has preoccupied Lévi-Strauss, who often refers to the law of mythical thought, "The transformation of metaphor is achieved in metonymy." [16] The clearest exposition, in my view, comes in a footnote to *The Savage Mind* (Lévi-Strauss 1966:150) pointing out the paradigmatic-syntagmatic bricolage in the life of Mr. Wemmick of Dickens's *Great Expectations*. The frame of Wemmick's home life is a bland suburban life and a residence which may be treated metaphorically as either a villa or a castle. What, as a "bricoleur," Wemmick "undertook and realized was the establishment of paradigmatic relations between the elements of these two [syntagmatic chains] . . . he can choose between villa and castle to signify his abode, between pond and moat to signify the entrance, between salad and food reserves to signify his lettuces." By what is in effect metaphoric assertion, Wemmick's suburban life (an inchoate existence, one takes it) is transformed into a "succession of ritual actions, the paradigmatic relations between two equally unreal syntagmatic chains. That of the castle which has never existed and that of the villa which has been sacrificed." The difficulty comes when we are told that "the first aspect of bricolage is thus to construct a system of paradigms with the fragments of syntagmatic chains. But the reverse is equally true . . . a new syntagmatic chain results from the system of paradigmatic relations . . . metaphors take over the mission of metonyms and vice versa."

These insights may be otherwise stated, in reference to the point of view taken here, in the following manner: in inchoateness of subjects within certain frames of reference[17]—suburban life, early childhood, those ultimate circumstances framed by birth and death—is concretized by metaphoric predication. Such predication incorporates into such frames elements of other domains of experience which, if not more clearly understood, are at least more sharply felt.[18] In a sense we may say that metaphoric predication takes an inchoate frame and incorporates into it a domain of objects and actions whose identity and action requirements we more clearly understand. The assumption is, as Pike (1967) has argued, that these frames of reference may be considered at any level of generality, from the individually specific (such as the space filled by our own bodies when we are brought to contemplate it) to that most general frame between the past and the future so problematic in highly transitional societies. The point is that within any frame there is a certain and finite class of appropriate metaphoric fillers. This class of sign-images which are associated by such similarity of function is the paradigm. The fifth mission of metaphor, then, is to enable pronouns to fill inchoate frames by incorporating experience in the form of sign-images from a metaphoric domain aptly included in the frame. In another vocabulary, one might say that metaphor is a mediating device connecting the unconnected and bridging the gaps in causality.

The frames in which metaphors appear are part of a larger syntagmatic chain, just as they themselves require, for their fulfillment, a sequence, a syntax of (in the case of ritual) ceremonial scenes. It is in that sense that the discussion is rendered difficult, causing Lévi-Strauss to point out that metaphors take over the mission of metonyms and vice versa. Metaphors give rise to a syntax of scenes designed to put them into effect, and in that sense they do take over the mission of metonyms (which is to represent and bring into association a larger context). Metonyms, on the other hand, take over the mission of metaphor in the sense that the elements of a syntagmatic progression can suggest themselves as a metaphor for the pronominal subjects of that progression. Jakobson (1960:370) points out how in Russian folk poetry a simile is presented in the shape of a temporal sequence. For example, in Slavic folklore the willow under which a girl passes serves at the same time as her image, or the horse a man rides comes to serve as his representation. Jakobson calls this "similarity imposed on contiguity" and quotes Goethe: "Anything transient is but a likeness." This is to say that in the process of syntactically playing out a sign-image, new metaphors may be suggested for the pronouns involved. In this sense the transformation of a metaphor predicated upon a pronoun is achieved in metonymy—in the performance of that metaphor. We do not, consequently, escape the fact that the distinction between metaphor and metonymy can be a slippery one. As Jakobson goes on to point out in respect to poetry, "similarity is superimposed upon contiguity and any metonymy is slightly metaphorical and any metaphor has a metonymical tint."

In extended discussion, in fact, the distinction between syntagmatic and paradigmatic relations is difficult to maintain. In linguistic analysis,

Lounsbury (1959:127) finds the notions of similarity relation and contiguity relation not independent: "linguistic similarity is nothing more than shared contiguity associations." If we think of this in terms of a matrix, we find that the substitution-distribution matrix A (i,j), where j is the paradigm of 1 to n frames and i is the class of 1 to n forms that will fill each of these frames, may be inverted to the substitution-distribution matrix B (j,i), where i is the paradigm of 1 to n forms and j is the class of 1 to n frames in which these forms may appear. What is a distribution paradigm in one sense—the set of frames into which a class of different forms may be fitted—becomes a substitution class in another sense—the class of frames defined by their ability to entertain the same set of forms. The same form may appear in different frames. This is a basic kind of transformation and accounts for the difficulty of categorizing the elements of expressive experience without having these categories undergo inversions, practically before our eyes.

From the nettles of this difficulty, however, can be grasped a useful analytic device (fig. 1). The Christian ceremony referred to, or any ceremony for that matter, suggests a cube of data the dimensions of whose cells are (1) the succeding frames of experience dominated by succeeding organizing metaphors or metonyms (core sign-images), which constitute the horizontal axis; (2) the particular scenes (Frake 1964) put forth and performed in order to fulfill the expectation of the metaphor, which constitute the vertical axis; and (3) the particular associations brought into play in each scene, which constitute the receding axis. In Christian ceremony, under the major metaphoric predication "Life is a sacrifice," one can identify the following sequence of underlying metaphors and metonyms: "I am the stained body" (metonym), "I am the fruit cut off from the vine" (metaphor), "He is the sacrificial lamb" (metaphor), "He is bread and wine" (metaphor), "He is the glorified lamb" (metaphor), "He is the Lamb of God" (metaphor), "We are the living body of the glorified" (metonym-metaphor). There are of course other and more abstract ways to state this metaphoric-metonymic movement: "I am the isolated," "He is the victim of our isolation," "He is the resurrected," "We are the living community." And, in still more abstract terms, one can talk of body becoming spirit. In ecclesiastical terms, one speaks of Penance, Eucharist, and Communion. The approach to ceremonial development from the perspective of underlying metaphoric-metonymic predications may seem contrived to one accustomed to more abstract categories, but there is good reason to believe, as I have argued, that the abstract categories are

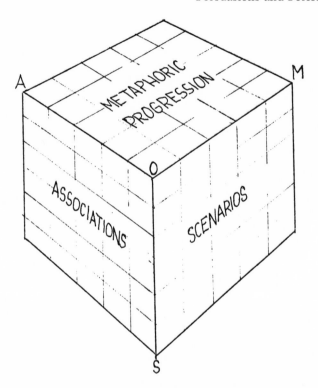

FIG. 1. Three dimensions of expressive events: M, core sign-images or organizing metaphors; S, scenes fulfilling the metaphors; A, associations brought into play by each scene; O, origin. Two faces, SOM and SOA, are displayed in figure 2.

derivative and the metaphoric predications primordial. They are the kernels from which has grown the edifice of liturgical and theological abstractions with which any established church is preoccupied. It is through the study of these metaphoric kernels that we better arrive at the movement of feelings involved in the ritual.

Figure 2 illustrates a two-dimensional analysis of that sacrificial ceremony in which an uncertainly perceived Lord becomes the Lamb of God and an inchoate devotee isolated by his stained condition is revived in his communal membership in the mystical body of that Lord.[19] Reading from the origin, one notes a progression of scenarios fulfilling the implications of succeeding metaphoric or metonymic predications. Each scene marshalls associations linked to the metaphor or metonym as a sign-image. The deeper one moves into the event, the thicker is the experience, for

| Secondary Associations | Primary Associations | | | | Penance | Offering | Invocation | Consecration | Communion |
	Color	Organs of Focus	Body Effluent	Corporeal Feeling Tone	"stained body"	"sacrificial lamb"	"He is bread and wine"	"He is Lamb of God"	"We are living body"
Individuation.	black	conative (endodermic) organs of gluttony and lust	tears and cloacal emissions	Corporeal collapse, the body overburdened.	Formulation of failings.	Entrance chant.	Laying of offering upon altar.	Prefatory prayers and praises.	Kiss of peace, embrace of fellowship.
Individuation.				Isolation, the body in ruins.	Entrance into solitary and obscure confessional.	Gospel lesson, life and times of the victim.	Mixing of the water with wine.	Isolation of priest and sanctification of altar.	Invitation of Congregation to the Holy Table.
Dyadic exchange.				Corporeal relief, the body unburdened.	The lonely confession.	Prayer of those assembled.	Invocation, insensation.	Plea for acceptance and intercession.	Partaking of the body of the glorified Lamb.
Dyadic exchange.						Offertory procession, or collection.	Handwashing.	Transformation of bread and wine into body and blood. (3d transformation)	Silent prayer and thanksgiving.
Dyadic exchange.						Oblation of the faithful through their gifts.	Prayer of fellowship, secret prayer of the priest.	Elevation and glorification of body and blood.	
The promise of community.				Reincorporation.	The absolution. (1st transformation)	Offerings transformed into bread and wine (2d transformation)	Dialogue of priest and congregation.	Commingling of body and blood, prayer to Lamb of God.	Blessing and recession.

FIG. 2. Three-dimensional analysis of Christian ceremony: $O \to M$, the progressive metaphoric rephrasings; $O \to A$, the associations brought into play by the progression (cf. fig. 1); $O \to S$, the scenario, or sequence of scenes fulfilling each of the first of these scenarios (penance).

these associations are reinforced, restated, and transformed (a process not illustrated here).

One can collapse this cube in various ways. One can, for example, collapse the sequence of scenes that puts the metaphor into effect so as to show the dominant associations brought into existence by succeeding metaphoric rephrasings of the ceremony (table 1). Just as Mr. Wemmick lives in a house among other houses which he metaphorically interprets to be either a villa or a castle, so the participant in any expressive experience lives in a body among other bodies which, all together, he comes to interpret as the living body of the Lord. But this overall transformation is accompanied by subordinate ones brought about by a succession of subordinate metaphors or metonyms. Each of these subordinate sign-images brings into play a set of associations linked to it in previous experience.

It is arguable that it is in the nature of human experience for these associations to have two sources: (1) the primary experience of corporeal life with its inner "textual" sensations of events and (2) the secondary life of the self in the external (structural) world (principally in the society of others) in the causal-functional context of social contiguities and discontiguities. The succession of metaphors and metonyms in any expressive event will be found, mainly, to be calling successively into focus different aspects of primary and secondary experience. The succession of sign-images not only shifts attention around within the primary experience, but, in most effective metaphors, extends the corporeal into the social and vice versa. The predication of these sign-images upon subjects allows them not only to concretize their inchoateness but often to link the corporeal and the social, socializing corporeal experience, as it were, and incorporating social experience. A metaphor is an assertion based on an inner sense of the pronoun's similarity to some aspect of the external world.

Metaphoric and metonymic predication in the end can only concretize a part of the inchoate whole of corporeal and social experience. When the exploration of the metaphor or metonym is fulfilled—when the condition in feeling or form of the sign-image is approximated—another metaphor or metonym appears to try to "return us to the whole." But, of course, it only succeeds in linking the subject to a partiality or an essentially false attribution again. This repeated search to "return to the whole,"[20] out of dissatisfaction, perhaps, with the "partness" of any of our devices of representation, may be called the sixth mission of metaphor.

TABLE 1

DOMINANT ASSOCIATIONS OF SUCCESSIVE METAPHORIC REPHRASINGS OF CHRISTIAN CEREMONY

ASSOCIATIONS	METAPHORIC PROGRESSION				
	"I AM STAINED BODY"	"HE IS SACRIFICIAL LAMB"	"HE IS BREAD AND WINE"	"HE IS LAMB OF GOD"	"WE ARE LIVING BODY"
Primary					
Corporeal feeling tone	separation, isolation (the body in ruins)	purposive solidarity (the body gathering its forces)	corporeal fractioning (the body reduced to its parts)	corporeal transformation (the body transformed)	corporeal exaltation (the body apotheosized)
Body effluents	tears and cloacal emissions	the sweat of our brow	the digestive liquids	blood	effluents mystically congealed
Organs of focus	conative (endodermic) organs of gluttony and lust	conative (mesodermic) organs	sustenential (endodermic) organs	organic parts transformed into a whole (heart)	ectodermic sensitivity to ambiance
Color	black	gold	brown	red	white
Secondary	the isolated individual	the family (as the offering unit)	the priest and the congregation (in dialogue)	the priest alone (as consecrator of bread and wine)	the Family of God

51

Associations in Complex

The motivation to put forth metaphor lies, I have proposed, in the need
to concretize the inchoateness of subjects within frames and obtain a more
satisfactory occupancy of quality space. Metaphors move us, and their
aptness lies in their power to change our moods, our sense of situation.
But this proposition, while it is subject to verification (by use of the
semantic-differential technique), does not describe the relationship between metaphors in a complex expressive event. It is not enough to say
that the metaphors within any expressive paradigm are associated on the
basis that they can aptly function within the same frame.

The study of the principles of association has generally been analytic,
concentrating upon either external contiguity relations or inner logical
relationships of ordination within the same domain or tree structure—
supraordinate (dog-animal), subordinate (animal-dog), and coordinate
(dog-cat) associations. But many of the most interesting kinds of associations for the student of expressive culture, and religious ceremony in
particular, are often thrown into a wastebasket class. These are synthetic
associations,[21] whose linkages seem very remote when considered by
reference to any principle of inner ordination or external contiguity. These
associations are obtained, it is generally recognized, by contrast or mediation.

The problems involved in the study of such synthetic associations
should not be underestimated. Very egocentric or culture-centric elements enter into them. Jung and Ricklin (1918), in their early and am-
bitious classification of word associations, point out that synthetic associations are usually not perceptually evident and are judgments taken with
marked reference to the ego and its values.[22] In the face of such subjective
constellations, they temper their ambitions (p. 119):

> There are possibilities of a series of coordinations which do not easily lend
> themselves to classification. In such cases impotence must be frankly admit-
> ted . . . consolation must be found in the fact that individual possibilities are
> incalculable, that no one scheme will ever be discovered by which all
> associations will be able to be classified typically and without a residue.

When we seek knowledge concerning systems of association in expressive culture, we are bound to recognize a range between those
systems which are systematically motivated and those which are much
more spontaneous and arbitrary in terms of the relationship between the

images put forth. Lévi-Strauss discusses the range in terms of Saussure's notions of grammatical motivation and lexicological orientation, the latter referring to the orientation towards the sign-image in itself and its right to appear in a system unconditioned. Lévi-Strauss is confident that the mind "continues to introduce a principle of order and regularity into certain parts of the mass of signs" (1966:154), but he also recognizes the complication presented by the irrational principle of the arbitrariness of the sign. Some languages are more grammatical and others more lexical. Jakobson (1955:79) has made a similar point: style in art arises from "a predilection for either the metonymical or the metaphorical device."

Anthropologists have long recognized variability in the concern for "logico-aesthetic integration" as we compare cultures (Thompson 1945) or as we compare cults within cultures or individuals within cults (Fernandez 1965, 1966b). In respect to the latter comparisons, one finds differences between cults in their interest in forming concepts about cult activities. Some cults and some cult members view the various events in cult life as a kind of agglomeration and feel it to possess only an "incoherent coherence." They focus on the experience of individual sign-images and are satisfied with social consensus. In other cults and in many cult leaders, there is a much clearer conception of total cult organization and a determination to submit the parts of the cult to the rules implicit in these conceptions.

This variability may be usefully referred to Vygotsky's (1962) classification of types of thinking in concepts: (1) Some religious leaders are anxious that one or several elements should run thematically through the ceremonies, binding the parts together through such common attribution. They have a very clear idea of general nuclei of association (I have labeled these as organizing metaphors) around which ceremonies are organized. (2) Others have a good notion of the chainlike relationship of parts but no overall concern with one or several principles of unity. (3) Still others are satisfied with a very diffuse notion that various parts of the cult have something to do with each other. Their cults tend to be highly volatile, and new ritual elements are readily added and others allowed to fall away. (4) Still others, in response to inquiry, will give a more or less concise conceptual account of cult activity which, however, upon inspection of the ritual, would seem to have little or nothing to do with what is transpiring there.

Vygotsky's classification and the notions of contrast and mediation mentioned above take us some way beyond Jung and Ricklin's sense of frustration. Of contrast association, in spite of its importance, there is relatively little to be said. In regard to structures of contradiction, as Lévi-Strauss (1966:95) admits, "The poverty of religious thought can never be overestimated."[23] The principle involved, basic to language coding, is also illustrated in the tendency of stimulus words—in word-association tests—to provoke their opposites. This occurs most generally in the case of qualities or adjectives. One can only speculate that the mind's inclination towards opposites at this level comes from a homeostatic principle involved in the mind's predication on inchoate subjects. The search for truth through qualification seems to be a process of narrowing in by opposites.

The associations that rest upon mediation merit more extended attention. In the study of these, we come to a better understanding of the overall progress made by a paradigm of metaphors than can be obtained through a study of the dialectical structures of contrast relations. Evans-Pritchard's (1956) discussion of the problem of associations is relevant here. He begins by recognizing the necessity in religion of linking inchoate concepts "to visible objects which enable the mind to hold them and keep them apart." In attempting to explain the various predications upon the Nuer notion of spirit, *kwoth,* [24] Evans-Pritchard feels it necessary to account not only for such predications as "crocodile is spirit"[25] but also for the more baffling "twins are birds" (Nuer) or "twins are salmons" (Nootka). It is these latter associations, seeming to express a plain contradiction, which, after all, led Lévy-Bruhl astray to his theory of prelogical mentality.[26] Though these associations may always rest to a degree on culture-bound and gratuitous or bizarre analogies (which it is the anthropologist's province to divulge), very often there is a latent factor involved. Statements such as "twins are birds" are made in relation to a third term: "They are statements, as far as the Nuer are concerned, not that A is B but that A and B have something in common in relation to C" (Evans-Pritchard 1956:142). The latent generic characteristic (what students of word association call a latent middle term) which they have in common and which associates them is spirit: they are both manifestations of spirit. There is a triadic relationship involved.

In this accounting for the association of sign-images by reference to a latent factor, it is obvious that the mind is, after all, one entity bound to realize the unity of its experiences at some level of abstraction. To say bizarrely of Frank that he is a clam, though for all practical purposes a metaphoric asociation of two quite distinct domains, is a predication within the same domain at a high level of abstraction. Both Frank and the clam are metazoa. To a sufficiently religious mentality, everything in the world can be brought into association as a manifestation of spirit. Certain kinds of metaphysical endeavor search precisely for those general principles by which the diversity of experience—the product of that logical dynamism, that drive towards categorization which is the object of Lévi-Strauss's study—can be integrated. In one of the religious cults I studied in Africa, *bwiti* in Gabon, a leader much given to the use of analogies (*efonan* likenesses) in his sermons remarked that such analogies make clear that all the world is one thing. By using them he was trying to teach his members that fact, and thus defeat witchcraft, which tries to break the world apart and isolate men in order to eat them (Fernandez 1965:911). This tendency in the cult leader comes very close to Lévy-Bruhl's "mystical participation."

What is useful in this recognition of the latent factors involved in associations is that it leads in the same direction as the recognition of the role of mediation in association and the recognition that a metaphoric predication is a hypothesis about the world or a part of it that responds to a specific intention or plan. Caution is surely in order when we set about to state those latent intentions which mediate and synthesize metaphoric objects to subjects and whose presence helps us account for the progression of metaphors in bodies of expressive culture. The search may too easily lead to outmoded notions of innate ideas or *Elementargedanken*. In every case the statement of latent intentions must be based upon careful study of the metaphor and metonym structure of the culture in question.

In simple predications of the kind S is O ("I [a man] am a bear"), I have hypothesized that the latent intention is to move the subject into a more appropriate position in the culture's quality space. But bodies of expressive culture give more complex predications than this, arising out of the formula $S^1 : O^1 :: S^2 : O^2$ ("I [a man] am to a bear as you [a woman] are to a bunny"). The latent intention for such a set of predications, in addition to placing the subjects more desirably in quality space, may be to state the dominance by size and power of male over female and, perhaps, the right of the one to lethargy and the responsibility of the other to reproductiveness. (More associations than this surely are pulled into our awareness by the metaphor; cf. Leach 1964.)

Matters of intention in expressive culture are more complicated; we have a paradigm of metaphors to account for. Returning to the Christian cult examined above, one asks what the latent intentions may be which bring together the metaphors in the paradigm. Under the organizing metaphoric predication "Life is a sacrifice," we have a series of metaphoric statements which constitute *points de repère* in the transformation wrought by the ritual. In one sense, the latent intention of these subordinate metaphors and metonyms is to put into effect the major organizing metaphor, and the latent intention of that metaphor is to affirm that life is necessarily a giving up of one valued condition for another in order to obtain a greater good—the giving up of corporeality for spirituality, as it were. But more specific things are learned about that intention by following the subordinate metaphoric statements. The succession of these statements is as follows:

(I : bodily appetites ::
He : sacrificial lamb),
(He : bread and wine ::
we : our bodily appetites),
(He : glorified lamb ::
we : his body).

One may formulate the progression of metaphors and metonyms in this ceremony in the following way:

$$(S^1 : O^1 :: S^2 : O^2),$$
$$(S^2 : O^3 :: S^1 + 1 : O^1),$$
$$(S^2 : O^2 + 1 :: S^1 + 1 : O^1 + 1),$$

where S is subject, O object, : a relationship of metaphoric (across-domain) predication, and : a relationship of metonymic (within-domain) predication. + 1 indicates a significant transformation, within a given ceremonial framework, of the original subject (in this case from singular to plural) and of the original object (in this case from negative to positive affect). (This formula, which does not pretend to be algebraic, may be compared with Lévi-Strauss's [n.24 above].)

We see, in respect to objects and subjects, the following transformations: the subject pronoun from singular to plural and the objects sacrificial lamb to glorified lamb and bodily appetites to mystical body.[27] There is an intermediate metaphoric predication, "He is bread and wine," and an intermediate restatement of the subject of the initial metonymic predication, the "I" becoming a "we." The transformation of the metonymic predication upon the pronoun—from "own appetites" to "other body"—and the transformation of the pronoun itself, from "I" to "we," are accomplished in the metaphoric predications of "lamb" and "bread and wine" on the significant other, "he." In this case the rule is: metaphoric predications upon a significant other bring about significant transformation of the inchoate subject in respect to its metonymic relationship to its parts. The seventh mission of metaphor is to rescue pronouns from a preoccupation with their parts.

Beyond recognizing the transformations in the subjects and objects of expressive events accomplished by metaphoric and metonymic predication, we also find suggested for us in such analysis the latent themes with which such events are preoccupied. On the evidence of the ritual considered here and on the basis of others I have examined, I would propose that in expressive events, and in religious celebrations particularly, metaphors and metonyms are being chosen to put forth three kinds of statements: statements of adequacy, inadequacy, and transformation or transcendence of state. These statements are predicated upon any of the society of pronouns, but primarily upon the self or significant others (in the case examined here, the "I," the "he," and the "we"). These statements are primarily comments about pronouns from either the social structural perspective, that of status and role experiences, or the corporeal perspective, that of biophysiological experience.[28] In the particular rituals referred to here we find statements of corporeal and social inadequacy of the "I" and the "he" followed by transformation, indeed transcendence, of the "he" and the "I." The ritual, through its predications, accomplishes the transformation of the "I" into a "we" and of animal into deity and, most subtly perhaps, in the final predication "We are the living body of Christ," an identification of the social, the transcendent, and the corporeal. Other rituals make different movements; I have elsewhere discussed a ritual whose metaphors make progressive transformations from statements of social adequacy of the "we" through statements of corporeal adequacy of the "we" and corporeal and status inadequacy of the "I" to statements of corporeal exaltation of the "we" (Fernandez 1977).

Conclusion

It should not be forgotten in reducing the very rich body of materials of expressive culture to some bare bones—the notions of pronouns in inchoate frames of quality space, of latent thematic social and corporeal preoccupations of pronominal subjects—that in the end the mission of metaphor and metonymy is to convert pronouns from their inappropriate and inchoate condition. Metaphor is that elementary form which lies at the heart of social life. It is the nature of that life to offer both periodic and exceptional conversions to the pronouns who pass through it. These conversions arise from the power men possess to metaphorically and metonymically "take the other." To so reduce the materials of expressive culture must inevitably provoke skepticism, particularly in anthropologists, who by reason of the character of fieldwork have a very rich sense of reality.

One may first be skeptical that metaphors are put forth by every participant, in a ceremony for example, in response to his inchoate and troubled subjectivity. And of course they are not. But one must postulate that at some point in the history of any expressive movement these metaphors were brought to bear upon the "I," "we," "they," "he," etc., by the visionaries or aesthetes who gave prophetic or artful impulse to that movement, whether cult or school. Metaphoric innovation, like any innovation, rests with the few. The many who are attracted to such statements and performances need only agree to their aptness. They need only entertain "social consensus," agreement about the appropriateness of actions required, and need have little concern for "cultural consensus," agreement as to the meaning of the metaphors upon which the action is based. But there are always some men who feel more strongly their inchoateness and their painful positioning in quality space. They have the imagination to leap to other domains to obtain recompense and movement. They have the strength of character to attract followers to the reorganization of existence represented in the acting out of their selected sign-images.

One may be skeptical in the second place that the participant in any highly organized expressive activity is paying exact attention to all the particulars of that activity. And of course he is not. There are important differences in "focus" (Pike 1967), in the level of activity of which the participant is aware or upon which he is concentrating. In fact, any participant may at certain junctures be so removed from the level of activity in the hierarchy of events qualifying a particular metaphor as to be "with" the ritual in body only. Nevertheless this hypostatization or removal of attention can never be so complete as to prevent the participant from recognizing those signals contained in any sign-image by which scenes are changed and new metaphors put into operation. In Puritan churches brass knobs on the end of long poles were employed to make sure that, at the least, one kept track of such clues. And in the Catholic church such attention is assured by rigorous genuflection.

One may be skeptical, thirdly, that we can exclude the awareness of

symbols, though we have argued here for the primacy of the study of
metaphor over the study of symbolism. And of course we cannot. Symbols
of various kinds are constantly appearing and being manipulated in expressive events. In their condensation of many meanings—their multivocality or polysemy—they are always likely to shift the members'
attention away from the metaphor at hand, either hypostatizing it at
another level or shifting attention to another meaning not appropriately
voiced in the metaphoric domain in which they are currently acting.

The metaphoric context in which a symbol appears tends to focus
attention on a particular meaning of that symbol (by reason of its multivocality it can appear in many contexts). Still, the symbol is volatile in the
sense that it is always likely to shift our attention away from the current
organizing metaphor. Symbols thus add the possibility of experience at
other levels of meaning at any time during the more basic transformations
here discussed. They fill out the universe of expressive experience and
give it a thickness and complexity which the discussion of metaphoric
progressions, however basic, does not fully capture.

One may be skeptical in the fourth place that the motivations in
expressive events are always the obtaining by means of metaphoric predicates of conversions in the subject's relationship to its corporeal and its
social contexts. And of course they are not. Many expressive events seem
to be devoted to either arousing or depressing the attention of the participants. Arousal in ritual, for example, is often obtained by confronting
participants with bizarre formations, whether men in animal clothing or
animal-headed gods, which in their incongruity invite attention. Whatever else may be said about them, they serve to raise the level of cortical
stimulation. Other rituals, through a slow and measured cadence, serve as
escape from overstimulation. Expressive events not only create a liminal
period for the readjustment of arousal, but also, by varying the normal
associations of things, enable learning to take place (Turner 1967:chap. 4).
But the bizarre features of ritual are simply an elaboration of what is basic
to metaphoric predication. That predication is a speculation upon the
varying possible concomitance of subjects and objects. And in that speculation lies arousal value as well. As the subject is brought metaphorically
to contemplate membership in a different domain than is customary or
metonymically to focus upon parts of himself that he is accustomed to
ignore, there must inevitably be some arousing or depressing of his
spirits.

The perspective espoused here, which might be labeled pronominalism,[29] is part of an emphasis in the social sciences in the last

decade upon the role of cognition and communication in interaction and more importantly upon the role of mental schema or images in mediating that interaction. Craik (1943) and Boulding (1957) made this point tellingly. The weight of such arguments against strict behaviorism was such that certain experimental psychologists were led to call for "subjective behaviorism" (Miller, Galanter, and Pribram 1960:213).

In anthropology, the interest in subjective thought processes is as old as Tylor and Boas. Recent developments in ethnoscience are an important refinement of that old tradition. The concentration of ethnoscience upon the defining features within given domains of experience needs to be complemented, however, with study of the way relationships are established between domains by metaphoric predication,[30] for such creative displacements are the source of the progress-conversion—in its profoundest sense—accomplished by the human animal. The study of such displacements tells us fundamental things about the way the subjective is related to the objective, the real to the imaginary.

What is the method of such study? One can promise no mechanical procedures or simple rules that will lead every student to the same result. As in so much of ethnographic or ethnologic interpretation, there is a considerable element of art involved, the intuitive grasp of essential relationships amidst a rich universe of possibilities (Burling 1964). There is always ellipsis as we pass from underlying metaphoric predications to ritual complexes. In our analysis of objects behaving, moreover, there seems always to remain something ineradicably subjective. We do not eradicate the copula. Scientific inquiry of this kind is not only hypothetical about objects; it is predicative upon subjects.

Nevertheless I suggest that more clarity can be achieved in the practice of such "subjective objectivity" if we study the structure of associations that arises in metaphoric and metonymic predication upon inchoate pronouns. The first requirement for such study is detail in ethnographic description. This means a following of the classic method of participant observation. This method gives us, as none other, an awareness of the many different domains of experience in a culture to which expressive events may, in their predications, be making a linkage. This method brings us into most penetrating relationship to pronouns and the object world they embrace. The collection of ethnographic detail should be guided by the following elementary assumptions:

1. Culture in its expressive aspects rests upon metonymic and metaphoric predications of sign-images upon inchoate pronominal subjects. These predications may be only persuasive, or they may lead to perform-

ance. These predications take place within an *n* dimensional cultural quality space and function to give affective definition to pronouns which seek to be more aptly located within that space. The social situation and the disposition of the pronouns which would seek to act within it motivate their metaphoric predication, their "taking of the other."

2. Predications are first evident in the "taking of the other" characteristic of the earliest childhood quest for identity and in the subsequent obtaining of identity by the mastery of these other objects (sign-images). Different cultures, it is postulated, choose these sign-images from characteristically different domans. There is thus a cultural lexicon of these sign-images rooted in earliest childhood.

3. The predication of sign-images upon subjects accomplishes significant movement of these subjects in cultural quality space. The study of the lexicon of sign-images leads to a dimensioning of that quality space. Within the quality space of a given culture, there are characteristic movements of characteristic subjects.

4. Complex expressive events consist of a chain of metaphors and metonyms, often operating under the organizing effect of major metaphor. Such complexes may be analyzed (*a*) in matrix form, by reference to the scenes devised to put metaphoric sign-images into effect and the associations marshalled by each scene, or (*b*) in formula form, by reference to the transformations in subjects and objects wrought by progressions in the relations between metonymic and metaphoric predications.

5. The study of metaphors with these assumptions in mind should lead to the exploration of the proposition that in expressive culture we find represented through tropes a limited number of latent intentions concerning the condition of pronouns in their corporeal and their social condition.

Whether such a set of assumptions can direct anthropological analysis towards the mastery the science seeks over the rich subtleties of expressive culture remains to be seen. Field study with the mission of the metaphor in mind can bring about a closer focus upon that interplay between the real and the imaginary by which social subjects deal masterfully with the object world, using that world to bring about significant conversions in themselves.

Abstract

The reappearance of the metaphor concept in ethnologic inquiry suggests the need for a clearer trope-ology than we now possess. Metaphor (and metonym) is defined here as the predication of a sign-image upon any of the set of inchoate pronouns—the essential social subjects. The study of metaphor is the study of the way these subjects take objects unto themselves or are assigned them—the way that, in the parlance of G. H. Mead, they "take the other" (or "another part of themselves" in the case of metonym). The overall mission of metaphor and metonym is to convert pronouns from their inappropriate and inchoate condition, but seven particular missions are to be identified: (1) the providing of an identity for inchoate subjects; (2) the enabling of movement in these subjects; (3) the optimum positioning of these subjects in quality space; (4) the providing of a plan for ritual movement; (5) the filling of frames of social experience; (6) the enabling of the subject to "return to the whole"; (7) the freeing of the subject from a preoccupation with its parts. It is shown that metaphoric and metonymic complexes may be analyzed either (a) in matrix form, by reference to the scenes devised to put metaphoric sign-images into effect and the associations marshalled by each scene, or (b) in formula form, by reference to the transformations in subjects and objects brought about by progressions in the relations between metonymic and metaphoric predications. The view is taken that valid ethnologic inquiry into expressive culture should focus upon the vicissitudes of subjects and objects as they are related in complexes of metaphoric and metonymic predication.

References

BERGGREN, D
   1962–63 The use and abuse of metaphor. *Review of Metaphysics* 16:238–58.
BLACK, MAX
   1962   "Metaphor," in *Models and metaphors*. Ithaca: Cornell University Press.
BOAS, FRANZ
   1911   "Introduction," in *Handbook of American Indian languages*. Bureau of American Ethnology Bullentin 40(1).
BOULDING, KENNETH
   1957   *The image*. Ann Arbor: University of Michigan Press.
BURKE, KENNETH
   1957   Revised edition. *The philosophy of literary form*. New York: Vintage Books.
BURLING, ROBBINS
   1964   Cognition and componential analysis: God's Truth or hocus pocus. *American Anthropologist* 66:20–29.
CHOMSKY, NOAM
   1965   *Aspects of the theory of syntax*. Cambridge: M.I.T. Press.

CRAIK, KENNETH
1943   *The nature of explanation.* London: Cambridge University Press.
DEESE, JAMES
1965   *The structure of associations in language and thought.* Baltimore: Johns Hopkins Press.
DIETERLEN, GERMAINE, and MARCEL GRIAULE
1965   *Le renard pale. Tome I, Le mythe cosmogonique fasicule I: La creation du monde.* Mémoires de l'Institut d'Ethnologie 72.
EDMONSON, M. S.
1971   *Lore: An introduction to the science of folklore and literature.* New York: Holt, Rinehard and Winston.
ENDLER, NORMAN S.
1961   Changes in meaning during psychotherapy as measured by the semantic differential. *Journal of Counseling Psychology* 8:105–11.
EVANS-PRITCHARD, E. E.
1956   *Neur religion.* Oxford: Oxford University Press.
FERNANDEZ, J. W.
1965   Symbolic consensus in a Fang reformative cult. *American Anthropologist* 67:902–29.
1966a.   Unbelievably subtle words: Representation and integration in the sermons of an African reformative cult. *Journal of the History of Religions* 6:43–69.
1966b.   Principles of opposition and vitality in Fang aesthetics. *Journal of Aesthetics and Art Criticism* 25:53–64.
1967   Review of: *Le renard pale,* by G. Dieterlen and M. Griaule (Travaux et Mémoires de l'Institut d'Ethnologie 72). *American Anthropologist* 69:527–28.
1968   Review of: *L'arbre cosmique dans la pensée populaire et dans la vie quotidienne du nord-ouest africain,* by Viviana Paques (Travaux et Mémoires de l'Institut d'Ethnologie 70). *American Anthropologist* 70:796.
1972   Persuasions and performances: Of the beast in every body and the metaphors of Everyman. *Daedalus* 101(1):39–60.
1977   "The performance of ritual metaphors," in *The social use of metaphor.* Edited by David Sapir and Christopher Crocker. Philadelphia, U. Penn Press, pp. 100–131.
n.d. *a* The power of positive pronouns. MS.
FRAKE, CHARLES O.
1964   "A structural description of Subanun religious behavior," in *Explorations in cultural anthropology: Essays in honor of George Peter Murdock.* Edited by Ward H. Goodenough, pp. 111–29. New York: McGraw-Hill.
GEORGES, ROBERT A., and ALAN DUNDES
1963   Toward a structural definition of the riddle. *Journal of American Folklore* 76:111–18. [AD]
GORHAM, DONALD R.
1956   Use of the proverbs test for differentiating schizophrenics from normals. *Journal of Consulting Psychology* 20:435–40. [AD]
HARVEY, O. J.
1964   *Motivation and social interaction.* New York: Ronald.
HAUGEN, EINAR

1973   Linguistic relativity: Myths and methods. Paper 1871, IXth International Congress of Anthropological and Ethnological Sciences, Chicago.

HYMAN, S. E.
1959   *The tangled bank: Darwin, Marx, Frazer, and Freud as imaginative writers.* New York: Atheneum.

JAKOBSON, ROMAN
1955   "Aphasia as a linguistic problem," in *On expressive language.* Edited by H. Werner, pp. 69–81. Worcester: Clark University Press.
1960   "Linguistics and poetics," in *Style in language.* Edited by Thomas A. Sebeok, pp. 355–73. Cambridge: M.I.T. Press.

JAKOBSON, ROMAN, and MORRIS HALLE
1956   *Fundamentals of language.* The Hague: Mouton.

JONES, W. T.
1961   *The romantic syndrome.* The Hague: Mouton.

JUNG, CARL
1958   "Transformation symbolism in the Mass," in *Psyche and symbol.* Edited by V. S. de Laszlo. New York: Modern Library.

JUNG, CARL, and FRANX RICKLIN
1918   *Studies in word association.* London: W. Heinemann.

JUNGMANN, J. A.
1955   *The Mass of the Roman rite: Its origin and development.* 2 vols. Translated by F. A. Brunner. New York: Benziger.

KAPLAN, BERNARD
1962   Radical metaphor, aesthetic, and the origin of language. *Review of Existential Psychology and Psychiatry* 2:75–84.

KEHOE, ALICE B.
1974a The metonymic pole and social roles. *Journal of Anthropological Research.* In press.
1974b "Ritual and religions: An ethologically-oriented formal analysis." *Proceedings of the IXth International Congress of Anthropological and Ethnological Sciences, Chicago.* The Hague: Mouton. In press.

KRAMER, SAMUEL NOAH
1963   *The Sumerians.* Chicago: University of Chicago Press.

LA BARRE, W.
1970   *The Ghost Dance: Origins of religion.* Garden City: Doubleday.

LACAN, J.
1966   *Ecrits.* Paris: Editions du Seuil.

LEACH, E.
1964   "Anthropological aspects of language: Animal categories and verbal abuse," in *New directions in the study of language.* Edited by E. H. Lenneberg, pp. 23–63. Cambridge: M.I.T. Press.

LÉVI-STRAUSS, C.
1956   The structural study of myth. *Journal of American Folklore* 78:428–44.
1962   *Totemism.* Translated from the French by Rodney Needham. Boston: Beacon Press.
1966   *The savage mind.* Chicago: University of Chicago Press.
1969   *The raw and the cooked.* Translated from the French by John and Doreen Weightman. New York: Harper and Row.

LOUNSBURY, F. G.
1959   "Similarity and contiguity relations in language in culture," in *Report of*

the Tenth Annual Round Table Meeting on Linguistics and Language Studies. Edited by Richard S. Harrell, pp. 123–28. Georgetown: Georgetown University Press.

MAUSS, M.
1923   Essai sur le don. *L'Année Sociologique*, n.s., 1:30–186.

MEAD, GEORGE HERBERT
1934   *Mind, self, and society*. Chicago: University of Chicago Press.

MELLI, CLAUDIA
1970   "Lacan: Psicoanálisis y lingüística," in *Estructuralismo y psicoanálisis*. Edited by José Sazbon, pp. 85–99. Buenos Aires: Sud Editorial.

MÉTRAUX, R.
1953   "Resonance in imagery," in *The study of culture at a distance*, by Margaret Mead and Rhoda Métraux, pp. 343–62. Chicago: University of Chicago Press.

MCCLOSKEY, MARY
1964   Metaphors. *Mind* 73 (290).

MILLER, G., E. GALANTER, and K. PRIBRAM.
1960   *Plans and the structure of behavior*. New York: Holt.

MORRIS, C.
1955   *Signs, language, and behavior*. New York: G. Braziller.

NISBET, R.
1968   *Social change and history*. New York: Oxford University Press.

ORTNER, SHERRY
1972   A kernel of truth: Some notes on the analysis of connotation. *Semiotica* 6:324–43. [DNM]

OSGOOD, CHARLES
1952   The nature and measurement of meaning. *Psychological Bulletin* 49:197–237.

OSGOOD, CHARLES, PERCY TANNENBAUM, and GEORGE SUCI
1957   *The measurement of meaning*. Urbana: University of Illinois Press.

PEPPER, STEPHEN
1942   *World hypothesis: A study in evidence*. Berkeley: University of California Press.

PIKE, KENNETH
1967   *Language in relation to a unified theory of the structure of human behaviour*. The Hague: Mouton.

POLANYI, M.
1964   *Science, faith, and society*. Chicago: University of Chicago Press.

QUINE, W. V. O.
1963   *Word and object*. Cambridge: M.I.T. Press.

SAPIR, E.
1934.   "Symbolism," in *Encyclopedia of the Social Sciences*, pp. 492–95.
1974   Haya metaphors for speech. *Language and Society*. Spring. In press.

SHANDS, H.
1971   *Compte rendu*: Anthony Wilder, *The Language of the Self*. *Semiotica* 3:280–87.

SHIBLES, WARREN A.
1971   *Metaphor*. Whitewater, Wis.: The Language Press.

SIMONIS, Y.
1968   *Claude Lévi-Strauss ou la "passion de l'inceste": Introduction au structuralisme*. Paris: Aubier Montaigne.

66 Persuasions and Performances

SKINNER, B. F.

1945   The operational analysis of psychological terms. *Cumulative Record,* pp. 272–86.

SPURGEON, CAROLYN

1936   *Shakespeare's imagery.* New York: Macmillan.

STEMMER, N.

1971   Innate ideas and quality space. *Semiotica* 3:234–40.

TURNER, V.

1967   *The forest of symbols.* Ithaca: Cornell University Press.

VAN DER LEEUW, G.

1938   *Religion in essence and manifestation.* New York: Macmillan.

VAN STEENBURGH, E. W.

1965   Metaphor. *Journal of Philosophy* 62:678–88.

VYGOTSKY, L.

1962   *Thought and language.* Edited and translated by Eugenia Hanfmann and Gertrude Vakar. Cambridge: M.I.T. Press.

WEINREICH, URIEL

1963   "On the semantic structure of language," in *Universals of language.* Edited by J. H. Greenberg, pp. 114–71. Cambridge: M.I.T. Press.

WHEELWRIGHT, P.

1962   *Symbolism.* Bloomington: Indiana University Press.

WHITE, LESLIE

1960   "Four stages in the evolution of minding," in *The evolution of man (Evolution After Darwin,* vol. 2). Edited by Sol Tax, pp. 239–54. Chicago: University of Chicago Press. [CLW]

Notes

The field research from which these ideas developed has been supported by the Ford Foundation, the Social Science Research Council, and the National Science Foundation. I am grateful. Wise commentary, for which I am also grateful, has come from many colleagues. I particularly thank Hoyt Alverson, Kenneth Bruntel, John Lanzetta, James H. Spencer, Jr., and Edward Yonan.

1. Compare Lévi-Strauss's conception of the constitutive nature of signs: "Images co-exist with ideas in signs." He sees signs as intermediary between "percepts and concepts" or "images and concepts" and linking the two (1966:18). Lévi-Strauss's whole object of study, the elements of mythical thought, is thus to be understood as the study of images as they receive some degree of conceptualization through syntactic manipulation. Lévi-Straus hunts and sings his hunter's songs in, as he himself says, "a forest of images" (1969:32) and not a "forest of symbols." The fruitfulness of the image concept in the analysis of cultural materials is seen in the work of Métraux (1953).

2. Metaphor and metonym are understood in this discussion to be the two basic modes of relating a sign-image to a subject, but "metaphor" will often be used synonymously with "sign-image."

3. Despite his determined pursuit of comparative evidence for the prevalence of "the theoretical attitude" and "logical dynamism," Lévi-Strauss has never oversimplified his argument or rested with transparent redactions. Thus the

reader of *The Savage Mind*, for instance, will be aware of a dialectic in the author's mind between his conviction that the objects of the natural world are to be simply treated as counters in the game of combinations and his recognition that they are sensible images and their content has some importance. On pp. 116–117 he asks us to recognize that he is giving precedence to ideological superstructures only because that is the purpose of the book. Elsewhere in his work there is plenty of substance—abundant content!

4. A main focus of the work of the structural psychoanalyst Lacan (1966) is the way that the subject, necessarily exocentric, relates itself to the other, "capturing" this other for purposes of constituting itself. The subject that does not either effectively relate to the other—is self-reflecting—or is overwhelmed by the other remains "strange to itself." It is the main object of psychotherapy to reduce or cure this estrangement, reconstituting the subject in its chain of associations. Lacan's writings are esoteric, hermetic, often contradictory. Recently they have received, as they must, a great deal of exegesis. My own interpretation of Lacan's view of the purpose of psychoanalysis is "to teach the troubled subject through talk to masterfully take the other." The notion of the inchoateness of the subject, though here put forth without Lacan in mind, seems comparable to his notion of the subject as imcomplete being ever-desirous of completing itself (constituting itself) through relating to the other. The assumption here is that the subject is ever desirous of giving some concreteness to its inchoateness.

5. The widespread shamanistic figure of the Master of Animals is discussed masterfully by La Barre (1970). In recent centuries this figure has been replaced by the Master Mechanic, etc. In Western societies the Master of Animals has turned into the "economic animal" (Mauss 1923:176) bent upon mastering exchange systems.

6. J. Edgar Hoover, Director of the FBI, referring to the former Attorney General, Ramsey Clark, November 1970.

7. This interplay is fundamental in social life. The subject always finds in any predicate that it contradicts itself; it is larger and contains multitudes. First among the types of such interplay is that between social action and cultural meaning, summed up in the tension between the signal and the symbol (Fernandez 1965:922).

8. In assuming here the predicative form so common in the Indo-European languages, in which the subject is linked straightforwardly to the object by the copula, I do not wish to ignore the variety of ways the verb "to be" is expressed in other languages and the lack of a discrete copula in many. All that is presumed here is that personal pronouns are a language universal and that at a deep level all language is concerned to link pronomial subjects to the world of objects. In any case, one must avoid Lévy-Bruhl's mistake—in his early work—of presuming the copula to be a universal, which argues for the identity of the subject and the object in those "prelogical" and nonanalytical societies in which quite bizarre predications are forthcoming. Lévy-Bruhl took their metaphor too literally. One should rather argue that in all societies the inchoate subject is anxious to predicate a concrete other upon itself, with the consequence not of the loss of self but rather, in the eventual progression of predications, of a fuller and more satisfactory sense of self. The subject, in other words, participates in the object for only a spell.

9. Both Black and Berggren make finer distinctions in the varieties of these metaphors than I feel it necessary to make here. For example, Black distinguishes between scale models, analogic models, and mathematical models. He also pre-

fers the term archetype to metaphor, probably because of the association of metaphor exclusively with poetics.

10. This may seem an opportunistic use of the semantic-differential dimensions, but it is not gratuitous. Van der Leeuw (1938) defined religion as a concern with power, will, and form and the relationship that should abide between them. His trichotomy seems notably congruent with Osgood's (the identity of ethics and aesthetics being presumed). Thinking in such a vein, it is tempting to speculate that somehow religious metaphor, in certain religions at least, tends to move the participants to the origin of the three dimensions (conceived in Cartesian format) defined as meaninglessness or nirvana. This final emancipation, in semantic-differential phrasing, would be absence of preoccupation with potency, activity, and evaluation; compare the Hindu view, in which emancipation represents a dying out in the heart of the threefold fires of passion, hatred, and delusion.

11. Osgood's own work on the semantic differential was based on this insight into the similarity between metaphor and synesthesis: "The relation of [synesthesis] to ordinary metaphor is evident . . . it seems clear from these studies that the imagery found in synesthesis is intimately tied up with language metaphor and they both represent semantic relations. . . . music synesthesis can be described as the parallel alignment of two or more dimensions of experience definable verbally by pairs of polar adjectives (Osgood, Tannenbaum, and Suci 1957:23).

12. The semantic differential has been used to measure changes in qualitative weighting of the inchoate self and important others before and after psychiatric treatment (Endler 1961).

13. The point of view evoked here is that of Miller, Galanter, and Pribram (1960), who understand images as plans for behavior and regard that behavior as controlled by information-processing and testing operations through which the consequences of behavior are checked against the image-plan.

14. One may employ an information-processing model, following Miller, Galanter, and Pribram (1960), to indicate this; see Fernandez (1977).

15. I have elsewhere attempted to discuss this "time-binding" consequence of metaphor using Black's view (1962) of the interactive nature of figures of speech (Fernandez 1966a).

16. Lacan has also confronted this problem, and his work, a synthesis of De Saussure and Freud, is equally difficult. One interpretation of his views (Melli 1970) is that the subject, in its endless search to constitute its incomplete self through the other (see n. 5 above), has two devices at its service: metonymic displacement and metaphoric substitution. The problem of the metonymic mode, since it only takes the part for the whole and can never realize the subject as a whole, is lack of significance to the signifier. The problem of the metaphoric mode, since it seeks to condense the subject and replace it with an other, is excess of significance to the signifier. The life of any subject, in Lacan's view, is to be regarded as an associative chain of metonymic and metaphoric attempts at constituting itself.

17. Though we have talked about the "inchoate subject" here, more properly speaking the subject does not exist by itself but within a frame which may be more or less inchoate in respect to his feelings and knowledge about his obligations to it.

18. Three basic terms employed here—frame, scene, and domain—are not coterminous. A frame is a segment of human social life conceived of as a syntactic progression. Frames, when filled, may be analyzed into scenes. The purpose of

scenes is to put into effect the metaphor(s) or metonyms chosen to fill the frame. A domain of experience is a set of objects or actions associated by a defining factor or factors they have in common.

19. I have in mind no specific Christian ceremony, but only the essentials of a generalized Christian ritual tradition. Christian religion is not my area of specialization. I employ it here only as an example which is widely known and from which the usefulness of this metaphoric approach can be more easily judged than if more recondite anthropological field materials were used for illustration. The evolutionary elaboration of Christianity challenges any intended analysis with vast detail (Jungmans 1955). But it may still be asked: is not this a surface elaboration on underlying metaphoric predications on inchoate pronouns? Jung (1958) offers a learned interpretation of the elements of the Mass more strictly within the Christian tradition. For Jung, however, the transformation of the self (the "individuation process") that takes place in the Mass is a process of symbolic merging of conscious and unconscious and not of progressive predications upon inchoate subjects.

20. Lévi-Strauss (1969:342) points out that "various forms of metonymy and in particular synecdoche celebrate the parts of experience while the more eloquent metaphors of myth refer back to the whole for significance." But the chain of metonymic predications may be said in a sense to seek to "return to the whole" by trying to grasp various parts of it. See also Lacan on this problem (n.17 above).

21. This is Kant's distinction between analytic and synthetic predications. Analytic predication is that judgment which is necessarily part of the concept in question. In synthetic predication, something is added which is not part of the concept; the concept is displaced from its customary domain.

22. Jung and Ricklin make the further point that knowing whether a judgment is analytic or synthetic depends upon knowing whether the subject was conceived in the particular or the universal. Thus "snake-green" is objectively synthetic, since there is no necessity of green in the thought of a snake. If it is the particular snake, the green mamba, which is in mind, the judgment becomes analytic.

23. Though out of such poverty Lévi-Strauss (1956) produces such a challenging formula as $f_x(a):f_y(b)::f_x(b):f_{a-1}(y)$, essentially a formula describing transformation in expressive events brought about by the sense of contrast $(a-1)$.

24. *Kwoth* can only appear in object position (in terms of English views of subject-object formation). This may be regarded as simply a subsequent theological transformation of the original predication of a concrete object upon the inchoate spirit. And spirit in turn may be regarded as an apotheosized pronoun, an alter ego.

25. Evans-Pritchard takes this predication to be metonymic, that is, crocodile is a manifestation of a part of spirit. He does not take it as metaphoric, that is, there is something crocodile-like about spirit!

26. Evans-Pritchard's discussion is mainly concerned to refute Lévy-Bruhl's notions.

27. This concentration on the vicissitudes of objects and subjects in expressive culture is found in the approach of Van der Leeuw (1938), who argues that "The Subject of Religion is, in the sense of Religion Itself, the Object, and its Object the Subject" and devotes attention to "Object and Subject in their Reciprocal Operation."

28. Harvey (1964:13) argues that all motivational arousal is the consequence of the disruption of certain relationships between the outside social world and the

subjective metering system encompassed in intraorganismic norms. He makes a distinction similar to the one made here between biogenic motives and sociogenic motives, the latter set off by discrepancies between subject and object arising in physiochemical changes in the internal environment. In either case, metaphoric or metonymic predications may be seen as attempts to reestablish appropriate subject-object relations by projecting subjects more appropriately into either corporeal or social domains.

29. I owe the term "pronominalism" to an assessment of this argument by R. P. Armstrong and E. P. Yonan. It assumes that any general account of society and culture must begin with the motives and relations of particular pronouns, for they point directly to the essential reality of social life and in their "taking of the other" are both the creators and the repositories of culture. Pronouns point to the real. All else is imaginary, that is, the embracing of sign-images.

30. The fact seems to be that men have, at once, both a sense of the continuity of experience—about which we can neither speak nor whistle—and a need to reduce that ineffable continuity to order and discrete categories. We both search for dichotomies and seek to escape them. This paradox is laden with an emotion often invested in intermediate and interstitial objects, a point well developed by Leach (1964).

Part II
PERFORMANCES

3

POETRY IN MOTION
BEING MOVED BY
AMUSEMENT, MOCKERY, AND
MORTALITY IN
THE ASTURIAN MOUNTAINS

> Science manipulates things but refuses to
> inhabit them.
>
> Merleau-Ponty, *L'Oeil et l'esprit*

In this chapter some examples of a rich tradition of "spontaneous" folk verse from Asturias in northern Spain are examined in the interest of understanding the qualitative movements they accomplish in the various subjects of the verse. A theory of social "shape-shifting" in cultural quality space animates the discussions. We shall argue that such "shiftings" or movements along the semantic dimensions of culture are accomplished by metaphoric and metonymic predications on the subjects of the verse. And we shall chart the "quality space" that is referenced in this collection of poetry: the "culture" within which this movement takes place. Any simple notion of movement is challenged, however, by an evocativeness, indeed a multivocality, in certain of these poetic images. This evocativeness summons some villagers beyond mere "movement." It calls them out of themselves and their social situation, as it were, to larger perspectives.

This paper has benefited from, and thus is in particular dialogue with, the work of two colleagues. First, it benefits from an important contribution to the method espoused here made by Peter Seitel.[1] He has shown us very clearly the component elements in metaphoric language as well as some of the semantic confounds which are the source of irony in that speech. Second, the paper benefits from the insight into Galician folk verse, similar to the Asturian, provided by Carmelo Lisón.[2] He points to a paradoxical quality in much of this "spontaneous" verse. He labels this "aggressivity in commensality" (agresividád en comensalidád). Indeed, while the poems we consider seek to manipulate, they are often enough vehicles of mutuality. How can this be so? Such paradoxes may help to explain why sometimes men and women are carried beyond the cheerful animosities and immediate manipulations of these rancorous rhymes to larger perspectives and participations. Such paradoxes, in any event, challenge the notion of movement in quality space.

The people from whom this verse was collected are cattle keepers of the Cantabrian mountains of Europe. Their chief source of income is from the sale of yearling beef. They practice subsistence agriculture: corn, potatoes, beans primarily. Social organization follows the characteristic bilateral family organization of peasant western Europe with some tendency towards the development of stem kindred. These people have Celtic and Visigothic as well as Iberian ancestry, and there are some vestigial traces of both cultures—the bagpipe, for example, and stilted granaries. In many respects these countrymen are closer in culture to the countrymen of central and western Europe than to the Mediterranean countrymen of central and southern Spain. The Asturian mountaineers have preferred to live close to their land—in tiny hamlets (aldeas)—rather than in population centers such as agrovillages. Their land is characteristically held in a multitude of tiny scattered parcels (minifúndia). There are few large landholders. The Mediterranean culture of family honor and shame is not an intense social dynamic among these countrymen. They now mostly speak Castilian. Their former language was Asturiano or Astur-leonés. A considerable lexicon of this dialect remains in their speech, and some of this is evident in this poetry.

I. The Joke: "Piononos en el Campoamor"

If the reader will sit down with me in the back of a bus speeding along between Oviedo and Arriondas on the north coast of Spain, we can cast our eye upon a spirited situation which has convulsed us all in the last six rows. We are in the province of Asturias (Oviedo) whose inhabitants have a dour reputation in the minds of most Spaniards. Indeed, the Cantabrian maritime is a humid and overcast climate easily giving rise to heaviness in character. It is said about the canny inhabitants of the humid northeast of the United States: "A Yankee is someone of whom you ask a question and must work like hell to get an answer." Likewise in Asturias there is brevity in human interchange and resistance to inhabitation by strangers. But however any people may stiffen up before strangers, if one is among them long enough, as the anthropologist tries to be, one is made aware of crinkly corners in their character where they can bend or double over. The Asturians are no different. They appear unbending at first. But they have their folding points.

The body image we employ here of public unbendingness and private doubling over exploits a characteristic personality dimension of American English between stiffness on the one hand and relaxedness on the other. This may be a universal dimension—a future anthropology may tell us— but it is not the preferred dimension of personality comparison in Asturias where it is rather the heaviness *(pesadez)* or lightness *(gracia)* which is remarked upon first. In many cultures public situations are felt as stiff or heavy, as the case may be, while private situations—familiar situations— are felt to be pliable, lighthearted, vivacious. It is shifts in such feelings that we are exploring here.

Behavioral situations are often complex and can be thickly layered. There are many ambiguities.[3] But we derive, I believe, useful insight by showing how personalities situate themselves within them. This process of situation can be described as taking place within a quality space of many semantic dimensions[4] such as those—stiff/relaxed, heavy/light—to which we have just referred. Just as we move constantly back and forth from the public to the private in social life, so our personas are moved about in quality space—we become stiff or supple, heavy or light, massive or inspirited. We may be moved without forethought or intention, the result of a congeries of shifting physiological and situational forces—the side of the bed we got up on, as we like to say. Or we may be moved about strategically in quality space as the result of adornments or disparagements communicated in interaction. In American English the primary dimension is that of up and down—we are put up or put down. In Spanish the primary dimension is size. We are made small *(achicar)* or made large, becoming *grandón* or *grandona*. In a socially mobile America one *achieves* height—one becomes high and mighty.[5] It is more the case in Spain that one has height *ascribed* to one as a result of inborn social position *(su alteza)*.

In this paper examples of Asturian folk humor, jokes, and poetic exchanges will show us varieties of this movement. But we should not oversimplify. There are complications and evocative ambiguities in this movement. The imagination does not sit complacently at the end of any set of continua. As our symbols are multivocal, our situation is, at the least, ambilocal. The end of one continuum can be brought to bear upon another. We find ourselves taking familiarities in formal situations. We stoop to conquer. That we are jocularly hostile or timidly pretentious and that both our placement in and the desirability of movement *along* a continuum are uncertain are also evocative. In any event, as the paper moves forward, we shall note some greater complexities of movement which will render us, as it has rendered these Asturian villagers, less confident in our explanatory manipulations and more contemplative— more mindful of wider and deeper patterns of existence.

But back to the bus. We have been hurtling along, and although the day is hot, with the windows closed so as to protect several hairdos in the broad seat rear. Three dressed-up young girls in their teens get on in Infiesto, look around nervously, and sit down primly, overly conscious of the eyes of others. The two younger girls not so far beyond puberty seem more nervous and stiff. In the second stop beyond Infiesto two tipsy middle-aged bachelors, shirttails and ties to the breeze, come aboard. They spot the three girls immediately as they lurch back to the rear. It turns out they are from a neighboring village. Taking their seats they immediately turn around and address the oldest girl:

> Aqui 'stais o! Oye! Mari Je, 'onde 'tuvisteis? Un entierro. Home!
> (There you are! Say! Mari Je. Where have you been? A burial.)
> Si supiéramos.
> (If we had only known.)

The girls, and particularly Mari Je, are trying to manage these familiarities in sotto voce without bringing in the whole rear section of the bus. But the two bachelors are a bit beyond modulation of voice. They focus in upon the two younger girls so fetchingly dressed:

> Guapatonas! Bajáis con nosotros . . . tomar algo al Bar Tito.
> (Big Beauties! Get off with us . . . take something at Tito's Bar!)
> Os guste? Al Campoamor, pues a comer pasteles.
> (You don't like to? Then to the Campoamor to eat pastries.)

Now here the fatter man with the weak eyes and the cane interjects the remark which brings laughter to the rear seats. He directs himself to the youngest girl:

> Pili! Comemos Piononos en el Campoamor.
> (Pili! Let's eat Piononos at the Campoamor.)

This is too much of a familiarity for Mari Je, who, more accustomed to *el verde*, responds tartly:

> 'Stá bien de Pio Pio en el Campoamor.
> (That's enough of Pio Pio in the Campoamor.)

The man with weak eyes, smiling, responds to this with a clever aside to his companion:

> 'Diz que 'stá bien de piojos en el Campoamor.
> (She says that that's enough of louses in the Campoamor.)

The two bachelors chuckle to themselves and redirect their attention, with a shout, to the driver far to the front. They endeavor to have him stop at an unmarked *parada*. The girls are obviously relieved at this redirection of interest—at the abandonment of this attempt to introduce familiarities into a formal public situation. They are even more relieved when the bachelors descend at the next stop, and they respond to their cheery farewells with a fleeting smile of relief.

There are at least two kinds of humor here: situational and verbal. The situational joke involves unexpected familiarity in the midst of what should be a polite and public, even though somewhat liminal, arena. The girls were all decked out for a polite and public scrutiny only to find themselves the object of public familiarities, abruptly moved to a familiar encounter. The anomaly of public familiarity is itself humorous. In most cultures the public meeting with a familiar is usually perplexing.[6] It was humorous to see the girls attempt a polite response to their interlocutors and, in the person of the eldest, finally respond tartly and familiarly— stooping to conquer, as it were. The verbal component, however, contained the clever element which moved the audience of passengers from private smiles to public laughter.

The familiarities, of course, hinged upon sexual innuendo. The invitation to the bar, for its inappropriateness, initiated that innuendo. Then, in changing the venue to the Campoamor Cafe ("lovefield cafe"), it was made more explicit.[7] The gross joke is the reference to the *Piononos* ("Pius the Ninths," literally), which are a chocolate covered, rolled (crepe fashion) pastry with a cream filling. This gross and impious reference brings a response, still in the spirit of verbal play, from the oldest girl: "That's enough chirpings of anxious desire." And finally as the men subside in their familiarities, the further verbal joke: "She says that's enough of importunate louses."

The main movements in the quality space of the participants in the scenario were from polite formality to ribald familiarity, from smallness to bigness (and vice versa), and from the funereal to the sensual. The petite and barely adolescent girls are made out as "big beauties" *(guapatonas)* by the roistering bachelors. This reference alone was playing along a dimension of considerable ambiguity and hence evocativeness. For in the life of the countryman and woman, "big beautyness" has been a desired trait, whereas demure prettiness is a citified value although of increased relevance in the country. As for the bachelors, they were in turn, *achicado* ("diminished") by the oldest girl as "plaintive fledglings"—a movement confirmed by the bachelors in their playful self-judgment as "louses." The somber and respectful public occasion for which the girls were dressed, the burial *(entierro)*, gave way to more vital and sensual preoccupations. And part of the humor of the occasion was the fact of the sensual imposing itself so abruptly on what was remnant of the funereal. This shift from the funereal to the sensual, not at all unusual in wakes and mortuary ceremonies after all,[8] was aptly represented in the Pionono pastry with its suggestive shape, its Papal name, and its sound of prudish denial— "*nono*." It is a veritable symbolic sweet, multivocal, with references to various domains of experience in tension.[9] At any rate, even for the bachelors the joking apparently reached a point of insupportable incompatibilities,[10] not satisfactorily embodied even in this key symbol. For the final movement was to turn the joke upon themselves and then cry out to the driver to halt the bus so that they might, with its movement halted, carry their revels to another and more appropriate locale.

II. Shifting Domains of Reference: *"Andando a Cantares"*

It may be the more appropriate to discuss this joke in terms of movement, because it is in the nature of humor to make a sudden movement or set of movements in the face of our composure and settledness of situation. This is seen most clearly in the practical joke where we are frustrated in some aspect of our accustomed practice and round of life. We find a cow in our college room or a whoopee cushion on our assigned seat at the table. We are frustrated because a customary domain of activity for which we are prepared—a dormitory study, a dinner table—suddenly gives evidence of elements belonging to another domain for which we are unprepared (the barnyard, as it were, in both instances). In this shifting of domains our identities as impractical students or well-behaved and polished dinner guests is brought into question. The joke depends upon the fact that we are never fully sure of our identity in any domain of life.

When we talk of movement we must be clear that there are two separate, though interdependent, kinds of movement involved in shifts in quality space. There is first of all the shift in the domains of reference of the activity and, second, there is a shift in the feeling tone or affect—the personal sense of quality—of the participants which accompanies that shift. The main shift in domain in the joke was from the preoccupations of the burial ground to the preoccupations of the field of love. And the main shift in affect was from petite and demure prettiness in the girls to big beautyness and from a hearty, overbearing ribaldry in the tipsy bachelors to a diminutive, dependent *(pio pio)* and parasitical *(piojo)* status. Of course, these two movements are related—a shift in domain of reference is accompanied by a shift in feeling tone: the "shock of recognition," as it is called, that two different domains of our understanding can be brought into informative association.

Such "movement" as we have described is taking place, in figurative time and space, by means of metaphoric and metonymic predications made upon the situation and the personages involved. In real time and space we were all together, still hurtling along, encapsulated in "Líneas Economicas" between Oviedo and Arriondas. Still, much of the most interesting and important "movement" in life takes place in such figurative terms. Of course, science likes to manipulate things in real time and space. It eschews the merely figurative. But anthropology as a human science, recognizing our powers of definition of situation, should seek equally such figurative inhabitation of space as we are examining here— and the manipulation of self and other that, by various tropic devices, takes place in that space.

Also important to the amusements of the incident we have examined is the verbal play—the metaphors and the movement between metaphors made on the basis of homophony (*Pionono, pio pio, piojo*). Anyone who has worked in Spain, surely in the North of Spain, will recognize how close the poetic—verbal play of various kinds and the indirect speech of metaphoric and metonymic allusion—is to the surface in the countryside. This may result from a filtering down from the Spanish Great Tradition, which is said to be essentially a "cultura literaria," something that can hardly be said of the American Great Tradition, for example. Or it may be because suffixing processes in the Romance languages, and Spanish in particular, lend themselves to ready rhyme. In any case the countryside *is* full of poetry.

The diversity and richness of this Spanish folk poetry, recurrently demonstrated since Joaquín Costa's time,[11] is most recently discussed in the insightful article by Carmelo Lisón[12] summarizing this aspect of his Galician work, but particularly focusing on the aggressive, competitive, improvised versification—*loias* and *reguifas* and *desafíos*—of Galician village life. This poetry either accompanies or follows upon occasions of communal celebration (*carnavales* and *fiestas*), of communal effort (*carretos*), or of commensality (*bodas* and *cenas*). Lisón is mostly concerned with the way these verses, particularly the *reguifa*, condense local values—the way they act for the common good, representing it as in a kind of *simulacro de auto sacramento* or morality play.

The words *competition, attack, opposition, tension, duel, conflict, rivalry, battle, defiance* inevitably arise, as he points out, in discussing this poetry. Lisón postulates aggressivity as the common denominator in all this verse—an aggressivity the more interesting, however, because it takes place on communal or commensal occasions. He focuses upon this *agresividad en commensalidad*, this *agape enfrentado* ("redemptive confrontation"), and he finds in it a poetic representation of village social structure, itself an example of conflicted solidarity and opposition in cooperation. Lisón suggests that this poetry has a particular power in its rhyme and rhythm, almost a "mystical power," perhaps, to deal in these contrarieties—the ultimate circumstances of village life, as it were. It is an instrument, par excellence, for negotiating the antinomies, aggression and conviviality, of communal solidarity. By provoking pleasure in the face of these contrarieties, it makes them endurable.

No doubt Lisón does put his finger on the paradoxical pulse of village life—aggressivity in commensality. It should also be pointed out that, appropriately, not only is this verse put forth aggressively in situations of social opposition, it also plays upon and manipulates semantic oppositions which we shall shortly detail. It is unlikely that the congruence between social and semantic opposition is accidental. One is reminded of Tarde's old argument[13] which we would now call a Durkheimian formulation, that the intellectual idea of opposition—in his view a prime and inescapable formulation of experience—arose from the experience of aggressive social encounters. The opposition of pleasure and pain arises, as it were, from the clearer opposition of horde to horde, clan to clan, or tribe to tribe. Whatever may be said of Tarde's argument—the cross-cultural occurrence of dualistic type thinking is just now receiving concerted attention from anthropologists[14]—the point is that the situations of manipulative social opposition which give rise to this verse find an intellectual counterpart in the semantic oppositions in the verse in relation to which subjects are manipulated. This may be only to say that these poems are very much a part—in the "models of"/"models for" sense—of the ongoing social life of the village. They both contribute to the understanding and tone of that life—its moods and motivations—as well as being a reflection of it.[15] As a singular expressive occurrence, they obtain, however, a kind of intriguing unity in midst of contrariety. This is Lison's point.

In any event, experience in Asturian mountain villages would surely confirm the degree to which the prevalence of this manipulative and aggressive poetry makes the hard life of the villages endurable—and, often enough, enjoyable. In the villages we know there are a variety of genres that make this contribution. For example, there are invariably two or three villagers with whom one can sit down and *"sacar romances"* by the hour. And there are usually one or two "manuscript" poets—men and women with a few years elementary education who painstakingly compose lyrics or longer romances with pen and paper. But it is most useful to concentrate on examples of that poetry called loosely *trobas* or *cantares.* In these there is greater evidence of that aggressive dynamic of which Lison speaks, more obvious movement. For not only does their characterization as "aggressive" imply movement, but the folk denomination of this activity as *andando a cantares* ("walking forth songs") or *discurriendo cantares* ("rambling, roaming, flowing forth with song") also clearly implies a figurative movement about. Of course, it is not simply a folk denomination. Castilian as a language, and Asturian no less, in its penchant for progressive and graphic tenses, grammatically fosters that dy-

namic. But where is this movement tending, and what are the
consequences of contrarieties in movement?

III. Alienation and Familiarization: *"Embárcate pa' Caracas"*

One of the first dimensions of movement is that which lies between the
forastero and the *vecino*, and a basic intent of these verses seems to be to
move their subjects from one quality to the other—to alienate or familiarize. For example, consider the following exchange between a handi-
capped veteran and a poor spinstress whose quick wit makes her a prime
source of *trobas* in the village. Her poverty lies in the fact that she has
very poor fields. And the veteran, possibly because of some other frustration, reminded her of this to her face. He rhymed:

Las tierras de Mamedián	The fields of Memedian
Salen cara las patatas!	Produce expensive potatoes.
Vale mas preparar el viaje	Better to take a journey
Y embárcate pa' Caracas.	And embark for Caracas.

To this the spinstress, Jesusa, was said to have responded immediately:

Tu pa Caracas nu vas!	You are not going to Caracas
Porque vas de mala gana.	You'd go with a heavy heart.
Nun quieres perder la paga	You wouldn't wish to lose the pay
De la mutilada en España.	Of the mutilated of Spain!

This basic movement, expressed pungently in such virtually universal
exclamations as "Go to," *"vaya," "fuera,"* etc., in Asturian poetry usually
takes the form of wishing emigration upon the auditor—a wish perfectly
compatible with the long historical experience of the Asturians in emigrat-
ing first to Castile during the reconquest and later to the New World,
most usually to Argentina and Venezuela. The fact of such long centuries
of emigration has meant that Asturian folk verse is full of the emotions of
farewells and welcomes after long absence.[16] It has also meant that there
is uncertainty and ambivalence about one's commitment to locality, one's
stability; hence, this kind of poetic movement, playing like the joking
reference to the adolescent girls' big beautyness upon a dimension in
which people feel uncertainly situated, is powerfully evocative. This evocation is most strongly condensed in the frequent deprecation of others as
gypsies.

We see this reference in Jesusa's poem (incomplete because she could not recall it all)[17] about a neighbor who went to market to sell goats and was taken in by the gypsies—and some gypsy spirit in himself—so that he came back with a cart instead of some more solid and settled and acceptable trade item for a husbandman, such as a cow or even a horse, to pull the cart. Not only was he putting the cart before the horse in village eyes, but as seen in the poem he was giving evidence of unsettled qualities and disturbing inclinations towards mobility:

Que mal oficio esti año,	What a bad deal this year,
El venderse las cabrinas	Selling the little goats.
Y emplearlas en un carro!	For a wagon!
Quería ser arieru	Wanting to be a wagoneer
Antes de tener caballo.	Before having a horse.
Con esas engatainas	At such gypsy tricks
El pueblu quedo· asustado.	The village is amazed.
Pal hecho no hay remedio.	But there's no remedy.
Un hombre desesperado.	A desperate man.
Quería celebrar a pascua	Wants to celebrate Easter
Antes de venir los ramos.	Before Palm Sunday.
Cuando compra cuando vende	In buying and selling
Que paez un gitano!	He looks a gypsy.

The continuum of movement upon which this poem takes place might be identified as that between the *paisano*—the condition of landedness and stability on the one hand—and the *gitano*—the footloose and endlessly mobile condition—on the other. Here, as in the case of alienation by assignment to foreign status, the *gitano* predication upon the subject of the verse is highly charged, for it evokes a basic ambiguity in their affairs and lives. The mountain villagers of Asturias, as cattle keepers, are almost all committed to short-term transhumance, and hence almost all have mobility between two locales—the village in the winter and the *caseríos* on the divides in the summer—built into the yearly cycle. The economic requirements of their existence leave them with an uncertain status between established and settled landholders and mobile cattle keepers. For some villagers as well, the thought arises that they are descended from the *vaqueiros*, a low-status and in some respects outcast people of full transhumance.[18] Some of these have settled into the villages in recent centuries, and the possibilities of such ancestry, admitted by no one, can be played upon in the poetry. In any case, one can alienate by suggesting that one has no landed commitment—is not family or a son of anything in the sense of family lands.

We should be clear that the dimension we have singled out here—
alienation-familiarization—along which poetic subjects are moved, is abstracted from a set of more concrete dimensions whose polar terms appear
or are implied by opposition in the poetry: *emigrante-vecino, paisano-
gitano, ganadero-arriero (arieru)*.

Alienation-Familiarization
Emigrante—Vecino
Gitano—Paisano
Arriero—Ganadero

While one may single out dimensions, one cannot ignore, we repeat, the
ambivalence in the vectors involved, which is part of their evocative
power. Take for another example the last one—that between *arriero* and
ganadero. The Asturian mountain villagers generally pride themselves on
being cattle keepers (*ganadero*), countrymen (*paisano*), and good neighbors (*vecinos*). But of course, the frictions of community life create desires
for emigration; the hard and confining labors of the land make the fiddle-
footed gypsies' life attractive; and the "servitude" of the cows (*esclavitude
de las vacas*), as they call it, makes the wagoneer's lot appealing. Rather
than being in servitude, the wagoneer is hauled and served by his
animals—hauled, moreover, from village to village and province to
province. He is the interstitial person, the bearer of extramural goods and
news, the man without a village and without the burdens of neigh-
borliness. Like any traveling man, he has a potential for the unexpected
and the ribald not permitted the *paisano*. Thus, though villagers may
pride themselves on their condition as cattle keepers, there is a certain
attraction to carting. And, of course, Jesusa was mocking the inadvertent
expression of that temptation in a "good neighbor," making her poem
especially evocative. It sings of the *vecino* who is *arrieru* and the
ganadero who is *gitano*.

While one may poetically move a *vecino* to foreign status, one can also
seek to move the subject of verse to a more fully integrated status as
villager and neighbor. Thus this same spinstress, Jesusa, spun out the
following verse in honor of my wife and me after we had sent her a gift by a
third party:

Esa señora Renate	This señora Renate
Y tambien el su marido	And also he her husband
Los mas buenos de Felechosa!	The best ones in Felechosa!
Vieron a Jesusa descalza'a	They observed Jesusa unshod
Y le compraron silenciosas.	And they brought her slippers.

Laudatory movement in this verse, and from this particular poet, is seen even more clearly in the following poem done in honor of the son of a neighbor who had done some passing kindness to her poverty:

En ese barrio de arriba	In this upper quarter,
El más rico es Anton,	The richest is Anton
Porque ha hecho tres casas	for he has built three houses
En el medio del Xerron.	In the center of Xerron.
En lugar de Felechosa	In the place of Felechosa
Ha llamado la atención	He has attracted attention.
Y ahora Jesusa le llama—	And now Jesusa calls him—
Grandón!	Grandon!

IV. Metonymic Misrepresentation as Movement: *"Todo Se Vuelve a Pepu"*

In the above exchange between the war veteran and the spinstress, we note the shift between direct and indirect reference, between the quality of polite evasion of direct reference, which is the characteristic of social life, and direct reference to physical or moral frailties in the person or group. Most of these *cantares* move toward direct *ad hominem* reference. This is an important feature of their aggressivity. In the veteran we see the direct refernce to the spinstress' poverty and her responsive reference to his mutilation. A sharp eye for human frailties is an important capacity in a folk poet of this genre. Thus while, as we see above, this poetry can move on occasion to praise singing and lauding of national leaders or religious figures, it prefers to reveal frailty. And characteristically it does this by what we may call "metonymic misrepresentation"—by moving to take the part of the person for the whole.[19] That part is usually a "weak part," a *punto flaco* ("thin point").

In revealing frailties, however, it is difficult to obtain an unassailable advantage, for frailties are widely distributed and are various. In the end, a sufficiantly clever person can make out a strength in any frailty and a frailty in every strength. An immediate strategy for one responding to some mocking reference is to discover another more telling frailty or to detect some weakness in a supposed strength. Thus, Ceferino de la Puente, a respected bachelor versifier,[20] responded to a neighbor who had been mocking his advancing baldness in the following manner:

Sepas tú ignorante,	Take heed, ignorant one,
Faltoso de entendimiento,	Lacking in understanding

Este calvo muy honrado	This honorable bald one
Ye de buenos sentimientos!	has very good judgment!
Mientras tú con melena	While you with your mane
Paez un burro penco.	Appear a raw-boned burro.
Quieu sabe en tu pellaje,	Who knows of your pelt,
Cuán habitantes habra dentro?	how many inhabitants within?
Córrete por alli peludo	Run along, hairy one,
Con melena de carnero.	With your ram's mane.
Vete y dile a tu amo	Go and tell your master
Que te lleve al asadero.	To carry you off to roasting.

Looking more closely at the poem, we see that we have both "metonymic misrepresentation" and the shifting of domains. Ceferino found himself metonymically misrepresented as the "bald one," for his neighbor took that part of him for the whole. Ceferino in turn took his neighbor's hairiness for the whole. But more than that, and impelled by the metonym, he jumped domains and predicated animality (the condition of a burro and a ram) upon his neighbor, a movement frequently enough encountered in the expletive *bestia*.

This is an instance of metaphoric transformation being found in a metonym, a transformation remarked on frequently by Jakobson and Lévi-Strauss.[21] In the poem under scrutiny here, the "partness" of the metonymic focus upon the neighbor's hairiness is given body, as it were, by associating him with a burro and a ram—the metaphor returns to a whole, although in a different domain. In any case, the main movement of both metonym and metaphor takes place on the qualitative dimension of intelligent mastery of one's affairs with a subordinate movement on the qualitative dimension of cleanness-unkemptness. Ceferino's metonym and metaphor smartly move his interlocutor to a situation of qualitatively less intelligent mastery and cleanliness while at the same time celebrating by indirection such qualities in the balding poet himself. More than most, this poem shows us the nature of aggressive movement: shifts in the qualitative states of subjects by metonymic and metaphoric predications upon them.

Another poem in which we see a metonymic shifting around on what may be called the "corporeal continuum"[22]—that is, from one frailty to another—was put out by Jesusa in response to a disparaging remark by two girls, sent up by the priest from another village in the parish to collect funds for a church celebration. They had collected very little and were supposed to have said that Felechosans were fat in the hips and thin in the pocket book:

Las mozas de Felechosa	The girls of Felechosa
Son muy anchas de cadera	Are very wide in the hips
Con los na'os de morcin	With the turnips of Morcin
Y la tonyá a la riega.	And the irrigated harvest.
Aquí en Felechosa	Here in Felechosa
Tenemos la cadera ancha!	We have the wide hip.
Vosotros teneislo arriba,	You have it there above,
La coxera en la garganta.	The storehouse in the throat.
Que todo se vuelve a pepu	Everything turns into a goiter
Del pulgo de las castañas.	From the husks of chestnuts.
De Felechosa no habléis!	Of Felechosa do not speak!
Ni siquiera pa'nunciala!	Don't even mention it!

Here we see Jesusa make a supposed defect, fatty deposits on the hips, a virtuous consequence of the fine blood sausage and the abundance (by irrigation) of the fall harvest. She then shifts attention to the prevalence of goiters in the girls' town: "everything," like the attention of the poem itself, "is converted into a goiter." This condition is a consequence of their malnutrition in subsisting on the food (chestnut husks) ordinarily given to pigs. After pronouncing the name of her town three times in this short poem, she prohibits that privilege to the saucy girls. *Qué tía!*

V. Metaphysical Domains and Final Movements: *"Qué Triste Fin a la Postre"*

While all the verses we have considered, and most *cantares*, are "aggressive and redressive" in the sense of making compensatory movements in the subjects of the verse, there are some subjects of village life that are beyond movement by their nature or are polyvectoral[23]—they move in several directions and often in such a counterposing manner as to result not in movement but in contemplation. One category of beings which is virtually beyond movement of the kind we have been discussing is the saints, who are characteristically objects of contemplation. On their feast days, to be sure, they make their ritual movements about the village or the province. But this is ritual reversal, for characteristically they are the very essence of composed stability and the goal and endpoint of movement—that is, of pilgrimage and veneration.

Indeed, the parish in which we collected these *cantares* preserves a very interesting one put out by the highly offended citizens of the nether village. The Bishopric of Oviedo, because of decline in the priesthood, had decided to consolidate the mountain parishes. The local priest interpreted that to mean that the Virgin of that village's chapel—a very old and beautiful one—should be "consolidated" as well. The villagers in angry demonstration put forth a rhyme composed years before in honor of the local Virgin whose chapel had withstood a great flood:

Aunque el mar se alborote	Though the ocean froths
Y el marinero se vaya,	And the sailor is lost
No se va la ramadora	The oarswoman remains
Que es la Virgen Soberana!	Who is the Sovereign Virgin!

Thus, while the villagers might admit to movements in the Virgin, it was not the tempestuous movement by men or the elements. They are very tranquil waters indeed in which the Virgin makes her stately progress.

The saints are beyond human movement. Of a woman married to a turbulent and sometimes violent man with every reason to abandon her house but who patiently remains, it is said, *"Ye una santa!"*[24] Of a student of ours, working up in the summer meadows, who had difficulty in learning to sleep with the cattle herders in the same *cabaña* bed and who, thus, slept alert and stiff and uncoordinated with others' movements, it was said *"Duerme como un santu."* Of anyone thus beyond the movement of human restlessness and human passion, it is said, *"Ye un santu."*

If the saints are beyond human movement, there are also saintly men and women who reach that contemplative, Archimedean point beyond the push and shove, the figurative jousting of village life, where they move, perhaps, but are unmoved. Such tranquil perspectives and sentiments are not unusual in the village. One encounters men and women who have become "unmoved movers," so to speak. Here is Ceferino de la Puente, moved to Whitmanesque contemplation of manure, that end product that is at once lowly and esteemed as the source of fertile fields. No doubt he had in mind the Asturian proverb, widespread in Iberia, *Dios y el cucho pueden muchu, sobre todo el cuchu* ("God and manure can do much, above all manure"). Ceferino carries the association between deity and manure a step further. He rhymed:

El cuchu es un cuerpo santo,	Manure is a holy body
Que a descirse la verdad,	That when the truth is told
Da yerba a los campos	Gives grass to the fields
Y frutos a la heredad.	And fruits to the property.
Gloria al cucho!	Glory to manure!

| Que sale de vientres | That comes from the belly |
| Y a vientres da frutos | And to the belly gives fruit. |

It would appear that the saintliness in this body lies in its embodiment of two contrary vectors, that of the lowest and the highest destiny, whose countervailing impulses reduce the poet to the contemplative attitude. And this may be, as well, the essential quality of the saint, himself the unmoved mover, who awesomely embodies many vectors of possible movement. In his polyvectoral quality the saint evokes in adepts and adorers many complex sentiments. He submits himself to many diverse petitions and to many possible costumings by those who, unsolicited by the hurly-burly of married life, remain to *vestir santos*.

In his later life Ceferino became became much less of an aggressive or redressive versifier. He became less spontaneous and was drawn to a more contemplative, intransitive, and composed verse, painstakingly copied out by hand. From the rapid movement of "riposte" and mockery of specific fellow villagers, incompatibilities of movement caused him to turn to gentler ironies about the foibles and contrarieties of mountain village life. Such long poems of his, fabulations really, as "The Marriage of the Villages," "The Marías of Felechosa," and "Juan de Juanes" are widely appreciated.[25] This is not for the piquancy of their particular attributions and retributions, but for the view they offer of the nature of village life.

In most of the versifiers we have considered here, incidentally, we note a marginal social position: they are unmarried or relatively poor by village standards. Those more centrally placed in the social structure—and thus obliged by and committed to its postures and sobrieties—are less free. The marginal position also gives a perspective that those more directly burdened by the hurly-burly of daily village life cannot as easily acquire. There is, in fact, in these marginal personages a relative lack of movement in respect to the normal processes of village life. But this, it would seem, gives them greater possibilities of poetically moving others—of *andando a cantares* and of making movement through verse. Those who do not move in village society may move in it through verse.

There seem to be really two possibilities for these marginal versifiers: to sally forth into village life with their verses or to withdraw from the "to and fro," the *va y ven*, of village life to a kind of "metaphysical" position above and beyond the "ignoble poetic strife." It is worth noting that the very lifeway of these cattle keepers recurrently offers this withdrawal as the solitary herders climb to their pastures and isolated *cabañas*. This loneliness of the mountain herding life is a sentiment richly contained in the "Asturianada" (the melismatic Asturian deepsong) which in its essence, although now much sung in bars and public places, and in its natural context is a solitary mountain air.[26] But there are plenty of these song poems that phrase the sentiments of the going out to the mountains and the return to the village—sing, that is, of the round of life rather than its isolation. And characteristically these poems are familistic and celebrate the going out from and return to sweetheart, hearth, and home. Here are three poems well known to the parish which have that theme—which sing of movement out to the mountains and gravitational attraction back. The first verse is more sentimental and serious and the last two playfully mocking of the attraction of village and family:

1. Maria, tú no me olvides   Don't forget me, Maria,
   Pasar a verte nun puedo.   For I cannot come to see you.
   Que estoy solo en la Mota   I'm here alone on the Mota
   Y no tengo compañero.   And I have no companion.

2. Dia Pachin pa la siega   Pachin set out for the scything
   y per camin acordóse   And recalled en route
   De la muyer y los fios   His wife and children.
   Y dio la vuelta y volvióse.   He turned about and returned.

3. Pachin fo pa la siega.   Pachin left for the scything.
   Marica quedó yorando.   Marcia was left crying.
   Ay! Mio Pachin del alma;   Ay! My precious Pachin;
   Dónde estarás carbruñando?   Where will you be hammering the
                                                   scythe?

But there are those who move entirely out of the orbit of village and family life and achieve a virtually "metaphysical" relation to the comings and goings, attributions and retributions, aggressions and redresses of that life. One of these in Felechosa was Santos Bandera, a man, disappointed in marriage, who took to wandering from *cabaña* to *cabaña* in the mountain heights. His poems, decades old now, are remembered more than most by the villagers who find them highly evocative. Santos Bandera mulled these poems over on the heights and then recited them on his occasional returns to the villages. One of his best known stills the village itself:

Estas calles no son calles,   These streets are not streets,
Esta puerta se cerró,   This door has closed
Este farol ya no alumbra,   This streetlight does not shine.
Nuestra amistad se terminó.   Our friendship is over.

And one of his final verses, moving but unmoved, is composed from a stillness in himself:

Adios mundo engañador	Goodbye world of deception
de ti me estoy despidendo,	To you I am bidding farewell
los años me lo permiten	The years permit it of me
yo la culpa no la tengo.	The fault is not mine.
Adiós mundo engañador,	Goodbye world of deception,
qué triste fin a la postre!	What a sad end for the conclusion!
una larga sepultura	A long interment
y un eterno pasaporte.	And a passport to eternity.

VI. Discussion

In this chapter we have moved from a provocative pastry that was the subject of a ribald joke to the sad, unrequited songs of an old cattle keeper become wandering versifier. In following our folk poets, we have, in our explanatory excursion, moved from an ephemeral, very physical hilarity to a more enduring, reflective, and metaphysical sobriety. The hope is that we can better understand what this folk poetry is mostly about: the movement of self and others in quality space. This poetry is aggressive and manipulative; it causes movement in its subjects by metaphoric predicating of various objects from other domains upon them or by associating them metonymically with various parts of themselves.

By and large, this poetry is a very physical poetry—a poetry of comestibles, of bodily disabilities, of lost legs, of fat hips, of goiters, of cows and donkeys and goats and carts before horses, of hairiness and baldness, of lice and of manure. And it is a poetry that is very much a part of the rub (*roce*) of social life of the village, contributing in its physicality to the vitalization of that life. But in the jousting of this poetry and in its very physicality, there are seeds of the metaphysical attitude, as we have seen. In part this is because some men tire of the provocative jousting and the jocular hostilities in this verse. The manipulation in this verse is mostly devoted, after all, to *achicar* ("diminishing") rather than to *agrandir* ("enlarging"). This is true whether it is a matter of pretentious material or social self-interest or of philosophical pretensions. The folk (usually at the lower, or smaller, end of the folk-urban continuum) more often than not embrace the deficiencies seen in them by the more urbane, and this is evident in much of this verse. In any case, some men come eventually to a hearty surfeit of physical and personal insufficiency—the endless transitivity—and act upon a desire for higher orders of integration in the universe (an integration, incidentally, which, as we see below, is implicit in metaphoric predication itself).

But can we ignore our own manipulation of the reader's understanding? There are, we see, certain major metaphors that keep reemerging in poets as they assess and represent to themselves their experiences of self and other. This is no less the case with students of human behavior who seek out paradigms and explanatory principles for that behavior. Our own primary physiological experience is one main source of these metaphors. That experience is extended out into the world extramural to the body itself to understand it, to familiarize ourselves with it. Time and again the experience of organic growth has been extended to social process itself. In this paper the basic metaphor used in our analysis is that of movement, and we assess our jokes and poems, just words after all, as to the movements they make in speaker and addressee. It is axiomatic to our discussion that men desire fruitful activity in themselves and take pleasure in effecting movement in others. And this is true for both real and literal and for figurative movement.

But the question remains: what is the nature of this movement? Our notion is that these poetic predications—these metaphors and metonyms—accomplish two fundamental, though related, kinds of movement: movement in lexical space and movement in quality space. The former movement is that from one lexical domain to another—to domain of men to the domain of animals is the predominant case here—a movement which is not only across lexical domains but up taxonomic hierarchies as well. For to predicate animals upon men is to recognize (integrate) their common characteristics (their common semantic features, such as organic, animate) at some higher level of the taxonomic hierarchy in which various domains of existence can be integrated. In this curious way the movement of metaphoric predication is at once an extension (a crossing of domains) and an integration of domains at a higher level of lexical abstraction. To say of George that he is an ox is to say that both poles of the predication are animate creatures. To say of him that he is a muffin is to say that both poles are organic entities. It is this integration above and beyond the crossing of domains which is implicit in metaphor that may well contain the seed of the metaphysical attitude we have identified.[27]

It is, however, the second kind of movement that has most interested us in this paper: the qualitative change of situation accomplished by this poetry—the qualitative resituation of interlocutors along various semantic dimensions which, in sum, constitute a culture's quality space. We have sought to identify some of these dimensions and the corresponding movements, the characteristic tendencies of this Asturian mockery and amusement. Our analysis is thus based on a metaphor lodged in primary experience, the primordial experience we all have of situating ourselves rightly and making appropriate movements in real space so as to escape discomfort. This metaphor surely has a resonance in the country to which we have applied it, Spain, where the sole political party is known as "The Movement." It certainly has resonance in this country from which I write. In the last decade a variety of politicians have appealed for our vote with the promise "to get America moving again."

The movement present in these poems may be shown graphically.[28] We may list, by first lines, the poems or joke situations we have considered and the main movements they make in the cultural situation of their subjects. As the first term of every dimension, we show in the vernacular what is generally felt to be the positively valued pole and as the second term the negatively valued pole. We can then indicate if the movement in the poem is in a positive or a negative direction. No poem avails itself of movement in every dimension, though most are moving in several.

Such a chart as this rests on the proposition common to an anthropology influenced by the linguistic point of view that learning culture is the learning of a set of dimensions of discrimination against which to judge our experiences in respect to some basic interests we have in them: their admissibility, desirability, belongingness, solidarity, trustworthiness, dominance, subordinance, etc. Poetry, particularly the variety of spontaneous folk poetry we have before us here, is a vehicle for "discriminating" in striking, though indirect, ways. It is a vehicle primarily for evoking affective response, for pungently changing the quality of its subjects—the consequences of poetic discrimination—by apt use of those prime vehicles of our understanding, metaphor and metonym. These act movingly on subjects by linking them in untoward ways to untoward objects.

This chart is helpful to our understanding in several ways at least. One cannot argue that it or any effort at the rating of affective response[29] is sufficient to our understanding. First of all, it enables us to note, were we to have an adequate sample of this poetry, what the preoccupying dimensions of movement of this country-culture are. On the face of what we do have, the preoccupying dimensions are two: neighbor-stranger and vil-

Oppositions (columns = characters/scenes, rows = semantic oppositions):

Pachin lo pa la siega: Maria	Pachin lo pa la siega: Pachin	muyer y fios: Pachin	Dia Pachin pal la siega: Pachin	Maria tu no me olvides: Maria	El cuchu es un cuerpo santo: cuchu	Aunque el mar: Virgin	Las mozas de Felechosa: visitors	Las mozas de Felechosa: local girls	Sepas tu ignorante: Celerino	Sepas tu ignorante: contrincante	En ese barrio de arriba: Anton	Esa Senora Renate: ethnographer	Que mal oficio: marketgoer	Las Tierras (exchange): spinster	Las Tierras (exchange): veterans	Piononos (exchange): bachelors	Piononos (exchange): girls	Opposition
					+											−	+	Familiar-polite (Campechanco-urbano)
−	+					+							−		−	−		Masterful-docile (Capaz-manso)
										−		+						Well fed-badly fed (Allmentado-hambrento)
										+	+		−					Rich-poor (Rico-pobre)
+	−				+					+	+							Good-bad (Bueno-mato)
		+			+		+	−			+	−	−		+		+	Villager-stranger (Vecino-forestero)
										−		+						Proper-frivolous (Forma'-vano)
+	−	+	−	−	+						+		−		−	+	−	Settled-vagrant (Aldeanc-vago)
											+					−	+	Big-small (Grande-chico)
										−		+	−					Administrator-spendthrift (Administrador-denochado)
	−				+												−	Spiritual-sensual (Sanic-corporeal)
										−		+				−		Human-bestial (Humano-bestial)
								−		−		+				−		Clean-dirty (Limpio-sucio)
			+					−									−	Up-down (Arriba-abajo)
										−		+						Composed-ignorant (Consciente-ignorante)

lager-vagrant. These dimensions we have previously abstracted as that of alienation-familiarization. This concern is constant in these mountain villages so subject over the centuries to emigration over the mountains, over the seas, and down to the mines and seaside industries. The uncertainty about the stability of one's family and neighbors is bound to express itself and to be a major dimension of poetic movement. Second, such graphic presentation is helpful in distinguishing between predominantly laudatory and predominantly disparaging verse. And it points up verse which is at least paradoxical and often ironical—that is, which makes at once both positive and negative movements in its subjects, which moves a subject to spirituality while emphasizing its visceral and cloacal character. The string of positive and negative movements are indicative of the undercutting, the contrary commentary, which is the essence of sarcasm and, in more subtle forms, irony.

VII. Objections to this Discussion

A significant presence in the two villages from which this poetry was obtained was that of the local schoolteacher, Don Antonio, an estimable *maestro nacional*. He was one side of that triumvirate of priest, mayor, and schoolteacher so important in most Spanish villages. In this case he was the only urban person and representative of the Spanish Great Tradition. Both the priest and the mayor were countrymen culturally, still rooted in the countryside. Don Antonio was a native of the province's largest city and a devoted apostle—he had been a number of years in training for the priesthood—of Castilian high culture. In our many long discussions he could not admit any of this verse as poetry. The *coplas* were mere *burlescos*, rhymed insults, or boasts. They did not have that loftiness of thought or dignity of milieu or subject matter characteristic of the Great Tradition. Argue as I might that, subject matter aside, this verse had the essentials of any poetry—scansion, rhyme, compression of statement, and more or less complex emotional movement—he would not or could not admit it. To his discrimination the verse was too gross (*grosera*), too much involved with matters of our animal nature (*abrutado*), to be admitted as poetry. It was not refined enough (*rafinado*). The semantic dimension lying between *abrutado* and *rafinado* was a central one in the schoolteacher's judgment of the world, of his experiences, and of his acquaintances.

In the Great Tradition in which we participate in the academies, we have to contend with and answer to a similar, though in important ways different, reaction to the understanding and appreciation of such verse as we have proffered here. One may argue that it is not refined enough. It concerns itself too much with "brute facts," as it were (and it *is* true that we are concerned with the semantic primitives of this mountain culture and in the emotion that rises out of the shifting between semantic poles). In modern anthropology where we have become aware of the extrinsic nature of culture and the human capacity for self-realization through symbol—the human capacity for the social construction of reality—the suggestion that experience is in some ways vectorial and that we move or are moved about in certain directions may seem to take us back to an older deterministic view of behavior as moving along intrinsic and innate parameters.

This is an important objection. One cannot wish to restore an old determinism. We have gained too much in diffusing our understanding, in opening our intuitions and imaginations up to the symbolic play of mind and imagination in culture. But as with any movement, we can go too far; we can become altogether too refined, too diffuse and extrinsic. In fact, our experience is not so extrinsic as to cease being anchored in our body with its endless internal motilities, its pulsings, its susceptibility to cramps in the short run and bedsores in the long, its search for new situations and resituations. Ours is an organism which is going somewhere or returning from somewhere. It has, if not its vectors, at the least a sense of potentiality of the space it or others might fill and the capacity to fill it. Our organism may flutter for a while, meditate, and be quiescent, but sooner or later it must get moving again—at least until it is cast into a final metaphysical mood!

To say that may not be saying anything necessarily about the mind as it *is* except that it is not perfectly superorganic and that, as part and parcel of constant organismic movement, it is endowed with a primordial appreciation of the need for it. In the end, of course, we do not yet really know how the mind is, how it exactly knows what it knows. Though it occupies space it may comprehend things simultaneously, in the relatively instant interpretation of multitudinous synaptic impulses. But in expressing ourselves, we must commit ourselves to movement or some other speculative image. We lay our thoughts out sequentially and linearize them from right to left, from subject to object, and up and down in generification and specification.

One must admit that our analysis here *is* metaphoric; it rests upon the metaphor of movement. While it is easy enough to recognize movement in a poem which seeks to dispatch its subject to Caracas, it may be more difficult to read "movement" into a poetic reference to a subject as a burro or to a subject's goiter. Still, it is hard to imagine what an unambiguously literal representative of these predications might be—how to give an analysis, in other terms, of poetic activity. Is there any analysis in the end which is not rooted in metaphor?[30] In any case and beyond that, while this analysis may be based upon a metaphoric extension, it may well arise—be extended—from a fundamental poetry in our nature that seems difficult to ignore, the poetry that lies in motion itself.

Quite another objection arises to our discussion, and that concerns our relative neglect, for an anthropological document, of the social and cultural context that would help us better to understand this country culture of repartee, of verbal riposte. It is true that I have been determined in ferreting out the semantic dimensions of movement and have neglected the larger situation—the pressures, for example, that the urban high culture exerts upon these country folk, making them too painfully aware of their inadequacies and quick to spot pretense in their neighbors and to pick it apart poetically. The subordinated circumstances of country folk in the European folk-urban continuum may cause them the more often to put down their fellows *(achicar)* than to support them or put them up.

Of course, there are more material facts of domination and subordination which the countrymen of Europe have long faced. Some of the verse we collected sought movement, even revolutionary movement, in the face of that situation. Under the regime, however, in which our verse was collected, the poetry of political movement was not much in evidence. It is much more in evidence in Costa's nineteenth-century collection of country verse. Our verse is more homely, *casera*, and pretends less to the reordering of society. It is a poetry of participation—turbulent, petulant, fretful participation perhaps—but not a poetry of mastery, of upheaval, and of new dispensations. In circumstances where countrymen feel unpretentious, often inadequate, they are quick to remark pretense in their fellows and mock it or comment upon it sarcastically or ironically before it can lay substantial claims on anything. In this sense, this poetry strives for an "equanimity" in village life at the expense of significant change.

The detailed level at which we have sought to examine our materials has, it is true, made us especially aware of local, homely change and movement. We may pay a price for such detailed examination in two ways. First, there may be some weakness in grasping the larger structure of social relations in which these poetic events are enmeshed. From time to time in social science that trade-off may be preferred to the weakening of our awareness of change and movement which occurs when we emphasize structure. For the dominant impulse in social science, perhaps inevitably, is that of determining where people are rather than where they are going. We want to put them in their place. We like to know their category. But however literal-mindedly men may classify themselves or be classified by category or by characteristic mood or temperament, they all fancy membership in other categories and undergo constant fluctuation in mood. There is a bit of the gypsy in every countryman, and every bumptious bumpkin is given pause—moments of quietude and unworthiness. In cultures of spontaneous versification, if many men and women are too busy to be aware of the fluctuating imagination, there are always these versifiers to remind them of it.

Our interest here, in any case, is that of grasping where the villagers are "going" as that is reflected in their verse. In grasping that existential, and surely figurative, mobility of human experience, as men and women by words in rhyme situate and resituate themselves—move here, move there in respect to each other's qualities—we come as close as we probably can to knowing who they are when they're at home.

Finally, an objection to this discussion may arise because, while we have shown the tangible qualities that are manipulated to obtain social affects in this village verse, we have not gone on to elaborate, in the Lévi-Straussian manner, the "logic of tangible qualities." This is because this verse is too brief to develop such a logic, such a "science of the concrete." These poems hardly qualify as "fabulations" and thus do not offer a complexity of movement from which a logic may be deduced.[31] Nevertheless, these poems are interesting in my view because they show us very clearly an important, indeed elemental, feature of poetic language in society—its manipulation of social subjects by proposing, that is to say, predicating or stating as a proposition, an associative relationship between them and empirical categories of experience.

VIII. Conclusion

We return in conclusion to our epigraph from Merleau-Ponty and to Carmelo Lisón's notion of aggressivity in commensality—a notion best typified, perhaps, in that impious pastry, the *Pionono*.

If anthropologists and folklorists are to inhabit the people they study, they must recognize the degree to which any people—and this is surely not the case of mountain people alone—experience, in ongoing social life, qualitative manipulation which is usefully conceptualized as taking place along various dimensions. The facts of social life are that people themselves manipulate each other by metaphor and metonym even while they inhabit the same community. Our anthropological inhabitation of people in part demands an understanding of that manipulation. This is the end towards which we have been moving in this paper. Of course, this poetic manipulation is rarely crass and cold spirited—purely instrumental. It emanates from inhabitation—common experiences of village barn and countryside from which evocative figures of speech can be taken. It provides savory verbal pleasures even for its victims and regularly offers the opportunity for riposte. This poetry, whatever its manipulation, celebrates that common experience and the mutuality of common language— of delectable metaphors and relished metonyms. To Lisón's phrase *"agresividad en comensalidad"* in describing this poetry, we may add "manipulation in mutuality."

This poetry, like any poetry worth its salt, speaks with many voices. It is multi-evocative. It is evocative in the first instance because it is based on this common inhabitation—common experiences of which it reminds its auditors. It is evocative in the second instance because it plays upon ambivalent dimensions where voices call subjects to and fro at once. It is evocative in the third instance because it brings the ends of various dimensions to bear upon each other—different voices moving in from different points of the quality space people occupy to speak at once. And it is evocative in the last instance, and most basically, because it extends images from their natural locus and centers of gravity into other domains: it makes arresting leaps of the imagination so that the subjects of the verse find themselves associated with unadmitted or unexpected arenas.

Notes

This is a revised and expanded version of a paper presented in November, 1974, at a conference in Galicia on northern Spanish folk culture. That version, in Spanish and now in press, carries acknowledgments to the many people, Asturians and colleagues, to whom I am indebted. But I should like to again thank Carmelo Lison, who organized the conference, and my coworker Renate Lellep Fernandez for her many insights. This revised version of the paper, pushing the notion of "quality space" and the notion of "vectors of semantic discrimination," was read at the 1975–76 Symbol Seminar at the Institute of Advanced Study, Princeton. I appreciate the comments of my colleagues in the seminar. I particularly want to thank Renato Rosaldo, who was kind enough to give an illuminating reading of the Spanish version.

1. "Haya Metaphors for Speech," *Language in Society*, 3 (1974), 51–67.

2. "Arte Verbal y estructura social en Galicia," in *Perfiles simbolico morales de la Cultura Gallega* (Madrid, 1974), pp. 29–60.

3. I have sought to emphasize this point in several places such as, for example, in a paper read at the Seventy-third Annual Meeting of the American Anthropological Association, Mexico City, 1974: "Seventeen Types of Ambiguity (Plus or Minus Two) in Explaining Human Behavior."

4. This theory of quality space is put forth in Chapters 1 and 2.

5. It may be a matter of vertical versus horizontal stratification. One is reminded of the American black comedian, Dick Gregory, when he advised his fellows: "In the North you can get as big as you want but don't get too close. In the South you can get as close as you want but don't get too big."

6. In the custom of the *abrazo* and the graceful *beso* among women, the Spanish manage public familiarities better than most cultures.

7. We have a shift, really, from secondary sexuality, the dalliance and flirtation of the bar, to the primary sexuality (on the basis of the sex and food association) of the *pastelaria* ("pastry shop").

8. It may be that the incorporative phase of rites of passage tends towards sensual innuendo simply as a reaffirmation of life after the celebration of death. The name *Campoamor* ("love field"), incidentally, is not an especially forced conceit, for many bars, *pastelaria*, and places of public gathering in the province, including the opera house in Oviedo, are named after the famous nineteenth-century Asturian poet, Ramon de Campoamor.

9. An interesting study in itself, in the structural vein, would be the names assigned in Spain, but especially in Asturias, to pastries: *huesos de San Esposito* ("bones of San Esposito"), *palmeros* ("pilgrim palms"), *casadielles* ("homebodies"), *frisuelos* ("fritters").

10. The rapidity with which the older girl tartly "put down" the men is not exceptional among Asturian women, who have a good deal of authority both in private and in public with regard to men. Some students speak of an Asturian matricentrism *(matriarcado)* maintained in part by a ready repartee and the brusque rebuff given by women to male presumption.

11. The classic work is by Joaquín Costa, *La Poesía Popular Española*, Obras Completas, VIII (Madrid, 1917).

12. "Arte Verbal y estructura social en Galicia."

13. Gabriel de Tarde, *La Psychologie Sociale de Gabriel Tarde* (Paris, 1910).

14. Cf. *Right and Left: Essays on Dual Symbolic Classification*, ed. Rodney Needham (Chicago, 1974).

15. This is C. L. Geertz's understanding of symbolic events in his "Religion as a Cultural System," in *Anthropological Approaches to the Study of Religion*, Association of Social Anthropologists Monograph No. 3 (London, 1965).

16. I have examined this sentiment in Chapter 4.

17. She does not read or write.

18. The authoritative and recent local study of this people in Asturias is that of Don Juan Uria Riu, *Los Vaqueiros de Alzada* (Oviedo, 1968). Maria Catedra is now working on the *vaqueiros* of Alzada. The first report of this research in her "Notas sobre un pueblo marginado: los vaqueiros de Alzada," *Revista de Estudios So-*

ciales, 6 (Sept.–Dec. 1973), 139–64, provides an interesting overview of the difference between the "quality space" of the *vaqueiro* cattle keepers and that of agriculturally oriented villagers.

19. Alice B. Kehoe has written insightfully about this process of taking the part for the whole in social interaction in "The Metonymic Pole and Social Roles," *Journal of Anthropological Research*, 32 (1976), 266–74.

20. Ceferino has some formal education—several grades—and is further self-educated. He has been to Cuba. There are influences of Spanish literary culture in his poetry. For example, he undertook a series of fables much influenced by the Spanish fabulist Samaniego. This particular poem appears to exhibit some of these influences.

21. This "rule of mythical thought" appears throughout Lévi-Strauss's *Mythologiques*, but particularly in *The Savage Mind* (Chicago, 1966). *Mythologiques* is the collective name for a series of monographs in which Lévi-Strauss analyzes myths. References for the *Mythologiques* are: *The Raw and the Cooked* (New York, 1969); *Du miel aux cendres* (Paris, 1966); *L'Origine des manieres de la table* (Paris, 1968); *L'Homme nu* (Paris, 1971). I discuss this, as well as Jakobson's view of the frequent imposition of similarity (metaphor) upon contiguity (metonym) in folklore, in "The Mission of Metaphor," p. 126.

22. Discussed along with the "gastro-intestinal continuum" in Chapter 1.

23. For complexity in tokens of communication various terms have been employed. Mircea Eliade refers to symbols as "polyvalent" in *Images et Symbols* (Paris, 1952), while Floyd Lounsbury prefers "polysemous" (Another View of Trobriand Kinship Categories," in *Formal Scientific Analysis*, ed. E. A. Hammel, American Anthropologist Special Publication [Menasha, 1965], pp. 142–85). Victor Turner uses the term "multivocal" in *The Forest of Symbols* (Ithaca, 1967). Because of the movement model employed here and the emphasis upon dimensionality, the term *polyvectoral* is the more apt.

24. There are sex role differences in movement with regard to one's house. A man can confine himself too much to his house. It is ominous and implies sickness to say of him curtly, *"no sale"* ("he doesn't come out"). Women are more installed and can come out too much. A principal desire of a girl is to marry and find her place in her home *(estar en su casa)*.

25. An essay on the life history and poetry of this most interesting man is in preparation.

26. See my discussion of the "typical" situation of this song in "Syllogisms of Association."

27. This integration is discussed, by reference to latent factors in association, in Chapter 1. But the creative element in this lexical abstraction—the filling of lexical gaps in our coding of experience—is cogently discussed in an important recent paper by Keith H. Basso, "Wise Words of the Western Apache: Metaphor and Semantic Theory," in *Meaning in Anthropology*, ed. K. Basso and H. Selby (Albuquerque, 1976).

28. Seitel, "Haya Metaphors for Speech," p. 65.

29. Robert J. Smith, for example, in "The Structure of Aesthetic Response," *Journal of American Folklore*, 84, No. 331 (1971), 68–79, has made a most interesting attempt to formalize the structure of aesthetic response in Peruvian fiestas and in two American folktales. He notes positive and negative responses in cognition and emotion to the various items of folklore of the fiesta. In respect to dealing with emotions, however, he notes a real dissatisfaction with such "meter readings." In

part this is because our conceptual tools for dealing with emotions are, compared to those for dealing with cognition, very inadequate. They pose major problems for validation. Smith's method is to obtain a profile of affective response, hedonic continua, by eliciting informant judgments at selected points in the telling of a folktale.

30. Steven C. Pepper, *World Hypotheses* (Berkeley and Los Angeles, 1942); Hayden White, *Metahistory: The Historical Imagination in Nineteenth-Century Europe* (Baltimore, 1974).

31. The references are to Lévi-Strauss's discussion of fabulation in *The Raw and the Cooked* (New York, 1969), esp. "Overture," pp. 1–32.

4

SYLLOGISMS OF ASSOCIATION
SOME MODERN EXTENSIONS OF
ASTURIAN DEEPSONG

This chapter will examine some aspects of a variety of folksong, the *Asturianada*, which is still very much alive in Asturian mountain munici- palities. In particular, we will account for the unexpected persistence of this genre among the miners. The municipality of Aller, in which most of these songs can be heard, extends from the divide fronting with Castile (Puerto de San Isidro at 1,530 meters in altitude) to the mining town of Moreda (at 298 meters), 46 kilometers to the northwest. This valley is one of those in the south central Asturias that have come to be known as the "Cuencas Mineras." The northern half of the municipality from the county seat, Cabañaquinta, to the line with the *concejo* of Mieres, has been devoted to deep mining of bituminous coal since the late nineteenth century; but, as is characteristic of Asturian miners, most men who work the mines still hold on to land. What cows they are able to keep graze in abundance in green meadows in the heart of the mining zone.

Cattle keeping is an ancient cultural pattern in Asturias, and the burden of hay making in the summer months falls in varying degrees on all valley dwellers. During the hay-making months, the mines go into reduced production—the inescapable acquiescence of coal to grass. In the upper reaches of the valley, cattle keeping is still dominant, though miners may be found in all seventeen villages and towns that make up the *concejo*. In the upper valley villages, a transhumant life is still prevalent. The cattle are moved in May (and stay through October) to graze in the high public pastures and divide-plateaus *(paramos)* so typical of the Cantabrian range. In former days, one or two family members accom- panied the cattle until the end of the hay season, when they were joined in the rough stone *caseríos* by the entire family. In recent years, however, the time spent by families in the *caseríos* has been much reduced because so many family members are miners who can devote themselves only to the haying but not the herding. There is more commuting back and forth from the village than before. Children have to be sent down in mid-September for schooling. There is still nostalgia for life under the peaks, but as more and more conveniences come into village life, extended sojourns in the uplands carry with them a sense of deprivation by comparison with village life.

One has to speak of a tension between two lifestyles that is present in every village, in many families and, often enough, in individuals. It is one thing to drive cattle to upland meadows to fatten them for a fall market; it is another thing to descend for daily wages into the depths of the earth. The former is a family-centered way of life, and though arrangements for herding may be made with other families, responsibility for one's cattle always rests finally within various generations of the family. In the miner's life, the male working bond is more important. Although it is rare for that bond to extend beyond four or five work companions in any truly effective way, there is a general sense of solidarity among Asturian miners. This, in part, accounts for the chronic strike situation that has long prevailed in the Asturian mines—even though, since the Spanish Civil War, the miners view themselves as having no labor organization that truly represents their interests. It is relatively easy to prevail upon Asturian miners to strike in their own interests, but it would be difficult, if not impossible, to prevail upon any cattle keeper *(ganadero)* to strike. This family-centeredness and unwillingness to cooperate in the interests of improvement of breed, prices, or conditions of marketing has been the despair of many a forward-looking veterinarian.

Many reasons account for the difference in solidarity between the two lifestyles. The family-centeredness of the cattle keeper's life carries with it the age-old enmity among families who are, in a sense, competing for scarce goods in a situation of relatively high human and cattle density. It carries with it all the enmities of generations of family interaction. The miner's life is no doubt subject to class-structure analysis. The miners are not really competing with each other in the exploitation of scarce resources, rather, they are thrown into a subterranean cooperation against what, in their view, is a superfluous class of well-off managers and owners who rarely descend into the mines. When the miner returns to the surface after his arduous and dangerous labor, his resentment is inevitably aroused by his contact with the clean-faced men who organize, manage, and, in some ways, own him, and who yet have no part in his dark feats of production. By contrast, when the cattle keeper returns to the village from the high pastures, the warmth of his homecoming is marred by his having to pass people to whom, for many reasons, he and his own family do not even nod their heads. Up in the mountain pastures during the day, the very strict stone demarcations of the *minifundia* landscape keep families apart more than they bring them together. Good stone fences keep neighbors in their place; they do not necessarily make good and helpful neighbors. These fences constantly remind one of family property, but they do not suggest interfamily solidarities. Farther up in the mountains, where herds graze in common on public lands, there is some collective herding and interfamily solidarity, yet the familialism of the valley reasserts itself in quarrels over the size of herds and limited grazing resources. There is a solidarity in life in the mountain heights for the cattle keeper, yet the familialism of the valley is the dominant mood. The solidarity of the mines is at odds with the familialism of the valleys, but it is not overcome by it. Miners are easily inspired to collective sentiments beyond the family; cattle keepers are not. Asturian deepsong plays an important role in that inspiration.

There are many kinds of social science analyses—economic, sociostructural, and political—that must be brought to bear upon the differences between miner and cattle keeper. Wage and class-structure differences alone may be sufficient explanations for many of the frictions. Yet these analytical categories are all epiphenomenal insofar as the Asturian villagers are concerned, and I believe that no explanations can be made that fail to allow for what is real experience for the miners and the cattle keepers: a tradition of song and verse that is still very much alive as a primary activity despite the overlay of newspaper, television, and dance hall culture now present in even the most isolated hamlet. In the solidarity and divisiveness of this song and verse, one may no doubt see other structures reflected. Songs and verses may not be final causes of interpersonal relations, but they are surely efficient causes for the way cattle keepers and miners represent their situation to themselves.

What I specifically propose to examine is the way the men and women of these Asturian mining valleys extend themselves into the lyrics of their deepsongs—lyrics that are, on the whole, quite short and simple. By using the term *extension*, I refer to that fundamental mechanism in the problem-solving process by which persons take experience from one

domain, where it is more concretely apprehended and more easily conceptualized, and use it as a model for a domain of greater abstraction and
much fuzzier and more ambiguous perception. In the expressive life, this
extension takes the form of metaphoric and metonymic predications upon
the various inchoate pronouns of social life (see Chapters 1 & 2). Such
predications instill qualities in pronouns when they, as subjects, are
brought into association with the objects of predication. What are the
qualities predicated upon or associated with the various Asturian pronouns as a consequence of singing of these songs? There is an important
problem of modernization involved, for deepsong has remained very
contemporary—very modern! How has it managed to do so when other
folklore has failed? How has a song largely rooted in an agricultural and
pastoral world become also the favored song of miners?

The Survival of Deepsong

As is everywhere the case, the Asturian mountain countryfolk have
suffered the inroads of mass communications and mass amusements. Men
and women used to memorize long historical romances in verse. In any
village, people can be found who can still recite these poems for hours on
end. The poems largely had a nineteenth-century locus, such as the wars
in Morocco or the Carlist Rebellion. But the didactic and entertaining
functions of these recitations have been appropriated—for those many
whose powers of reading still do not enable them to take to the paper-
back novel—by the serial *novelas* and the dramatized twentieth-century
newsreels *(España Siglo XX)* on television.

There was also a rich lyrical tradition in courtship songs and the lyrics
accompanying the variety of folk dances; the characteristic Asturian
Giraldillas, the *bailes de pandero* of the *vaquieros de Alzada*, the *bailes
de los pollos* were typical.

In E. M. Torner's classic collection *Cancionero musical de la lírica
popular Asturiana* (1920), more than half of the lyrics collected—261 of
500—are associated with dances. The greatest proportion of these, 182,
are lyrics for the Asturian *Giraldilla*. These songs and dances are no
longer popularly maintained—they are defunct in the villages—though
the Spanish National Movement is making efforts through its feminine
section to keep them alive. (This was written in 1973.) They have been
replaced by the pop music of the village dance halls *(las pistas)*, which,

though an old institution in the cities of Asturias, do not date beyond the 1930s in the *pueblos* and *aldeas,* and are really a development of the postwar world.

The rich repertoire of courtships songs *(canciones de Ronda)*[1] is also much depleted and scarcely heard today because young men no longer form singing groups and spend their evenings courting in other villages. Village girls now attend school for four or five years and, with their new reading skills, have turned from the folklore of such itinerant courtship to the *fotonovelas*—jejune accounts in many pictures and few words of pubescent intrigue. These days young men and young women congregate weekly in the steamy hubbub of the overcrowded dance halls—hardly a lyrical arena, whatever other fancies may be titillated.

As the villages have experienced decentering—the failure to maintain themselves as the focus of life for their inhabitants—so also have those songs of communal labor vanished, whether in the interest of village improvement *(sextiferia),* or in group labor in the fields *(andecha).* Like the folk dances, they once celebrated a community spirit beyond the family.

Nevertheless, deepsong maintains its strength in these mountain communities. By Asturian deepsong[2] I mean that highly personalized song, also called *Asturianada* or *canción Asturiana,*[3] in which rhythm is of the least importance and in which the singers, male or female, seem to search deep within for those resources of endurance and timbre that they can bring to bear, with high emotional expressivity, upon relatively simple lyrics. The intense concentration upon melismatic vocalization of each syllable means that very often the lyric seems lost in the song production. But the lyric is always there, and its meaning can be of equal interest to listeners, however caught up they might be in the quality of vocalization.

Our inquiry here will be directed primarily at the songs sung by men. However, this genre formerly belonged to both men and women. In the provincial championships this is still the case, as there are equal numbers of participants from both sexes, and male and female champions are chosen. In an overview, no striking difference in the content of the songs chosen by men and women emerges. There is no differing commitment to lyric or narrative deepsong, for example. In fact, in the provincial championships, women sing mining songs about as frequently as men.

Asturian deepsong, when well done, presents profound challenges to the human voice. If there is any cultural preparation on the listener's part to receive it, and if the singer's voice can rise triumphantly beyond the obvious physical effort, then these *Asturianadas* can be moving indeed. Annual championships in this song genre pack provincial opera houses; the unruly crowds from the countryside, quick to catcall inadequate singers, are as quick to manifest admiration at some powerful voice especially fertile in the intricacy of its melismatic embellishments.

There are many reasons why this genre persists. Its intensely personal quality is one vital factor. Traditionally, the *Asturianada* was the song of the lone countryman or woman, sung late in the evening, while climbing with the cows up to the pastures after milking them or winding down a long trail after cutting hay. This song *in situ* should properly be heard in early morning or late evening, across a valley. The singer cannot be made out, but the intricate song drifts clearly across the void. Though it bursts out regularly in bars or public gatherings, it is not, and never was, a song for active group participation. Either the group may go on in its hubbub ignoring the singer, or the singer's voice and song commands their attention, and people fall silent in appreciation of the singer's efforts. A fine voice may sometimes be exploited by a group of men in *juerga*, moving on a Saturday or Sunday afternoon from bar to bar. The voice may not even belong to a man who has previous comradeship with the group or who by class belongs in the group. He is invited along to intone *Asturianadas* in bar after bar in order to impose the group's presence—through its association with his voice—upon the bar. Such abuse of deepsong, which should more naturally arise as an end product of intense communication either with the self or with others, is quite naturally resented by many if the voice is not of sufficient quality.

As the communal spirit has gone out of Asturian villages under the impact of wage labor and the individually oriented attractions and amusements of the modern city culture (magazines, books, movie theaters, television), so the folklore that was a part of that communalism—the dance lyrics, the lyrics of courtship—has also died. In an epoch of increasing family autonomy and economic individualism, the old group songs have appeared less appropriate to the age. But the genre that is individualistic *par excellence* appears even more appropriate to an age that more and more celebrates the individual—or the individual celebrity. In this age the *Asturianada* is fully at home. The singer in any gathering is always a celebrity. He does not demand the appreciation of the crowd, only silent, and not necessarily positive, spectatorship. There is certainly intense communication involved in the *Asturianadas*, but it arises from personal display and not from group participation. If collective sentiments are finally provoked by the *Asturianada*, this occurs because the singer has managed to raise the song to the status of a symbol with which all listeners may merge their identity, and not because all participants are merged collectively into the act of singing the song.

The *Asturianada* has also survived—indeed it flourishes—because it is a song style that has proved congenial to the Asturian miners who, for courtship, prefer the hurly-burly of the dance hall to the straggling about in *ronda* and who, for group amusement, prefer the camaraderie of the bars to street dances and celebrations. *Rondas* and street-dance songs are not their style—*Asturianadas* are. Thus, this song can be heard in solitary rendition in distant galleries of the mines. And after several glasses of wine, it almost inevitably rises to the surface in the bars as an alternate and deeper mode of communication among drinking comrades who in ordinary discourse are limited to a public language (Bernstein 1959) with all the tough-minded restrictions on subtle communication of any kind.

As men in the bars, in their increasingly flushed intercommunication, arrive at the speechless level, they turn to Asturian deepsong for deeper sentiments and deeper meanings. Deepsong thus becomes a form of profound comunication among three or four drinking companions as first one and then another tries his voice on a *tonada*. It is not only among miners that drinking produces this musical effect. Cattle keepers with a wineskin who are gathered around a pot of stew (*cazuela*) in the *caseríos* soon turn to *Asturianadas* to communicate more deeply among themselves. Countrymen of the old culture seem to have had a wider and more subtle range of verbal art at their disposition (*refranes*, for example) and were not as committed to a shallow public language. Indeed, Asturian villagers love stories of the simple-minded sagacity of the countrypeople who, having no sophisticated language at their disposal, make observations of an outrageous obviousness that, on second thought, show a deeper understanding.

In village bars, where there may be no miners present, unmarried countrymen not long in their cups soon are caught up in deepsong. These musical exchanges almost always occur between bachelors celebrating a camaraderie that will be lost when they are married and begin to take up the burden of family quarrels—begin, that is, to fit into that network of social resentments that will make it increasingly difficult to break out in deepsong in the bars of their own village. On trips to other villages, old comrades of the summer's high pastures or of cattle- or horse-trading ventures may be encountered in bars, and their camaraderie, unfettered by family antagonisms, soon leads to deepsong.

Breaking into Deepsong

What are the profound emotions communicated by deepsong? What does the song mean and what do the lyrics mean? In many cases, it is the breaking into song that is meaningful, and little attention is paid to the lyrics. Still, how is one to say what breaking into song means? It is an event that surpasses understanding and about which it is difficult to elicit comment. The situation seems ripe; a companion has confidence in his voice, so he launches into song for any number of reasons. His song may be an attempt to express the ineffable, and is equivalent to saying; "Our comradeship has qualities that cannot be expressed in words, and I propose now to sing you a song." Such a move must both flatter and slightly embarrass a comrade, for it is a shift to a level of feeling higher than is normal in the public relationship of men. As in most communications between comrades, there is also an element of challenge—a kind of throat wrestling. As one launches into song, there is also, therefore, the statement: "Match this if you can, my friend." Indeed, this may be the dominant statement in many songs.

The Attachment to Place

If the voice is a very good one and the song well done, then the event becomes symbolic, that is, it comes to stand for much more than itself and the immediate participants. Such a song, regardless of the meaning of its lyrics, raises in the Asturian listeners pride in their province and its lore; at the very least, it arouses local pride. Approval of the song may be murmered or shouted: ¡Vaya guaje ésto es de cantar!", said in the sense and spirit of "That's what it is to be an Asturian!" or "That's what Asturias is all about!" or "That's what it is to be from Bimenes (or Langreo)!" or "What a splendid thing it is to be an Asturian (or a Langreano)!" or "What fine songs and what fine singers we Asturians have!" Thus it is that the lyrics of many of these songs do little more than celebrate a provincial or local origin. They mainly add color to locality with words conveying hardly any meaning. The title of one of these songs, "Viva el lugar," is exactly what they are all about. They celebrate province (*concejo, pueblo,* or *lugar*). The song "Soy de Langreo" ("I Am from Langreo") has various endings, all difficult to decipher, so overshadowed are they by the fourfold repetition of the *pueblo* identification. Because of melismatic elaboration, · the song takes much longer to sing than might be suspected; the elabora- tion is primarily expended upon the four-line claims to local identity:

1. Soy de Langreo — I am of Langreo
   Soy de Langreo, mira — I am of Langreo, look you
   Soy Langreano — I am of Langreo
   Soy Langreano, mira — I am of Langreo, look you
   Soy Langreano, y minero — I am of Langreo and a miner
   Y de eso muy fiero. — And of this fiercely proud.

Or the song, still concentrating on the same first four lines, may conclude:

1a. Por darte un beso suave — For giving you a soft kiss
    Lloraba tu madre un día. — Your mother cried one day.
    Para darme, tu, un a mi — For you to give one to me
    A ver si lloraba la mia. — Let's see if mine will cry.

The provincial champion of 1971 (a male) sang as one of his championship songs his own composition, which follows:

2. Soy del pueblin de Bimenes — I am of the little town of Bimenes
   Baxe de una montaña. — I came down from a mountain.
   Que me mandan a cantar — They sent me to sing
   Una canción Asturiana. — An Asturian song.

It is clear that the *campanilismo* is the important motive in the song, the fact that he and his song represent, are *naturales de,* Bimenes.[4] Though it is difficult to be equally proud of more than one place at a time, men can and do develop loyalties to several villages, and there is also a slight tendency toward uxorilocality in Asturias. Here, in its entirety, is a deepsong that handles the problem with a touch of humor[5] and with what faithfulness is possible to four locales:

3. Nací en la Pola de Lena, — I was born in Pola de Lena,
   Cortexé en Pola de Sierro, — I courted in Pola de Sierro,
   Caséme en Pola de Tsaciana, — I married in Pola de Tsaciana,
   Y vivo en Pola de Somiedo. — I live in Pola de Somiedo.

Even though the singer may not associate himself with a place in the song, place names figure boldly in most songs. Here is an example:

4.	Entre La Pola y el Pino	Between La Pola and El Pino
	Hay una piedra redonda	There is a round stone
	Donde se sienten los mozos	Where the young men sit
	Cuando vienen de la ronda.	When they come from the *ronda*.

In support of the theory that these songs are primarily a celebration of place with little additional meaning is the fact that neither the inhabitants of El Pino or La Pola (Aller), pleased as they were to hear their towns mentioned in the song, knew of any such rendezvous stone as the *piedra redonda*. Some people pointed to a kilometer stone between the two towns, but it was, in fact, put up well after the song had obtained currency. The song was originally collected as a dance song from a town neighboring the two towns mentioned (Torner 1920:113). For the same locale, this song, like example 1a, deals with unifying of separate personalities through a common action:

5.	La primera vez de mia vida	The first time in my life
	Fuiste al Carmin de la Pola	You went to Carmin de La Pola
	La primera vez de mia vida	The first time in my life
	Que fui al Carmin de la Pola	That I went to Carmin de La Pola

There may be romantic references in these songs, as in the woman's version of the Langreo song, but they still are subordinate to the place element and are mainly vehicles for deepening the tenor of the song. This is well seen in the following song:

6.	Asturiana, Asturianina,	Asturian woman, Asturian girl,
	Como quieres tu	Why do you wish
	Que yo non te quiero?	I should not love you?
	Asturias, Asturias!	Asturias, Asturias!

After addressing itself to an Asturian girl, the song transforms her into Asturias itself; the attachment to person transforms itself into attachment to place.

In Asturian folklore, there is a very powerful association of women with the province. The province has a feminine quality assigned to it—*Las Asturias*. And the matriarchal quality of family life is readily recognized by Asturian men: *"nuestro matriarcado,"* men say ruefully! Women (*Asturianas*), it is often said, are strongly attached to the province and will not leave it: "Marry an Asturiana, marry Asturias." There is an historical basis to this attachment. Men have been leaving women behind to maintain the home and village in Asturias since the time of the reconquest. They went off to battle across the mountains in Castile and stayed to settle. They also have been going to the New World since its discovery, but particularly emigrated in the nineteenth century. And Asturian men coming from the rich grass country of the Cantabrian slope have long been in demand as mowers and reapers in northern Castile and León; and in the late summer and early fall, they leave the province, scythe over shoulder, to spend several months in the grass and grain fields of León, Zamora, and Valladolid. At the present time, many more men than women migrate to jobs in the rest of Europe, though the rate of labor migration is below that for other Spanish provinces. Considering all these masculine vagaries, there is ample reason for the association between Asturias and its womenfolk and for the large number of *Asturianadas* that play upon the deep emotions aroused in men by the accustomed farewells both to the province and to its womenfolk:

7. Cuando yo salí de Asturias	When I left Asturias
De la mas alta montaña	From the highest mountain
me dexaron prisionero	They left me prisoner
Los gueyos de una Asturiana!	The eyes of an Asturian woman!

Or the same emotion and identification in a well-known song called "Adios Asturias":

8. Pasé el puerto de Payares.	I passed through the port of Payares.
Pasé el puerto de Payares.	
Pasélu con una grande pena.	I passed through the port of Payares.
Pasélu con una grande pena.	
Porque dexaba la mozà,	I passed it with great pain.
Pasélu con una grande pena.	I passed it with great pain.
	Because I was leaving the girl,
	I passed it with great pain.

A final testimony to the evocation of place in Asturian deepsong is one of the longest—and least spontaneous—songs composed in this mode:

9. Soy Asturianiana.	I am a true Asturian girl.
Soylo de verdad.	I was born in La Corridoria.
Nacida en la Corridoria.	He who was born here in Asturias
Todo el que en Asturia nace	Can say he was born in glory.

Puede decir que nació en la   Blessed land where I was born
  gloria.   I cannot live without you Asturias.
Bendita tierra donde nací   I adore her so much
No puedo Asturias vivir sin ti.   That I cry for her and would die for
Es tanto lo que la adoro   her.
Que por ella lloro y por ella   I cannot live without you Asturias,
  morirá.   Blessed Asturias.
No puedo Asturias vivir sin ti,
Bendita Asturias.

A fundamental meaning of Asturian deepsong, then, is some locality or set of localities within Asturias and, in the larger context, Asturias itself. Since Asturias is strongly associated with its womenfolk, a relationship to a women celebrated in a deepsong may easily transform into the celebration of a relationship to Asturias. The opposite transformation may also occur. Examples 6 and 7 typify these transformations. Although the collective sentiment aroused by a singer is the sentiment of belonging to a locality, a fine singer will arouse in many of his hearers who are not of his locality—a sentiment of belonging to Asturias itself. Any of the following forms of the statement is possible:

Ordinary singing provoking exclusive feelings:

> I am [we are] to Langreo
> As you [singular or plural] are to Pravia.

Fine singing provoking inclusive feelings:

> I am [we are] to Langreo
> As we all are to Asturias.

Various forms expressing the sentiment of attachment to the opposite sex and hence to Asturias are possible:

I [male] am to you [female] as we are to Asturias [example 6].
I [male] am to Asturias as I am to you [female] [example 7].
I [female] am to you [male] as Asturias is to you [us] [no example given].
I [female] am to you [without gender] as Asturias is to us [example 9].

The evocations of collective sentiments of locality continue to be a main characteristic of deepsong even though, relative to emigration in former years, the development of mining and heavy industry in Asturias has made possible more local employment and, as a result, there has been much less movement of men to the outside world. Industrialization also accounts for the rural exodus, a decentering of the villages and a lessening of allegiance to them. Asturians still think of themselves as mountainlocked on the Cantabrian Sea with poor communications with Castile, although there is much more coming and going than there was formerly. Although men and women may live in the industrial center, they still identify with, return to, and frequently hold land in, their native villages. Regionalism—in this case, provincialism because Asturias, the region, is coterminous with the province of Oviedo—is still pronounced, and so is a kind of nostalgic localism. There is, therefore, plenty of sentiment—both attachment to place, and an associated attachment to women in their various manifestations as sweethearts, mothers, or wives—that can be played upon by deepsong, employing the predominant traditional idiom. Deepsong in this sense retains its modernity by remaining the same. The association of womenfolk with locality no doubt reinforces the persistence of deepsong.

More Subtle Sentiments and Associations

While the simple celebration of place is present in many *Asturianadas* and may be a part of the meaning of any deepsong, more subtle meanings may be discovered in the lyrics of many of these songs. I give below an example from an *espicha* I attended in a village in Alto Aller. An *espicha* is a celebration at which the first barrel of relatively green cider from the last harvest is tapped. There is much food, dancing, and general hilarity.

In this particular case, there were about equal numbers of miners and cattle keepers. Characteristically, the miners gathered more boisterously in the center of the room and around the barrel while the cattle keepers sat quietly at the tables around the side of the room. I was with a group of miners and one older, retired miner (the father of one of them), when we were accosted by a small, powerfully built, dark-haired man from a neighboring village. Formerly a miner, but now retired with mild silicosis,[6] and an owner of a small bar, he began immediately, with arms around one of the young men, to tax him about the easy conditions of present-day work in the mine. He described how hard conditions used to be. "But now, with all this injection of water into the seams to hold down the dust, and all the machinery, mining is soft work," he said. The young man responded with a lively defense of present-day work conditions, the higher wages, and the greater productiveness—better mining in every way. "How could the older miners ever have worked for such slave wages?" he asked. He seemed to be getting the better of the debate when the older man suddenly stepped back a bit from him—still remaining quite close—and broke into song:

10. San Xuan creó les cerezes.	Saint John created cherries.
San Bartolomé la escanda.	Saint Bartholmy the spelt wheat.
¡Viva San Bartolomé!	Long live Saint Bartholmy!
Que les cerezes son piedra y agua.	Cherries are stone and water.

The reaction to this song was impressive. It brought tears to the eyes of the other older, retired miner in our company. "*Cuanto me emocionó,*" he said later. And it brought a smile to the face of the young man who had been in argument with the singer. At the end of the song, the young man intoned, "Whey ohh!" and encouraged the bar owner to repeat his deepsong.

Beyond the music and the quality of voice were the associations brought to mind by the lyrics, moving in themselves. In the first place, the patron saint of the village in which the *espicha* was taking place was San Bartolomy—also patron saint of spelt wheat *(escanda)!* A small chapel dedicated to him was directly across from the bar where the tapping was taking place. A reference to and a *viva* for the local patron saint were bound to provoke emotion and promote feelings of solidarity. But beyond that, the reference to cherries and spelt wheat was very apt in this context. The discussion had been mainly concerned with the injection of the water into the coal seams as protection against silicosis. And the reference to water in the mines and water in the cherry may have, more than with the patron saint, associated the song with the situation in the singer's mind. The aptness lies in the singer's association of the young miners with the cherry; although fat and "sweetened" by high wages, they were still just water and stone (the old miner had suggested that there was no more good coal left in the mines).

At the same time, the singer was linking himself to spelt wheat: the ancient cereal crop *(Triticum spelta)* cultivated until very recently in the poorer soil regions of the Cantabrian and particularly in the mountains. Spelt wheat is smaller and tougher-bodied than bread wheat *(Triticum vulgare)*. It possesses a double hull, which is difficult to thresh free from the grain and which protects it much better from cold and the year-round rains, mists, and sleets of the Cantabrian Mountains, where common wheat would hardly grow. Spelt wheat has a very tough and spiny body, exactly the characteristics the singer had been lauding in the miners of old and which were evident in himself. Quite beside his own linkage to spelt wheat, a reference to it in the song was bound to be evocative, for as flour has become more readily available, more and more attention has been paid to the planting of potatoes and corn. The growing of spelt wheat has been largely abandoned, though, as with seasonal pastoralism, not without nostalgia. For example, to everyone's regret, common wheat flour has replaced *escanda* in the making of the bread offerings *(Ramu)* baked for patronal festivals and auctioned after the Mass. The dark flour of *escanda* is felt by many to be the only proper ingredient for the bread on this occasion.

I would suggest a further level of meaning very likely touched by this song: the distinction between the mountain people of Asturias and the maritime peoples of the same province, that is, between *maraniegos* [the maritime people] and *maraguellos* [the mountain and upper valley people]. Although cherry trees appear occasionally in the mountains, the fruit zone is the Asturian littoral, and cherries are primarily associated with seaside valleys.

The mountain people have always felt they were different from the people who lived near the sea. This feeling is complex and is, in part, due to admiration for the greater fertility and productivity of the lands by the seaside, the greater size of the seaside cattle, and the greater worldliness of the maritime people. But there is also a feeling of a greater toughness in the mountaineers, who are the products of a much harsher climate. The difference is aptly represented in spelt wheat and the cherry. In the social interaction preceding the song, no reference was made to the mountain/ maritime distinction, but enough such references are made in the bars and in village life to justify the view that the "spelt wheat/cherry" contrast brought to mind differences between the mountains and the maritime, and worked on the young miners' sense of solidarity with their heritage in the following way:

> I [the singer] am of San Bartolomy and spelt wheat
> [Which is tough, durable and of us mountaineers]
> As you [young miners] are of San Xuan and cherries
> [Which are soft, ephemeral and of the other
> Asturians].

The celebration of place—in this case, the mountains—still is important in this song, but it is under-and overlaid with these more subtle sentiments of association.

The old miner went on to sing one more song that, though less emotive for his listeners, was instructive as well. He sang:

11. Tengo que comprarte un areu   I must buy you a plow
    Que revuelve bien la tierra;   That turns well the earth;
    Que tu pa' mayar terrones,   For to break the earth,
    Tienes muy mala ma'era.   You have very bad wood.

This song is generally understood as a courtship song and was so described by participants. In it, the man figuratively offers his services as plowman to the woman because she has very bad wood for turning and breaking up the earth. Men and women participate together in the plowing, but it is the men's job to sink and force the plow, and the women's job to pull and guide the cow team. Women, physically speaking, do not have the "wood," or the physique, to handle the plow, which, in any case, is a male-associated instrument (no doubt sexual associations are present in this song as well). In this noncourtship context, the song was aptly chosen by the singer. It is apt, first, because the exchange of deepsong among men in these small-group situations has something of the air of courtship about it: high affective evaluation of one another and a desire to win the other over to one's viewpoint.

Second, the song was apt because the old miner had been attacking the young miners for having lost the real skill of mining with pick and shovel. Everything has been appropriated, he said, by machinery and the mere leading about of machines. The young men did not really know how to bust up the earth, and so their constitutions, their "wood," were the worse for it. The equation is as follows:

Mining with machinery is to old-hand mining
As the women's dragging about of cows is to the
Hard work of forcing the plow to break up the earth.

Here again we see the singer play upon nostalgia for a former way of life to which all the miners to whom he sang were still in some way committed, if only to such tasks as mowing, in the summer. And we see in this song how a traditional agricultural subject, on the face of it inappropriate to a friendly argument between mining men, can still subtly serve as apt commentary upon that argument.

One could provide countless examples from contemporary bar life in which deepsong is used to communicate more deeply than public language. In many of these "spontaneous" songs, there is a subtle aptness as traditional topics are reworked for modern application—agriculture to mining—and as topics more appropriate to one domain, such as courtship, are applied to another, such as jocular rivalry between male working companions. This adaptability of deepsong is certainly another explanation for its vigorous survival in the modern Asturian world.

The extension of experience from one domain into another for purposes of more concrete comprehension is present throughout the more traditional deepsong. Such metaphorical and metonymic linkages to the subjects of these songs should hardly surprise us, for such topic extensions are fundamental to folklore. What may be more surprising is the ease with which the lore of the agricultural life can be aptly employed for communication between miners. In part, this power to speak about the affairs of miners in agricultural terms arises because practically all Asturian miners are *mixtos,* which means they preserve, by choice or necessity, some tie with the agricultural life through possession of cattle and responsibilities to haying. Metaphoric references to the agricultural life are not dead metaphors to them.

The principal metaphoric and metonymic linkages made to the pronominal subjects of Asturian deepsong (the *I* of the singer, the *he* or *she* of the courtship songs, the *they* of other towns, other parts of the province, or other provinces, and the *we* of the same town, valley, region, or province) are a study in themselves. It has already been shown that some of these linkages are locality-related. Others have just emerged:

We [mountain Asturians] are spelt wheat;
They [maritime Asturians] are cherries;
We [men, or old miners] are tough wood of the plow breaking the earth;
They [women or new miners] are the soft hand tugging at cows.

Asturians themselves are well attuned to the metaphoric mode (Armayor 1962). A reading of the 500 songs collected by E. M. Torner (1920) shows young courting men *(mozos, galanes)* being represented or representing themselves metaphorically as mules, fishes fished from the river or the sea, lost sheep, the sun, a bull bellowing to enter a meadow, mail carriers wandering around the town with intimate letters for every girl, trees, the wood of various trees (oak, ash, or, at a later date, softer woods), and metonymically, as handkerchiefs (part of the courtship attire). Women in courtship *(mozas* and *mozaquinas)*are represented as flowers, doves invited to perch in trees or locked in the cages of their fathers' homes, the moon, a magical snake *(cuelebre)* singing its enchantments, the mountain stone hut into which the pastor desires to drive his cattle, a meadow lush with grass into which the bellowing bull or the herd of cattle desires to enter, a Moorish castle difficult to besiege, a white flag announcing a war in which a young man would feign to enlist, a thorny rosebush, a willow wand, a gardenia bush, and, metonymically, a white underskirt. Married women are represented as old leather bags, unpredictable jumping goats, bundled corn stalks, muddy roads. Married men hardly ever appear in Torner's collection, except indirectly as fathers opposed in some way to a prospective marriage. They appear generally in pronominal reference unqualified by metaphoric or metonymic predications.

Not only personal pronouns but also impersonal ones—particularly the *it*[7] of courtship and lovemaking—obtain metaphoric elaboration. One of the prevelant metaphoric modes for this activity is sating one's thirst or bathing with water. The invitation to come drink from a crystal mountain spring represents an invitation to make love. Lovers' trysts are made at favorite springs. A lover invites his loved one, figuratively, to go swimming with him though neither can swim a stroke. A member of one sex gazing down at water flowing under a bridge is reminded of his or her loved one or of their love together. It is not surprising that this association, when taken together with the association of threshing, mowing, haying (the separation of the seed or the fruit from the plant) with love making, should make the miller and the miller's life highly suggestive. He or she grinds seed by the power of falling water. The milling gear is itself suggestive. The miller, his wife, or his daughter appear in these songs as evocative representations of the *it* to which the singer by indirection is concentrating his attention.

The Emergence of Miners' Songs

If millers, their situation, and their trade seem so evocative of the sensual life in the Asturian mountains (and not only there, as Chaucer's "Miller's Tale" teaches us), then surely miners in their trade and situation, delving in the bowels of the earth, would be evocative as well. In fact, in a well-known, late nineteenth-century Spanish novel of life in these mountains, *La aldea perdida* (1903), written by the Asturian Palacio Valdés, the dark and debauched life of the miner is set against the ruddy pastoral virtues of the countryfolk. The villain in this book is a dark-featured, violent-tempered miner who attempts to waylay sexually the heroine in an abandoned mine shaft. The association between mining and sexuality has long been present in Asturias, but miners hardly appear in Torner's collection. Only two songs out of the 500 make any reference to miners, and these, only indirectly. In example 12, collected by Torner (1920:45), the miner, referred to diminutively as *un pobre carbonerillo*, is the victim of his sweetheart's whims. As in so many songs written of the miners, his most attractive quality is found in the money he earns:

12. Una nina bordadora	A seamstress girl
Cuando sale de bordar	When she leaves her seams
Mande razon a su amante, el minero	Directs her lover, the miner
Que la venga a pasear	That he should come and walk
Y que la lleve al cafe.	And take her for coffee.
Y el pobre carbonerillo, el minero	And the poor little coalman, the miner
Triste, afligido, se ve.	Appears sad and afflicted
No lo puede remediar;	And cannot respond;
Una peseta que gana el minero	The peseta that the miner earns
No tiene para gastar.	He does not have to spend.

Regarding the only other song referring to miners in Torner's collection (1920:76), example 13, the compiler has to explain in the footnotes that it is a song of mockery. The people of the *concejo* of Aller are sung of by miners from a neighboring *concejo*, Quiros. The association of the miner with sensuality is present. The men from Quiros have been living in Aller close to the mines and now, returning home with their savings, they call out to the Alleranos to take good care of the children they have sired and are leaving behind. Mining is still a temporary thing in the song. Countryfolk come down to the mines, but they soon return to the land:

13. Adios concejo de Aller	Good-bye valley of Aller
Adios nobles Alleranos	Good-bye noble Allerians
Teneis que criar los fijos	You must care for the children
De los mozos Quirosanos.	Of the men of Quiros.

The lack of miners' songs in Torner's collection has a number of explanations. He does not seem to have purposely ignored these songs, although he may have phrased his interest in collection in a way so as to encourage songs of the nostalgic past—exclusively agricultural-pastoral rather than industrial. The lack of such songs is first explained by the fact that the great majority of songs available to Torner, the most popular songs of the period, were either courtship songs—*rondas*—or dance songs in which both men and women were involved. The content of these songs would more naturally refer to the agricultural-pastoral life in which men and women participate together virtually even-handedly, rather than to the mining life, which is exclusive to men. Second, given the *ruralismo* that Austurians ascribe to themselves (Cabezas 1964:138–164), there has been resistance to thinking of mining songs as being in any way typically Asturian. There has been, and this was surely the case in Torner's time, a tendency to think of mining as a way of life that was curious, amusing, sometimes threatening, and surely dangerous. Still, as in example 13 above, it was regarded only as a temporary occupation and not truly an Asturian one. Third, since the more traditional songs of field, meadow, and high pasture could by extension be made relevant to the concerns of miners, who as *mixtos* kept one foot in the agricultural and pastoral life, there was less pressure from them to change the content of deepsong. They could revitalize the old songs by extension. Since a great many Asturian miners, moreover, continued to live in the villages along with agriculturalists mixing with them in the bars, they have hesitated, in my experience, to impose mining songs. Finally, there was a satisfaction for the miners in singing the old songs.

Nevertheless, Asturian song has always valued spontaneity and contemporaneity; the ability to compose rapidly and sing topical verse (*andar cantares*) has always been much admired. Jovellanos gives us an example from the late eighteenth century of a group of youth in *romería* improvising a song of jocular defiance to a local prelate who thought to prohibit their festivities (Jovellanos 1884:591). Experience today in practically any Asturian village would reveal two or three villagers well known for their abilities to *andar a cantares* [walk-forth songs] of a mocking or laudatory character. Even at the time of Torner, there were, no doubt, a great many songs being sung about miners and the mining life—active mining had then been in existence more than fifty years—but probably they had not achieved the status of "traditional deepsong repertoire." They were not regarded as Asturian.

But events occurring since Torner published his collection—the Asturian miners' union movement of the first three decades of the twentieth century, the miners' 1934 revolution in Asturias, and the central role played by the miners in the Spanish Civil War—have permanently linked Asturias with its miners both in the minds of Asturians and in the eyes of all Spaniards. Deepsong directed to miners (and mining as subject matter) is now everywhere recognized as Asturian deepsong and not simply as a curious and ephemeral hybrid. Moreover, while most Asturian miners preserve strong ties with country and cattle, an increasing number of miners—most from outside the province—live in urban housing projects and devote themselves solely to mining. Deepsong is heard in these projects, but it is a deepsong tied less to the agricultural-pastoral tradition. There is still no adequate collection of the folklore of these mining communities.

In the provincial championships of deepsong in the spring of 1971, mining songs had a more realistic representation; still, only five of the forty songs presented in the competition could be so categorized. This was the case even though at least half of the twenty competitors had worked in the mines. Since the Civil War, there have been, no doubt, constraints upon the miners' self-celebration in public performance, particularly at times when illegal walkouts were in progress.

The five songs below, recorded during an actual performance, give a representative range of deepsong devoted to mining. The two shortest songs (with respect to the lyrics) celebrate in a simple way the miner's role. Example 14 is a simple *vivar;* example 15 is a pious hope for the salvation of the miner, a role easily associated with the infernal depths of earth and the devil's work:

14. Viva la xente minera'	Long live the mining people
De Laviana, Carbayin,	From Laviana, Carbayin,
La xente minera!	The mining people!

15. Dios quiere que	God desires that
Al cielo vaya	To heaven should go
El alma de los mineros.	The soul of the miners.

The longest song in the competition, unusually long with respect to lyrics, concentrates its attention, as do so many miners' songs, upon the tragic accidents to which the miner's life is exposed. This song also celebrates a family solidarity between brothers and their mother, which is unusual. Generally, miners' songs celebrate the solidarity of *we*, that is, all the miners, as in songs 14 and 15 above:

16. Dexame pasar que voy.	Let me pass I am going.
Quiero baxar a la mina.	I want to go down in the mine.

Tengo el mio hermano	I have my brother
Encerrado y quiero sacarlu,	Trapped and I wish to free him,
Salvar la vida.	Save his life.
Aquel hermanin, madre.	That little brother, mother,
Que siempre fue un gran minero.	He was always a great miner.
	I will free him alive.
Voy a sacarlu con vida.	If not I will die of pain!
Y si non de pena muero!	

The final two songs celebrated two talents for which the Asturian miner is famous: his skill with dynamite and his skill in organizing demonstrations and strikes. In the first of these songs, sung by a woman, the miner is slightly mocked,[8] for with all his powers of dynamite, he is not able to buy her a coral necklace. This readiness to mock a pretentious male role and particularly that of the miner is a recurrent expression of the matriarchal orientation in deepsong. There is an association in this song between opening the mine with dynamite and opening a way to the girl's heart with a red coral necklace. The same kind of association is present in example 11: opening the earth with a good plow and opening a way to the girl's heart with a present:

17. Si yo fuera picador	If I were a picador
A mi amor le compraría	I would buy my love
Un collar de rojos corales	A necklace of red coral
Como quince cartuchos de dynamita.	Like fifteen sticks of dynamite.
Y no me pudiste comprar collar de rojos corales.	And you couldn't buy for me a necklace of red coral.

In the second song, sung by men, the solidarity of the *we* is suggested by a metonymic reference to a common item of clothing—the countryman's beret. There is something of a boast in this, for it is the custom to wear hard hats in the mine and not berets. It serves also as a reference to their status as countryfolk first, rather than miners—an identity that brings them readily out of the mine in protest, as the song goes on to say:

18. Los mineros del Fondon	The miners of Fondon
Todos gastamos boina.	All of us sport a beret.
Con un letreru	With a placard
Todos salimos de la mina.	We march out of the mine.

There have been at least three moods to the deepsong of miners and mining: (1) the mood of mild mockery of miners by countryfolk and, particularly, by the Asturian matriarchate (examples 12 and 17) or the reverse, a mockery by the miners of the countryfolk (example 13); (2) the vaunting mood of miners lauding their powers and solidarity (examples 14, 15, and 18); and (3) the mood of pathos most often thought of as the essence of the miner's deepsong, in which the tragic nature of the mining way of life is explored in its various aspects (example 16). There has been, over the years, a tendency for the deepsong of the mines to move away from the first mood to the second and, finally, to the third. There is much that is politic about this development. There has also been a tendency toward greater narration than is characteristic of the more traditional deepsong.

Conclusion: Deep Moods and Deep Arguments

This paper has explored some of the moods and associations evoked by Asturian deepsong in an attempt to account for its continuing vitality. Deepsong is first of all a genre that is in accord with the personalism and celebrity orientation of modern western Europe. It is, second, in its celebration of place, evocative of provincial and local sentiments still very much alive in Spain and Asturias despite increasing decentering of the rural villages. It is, third, a kind of folksong that continues to appeal to miners, whereas this is not the case for other kinds of song. It appeals in part because it takes reservoirs of strength and endurance to sing deepsong well, and this requirement conforms to the miners' image of themselves. It appeals also because most of the Asturian miners are *mixtos*, who keep some interest in the land and in cattle and have to work at these concerns some part of the year. The *mixtos* preserve a nostalgic interest in the subject matter of the more traditional deepsong. Even if there is no interest in the song itself, the subject matter can be reinterpreted and figuratively extended to cover quite contemporary situations.

Despite the presence of mining in the central mountain valleys of Asturias for almost a hundred years, the development of deepsong with a strictly mining content—its modernization in this sense—has been slow. This is explained in part by the reasons already given for its persistence, and in part by the "ruralism" of the Asturian and his resistance to thinking of the miner's deepsong as typically Asturian. Recent history, however, has firmly linked the miners to Asturias, and there has been some development of mining deepsong. The tendency in this song has been to move from a mood of mild mockery between miners and countryfolk to a mood of pathos. Such observations as these, however, and indeed all the explanations for the modernization of deepsong, can be treated only as propositions that must be used to confront a fuller compilation of the materials. Present collections of deepsong are not adequate for conclusive explanation.

Underlying our exposition has been a more theoretical interest in what might be called *syllogisms of association*. We have also delved into the connections between extensions in figures of speech and extensions of human experience in time, which is *modernization*. While *Asturianadas* are often simple songs that seek only to establish certain moods about people and places, some of them make an argument that lies beneath the mood they establish. In this sense, they are syllogistic: if one admits their premises, one is led to necessary conclusions. Of course, the logical necessities are those not of identity but of analogy and association by similarity and contiguity. They look like this in a courtship song such as example 6:

> I [male] am to You [female]
> As You [female] are to It [Asturias].
> Therefore I [male] am to It [Asturias].

Or consider example 10:

> We [old miners] are to spelt wheat
> As You [young miners] are to cherries.
> Spelt wheat is to Us [mountain Asturians]
> As cherries are to Them [lowland Asturians].
> Therefore You [young miners] are of Them and not of Us.

Such deep arguments are still persuasive because the metaphors upon which they are based exploit domains of experience that remain vital to the great majority of Asturians. They are a people who, amid extensive mining operations and a large steel industry, continue to retain a strong allegiance to the rural character of their province and their localities. It remains to be seen whether this allegiance will continue to survive the superficial excitements of dance hall culture and mass communications; these purvey a metropolitan popular culture with very little of the flavor or substance of rural locality. The evidence from miners is heartening. Not only do they subtly extend the rural to their contemporary situation, but, insofar as their experience has shifted away from the rural, they have yet stayed with deepsong, inventing new content, and continuing to find in it one of the very best methods for passing beyond a superficial public language and a canned popular culture to real depths of feeling and association.

References

ARMAYOR, OLIVIA
   1962   La metafora y la fauna de caso [Metaphor and fauna in Caso]. *Boletín del Instituto de Estudios Asturianos* 47:5–22.
BERNSTEIN, BASIL A.
   1959   A public language: some sociological implications of a linguistic form. *British Journal of Sociology* 10:311–326.
CABEZAS, JUAN ANTONIO
   1964   "Asturias," in *La España de Cada Provincia* [The Spain of each province]. Madrid: Publicaciones Españolas.
CASTELLANO, LORENZO RODRIQUES
   1970   "El dialect Asturiano" [The Asturian dialect], in *El libro de Asturias*, 210–232. Oviedo: Prensa del Norte.
FERNANDEZ, JAMES W.
   1970   "What it means to be moved; the operation of metaphor in religious behavior." Unpublished manuscript.
GONZALEZ GARCÍA, ISABEL
   1970   "Asturias folklórica y ethnográfica," in *El libro de Asturias*, 170–207. Oviedo: Prensa del Norte.
JOVELLANOS, GASPAR M.
   1884   "Romerías de Asturias" [Asturian romerías] in *Cartas a varias personas*. Reprinted 1925 in *Costumbristas españoles*, volume 1. Madrid.
TORNER, E. M.
   1920   *Cancionero musical de la lírica popular asturiana* [The songbook of Asturian lyrics]. Madrid: Akal.
VALDÉS, PALACIO
   1903   *La aldea perdida* [The lost village]. Madrid: Espasa Calpe.

Notes

The deepsong discussed in this paper was heard either by my wife or me in the municipality of Aller. However, it is surely not exclusive to this locale. Songs recorded at the provincial championships of 1971 are also discussed, as are those in the collection of E. M. Torner (1920). We are indebted to the National Science Foundation for their support of the research on comparative culture change in the Asturian mountains. I have also benefited from the comments made on this paper by Richard Detwiler, Sidney Kasfir, and Juan Noriega.

1. Forty-nine of the songs in the Torner collection were specifically labeled *de ronda* by his informants. One hundred and eighty-four songs in the collection

were not labeled, but of this number ninety-two would also seem to be of this usage.

2. To call these Asturian melismatic airs *deepsong* brings to mind the Andalusian deepsong *cante hondo*, which, in my view and in the view of others who have heard the Asturian song, is similar. A first response of many listeners to the *Asturianada*—as to *cante hondo*—is that it sounds very Arabic. No doubt this comparison rises to mind because of the arhythmic quality and the melismatic quavering in the voice. I know of no extant study of deepsong in Asturias—one of the few parts of Spain that effectively resisted Moorish domination. This Arabic quality may arise from the Mozarabic influx into the kingdom of Asturias in the first several centuries after the Moorish conquest of the rest of Spain. In any case, I employ the term *deepsong* not for musical reasons but because, in the *Asturianada* as in *cante hondo*, the singer seems to be reaching within himself to give voice to very deep sentiments.

3. The question of nomenclature for the *Asturianada* is a difficult one. At the present time and in the biannual championships, it is known as *Canción Asturiana*. But I agree with Gonzalez Garcia that the term *canción* should be applied to nonmelismatic song in which rhythm is important. The *Asturianada* should fall under the category of *cantar*. As she points out: "el cantar sería de indole más subjetiva, propia para la entonación a solo, mientras que la canción sería menos susceptible de posibles variantes y podría ser cantado por un coro . . . al cantar corresponde en Asturias la melodía arritmica . . . la canción propiamente dicha, esta compuesta por las melodias acompasadas" ("Asturias folklórica y etnográfica," in *El libro de Asturias* (1970:180). Striking a distinction between *cantar* and *canción* is much more difficult in respect to our interest here: the content of the lyrics. They may both treat the same subject matter with rather more light-hearted lyrics characteristic of *canción* and somber declaration of *cantar*.

4. We are dealing with a folk tradition in which there is both stability and change in the elements. There are, for example, a series of well-known songs celebrating places—"*Soy de Langreo*" or "*Soy de Pravia*," both collected by Torner (1920:41, 185)—but the elaboration of their lyrics may change according to the singer. In the case of the Bimenes song, we have virtually a new composition, in the view of the singer. But countless other very similar place-celebrating songs have been heard in Asturias. Also to be noted in these songs are elements of the Asturian dialect, Bable, and, in particular, that of Bable central (Castellano 1964:210–232).

5. Part of the humor in this song develops from the allegiance declared to four different *Polas*—the Asturian form of *Puebla*. These municipal entities created in the Middle Ages (the twelfth or thirteenth century) by Royal Letters of Privilege are readily recognizable as Asturian town names, but are quite exceptional names in the total provincial nomenclature.

6. Silicosis, or black lung, is a grave problem in the Asturian mines, for the coal is very dirty and the conditions of extraction very difficult. Until recently, the expected working life before onset of silicosis for *picadors* and *barrenists* was between twelve and eighteen years. The reduced lung capacity brought on by this condition greatly hampers the ability to sing deepsong and is one of the consequences of black lung most regretted by miners.

7. Readers who feel that this pronoun does not have the referent implied may wish to recall Clara Bow, the "It girl." She had "it"—sex appeal—to employ the barbarous abstraction. But the Asturian mountaineers have more resource of

metaphoric and metonymic image than to content themselves with such a barbarism—one that leaves the pronoun in this manner exposed.

8. In other versions of this song quite a different mood is established shifting this "matriarchal mockery of the male" to the tragic view of the miner and his life. Killed by dynamite, the miner is unable to bring a present, reminiscent of that very dynamite, to his loved one.

5

LEXICAL FIELDS
AND SOME MOVEMENTS ABOUT,
WITHIN, AND BETWEEN THEM

> La llingua, al mio mo ver, ye un muñon, qu'est-
> rema una cultura d'otra. Pero una cultura ye la
> xuntura de munchos muñones ademas del llin-
> güisticu. Por eso camientome que pa recuperar
> la nuestra cultura tien que recuperar too aque-
> llo que pertenaz a la historia del pueblu as-
> turianu."
> X.LL. García Arias,
>
> Llingua y Sociedá Asturianu
>
> (Language, in my way of seeing, is a field
> marker that separates one culture from another
> although a culture is a conjunction of many
> such field markers besides linguistic ones. For
> this reason it seems to me that in order to
> revive our culture we have to revive all that
> which belongs to the history of the Asturian
> people.)

The above epigraph, in the Asturian language, is taken from the writings
of one of the chief proponents of the restoration of that language. We see
him make use—amidst a more or less abstract argument—of a characteristic rural metaphor: the stone fieldmarker. Anyone who has lived rural
life in the *minifundia* landscape of Asturias with its myriad scattered
family fields and meadows, with its recurrent family anxieties about the
just and equitable inheritance of these fields, and with its folklore and
recurrent village rumors about the surreptitious shifting, "inching" (*cor-
riendo mojones*), of these markers in the dead of night in slow aggrandize-
ment of someone else's land will recognize how evocative the metaphor is.
It aptly evokes such possessive and proprietorial feelings as are useful to

García Arias in his attempt at convincing his Asturian fellow countrymen to protect and revive their patrimony—principally the Asturian language. No doubt men's experience of material possessions, here spatial possessions par excellence, have very much to do with their experience of intellectual possessions, here language par excellence, which do not really occupy space but seem to be, very often, best understood as if they did. We will be mainly concerned in this chapter with trying to understand the evocativeness of this provincial language, with what "space" it occupies in provincial experience, and in what way use of this language moves its speakers. What is it to possess a language and to lose that possession, and how does this possession relate to more concrete patrimonies such as the possession of land?

It ought to be made clear to begin with that Asturian language does not enjoy the same status as the other peninsular regional languages of romance origin which are much better known and much better established: Portuguese, Galician, and Catalan.[1] Nevertheless, and although Asturian—which in any case is no longer spoken in its purest form—is presently considered as a dialect at best, or more generally as a simple lexical diversion, it is or was as much a language as these others considering its common origin in Latin and the evolution and diversification from that Latin base that all romance languages of the peninsula have experienced. At the present time, perhaps, given the general state of abandon in which Asturian is found, it would be possible to demonstrate clear differences (and deficiencies) between Asturian and Gallego, for example, which would justify labeling the first a dialect and the second a language. But taking our measure from those few zones in which Asturian is still currently spoken or reading Asturian written in its proper form—that is to say pure Asturian, not Bable (Castilian spiced with dashes of Asturian), which is the present form of the language—it would be difficult to make invidious comparisons. If Catalan is accepted as a language, so also must be Asturian.

It is, of course, a very interesting question why Asturians have largely abandoned the Asturian language, particularly when we compare its fate with that of Catalan. This is not our problem here and we will take the Asturian language as we found it—as a dialect of Castilian salted with Asturian. But it would be useful as a background of our discussion to offer several suggestions which point us toward an explanation for this decadence. In very general terms, the decadence has to be explained by reference to such conditions as rural poverty, relatively early industrialization, the out-migration of Asturians in the reconquest and in the opening up of the New World and the in-migration of southerners, the Castilian culture esteemed and desired by the middle classes, a relatively sparse vernacular literature, a relatively positive attitude toward Spanish identity, and a pronounced sense of the role of Asturias in the history of modern Spain. But let us pick up our theme.

The Corporeality of Words

Our discussion will be most solidly based and revealing if we note some of those daily situations in which Asturians, who are normally Castilian speaking, make use of Asturian words or expressions. This usage is characteristic of the great majority of the inhabitants of the province. The usage reveals the aptness, grasp, vivacity that still exists in this vestigial tongue. For example, we have before us a mild dispute in a restaurant as regards the real identity of the meat offered on the menu. It is featured as roast veal but it proves to be, in the eating, from an animal of more advanced age and rather tougher to the teeth than is to be expected. Very likely it is meat from a milk cow of advanced age and of declining milk production. The waiter is circumspect in face of the objection and insists that the menu description is accurate. But the client easily causes him to laugh and leads him to a situation of more open exchange of opinion by asking him in Asturian, "Matastelu tu?"[2] ("Were you the one who killed it?") The humor here and the aptness of the expression arises from its pointing up of the urban situation, far from rural life or the slaughterhouse, where the waiter would have been able to have first-hand knowledge of the quality of his meat. The Asturian expression, which itself evokes the rural life, created a solidarity between the client and waiter for both are of rural origin.

Asturian words and phrases frequently appear in situations which can be labeled as "primary" or "corporeal" . . . that is to say, in situations where it is a matter of processes and movements of the body itself as, for example, the various kinds of alimentation. In such situations the Asturian lexicon is particularly rich and expressive. For example, the Asturian word *fartucar* which is widely employed expresses better than the corresponding word in Castilian, *hartar* (to be full, replete to excess) that state of satisfying satiety and corporeal fullness—to the point of bursting in some cases—which is desired in an Asturian banquet. The stranger cannot be long in the Asturian countryside without being offered this or associated words (*fartura*—a completeness) for his own use making him conscious of their expressivity as regards truly ample and fortifying meals. The question, after a prolonged meal with abundantly heaped plates, is simple, brief, direct and forceful: "Fartucaste?" The appropriate response ought to be, itself, direct and forceful, "home!" (man). It will be accompanied by gestures of repletion indicative of *la buena fartura* (a good satiety). Castilian, or at least the Castilian spoken in Asturias, does not offer this exchange of nutritive impressions—profoundly corporeal and satisfying.

We leave to the side and for another day the importance in the province of strong eating and strengthening foods. There is a provincial feeling that beyond its frontiers one does not eat well. It is possible that there is good food elsewhere but it will not be substantial or strong enough. It is not surprising that the typical dish of Asturias, *la fabada* (a variety of cassoulet with chorizo sausage, blood sausage, salt ham and pork and white beans), is the strongest and most filling of all Spanish regional dishes. It is also a meal which is complete in itself. It is also a meal perfectly adapted to Asturian rural life—a daily life of ascending and descending steep mountains in the preoccupations of the cattle keeper.

The Sociability of Words

As in many parts of Spain there is local pressure to install Asturian in the primary schools. At the present time (1978) the campaign, *Bable en les Escueles*, is especially intense. Schoolteachers, functionaries of the state after all, find themselves in the cross fire between the Castilian in which they teach and the speech of their province. Naturally they vary in their attitudes toward and their loyalty to Castilian as well as in their feelings for the vernacular. The situation is almost always ambiguous. The same person can maintain contradictory attitudes. Take, for example, an esteemed teacher, Maestro Nacional, a friend, who has publicly and again and again been decidedly against the local dialect: "What culture do its speakers have?" Nevertheless, when it is asked of him that he read an "old peoples' story" published in a regional paper,[3] he begins to laugh in spite of himself and in spite of his criticism of the spelling errors in the text. The story concerns a country couple, old but affectionate, just come into the city and showing off their sober holiday dress. Observing the young couples in the streets, they remember their own courtship. But the dress

of these young couples amazes them. The two paragraphs which caused
the most laughter were the following:

"Son los tiempos, Pachu, que tou lo cambién, pero a tous estos dudosus
rapaces, pa conocelus bastu mirayus la delantera i prontu se sabe de que sesu
son. Comprendísteme?
    Sí, Xuaca, compreníte bien peru le dicite que non y siempre de razón lo
que me dies, placertar; pos hay muyeres que tienen does espaldes. Si todas
fosen come tu que yera rispetable la to delantrera, que mialma munchu
apetecía masuñar non habia d'haber confusiones."⁴

It's the times we are living through, Pachu. Everything is changing. But for
all the doubtful identity of these youngsters we can still know the difference
if we study the front of them. That will quickly reveal their sex. Do you
understand me?
    Yes, Juana, I understand that very well but I have to tell you that your
advice is not always helpful because there are women who have two backs.
Ah, if they were all like you, so "respectable" from the front view—a
respectability that always gave me a great pleasure to massage [masuñar]—
there would not be any confusion.

The pleasures in this text are various. The enduring themes of the rustic
in the city and the misunderstanding in the relation between the generations is here present. But above all the text possesses a certain familiarity
or intimacy, a sensuality that amuses for being found in such a public place
as a newspaper and between such "respectable" persons—there is a play
on that word—as an old couple dressed in black.

This sensuality was, for the teacher, perfectly expressed in the word
masuñar (massage). The word carries a combination of meanings—rubbing, stroking the dressed body, palpating sensually. It is a word whose
evocative intimacy does not exist in Castilian. The teacher in trying to
explain the word was forced to demonstrate its sense with gestures over
his own body as if no other words, in Castilian at least, were adequate to
the sensations aroused.

The teacher continued reading the text, enjoying other delicacies and
confidences therein contained. But, upon finishing, he threw the clipping
aside exclaiming, "Bah, nothing at all," thus summarizing in a deprecatory
gesture a "professional" attitude and an attitude very typical of public
reaction to the vernacular in the province. But the denial could not
change the pleasures and profounder sentiments provoked by the reading
of the piece.

The content of this story evokes the corporeal element in existence referring us to human relations lived at their most intimate levels. Indeed, Asturian words and phrases appear with particular aptness in social situations that tend toward the intimate: relations within the extended family, for example, or with neighbors of the same parish. It is a matter of social relations in which the corporeal is inescapably present. Let us take, for example, those social relations in which the stranger finds himself involved when he is offered the hospitality of a house or a locality. The consequences of this hospitality are put into question—it is thematic in Spanish culture. Was it sufficient so the stranger found himself at ease? Did he have the impression of being in his own house?[5] But to Asturian ears the phrase "be at ease" *(encontrarse a gusto)* has a certain formality that does not evoke corporeal realities in finding oneself newly related to strangers. The Asturian verb *atoparse* (to strike up against) does have this sense. Even more satisfactory in expressing these sentiments of being at home in foreign circumstances is the adverb *atopaizo,* a word that suggests the atmosphere of rubbing and bumping together which is involved in "being at home."[6]

In these two words, *fartucar* and *atopar,* we note a positive corporeal quality when we compare them with their Castilian equivalents. *Harto* and *hartar* (for an Asturian) are words that sound deprecatory—they imply the vice of gluttony, a fullness that much surpasses an appropriate pleasure and proper enjoyment. The Asturian words carry, rather, the sense of a state of repletion in which the appetite is fully satisfied. It is a state which serves to testify to the abundance of the house and which justifies the word "splendid" *(arrogante)* as to the meal. The Asturian word permits, therefore, a plenitude that is more positive and less ambiguous. The same positive emphasis is present in *atopar.* Where the Castilian equivalent suggests an uncomfortable shock, the Asturian carries the sense of a direct but agreeable encounter. *Atopaizo* is that state implying a primary contact of the body with all its senses alive—and a contact with familiars. The word contrasts with the Castilian where there is more formality and distance.

Asturians make abundant use of the vernacular lexicon when they approach the nexus of social relations. There are a whole series of locutions in Asturian which serve much better than Castilian locutions— *Buenos días, ¿Como está? ¿que tal?*—in relating people in brief encounters and ephemeral contacts when there is no need to exchange significant points of view but where there does exist the need to manifest, once again, affective co-existence. In this realm Asturians mock that which appears to them to be something rather too false and forced in Castilian forms of address. More traditional Asturians resist the *Buenos días* or the *Buenos tardes* of the Castilian, feeling that these are very superficial formulae hardly acknowledging the existence of another. These Castilian formulae seem to be affable but most often they are formulae useful to maintain distances and avoid involvements. The Asturian dialect thus prefers formulae more specifically formulated which, while they do not impede the daily round, do show a localized and specific interest in the activity and intentionality of one's neighbor. "You got up early, huh! So you are in the Xerron! You're going up to the cows? Is the boy better? Good to hear!" One Asturian, presently a lawyer and secretary of a municipality outside of Asturias—and as a bureaucrat obliged to many polite formulae—remembers that during his years in university he had great difficulty saying *Buenos días* or other superficial Castilian greetings in making his entrances into classrooms. These seemed to him false and hypocritical expressions not well or sincerely related to the people present.

This same man when he thinks of the Asturian spoken during his childhood often remembers an experience that moved him greatly and that symbolizes Asturian to him. As it happened his grandmother became senile in her old age, to the point of confusing members of her own family. One day coming over to her bed, the lawyer, then a child, found himself embraced and caressed by the old woman who, however, employed the name of his father—her son—rather than his own. A little after, the father himself entered and, noting the situation, reminded his mother tenderly that she was talking to her grandson. The grandmother began to laugh to cover her confusion, saying in Asturian, "Ay, que xera me xeva!" (Ay, what a task it is to distinguish!). The anecdote is simple but it has profound import and that import is represented—symbolized—for the lawyer in the Asturian phrase.

Our emphasis here upon the expressivity of Asturian words in social relations has caused us to emphasize positive sentiments. We have considered narratives in which Asturian or Bable has acted to make primary relations more affectionate. But, of course, the Asturian vernacular is most reputed to possess strong words of great usefulness in quarrels and acrimonious disputes. This aptitude is celebrated, for example, in Asturian comics such as "The Adventures of Xuanón"[7] appearing in regional periodicals and drawn by the Asturianist Adolfo Iglesias. Almost always the plot of this comic concerns a misunderstanding or dispute caused by

Xuanón in which Asturian insults are very useful. Surely Asturian has an aptitude in both directions, positive and negative. But it would seem to be more important to neutralize the widespread impression that Asturian is mainly a lexicon of insults. The lexicon contains so much that is affectionate and supportive.

Let us conclude with an event concerning a village simpleton, victim of meningitis in his childhood. He has come down by bus to the municipal seat and is awaiting the bus to return. The people at the bus stop joke a bit with him: "Pepin, what are you doing here, eh? Paying your taxes?" But very quickly two women of the zone who had been speaking Castilian to each other turn to the simpleton and begin to speak to him in a Bable much more Asturian. "Fiu mio," they say and with tenderness straighten his tie and the lapel of his jacket and, above all, caress him with the vernacular language.

The Territoriality of Words

To argue that the Asturian lexicon organizes semantic space in a different way than the Castilian and gives to the speaker other possibilities to know and express the world commits us to a certain metaphor of analysis. It is a metaphor although we can demonstrate semantic space quite graphically. For example, one can show that the summer months in Asturian are not distinguished as in Castilian and that we have one long month of work in the fields, *xunu,* marked with a diminutive to indicate its concluding phase *(xunetu).* One can show that the clear distinction between bull and ox in Castilian—a distinction so central in bull-fighting—does not exist in Asturian or, at the least, if it exists considers the ox as the focal animal and places emphasis on the capacity for hauling and not upon reproductive capacity or defiance. Nevertheless, the notion of semantic space is still metaphoric—it organizes our experiences, which may be quite other, by a spatial metaphor.

Such intellectual strategies may be inescapable and there may be no stance more secure than the debating of apt metaphors of analysis. Still there is a more grounded way of demonstrating the territoriality of words and laying out a real semantic space. We can take down the Asturian names for their country and its parts and we can note the evocativeness of these names. I was frequently told that if one wishes to become real friends with an Asturian one has to walk the paths and byways of Asturias with him: the mountains if he is a mountaineer, the riversides if he is a fisherman. "To walk is to learn" *(Caminar es aprender)*. To know Asturias, one is told, is to learn the Asturian names associated with the peaks where the chamois hide or the river pools where the trout lie.

Of course, it is not unusual in the world that the names on the land embody ancient associations and recall other lives and other cultures— other long-gone civilizations. Territorial topography persists even when the cultures and tongues which used such names are dying or extinct. In many places these names remain absorbed and lost in the general lexicon—scarcely suggestive except for arcane or poetic purposes. In Asturias, however, there still exist strong sentiments and resentments about provincial nomenclature. There is the most lively interest in local place names and many provincial scholars have dedicated themselves to the study of these names. This is not surprising in a province where there are so many nostalgic feelings attached to the land.[8]

The resentment arises over the imposition of Castilian or Castilianized place names. For example, there has been a resentment for many years over the fact that the province carries the name of its capitol, Oviedo, and not its proper and ancient name, Asturias. The importance of the territoriality of words was at once recognized by the promoters of a return to Asturia (called *los nuevos Bablistas*) and above all by the Conceyu Bable. Almost from the first in their publications they presented lists of local names changing the Castilian form into its Asturian equivalent. This effort gained almost at once the enthusiastic support of young sympathizers who began to paint over with a spray can all the names written on provincial highway signs: Uvieu for Oviedo, Xixón for Gijon, El Quempu for El Campo. Thus were reclaimed for Asturias places which had been, in a certain measure, "alienated" by the imposition of names showing the language preferences of the Ministry of Public Works.

The alienation, on the one hand, or the familiarity, on the other, that one feels for his land is expressed in the control he possesses of its nomenclature. We can see that in an extended family of miners. The men are of Galician origin, some in their second generation in Asturias. The women are all of Asturian lineage. The men confess that they do not feel themselves well rooted in village life in part because they do not have full control of all the local place names of the land that surrounds them: the peaks, passes, slopes, canyons which carry such names as Pico Lacixa, Gumial, Retinon, La Redondiella, Los Cuayos, Cuirgu, Xomba, Pando,

Caserón. Repeatedly their wives instruct them in all the pertinent names but they confess with resignation: "Ay, we work in a different mine!"

Even more difficult to learn in this country of tiny scattered fields are the multitude of names of meadows, gardens, and plots. These, more than the peaks, passes or hills, are the scenario of daily life—its heart. If one does not control these names—El Ateyu, Mayalín, Ruetxá, La Texera, Peorneu, Coxa Mayor, El Xerián, Sola Mota, La Xanutra—it will be difficult to participate in that topic which with the greatest frequency enters into everyday conversation—the state of the land and its parts. It is the most enduring preoccupation of the life of the village—attention is constantly directed toward landed property and its divisions and re-grouping generation by generation. To be excluded from this lexicon is to be excluded from that which is most fundamentally past, present, and future. It is to be excluded from the most concrete representation of time. In this vein one can understand how the imposition of Castilian names creates for the Asturian an alienation from some fundamental aspects of his experience. To lack knowledge of the field names is to be deprived of important mental movements which regularly take place in local life: that movement which is the going and coming in the landscape of the imagination from, for example, the hillcrest Coxaroces to the riverside meadow El Furiosu, the latter a little too humid and shady and the former sunny and exposed to the wind. In the lexicon of fields there repose not only economic matters but imaginative ones as well.

The capacity to move oneself or be moved which is given by knowledge of the local lexicon can be seen in an encounter in the high peaks. The Asturian mountains, in particular the spectacular Peaks of Europe, quite naturally carry Asturian names: Jultayu, Canal de Trea, Porru Llagu, Gueyos del Jungumiá, Requexon, Jou Santu, Llampa Cimera. Knowledge of these names is a necessary attribute of the Asturian mountaineer. It gives evidence of his capacity to move in the mountains. For example, we are present in the Collá de los Horcados Rojos looking down upon Uriellu and the Jou de los Boches. Two Asturian mountaineers are offering coun-sel to two from Madrid. Though experienced mountaineers the Madrileños, nevertheless, are strangers to the zone and do not know the local names. A snow flurry is blowing. It is a very uncertain situation for the Madrid pair and they are offered abundant and redundant counsel. Strange names swirl around them. Their maps are precise in the contours of the place but exiguous in local nomenclature. The Asturian knowledge of their locality, by word of mouth only, becomes undeniable and the two visiting mountaineers decide to abandon their plan of traverse and agree to follow the Asturians to the refuge. Actually the weather is not that bad. But during the long and prolix advice-giving, it gradually becomes clear to the Madrileños—and each new Asturian name makes it clearer—that they are alien to the situation. More than anything it is the lexicon that convinces them.

One can argue that in this event all that is being demonstrated is familiarity. But there, precisely, is the point. The demonstration of familiarity and the anxious awareness of alienation are based upon the lexicon—and in the control or lack of control of it. In a certain sense we have there that which is fundamental in linguistic revitalization in Asturias. That revitalization seeks to define or redefine a territory in which the Asturian can move himself with familiarity—a territory to some degree alienated under the influence of a foreign tongue. One is made anxious in not controlling the names of a territory. That is seen in the reactions of the Asturian mountaineers. It is seen in villagers when they go over to another parish or over to other valleys or mountains where they do not know the names. It is seen in the marriages between parishes or municipalities where one of the first responsibilities of the alien spouse is to learn local topography and, in that learning, obtain adaptation to his or her new life.

Contexts of Use and Explanation: Totalities and Partialities

The materials of this chapter have been presented in such a way as to follow the tradition of linguistic analysis proposed by Malinowski. His was an inductive tradition that did not undertake to explain linguistic facts until they had been presented in their context. This "after the fact" kind of explanation gives maximum importance not to the logic of language *per se*[9] but to speech context in the understanding of speech acts. One need not follow the Malinowskian point to the extreme of denying that there is any useful analysis outside of context. But for the anthropologist the context is of inescapable importance in understanding what is being evoked by words . . . in understanding how words are as much modes of action or inaction as they are countersigns of thought.[10]

The idea of context includes, evidently, a wide variety of facts in various spheres and at various levels of experience. In respect to the Asturian language and the Bable dialect, it implies historical, economic, geographic, and political facts all of which enter into Asturian experience and into choices made in regional expression. We have not tried to treat historical contexts here nor economic or political ones either except as these are incidental to the primary contexts—corporeal, social, and above all territorial—which we have treated. But we do see in these primary contexts that Asturian words and Bable phrases carry certain associations—and are apt in certain ways—that cannot be evoked or argued by Castilian. In fact, Castilian may actually—it is the feeling of some Asturian intellectuals—inhibit such associations.

Our focus on these primary contexts of speech also follows Malinowski, who emphasized in various of his works three fundamental contexts in the creation of significance: ongoing bodily activity, the ongoing "narrative situation" by which what is occurring is being formulated, and the "phatic" situation or the establishment of social interaction by speech relationships irrespective of any other considerations of significance. The corporeal and social contexts here considered fit quite easily within the framework of this theory. The territorial context which, because regionalism is such a pronounced issue at the present time, we consider of maximum importance, does not fall within Malinowski's discussion in the specific work referred to here although the importance of territorial matters in human behaviour is amply recognized by him elsewhere. We do not consider the narrative context, leaving that aside for another place and for broader treatment of the "Asturian Monologue"—the archetypal narratives of the province.

There is one further important point in Malinowski's theory. He maintains that his understanding of human language as intimately tied to context and implicated in social relations and actions brings us closest to grasping the primary function of this communicative instrument. For it is in such context that the child learns his language—that is to say, the child learns language as just one more element in a dynamic totality. Learning to use language as an instrument of thought, more or less distant from a particular context, is a later kind of learning linked to scholarly learning and literacy. But a language always preserves some intimations of the "original totality" of its first contexts of use, although very often these "intimations" are transformed or suppressed by scholarly requirements. These transformations away from a "familiar totality" may be even more marked when the school idiom differs from that spoken at home. Such is the situation in rural Asturias and such are the familiar transformations and recapturings of a totality that the use of Bable or Asturian achieves.

Precisely here, in this primordiality—and on this point Malinowski lays emphasis—is where non-written languages offer us a more profound understanding of language in its relation to the context of emotive interaction. Non-written and non-studied (in the objectifying sense) languages better preserve the force of the original totality—better preserve the inclusion of language in lively interaction.[11] As Asturian has been a language with very little written literature, it is possible that it preserves those "intimations of totality" in a more intense and evocative form. For that reason, it would be a particularly powerful vehicle of those nostalgias (añoranza, or morriña in the case of Galician) which are such characteristic sentiments in the provincial life of northern Spain, nostalgias for the pristine and mundane daily world of the maternal hearth—that is to say, of the matrix.[12] These primordial sentiments have been, for a variety of reasons, repeatedly celebrated in regional literature and have come to characterize Galician and Asturian attitudes. Without entering into all the complexities of the meaning of añoranza, it must certainly have something to do with the abrupt change of language or dialect on passing from the hearth to the school. In any event, time and again in Asturian daily life one recognizes that Bable or Asturian, much less formalized and studied, is a much stronger vehicle of añoranza than Castilian which is a language, so to speak, more analytic, abstracting, and desiccating in the experience of Asturians . . . a catabolic rather than an anabolic instrument.

It is Bable or Asturian that has the power for immediate and concrete synthesis of contexts. It can totalize, as it were, without doing this by semantic abstraction in semantic hierarchies. The sense of wholeness in the provincial language is clearly what attracts contemporary provincial poets and what compensates them for the public they lose by expressing themselves in a language no longer widely understood.[13]

Popular Dichotomies and Poetic Vitality

It should hardly be necessary to say that what we remark to be the case of Castilian in Asturias—its partiality, specificity of function, and tendency toward vitiated abstraction—constitutes no judgment on Castilian *per se*. In its own situation, quite naturally, Castilian possesses ample resources of emotional movement within and between corporeal, social, and territorial domains.[14] In the Asturian, as in many provincial situations where Castilian has been imposed as an official language, a polarization has occurred—university intellectuals speak of a "colonization." The official language relegates the local language to the rural and domestic life, causes it to appear backward, and installs itself as the medium of bureaucratic communication and of communication between the educated. While this polarization seems to work to the obvious advantage of the dominant language, it also acts to vitiate that language in respect to its most human qualities. At the same time the local language, however subordinate and marginated, *is* fecundated and enriched in its primary possibilities. These qualities persist even when, as in the case of Bable, the language becomes vestigial—a lexicon and little more. Margination to the country life and the hearth, to the primary routine of rural life, can yet act to maintain certain vitalities. Very likely this polarization acts in any situation where a language installs itself as an instrument of administration, of public power, and of social mobility. But there is also the question of emotional mobility . . . transformations of moods.

It is the transformative possibilities of the local language that is attractive to certain groups of local poets. Thus in a discussion arising after an evening of poetry in Asturian—conducted under University auspices[15] and titled "La Nueva Poesía en Bable"—the five poets present argued with much animation about the resources of the local language that caused them to prefer it to Castilian. They mentioned such qualities as "coloration," "direct reference to nature and natural processes," greater fidelity to the reality of "human experience," "concreteness and expressive vitality," "local definition," "potentiality and plasticity," and "metaphorical flexibility." All these appreciations of Bable or Asturian were taken in opposition to Castilian, a language that, for all its immense resources, the poets argued was "abstract," "formal," "generic," "inflexible to metaphoric invention"—in short, of limited "potentiality" for an Asturian who was most likely to feel in respect to Castilian "the suffocating weight of its immense literature overloaded with over-threshed phrases" (*supercargados de frases trilladas*).

Another similar comment is that of the local schoolteacher who was strongly opposed to the teaching of Asturian or Bable in the schools but on reading a short story in the language nevertheless found himself positively affected. Reflecting over this reaction he admitted that Bable had its advantages. It was, he reasoned, "a language of the senses." To speak Bable was to see, hear, touch, smell—it was "to have all the senses especially alive." Possibly, he said, it might be argued that Bable was "the language of common sense." But in any event Castilian was the language of the brain, of the reasoning process, and of all that which exalted mankind amidst all other living and animal beings.

There is a good deal of discussion in Asturias at the present time about these two languages or dialects. These discussions almost always and relatively rapidly move to a popular dichotomy—a set of two lexical fields—which would remind any anthropologist of the qualitative distinctions often struck in the literature of anthropology between the Great and the Little Traditions, or the urban literate and the rural (oral) traditions. The popular dichotomy would look something like this . . . all the words in these two lexical fields are culled from actual discussions of the two languages:

Asturian (Bable)	*Castilian*
concretion	abstraction
body	brain
ingenuous	courteous
content	form
proximity	distance
solidarity	individuality
country	city
vivacity	monotony
specific	generic
house	office
fluid	stable
flexible	rigid
family	bureaucracy
direct	indirect
talking and recounting	speaking and writing
chaotic	well-defined
spontaneous	orderly and well-planned

As schematic as this arrangement may appear and as simplified—in relation to the complexities of qualitative discrimination in experience—it nevertheless constitutes a set of categories or lexical fields very real and relevant to contemporary Asturian behaviour. For it seems clear that—as ongoing argument and discussion both expresses and motivates—many Asturians feel themselves overly confined by modern life in one field (or pole) and anxious to move to another field as this movement can be accomplished by language revitalization. It is such a transformation that the Bable revival is all about.

At the same time, though our focus here is Asturian, we recognize that this popular dichotomy and its associated dynamic is by no means limited to Asturias. We find a similar sort of dichotomy wherever the rise of literacy in urban milieus has created the distinction between the Great and the Little Traditions. Such popular dichotomies and resultant dynamics seem to arise wherever we find a tradition which is predominantly oral and homely brought into contact with a tradition produced and maintained by the "literati," in Robert Redfield's terms.[16] And even in societies like the North American one not ordinarily associated with the Great Tradition-Little Tradition dynamic, we find it present in certain milieus. Thus Myerhoff in a moving account of a Jewish old-age community shows us the residents negotiating their allegiance to the Great Tradition of Judaism on the one hand—its abstract, austere, eternal verities, its remote, great centers of learning—and their feelings of belonging to the familiar satisfactions of European *shtetl* culture from which they derive on the other. In presenting the local tradition derived from *shtetl* culture, Myerhoff defines it with reference to primary experience and in terms similar to those employed by Malinowski in speaking of speech in its natural milieu before it has been appropriated by intellectuals:

> Local traditions are matters of daily life occurring first and foremost in the familial setting in association with the child's earliest experiences . . . they have a kind of sacrality despite their mundane nature which comes from being . . . learned pre-verbally and intertwined with nurturance and survival occurring in the form of the small physical and sensory events and experiences . . . the profoundly familiar mix of household odors and habits, gestures, sounds, tastes, and sentiments which set down the deepest roots in the individual.[17]

It seems clear that the Asturian dynamic is part of a general dynamic in cultural evolution.

In Search of Regional Personality

Let us remind ourselves of the linguistic situation in Asturias. There is the Asturian or Astur-Leones language—the romance originally spoken in Asturias. Over the centuries the closely related language Castilian has imposed itself and become the official language—the language of the Great Tradition. A variety of vernacular dialects which show various degrees of influence from Castilian have concurrently appeared called Bable—there are really a diversity of Bables. This Bable or these Bables are in major part Castilian showing Asturian influences in lexicon, in syntax (suffixation of pronouns), and in phonological forms and in intonation (endings in "u," circumflex curve in the final inflexion). For many Asturians, instead of speaking of two languages it would be more accurate to speak of a range of expressive possibilities. On the one hand, for those who speak a relatively pure Castilian there are the possibilities of adapting in such appropriate circumstances as we have detailed certain words or stylistic turns of phrase more or less Asturian. And, on the other hand, there are some in the villages who are constant speakers of Bable yet who, on visits to municipal officials, for example, are able to make use of a much more Castilian turn of phrase. In the situation of diglossia where there is a Great Tradition and a Little Tradition language—the classic diglossic situations are those of Greece or the Arab countries where we have a classic language and a vernacular—we get more of a separation of the two languages than is often the case in Asturias where there is a greater range of possibilities between speaking *fino* or *paisano*. There are greater possibilities of speech variation than are captured in the concept of diglossia. Gumperz's term for such a situation of variation, "bilectualism," is perhaps the better concept.[18]

There are several important consequences of this bilectical situation. First, speech variation gives to speakers who can master it certain expressive possibilities that are not found in a monolingual situation. The enjoyment of poetry or short stories in Bable, even by those who do not speak it or who deny its importance, show these possibilities. And while many Asturians enjoy passively the possibilities of this variation, many Asturians have an active virtuosity in shifting between variants. At the same time and despite this expressive potential, the sense of inferiority so often associated with diglossic situations is also present in Asturias. In a situation where a Great Tradition language is imposed on a local situation, local speakers lose confidence and have the feeling of speaking badly—a feeling of language inadequacy that is, in fact, widespread throughout Spain. It is found in almost every province in the peninsula.[19] The opposite side of the coin of virtuoso possibility in language styles is the feeling of not speaking *any* language well. In fact, the varieties of Bable and the differences in lexicon that prevail as one moves from valley to valley constitute proof for many that there is no Bable or Asturian language. The impression of speaking badly or of speaking many Bables leads to an inhibition in communication as much as it suggests virtuoso possibility. Language events become occasions of invidious comparison and deprecation—of pretensions of control or lack of control of language. They become occasions for the putting up and putting down of persons.

The university intellectuals who are now seeking to revitalize Asturian seek to respond to both these consequences of bilectualism. On the one hand, they seek to defend the dignity of the Asturian language and of the speakers of the various Bable dialects influenced by it. They seek to do this by showing that the provincial language can be normalized, standardized in phonology, syntax, and lexicon and thus brought within the reach of all Asturians as a language option. The word "option" is important because with all this effort at standardization there is little interest in replacing Castilian. To the contrary, and although it appears paradoxical, the New Bablistas, as they are called, repeatedly argue that the study of Asturian will lead not only to a better control of that language but to a better understanding and control of Castilian.[20] For, they argue, it is precisely that situation where there are badly misunderstood interferences and intermixtures which leads to the feeling of language inadequacy they seek to combat. Thus, on the other hand, they value and defend the expressive possibilities of several interacting provincial languages—interacting on a basis, however, of equality.

The argument that by better knowing Bable or Asturian one can better know Castilian, paradoxical as it sounds, is much the same as another quite regionalist argument according to which the region with fully developed regional personality will better participate in the Spanish state.[21] The arguments are much the same because—and this is particularly true in Spain whose culture is more literary than technical-scientific—expressivity in language is such an important aspect of personality. In Spain, particularly, where "making use of the palabra" is so important in public and political life it can be readily seen that the negative consequences of "bilectualism" will be sharply felt as a problem for regional personality. Before the increasingly insistent question "What is it to be an Asturian?"

there can be no adequate answer that does not take into account the provincial language situation.

The New Bablistas thus recognize clearly the very close relation that prevails between regionalism and language.[22] They recognize that politico-administrative decentralization in the search for regional autonomy, while necessary, is not sufficient. It is not sufficient because politico-administrative structures are above all structures of communication. Where that communication remains afflicted by incomprehension and linguistic deprecation, decentralization may be illusory.[23] To pretend that equalization of opportunities is only a matter of economics is to ignore that language can be a value and a source of inequality . . . the inequality of being unable to express one's self adequately either in vertical or horizontal structures. The Asturian language revitalizers have in mind a regional personality at once confident in the dignity and potentiality of the local language and in possession of the rather different expressive possibilities of the several languages.

The Movement between Levels . . . between Fields

It is most useful to proceed from a psychology which recognizes that personality is a process of negotiation rather than a formulated entity.[24]In the Asturian context the obtaining of regional personality, then, means the freeing up of powers of negotiation, not simply in that obvious and usual sense of the wresting of such powers in the negotiation of regional economic and political interests vis-á-vis a central government but in the deeper sense of the release from ignorance and inhibition for the fullest use of the differing expressive possibilities of provincial languages and, in particular, for the fullest exploration of different lexical fields. What the Asturian language revitalizers, the New Bablistas, seek is, it seems to me, just this freedom—the freedom to move back and forth between lexical fields, as it were, without inhibition.

Just here the history of language revitalization in other regions of diglossia in the Mediterranean might cause us to misread what is intended in Asturias. In Greece, for example, there has been a bitter battle between proponents of the classical Greek of the Great Tradition, *katharevousa*, imposed in the nineteenth-century revival and the modern vernacular Greek, *demotiki*. Feelings in Greece run very high on this issue and the prevailing sentiment is in favor of replacing the inhibiting

classical Greek with *demotiki* in every relevant domain.[25] But this desire
for replacement and the establishment of a single lexical field is not the
predominant objective in Asturias.

There is surely one very good reason for this: Castilian outside Asturias
and outside Spain has, unlike classical Greek, widespread valency. But we
must argue as well that the preference for the negotiation between lexical
fields is compatible with provincial experience in a *minifundia* landscape
and with a mode of life which emphasizes itinerant cattle keeping and
short-term transhumance in such a landscape of scattered family fields. It
is a life of sampling many fields. The linguistic personality sought by the
New Bablistas is thus compatible with a personality formed in the Asturian landscape and by its mobile mode of life. We might, in fact, speak
metaphorically of the *latifundia* option (imposition of one language) or the
minifundia option (preservation of a plurality of linguistic options) in
language revitalization.

Behind such perspective is the axiomatic supposition that men and
women in confronting problems in secondary realms of being—such as
that of provincial politics—metaphorically extend to these less well understood realms experiences from their primary realms of being.[26] In this
sense the primary experience of Asturians with cattle-keeping itinerancy
in a *minifundia* landscape of scattered family fields is extended to something as difficult to grasp, formulate, and understand as the Asturian
language problem. That extension is the basis of our playing—quite
seriously—on the analogy between lexical fields and real fields of mountain pasturage. The analogy is, we have seen, present in our epigraph: "La
llingua ye un muñon." Surely human experience with the terra firma and
its particular divisions aids in the understanding of something as "infirm"
as language problems. Treating the Asturian language situation with this
analogy in mind, in any event, gives us insight into the particular kind of
"negotiation of fields" and "maintenance of boundaries" Asturian regionalists and revitalizers have in mind. We need all the insight we can get
because Asturian regionalism has long been enigmatic and difficult to
decipher for students of the subject.[27]

It is obvious that regionalist sentiments will be sentiments profoundly
attached to territory—they are in part sentiments that arise in defense of
territory. But what is that territory? Here we have regarded our *minifundia* landscape as, in the deepest sense, those lush and fruitful emotional
fields of the primary experience of the body and the hearth and of village
society. These fields are not, in Asturian experience, well cultivated by

the Castilian lexicon and, in truth, are often alienated by its employment.
There are also inhibitions in employing the Asturian lexicon. The importance of cultivating in an affectively productive way these primary fields of
the imagination is a fundamental animus in Asturian regionalism seen
from the linguistic point of view. It is fundamental, though perhaps a
paradoxical objective, that the boundaries of these emotive fields be
maintained against alienation and at the same time made less inhibiting.
Emotional fields have their reality in human behavior as the earth and its
divisions have their emotional reality. Such realities may be mostly implicit—a hidden agenda amidst the more strenuous and explicit political
and economic debate in regionalist struggles. But that is no reason to deny
their existence nor neglect them when fieldstones are turned up which
reveal them to us.

Conclusion: Regionalism and the Evolution of Levels

Contemporary regionalist activities in Asturias, elsewhere in Spain,
and elsewhere in Western Europe are another phase in the enduring
scenario of human culture: the dialectic or, as we prefer to call it, the
negiotiation between levels of cultural evolution. Cultural evolution, on
the one hand, proceeds at a general level toward more and more specialized and uniformly diversified forms. On the other hand, it proceeds at
the specific level toward forms of cultural life which are purely local and
which are recombinations of diverse possibilities of a quite local
character.[28] Very often the dialectic or negotiation between—seeing it
very simply—the Great and the Little Traditions, which is otherwise, as we
have endeavored to show, the negotiation between two lexical fields in
Asturias, takes on the character of the negotiation between general and
specific evolution.[29] Certainly in Asturias Castilian has come to signify
bureaucratic specialization and diversification and semantic abstractness
while it is Asturian and the Bable dialects which signify the groundedness
of locality. Thus the debate about lexical fields and the desire to free up
the negotiation between them are not just transitory political or economic
battles but another scenario in the enduring negotiation of culture in
evolution.

It is important to recognize how greatly literacy, and the communication it has brought about between past and present and between parts of
the present, has affected cultural evolution. For by freeing up communi-

cation from the transitory face-to-face oral situation, it has contributed to general evolution by facilitating the possibilities of self-distancing in the abstract and the general. And it has facilitated the creation of specialized functions and administrative hierarchies. Literacy in short has facilitated that "alienation" from the sentiments of local and everyday reality. Just here the Asturian language revitalizers face a paradox. For, as they seek by many different efforts[30] to alphabetize, standardize, and institutionalize the Asturian language, they risk vitiating its very particular vitality—its primary local quality. The drive to enforce the teaching of Bable in the grade schools (Bable en les Escueles) risks such generalization and vitiation.

Perhaps for that reason some Bablistas who have devoted many years to the study of Asturian oppose a forced recuperation of the tongue. "Language is spoken, not recuperated," they argue.[31] Such skeptics are confident that the dialects of the Asturian language will continue to maintain their presence in the province without special measures. And they believe that special measures of any kind will have a "falsifying" impact on the "place" of the language—will alienate it, in effect, from those particular lexical fields that it cultivates.

Whether without the present efforts at revival—these are not the first in the province[32]—any form of Asturian could maintain its place, however, is open to question. For Asturian, in the form of the Bable dialects, has receded before Castilian over recent centuries and it may be that only through institutionalization—whatever the paradoxes involved and whatever the possibilities of diglossic conflict it portends—can the language be preserved in an increasingly literate and homogenized age.

While the Asturian intellectuals who are Bablistas face this paradoxical problem of revitalizing Asturian without vitiating it of its primary qualities, for most Asturians there remain the bilectical negotiations of everyday life between the two lexical fields. Of course, the popular dichotomy which we have produced out of local commentary is a simplification of the situation in which Asturian language behavior has developed and is developing. It ignores the variety of intermediate stylistic combinations of Asturian and Castilian—the variety of Bables which Asturians employ. Nevertheless, it reflects the dualistic tendency in local thought as well as certain strategic realities in local social life. The dichotomy does suggest the dimensions of the quality space—that emotional landscape—in which Asturian speakers by choice of dialect and style move themselves and move each other. For the Asturian speaker can negotiate destinies in much the same manner as the folk poets (whose verse we examine here in Chapters 3 and 10) move their own and each other's reputations in the agitated quality space of village life. But while the folk poets work their movement by the argument of local images and by metaphoric and metonymic manipulations, practically every Asturian can work movement in quality space simply by choice of lexicon and by stylistic phrasings.

In the end what is interesting about linguistic regionalism in Asturias is that those University intellectuals who call themselves the New Bablistas, although firmly committed to an intellectual worldview in one sense, yet at the same time espouse and fight for the values of the rural tradition which repose in the provincial language. This effort should not surprise us. There is a long tradition of "university extension work" in Asturias that has tried to carry the university to the countryside and vice versa.[33] Nor should we be surprised by the rural orientation. It has been said of Spain that it is, by history and propensity, one of the most rural states of Europe and one in which, until recently, the urban-oriented mentality, the bourgeoisie mentality par excellence, has had least influence. Whatever may be said about the attraction of the town in other parts of Spain, this rural orientation is certainly true of Asturias. It is seen in the frequent *romerías* and other country festivals which all manifest a strong attraction to a rural return. It is seen in the desire by the great majority of Asturians to retain—even those families long urbanized—some family fields and to return periodically to them in order to *gozar la propriedad*—to enjoy those "estates" which are really estates and that property which is really property.

No doubt in the modern world there is romanticism in whatever ruralism. But in the case of the Bablistas it is a romanticism that is conscious of political realities—on the one side the necessity of conserving and restoring the particular pungency of rural expression and on the other the necessity of freeing up to the fullest the provincial personality conceived of as a personality empowered to negotiate the various fields of expression. There must always be, as there is, paradox, tension, and ambiguity in such efforts to promote fuller negotiation between the Great and the Little Traditions, between the general and the concrete and immediate, between the highly specialized and the diffuse and spontaneous. Regionalism has many aspects. But the debates swirling around the various fieldmarkers of Asturian and Castilian language and culture give us some deeper insight into that landscape and those fields which are in question.

Notes

1. To judge by the new Spanish Constitution written, debated, and promulgated in 1978, there are three categories of Peninsular languages: the official language (Art. 3.1.), the remaining languages of the various autonomous regions (Art. 3.2.), and various dialects or manners or modes of speaking (modalidades) (Art 3.3.). The Bables or Bable of present-day Asturias are listed in the third category, and it is the object of the present language revitalizers, the New Bablistas, to convert the local idiom from the third to the second category.

It is important to note a rather different designation employed in this chapter to refer to the romance of Asturias. We will call it Asturiano after Menendez Pidal's designation, "Astur-Leones." We will refer to the diversity of present dialects of Asturiano—all strongly mixed with Castilian—as Bable or the Bables of Asturias. Presently in Asturias these dialects are referred to as Bable. Present-day students have mostly accepted and put a good face on the term Bable though it was initially, in the eighteenth century, deprecatory and still continues to be.

2. We see here the resistance in Asturian to compound tenses although at the present time the verb system is unstable and under the pressure of Castilian compound forms which have been introduced. We also see here the Asturian tendency to locate atonic forms of the pronoun after the verbal nucleus.

3. "Fiestes de Amor" by Belarmino Prada Gonzales in *La Voz de Asturias*, 21/9/77, p. 16.

4. The Castilian word would be *manosear*, which carries with it more the sense of running the hand brusquely or harshly over something. The Asturian association carries more the sense of massaging.

5. As in well-known welcome to strangers—"Está(s) en su casa."

6. In Castilian, or at least the Castilian of Asturias, *encontradizo* has more the sense of casualness of encounter.

7. In the 1970s this comic appeared from time to time in the regional paper, *La Nueva España*. The author has published other illustrated adventures of Asturian villagers, for example, *Pin y Tielva*, Oviedo 1972.

8. The best and most complete of these Asturian toponymic studies is that of José Manuel Gonzalez, *La Toponomia de Una Paroquia Asturiana*, IDEA, Oviedo, 1959.

9. As an example of such purely logical interests, there is Katz's view that semantic studies are not datable and do not possess temporal properties or bear temporal relations. (Jerrold J. Katz, *Semantic Theory*. [New York: Harper & Row, 1972], p. 38). The anthropologist's interests are, on the contrary, very datable.

10. B. Malinowski, "The Problem of Meaning in Primitive Languages," in C. K. Ogden and I. A. Richards, *The Meaning of Meaning*, 10th ed. (New York: Harcourt Brace, 1966), p. 297.

11. Interlocutors in the villages of Alto Aller, Sobrescobio, and Laviana where this research was undertaken in 1971–72 and in 1977 would, in fact, insist on the impossibility of writing Bable: "We speak badly here, the way we speak cannot be written down." In 1978, on returning to the valley, one of these interlocutors confessed to me his surprise at seeing Bable written on one of the political posters for a by-election. In presenting this rather reluctant claim by villagers that theirs was an unwritten language—one that, in effect, couldn't be analyzed into parts and written—we don't want to ignore that there has been for many centuries a modest literature in Asturian or Bable although not comparable to that in Catalan or Galician. That vernacular literature is less well known in the countryside in any case.

12. The justification for this word lies in the phrase *lengua materna*.

13. The new poets writing in Bable sometimes adopt the strategy of mixing Castilian into their poems in order to obtain greater understanding.

14. Neither should this judgment predjudice the Castilian perfectly controlled by many Asturians. After all, Asturias has contributed considerable talent to Castilian literature. To name just a few: Jovellanos, Clarin, Campoamor, Palacio Valdes, Perez de Ayala.

15. In the Faculty of Arts and Letters at the University of Oviedo, 21 April 1978. Five poets participated: X. LL. García Arias, X. X. Sanchez Vicente, Manuel Azur, Manuel Amaro, and Faustino Alvarez.

16. Put forth in *The Primitive World and Its Transformations*, Ithaca 1952.

17. B. G. Myerhoff, "We Don't Wrap Herring in a Printed Page: Fusion, Fictions, and Continuity in Secular Ritual," Burg Wartenstein Conference No. 64:1974. Conference Paper.

18. John J. Gumperz, "Speech Variation and the Study of Indian Civilization," *American Anthropologist* 63:976–978.

19. In a conference on Spanish regionalism held in the Canary Islands in May 1978, under the auspices of the University at La Laguna, Tenerife, it became apparent that the feeling of "speaking Castilian badly" was very widespread in the Iberian peninsula and was found in Andalusia, Extremadura, Valencia, Catalonia and the Basque country. The role of this very general language inhibition in Spanish life has not been assessed nor has its evident role in energizing the search for regional cultural autonomy, the search for regional "personality," to use the frequently employed term.

20. There is, indeed, an inhibiting amount of confusion in Asturias about what constitutes Castilian and what Asturian. Asturians find it difficult to distinguish. Under the pressure of a question they may say such things as, "It must be Bable. I, at least, never heard the word when I was in Burgos." The average Asturian recognizes that, provincially, he employs turns of phrase that identify him as an Asturian but he is not sure of them.

21. This argument of lack of personality was made by regionalist groups who refused to participate at the investiture of the young Don Felipe as Prince of Asturias in Covadonga in November of 1977. As Asturians did not have or had not been granted the means by which to achieve their own personality *(personalidad propia)*, they observed, they could not assist fully in the ceremonies.

22. As seen in a whole sequence of publications and most notably in these works: J. L. Garcia Arias, *Bable y Regionalismo*, Oviedo, 1975: X. LL. Garcia Arias, Llingua v Sociedá Asturiana, Oviedo, 1976; X. X. Sanchez, "Concencia Rexonal y Llinguistica," *La Nueva España*, Feb. 20 and 21, 1978.

23. It is useful to recall that communication, socially considered, moves in two directions: vertical (ascending or descending) and horizontal. The majority of societies keep vertical, descending communication very well organized because it serves structures of authority. Many societies, and particularly authoritarian societies, neglect or constrain vertical, ascending communication. In Spain, where Castilian has been employed primarily as an instrument of vertical, descending communication (and particularly in regions where the romance languages had antecedence), to continue with this inheritance although other attributes of regional autonomy were achieved would not respond to present regionalist desires. It would be to continue with a deprecation implicitly if not explicitly vertical, descending. Vertical, ascending communication would remain inhibited. An important goal of many regionalists is to obtain within bureaucratic-administrative

structures a much greater degree of horizontal communication than presently exists, while ensuring that vertical communication is effectively two-way, not preponderantly descending.

24. Melford Spiro, "Culture and Personality: The Natural History of a False Dichotomy," *Psychiatry* 15:19–46, 1951.

25. See, for example, the discussion by Dmitri Sotiropoulos, "Diglossia and the National Language Question in Modern Greece," *Linguistics*, No. 197, 1977, pp. 5–31.

26. For an argument in anthropology that the ontogeny of knowing is greatly facilitated in culture by metaphoric extension of experiences from primary and literal realms of being to secondary realms, see F. L. Lounsbury's discussion of this in respect to the extension of primary kin-terms to secondary kin relations: "Another View of Trobriand Kinship Categories," *American Anthropologist*, Vol. 67, No. 2, Part 2, pp. 142–185. A cautionary note on the difficulty of distinguishing between the literal and the metaphorical and the possibility that secondary realms of belonging may seem as real and literal—if not more so—as primary realms; see Gary Witherspoon, *Language and Art in the Navaho Universe*, pp. 91–95. Ann Arbor: University of Michigan Press, 1977.

27. The enigmatic and paradoxical nature of Asturian regionalism baffled the analysis of a team of Madrid sociologists who approached it by means of questionnaires in *La Conciencia Regional en España*, Jose J. Blanco et al., Madrid: Centro de Investigaciones Sociológicas, 1977. While Asturians showed a marked regional consciousness in the sense of devotion to regional symbols and modes of life, at the same time they maintained significant allegiance to general Spanish culture and Madrid centralism.

28. The specific level of evolution is, par excellence, the level of "bricolage," that is to say creative if relatively spontaneous and unplanned recombination of a limited number of diverse and locally available elements. In evolution at the general level, the weight of tradition is much greater and we have much less possibility for abrupt makeshift recombination.

29. For the distinction between general and specific evolution, see M. Sahlins and E. Service, *Evolution and Culture*, pp. 12–13. Ann Arbor: University of Michigan Press.

30. For more than a decade an association called "Los Amigos del Bable" has been at work in Asturias. The members have dedicated themselves to the publication and circulation of classic works in Bable, poetry above all. This association, it might be said, has tended to concentrate on the corporeal, social, and territorial satisfactions of the languages. In 1974 a much more active organization was founded, El Conceyu Bable. It was decided, almost from the first, to take political postures. Of course, it has worked in favor of the vitalities here mentioned but its political orientation, comprehensible in post-Franco Spain, is so marked for some that it impedes their enjoyment of the delights of the local language such as brought to their attention in the verse circulated by Los Amigos. Many members of this latter group are angered that their familiar and well-loved language has been converted into a political slogan. The response of the members of the Conceyu is that such Amigos of Bable were almost always bourgeoisie of a certain privilege who treated the language as a diversion and a delectation and never seriously sought to recuperate it. The restoration of a language, they argue, demands a politics. We have not treated here the fascinating problem of the politicization of Bable.

31. These were the words of Jesús Neira, Professor of Linguistics in the Univer-

sity of Oviedo and one of the first authorities of Bable. He was reacting to the general enthusiasm for revitalization and particularly to the remarks of D. Luis Michelena, the Basque linguist, who was comparing the rescue of Bable with the rescue of Basque at a colloquium on Asturian revitalization held at the University of Oviedo in April of 1978.

32. The effort at restoration of Asturian or Bable occurred periodically in the last century almost always with university input: for example, there were notable efforts in the 1870s and again in the 1890s and also in the 20s of the present century.

33. The Asturian columnist and provincial savant M. Avello makes reference in this regard to the experience of the novelist Perez de Ayala when he was a student at the University of Oviedo at the turn of the century: "The professors wore the peasants' wooden shoes [madreñas] to class." Avello adds, "Formidable people those professors wearing village gear on the feet but full of wisdom, tolerance, and European substance in the head and heart" (La Nueva Espana, Thursday, May 18, 1978). In short, they were skillful negotiators of the Great and the Little Traditions.

6

REFLECTIONS ON LOOKING
INTO MIRRORS

> Half asleep (on the plane) I looked out into the
> night and saw my father's face looking in
> squinting, trying to see something. I sat up.
> But of course it was my own face, my reflection
> in the glass squinting, trying as see something
> looking out.
>> Michael J. Arlen, *Passage to Ararat*

> In this room a mirror has been hung in the
> background in order to duplicate the distance
> of observation. If we look at the floor it is easy
> to persuade ourselves that it is a continuation of
> the one we occupy as spectators . . . the sensa-
> tion of relief is absolute.
>> A. J. Onieva, *The Prado Gallery* A Museum
>> Guide—Comment on Velasquez' 'Las Men-
>> inas'

The Ancestor in Everyman[1]

On my passage out to Equatorial Africa in 1958 I had occasion to pass
through Madrid and return once again to visit the Prado. I there spent,
like so many visitors, considerable time in the room devoted to the famous
picture by Velasquez, *Las Meninas* (The Ladies in Waiting).[2] In this
picture there is a subtle play of mirrors both within the picture and by
means of an actual large mirror set up in the small room entirely devoted
to the canvas. The trick—the duplicity—in the duplication of mirrors is to
persuade the observer that he is part of the scene figured, a gathering of
the Spanish royal family. I have always had difficulty in suspending the
disbelief of visual, not to mention social and historical distance, long
enough to enjoy this effect. And, contrary to the claims of the guidebook,

157

the sensation of relief I experienced was that of leaving the room and my frustrating efforts to get into the gestalt of the thing—to feel my speculating figure grounded, as it were, in the royal chambers of Philip the Fourth. One could even, and I suppose that this is the main available sensation, be identified with the royal couple themselves. For it is they who are reflected in the mirror in the painting in such a way as to seem to be occupying the position of the spectator. If the trick works, and I am told that it often does, the mirror should show the king and queen in every man and woman.

These frustrations in obtaining objective self-awareness in a seventeenth-century scene may account for the exceptional interest I subsequently took in a feature of initiation into the Mbiri-Bwiti religious movement complex among the Fang of western Equatorial Africa.[3] Initiation into this movement is achieved by the ingestion of large amounts of the psychotropic plant *eboga (Tabernanthe eboga)*.[4] The visionary excursions produced by higher levels of dosage are sufficient unto themselves in many chapels. But often the initiation is aided by placing a mirror on the ground some six to eight feet directly before the initiate, who is also sitting spreadlegged upon the ground. Sometimes the mirror will carry a design in white paint, an 'X' or a facelike configuration, and sometimes it will be unmarked. It is never so completely marked that the initiate cannot make out his own face reflected in the mirror.

A significant moment in initiation comes when the initiate, now deeply under the influence of *eboga*, recognizes his or her ancestor or troubling spirit in the virtual image of the mirror. He recognizes *Bwiti*, as it is said. It is a moment of singular import, for the initiate may well have been staring intently, often leaning forward in a strained position, for several hours. What was his or her face or an ambiguous mark becomes transformed into the significant other with whom the religion or curing cult is seeking to come into communication. When the other is finally seen— there is always some question whether the initiation will work—the relief is indeed absolute. The initiate, his initiation confirmed by this manifestation, can now pass on to a new state of being—that of incumbent of the chapel or 'angel' *(Banzie)*. Having seen the ancestor, the initiate can now be removed to a chamber outside the ceremonial arena where, stupefied and soon falling asleep, he can continue his visionary excursion in the land of the dead.[5]

Inevitably there are various explanations for this phase of the initiation. Some members of these movements say that the ancestor or afflicting spirit has come directly into the mirror out of the ground. Others say that the ancestor simply manifests himself in the mirror. Others say that the event is indicative of the stage in the ingestion of *eboga* in which the initiate can no longer see the things of this world. One subtle-minded informant said that the initiate was really seeing himself but that this was what the religion was really all about—the enabling of one to see oneself more clearly, more at a distance as it were. The self-objectification by means of a mirror to which this informant seems to be referring is compatible, incidentally, with the sense of distancing from self—or at least the sense of observing one's own body from a distance—produced as a psychoreaction to the *eboga* plant,[6] which as Bwitists say produces the sense of "I am here and my body is there."

In any event, no member offered the explanation which I think is the most fruitful one: This is the explanation that the trick of the mirror accomplished an identification of the dead ancestor behind the looking glass and the living descendant before it. If there was not an identification, there was at least a recognition that the one and the other were reflections of each other—a condition essentially true for cultures like the Fang which emphasize genealogical continuities between the living and the dead and reject any sense of pronounced discontinuity.[7] Indeed, these religious movements are seeking to reestablish continuities between the living and the dead—continuities disturbed by the missionary attack upon the immanence of ancestors and by other secularizing and depersonalizing processes of the colonial world. More than the colonial, perhaps it is the modern world! For these processes of 'discontinuity' surely were at work on Michael Arlen, to refer to our other epigraph, animating him to fly back to Ararat in search of his Armenian ancestry. And his is only the most notable of much recent literature in search of 'ethnic communion'.

African Uses of Mirrors and Other Reflecting Surfaces

There is precedence for this use of mirrors in western Equatorial Africa. Among Fang themselves mirrors were sometimes used in ancestral cult initiations . . . after, however, rather than before collapse from the taking of hallucinatory drugs. (In the Fang ancestral cult the psychoreactive plant was not *Tabernanthe eboga* but *Alchornea floribunda malan*.) When the initiate had collapsed, he was rushed from the village into the forest precincts and revived. Behind him the skulls of the ancestors were taken out of the reliquaries and placed on a platform. When the initiate was sufficiently revived, he was propped up before a mirror in such a way as to see the skulls reflected in it. He would later be shown the skulls directly and he would participate in their washing. It was felt that if he were first directly shown the skulls the shock would be too great. In point of fact, the reflection of the skulls in the mirrors seems to have had more psychological effect than direct viewing.

The use of mirrors for religious purposes along the equatorial west coast has been long remarked, particularly among the Loango or Bavili (Pechuel Loesch 1907 passim; Dennet 1906: 30, 51, 84), where magical mirrors were used by diviners and where the light thrown from mirrors was felt to have grievous consequences. Reliquary and other religious figurines often had bits of mirrors embedded in them with the intention, very likely, of protecting them and adding to their power. Trilles (1932: 178–180) argues that the origin of this mirror use may well lie with the pygmies and their use of the magic mirror (although surely mirror use in this part of Africa must be traced to very early contact with Europeans as well as to the belief that the dead dwelt at the bottom of streams, lakes, and pools—behind or beneath reflective surfaces, as it were). Among western equatorial pygmies Trilles says the mirror was used in divination in order to conjure up the more or less distinct physiognomy of the guilty party, the enemy of the patient. The face would be less distinct because the pygmies employed a polished piece of copper. Before the acquisition of this metal they employed a very still pool of water deep in the forest—*fontaine des esprits*—for reflective divination. This practice is reinterpreted in the Bwiti religion, which regards such deep forest pools as the sites where the souls of the newborn are first sent before they are conceived in the womb. Pebbles representing souls are fished out of these pools and transported into the chapel house. Fang have long believed that the essential self is seen in water reflection (Tessman 1913:II.35), particularly in still pools.

Trilles also discusses the consecration of the pygmy mirror. It is consecrated to the sun, which sees everything, and some of whose all-seeing light is confined in the mirror for future use. But there is surprisingly little ethnographic data on the use of mirrors from elsewhere in Africa. Since the earliest use of mirrors seems to have been in Egypt, there has long been opportunity for diffusion into the rest of Africa. This opportunity is enhanced by widespread Islamic beliefs—similar to those in Europe—

that the mirror image is the embodiment of the soul and hence to be avoided, particularly at times of funerals when one's own soul might be stolen away by the departing. Among Zulu, who divined traditionally by dark reflecting pools and who regarded, it is said (Calloway 1868:342ff), any reflecting surface with respect if not awe, the custom still persists of covering or turning mirrors to the wall during lightning storms, lest the mortal bolt of such a supernatural event be reflected directly into living quarters. There was also the belief among Zulu and other southern Nguni that a mirror properly adjusted to reflect the heavens could kill enemy warriors.

There is plentiful evidence for the use of mirrors elsewhere in the world, particularly in East Asia, Southeast Asia, and the Pacific, as well as in aboriginal America. Among the Plains Indians, for example, mirror boards were used in war expeditions to make the bearer as difficult to capture or injure as light from a mirror, and latterly they were employed in the Sun Dance and Ghost Dance (Kroeber 1907:356). A review of the folk literature motifs involving mirrors gathered by Stith Thompson (1958 Index Volume:509) shows worldwide provenience from Japan through Siberia to Iceland. The mirror apparently, perhaps because of the "trickiness" we discuss below, is a device which easily becomes a repository of significance—a collective representation. But what it represents is, characteristically, variable from culture to culture. Thus in English, French, Welsh, and Italian folktales the devil appears when a woman looks at herself in a mirror after sunset. In Jewish tales, the same theme is transformed and the mirror acts as a chastity index justly reflecting the degree of a woman's devilishness. Similarly, while in the English tradition a broken mirror is an evil omen, in Armenia and Japan a mirror gradually grows dark as an individual's life prospects dim. In either case the state of the mirror is tied up with the fate, health, and future of the person whom it reflects. Thus God or Saint Peter or other 'weighers of souls' can make use of a mirror on the judgment day. For it will faithfully reflect the virtues or vices of the spectator's life.

The mirror's self-sufficient tricks also provoke the playful or absurd in folktales: tales where characters stand in front of a mirror with their eyes shut to see how they look when they are asleep or where they take mirrors to bed to see if they sleep with their mouths open. In cabalistic thought there are the seven mirrors for each day of the week, dedicated to each of the seven planets. Having different reflective surfaces, they are consulted for different purposes. Tuesday's Mars mirror of iron is consulted as to imminent enmities and lawsuits. Friday's Venus mirror of copper is consulted as to questions of love.

Of course, the literature and folklore of exploration and western expansion is replete with accounts of native amusement or amazement upon first setting eyes on European mirrors—pocket reflecting pools as they must have seemed. But this literature, often quite elaborated, lacks ethnographic value and may reflect, as much as anything, the mirroring effect that Europeans themselves were encountering amidst strangely familiar men and women in barbarous climes.

The Mirror's Tricks

Mirrors play at least two tricks. They reverse the horizontal plane while maintaining the vertical and they give the see-through effect. That is, they locate, as anyone who has tried to photograph a mirror knows, the virtual image as far back of the mirror, apparently, as the objects in view are in front of it. These tricks act to create an interesting arousal and state of wonder, susceptible, as we see, to a wide variety of cultural uses. One may speculate to begin with that human reactions to mirrors have something to do with the principle of bilateral symmetry in organisms, by which the left side of an animal is a mirror image of the right. At the same time, organisms usually do not develop their two sides symmetrically but, in fact, give emphasis to one or another side. An example is the prevalence of right- or left-hand dominance in humans. Arousal in the presence of mirrors would arise then—this is the speculation—from the fact that an acquired sidedness, often painfully enforced by culture, is apparently reversed. The effect is that of having a dualism which has been resolved in dominance suddenly reversed—transformed by the transitory reassertion of the basic fact of symmetry. The world is transformed without being turned upside down.

The reversal of an otherwise identical representation—what is called the enantiomorphic effect (Ogden 1967)—has been suggestive as a metaphor for the condition of the dead, particularly in societies which emphasize their continuity and similarity with the living. Among the Cuicatec of Central America, for example, Eva Hunt (1976) shows us the enantiomorphic relationship between the present time and space of the living, and the past time and space of the dead. Though the one is visible and the other invisible, they are reflections of each other—that is to say, identical but reversed. The effect is very much like that of walking on top of a mirror—the living of this world moving about above and the dead of the past and future world walking upside down below. Something of the notion of the world of the dead as a mirror image of the living is found in western Equatorial Africa—in notions that the ancestors live under the reflective surfaces of pools and watercourses in villages of the dead both the same as and different from the villages of the living. MacGaffey has pointed out (1969: 144–145) that in Kongo cosmography "a world is separated from its antithesis (its mirror image) by a body of water . . . the other world is reached by going through or across this water which may be identified in appropriate contexts with any physical body of water . . . and even a bowl of water or a mirror." In my experience, these quasi-enantiomorphic notions are not, however, as well worked out as in Mesoamerica. Still, their presence may well account for the religious uses made of the mirrors in this part of Africa—the ease with which it is believed that a mirror can give us a view of the dead, if not of the unseen land of the dead.

This widespread notion of being able to pass through the looking glass into other unseen realms—most relevantly here the land of the dead—is particularly abetted by the mirror's second trick, the trick of locating the virtual image equidistant behind itself. This behind-the-looking-glass effect has long been apparent to Europeans and emerges particularly in Lewis Carroll's books. It is also present in the production of Sartre's *No Exit* where stage directions prohibit any use of mirrors. The characters are not to be allowed even this possibility of escape beyond these, their ultimate and immediate circumstances. There are plentiful instances in the ethnographic literature of local beliefs in being able to see deep into the world of the spirits through mirrors or to see one's spirit-world soul in one's reflection.

Lust of the Eyes—Lust of the Mind

If the tricks of mirrors lend support to the notion that in them one can see beyond this world to the next world or the world of the imagination, at the same time mirrors do reflect the physical facts of this world. Indeed, as parents of teenagers are painfully aware, mirrors tend to lend too much credence to the facts of this world—the facts of physical self. The possibilities for the gratification of concupiscent self-interest—the pleasures, not altogether unambiguous, of visual self-inspection—which are presented by mirrors lead to their banning in nunneries and other ascetic and self-abnegating institutions, lest they exacerbate what St. Augustine called the "lust of the eyes."

On the other hand, and paradoxically, it is also believed, often in the same culture, that what a mirror reflects is the essence or the perfection of physical being. This belief is similar to the belief that what is actually seen in a mirror is the soul—the essence of being. Thus Benedict, in discussing the Japanese, points out how they use mirrors to recapture the purity of the earliest "side of themselves" built up in childhood (1946: 288–289) . . . a purity unhampered by the "observing self."

> That side which is built up in the earliest period is the "self without shame" and they test how far they have kept it when they look at their own faces in the mirror. The mirror they say "reflects eternal purity." It does not foster vanity nor reflect the "interfering self." It reflects the depth of the soul. A person should see there his self without "shame" . . . Japanese feelings about the mirror are derived from the time before the "observing self" was inculcated in the child. They do not see the observing self in the looking glass. There their selves are spontaneously good as they were in childhood without the mentor of "shame."

One may, of course, be passionate about other things besides physical being, purely or impurely regarded. Many a mind—and not only a Platonic mind—is passionate to escape mere being itself, lusting after the perfections of abstraction. Mirrors, as devices by which essence or perfection can be perceived, can serve that purpose as well. This may explain why engines of evil such as vampires could not be seen in mirrors; they have no perfection. Another explanation is that such evils are actually disembodied presences. They are not really there in any physical sense and mirrors are bound to reflect the vacuous fact. Or it may simply be believed that evil destroys itself in a mirror by being brought to recognize itself.

The notion that mirrors reflect the essence of things, with the possibility of suggesting the perfection of things, should be familiar to anthropologists, for we have from time to time conceived of our purpose as that of holding a mirror up to a man in which, by seeing ourselves strangely (or darkly) in another culture, we can discover the essence of our humanity if not the possibilities of its perfection. The more modern notion—which we shall consider below—is that the mirror we have been holding up first of all reflects ourselves, the makers and manipulators of the mirror.

In any event, the notion that the reflective process may be a process of the perfection of being is seen in the inclination to consider the perfect or near perfect beings of our existence as mirrors themselves. Most notable is the Virgin, who has been considered as the *Specula sine macula*, the "mirror without blemish." In a believing Christendom it is to be much preferred that a picture of the Virgin or the Savior should be found in young people's chambers rather than a real mirror. For in those pictures will be reflected all the essential virtues of Christendom such as a mere mirror could not reveal. In the same way, extended contemplation of any picture of Abraham Lincoln, *maculas* and all, will cause in us reflections upon the essential virtues of our Republic . . . for they are to be found there in as nearly perfect a form as they are likely to be embodied in a Republic.

It is not only in the human face that we can see reflected the essence or the perfection of ourselves. Anyone who has worked among cattle-keepers of East Africa will recognize what a reflected sense of satisfaction is found by contemplating the family herds. Cows can be mirrors in many parts of the world. The following is a translation from the Spanish novelist, Concha Espina, found in her story, *El Rabion* (1948:69), which takes place among cattle-keeping peoples of northern Spain.

> The other cows docile in their accustomed route had just crossed over the river confidently without hesitation and Martin harassing them from the bank with shouts and whistles saw them walk slowly away towards the village. Then he ran in search of the saucy companion, the best one in the herd, in which the family saw themselves as in a mirror. [*se miraba como en un espejo*]

For the rest, Evans-Pritchard (1965) has shown for the Dinka (as for the Nuer) how many images are reflected back to them when men sit back to contemplate their herds . . . and how these images bouncing off the cows, as it were, associate cattle in complex ways to other beings in the animal world and both to the various relevant domains of human experience.

Self-Objectification and Back

In our discussion so far we see the mirror employed both literally and figuratively. On the one hand, by literally looking into mirrors we obtain a sense of ourselves as object—as something to be seen by others. This is the sense of the term self-objectification. On the other hand, in a more figurative sense, we see that objects can be mirrors reflecting us or aspects of ourselves. We might call this object-subjectification (with a high tolerance of cumbersomeness): the discovery of self by recognizing a convincing association with objects which reflect us . . . which we are well satisfied to let stand for us.

It has been made plentifully apparent in the writings of Jacques Lacan that in addressing ourselves to mirrors we are not simply exploring an interesting artifact with some wonderful properties. Rather, we are addressing ourselves to an artifact which is central and crucial to the achievement of identity. It is probably primordial. Lacan (1949, 1953) has spoken at length about the "joyful assumption of their specular image" by children, and he points this out as the necessary stage, "stade du miroir" as he calls it, in the precipitation of the "I" into that dialectic of identification between the object and the subject. Before the subsequent taking from 'the other' of language and the predicative process, an acquisition that restores to us our subjective existence, we must pass through the mirror stage of the alienated self—the stage of the *moi*.

Lacan, moreover, actually examines the narcissistic fascination of the young with their image—their attempts to control their own image in a mirror in the early phases of their growth. It is this primordial mirror play which interests him, as it interests us here. Indeed, he makes reference to animal biology, where experiments show that the proper maturing processes of animals demand a perceptual relationship to another of the same species. Where this is not possible, the substitution of a mirror in the animal's cage can itself provide for the normal tempo of development. How interested Lacan might be, therefore, in recent experiments in psychology on subjective self-awareness by Robert Wicklund and others. These researchers force their subjects to fail or succeed in their experiments so as to induce discrepancies, positive or negative, between images of self and actual performance. Then they place these controlled groups in rooms with a mirror where they can't avoid inspecting themselves and which create, therefore, objective self-focusing. Those who have failed, and suffered in self-esteem, show a significantly reduced tolerance of the room itself (Duval and Wicklund 1972: 16–20). Wicklund and his associates have engaged in a variety of mirror manipulations of the experimental kind, practically all of which show how much a mirror has to do with one's sense of identity, situation tolerance, and self-rating. They have also shown that subjects who have just undergone "induced positive performance" show a significant increment in the number of first-person pronouns they employ when speaking about the experience in the presence of a mirror, as compared to a 'no-mirror' situation (Davis and Brock 1974.) Subjects are also given the opportunity (Wicklund personal communication 1975) to cheat on a mock exam with important rewards. There is significantly less cheating in the presence of a mirror.

These are examples of a resourceful scientific objectivity in action—that lust of the mind which is the dominant characteristic of our age. However we are to interpret the meaning of the mirror itself in these experiments, the self or other presence it brings to bear on the subjects (including the thought that they may always suspect a two-way mirror—that is, no mirror at all) they suitably bring into focus the notion of alienation, distancing from self and from others, which the mirror suggests. If all we learn from mirrors is their initial lesson, self-objectification, and if we forget their subsequent lesson, object-subjectification, then we are easily led into a rather arrogant objective paradigm—that alienation from the dialectic of reflexivity with which we are here struggling and which is an inevitable feature of the study of the other. The culture of science may demand Piagetian decentering and self- (and other) objectification. But those of us interested in passage over to a deeper grasp of the fabulation of culture and the ongoing search for identity will recognize that it is a reflexive process—reciprocal in an inseparable way—the "mind reflecting upon itself" as Lévi-Strauss says of myth making, both his own and that of others, the subject seeing itself in the object, the object living itself in the subject. In short, it is the mind in the mirror.

Conclusion

If an ape peeps in will an apostle peer out?
George Lichtenberg

These final difficult issues demand to be addressed in a variety of ways. We must look into many mirrors. Here we have been interested in mirrors themselves. The mirror, it appears, is par excellence the instrument of paradox—the paradox we are exploring here. It presents a direct and recognizable image which is yet an inversion, a reversal. It presents something in itself which is yet behind itself. The paradoxes of reflectivity which are passively present in mirrors are actively present in the eye—

that primordial mirror—of the beholder. From very early on in human experience we have had to contend with reflective surfaces. To the degree that we accept, like Merleau-Ponty (1962), the primacy of visual perception as the dominant mode of "making things intelligible"—to the degree that we accept that thinking is reflecting[8]—we see that we are inescapably confronted with that paradox: in looking upon another we see ourselves, in looking into ourselves we see another.

Beyond that, the mirror is and always has been a crucial device of extension and linkage. Given the essential solitary quality of the human condition, the mirror has been a device for escaping the fate of isolation. It is a device by which we can extend ourselves into the other while, at the same time, linking ourselves with that other. We know, in point of fact, precious little about others and although we live amidst a welter of impulses and habits, precious little about ourselves. The mirror shows us a fundamental truth about human affairs. The way that we discover ourselves is precisely the way we discover others and these discoveries are in reflexive relationship.

The mirror then is one of those devices, perhaps the fundamental one, by which we can gain some enthusiasm to base a sociable life plan upon. It can give us, as we see, some feeling that there is something of our fathers in ourselves and something of ourselves in them. It can give us some feeling that there is something of the king in everyman and something of everyman in the king. If the mirror can give us such feelings—to return to our epigraph again—the "sensation of relief" may well be absolute.

Notes

1. This paper was originally presented at the 75th Annual Meeting of the American Anthropological Association, November 19th, 1976, Washington, D.C., in the session *Rituals and Myths of Self: Uses and Occasions of Reflexivity*, Barbara Myerhoff, Michelle Rosaldo, and Barbara Babcock organizing. I appreciate their comments and those of David Crabb.

2. It is this painting that inspired Michel Foucault to a lengthy introductory chapter in *The Order of Things* (1970), his archaeology of the shift in recent centuries, concomitant with the development of the human sciences, from the objective to the subjective paradigm, from the self as an adjunct to an assumed objective and orderly reality to the self as a center of composition, as a center of representation of a variety of perspectives. Since the spectator occupies a vacuous center of attention in this painting, it is highly suitable to his purposes. He has some interesting things to say about "the play of metamorphoses" between spectator and mirror, but he does not consider the actual mirror hung in the observing chamber by the Prado Gallery and its intended effect.

3. This new African religion has recurrently been discussed in the literature of Georges Balandier (1970). See also Stanislaw Swiderski (1973).

4. The use of this plant is discussed in H. Pope (1969) and also in J. Fernandez (1972: 237–260).

5. A mirror frequently appears in the visions themselves, which are stereo-typically presented as an excursion along a red path through the forest back up to a savannah upland. There appear buildings of strange construction on these envisioned "uplands"—globes covered with mirrors or a house with a hall of mirrors in which a cadaver is laid and suddenly resurrected by the action of reflections upon it.

6. See the discussion of the components of the physiological-perceptual reaction to *eboga* in Fernandez 1972: 254–258.

7. The fact of the continuity between the living and the dead in African ancestor worship is argued by Kopytoff (1971). Among Fang this continuity is symbolized in the recitation of the genealogy, in which living and dead are undifferentiated. There is, incidentally, an interesting "enantiomorphic" effect in Fang genealogy, for a man or woman's last name is his or her father's first name and as genealogy is recited, there is the effect of the sequential reversing of names.

8. Indeed among Fang, whose mirror experience we examine, the most accurate translation of the verb *siman*, which is usually translated "to think," is rather "to reflect," as it is derived from the root *sim*, "to pause and look back," to recall, in other words, the vestigial experiences of the past and their relevance to present experience. There is some notion of the mind (which reposes, however, in the heart and not the head) as a kind of retentive mirror whose former reflections can be re-collected for comparison with what is presently reflected. I am elaborating a bit on my fieldnotes but Fang do differentiate people as thinkers according to how well they can recall former experiences. In the raising of children, they will often test them by asking the young to recall such and such an event in as great a detail as possible. This practice in the lawyerly art of recall—of knowing precedence—serves Fang men well in the endless litigations which characterize adult life in the men's council house.

One should be cautious here so as not to fall into the old stereotype of primitive intelligence as consisting essentially of strong memory. By no means does experiment easily confirm memory strength among nonliterates (cf. Cole and Colby 1973). Without denying the various aspects of thinking among Fang, I wish to point out the reflection metaphor in use among them as compatible with their use of the mirror and with the form of debate and litigation in the council house.

This metaphor of the mind as a mirror is, of course, of much wider currency. Examples occur constantly in the literature of neuropsychology. For example, the work of P. D. Maclean is extensively quoted by Earl Count (1973:180–185). Here the evolution of the central nervous system is seen fundamentally as an adaptive process by which a clearer and clearer screen has developed in the cortex, less and less clouded by proprioceptive internal events and more and more accurately reflective of external events.

References

BALANDIER, GEORGES
  1970 *The Sociology of Black Africa*, trans. by Douglas Garman. New York: Praeger.

BENEDICT, RUTH
1964   *The Chrysanthemum and the Sword*. Boston: Houghton.
CALLOWAY, CALEB
1868   *The Religious System of the Amazulu*. Capetown: Shuter and Shuter.
COLE, M. and COLBY, B.
1973   Culture memory and narrative. In *Modes of Thought*, R. Horton and R. Finnegan (eds), 63–91. London: Faber.
COUNT, EARL
1973   *Being and Becoming Human: Essays on the Biogram*. New York: Van Nostrand Reinhold.
DAVIS, DAVID and BROCK, THOMAS C.
1974   Heightened self-awareness, self-esteem, and ego-centric thought. Manuscript Referenced in R. Wicklund 'Objective self-awareness'. In *Advances in Experimental Social Psychology*, Vol. 9.
DENNETT, RICHARD EDWARD
1906   *At the Back of the Black Man's Mind: Notes on the Kingly Office in West Africa*. London: Macmillan.
DUVAL, SHELLY and WICKLUND, ROBERT A.
1972   *A Theory of Objective Self-Awareness*. New York: Academic Press.
ESPINA, CONCHA
1948   *Pastorales*. Madrid: Espasa-Calpe.
EVANS-PRITCHARD, EDWARD
1965   Imagery in Ngok Dinka cattle-names. In *The Position of Women in Primitive Societies and other Essays in Social Anthropology*. New York: Free Press.
FERNANDEZ, JAMES
1972   *T. eboga* and the work of the ancestors. In *The Flesh of the Gods*, P. Furst (ed.) 237–260, New York: Praeger Publishers.
FOUCAULT, MICHEL
1970   *The Order of Things*. New York: Pantheon Books.
HUNT, EVA
1976   The Quincunx: A root paradigm in Cuicatec Indian religion. Unpublished manuscript.
KOPYTOFF, IGOR
1971   Ancestors as Elders in Africa. *Africa* 41 (2), 129–143.
KROEBER, ALFRED LEWIS
1907   *The Arapaho*. IV Religion Bulletin of the American Museum of Natural History, Vol. XVIII. New York.
LACAN, JACQUES
1949   'Le stade du miroir' comme formateur de la fonction du Je, qu'elle nous est revelee dans l'experience psychoanalytique. *Revue Francais de Psychanalyse* 12, 449–455.
1953   Some reflections on the Ego. *International Journal of Psycho-Analysis*, 34, 11–17.
MACGAFFEY, WYATT
1969   The 'Beloved City': Commentary on a Kimleanguist text. *Journal of Religion in Africa* 2, 129–157.
MERLEAU-PONTY, MAURICE
1962   *The Phenomenology of Perception*. London: Routledge & Kegan Paul.

OGDEN, CHARLES
    1967   *Opposition: A Linguistic and Psychological Analysis*. Bloomington: Indiana University Press.
PECHEUL LOESCH, OTTO
    1907   *Die Loango*. Berlin: Erdmann.
POPE, H.
    1969   *Tabernanthe eboga:* An African narcotic plant of social importance. *Economic Botany* 23 (2), 174–184.
SARTRE, JEAN PAUL
    1974   *Huis-clos suivi de Les mouches*. Paris: Gallimard.
SWIDERSKI, STANISLAW
    1973   Notes biographiques sur les fondateurs et les guides spirituels des sectes syncretiques au Gabon. *Anthropologica* N.S. 15(1), 37–88.
TESSMAN, GUNTER
    1913   *Die Pangwe,* 2 vols. Berlin: Ernst Wassmuth.
THOMPSON, STITH
    1958   *Motif-Index of Folk Literature*. Bloomington: Indiana University Press.
TRILLES, HENRI
    1932   *Les Pygmees de la Foret Equatoriale*. Paris: Bloud.

7

Edification by Puzzlement

By indirections find directions out!
POLONIUS
He gives me ideas even when I don't under-
stand him.
E. LEACH ON C. LÉVI–STRAUSS

Administered Intellectuality

The colonial mentality is generally associated with a set of racial attitudes produced in a privileged class of administrative, merchant, or sometimes, missionary plenipotentiaries well suited to justify and preserve privileges and exclude the claims of the administered peoples upon those privileges. These attitudes most often were expressed in observations on the moral behavior of native peoples such as their irresponsibility and deviousness or their lack of the more refined feelings. But the colonial mentality was also a set of beliefs about mentality itself. These beliefs were most often expressed in observations on "time sense," childishness, or prelogical reasoning. To the very end of the colonial period, colonialists bewailed the granting of independence to local peoples who wouldn't have the wits to run things, whether it was the Suez Canal—these days it has been the Panama Canal, one of the last outposts of the colonial attitude in its purest form—the Kariba Dam, the Katanga copper mines, or the Ghana Cocoa Marketing Board. Of course, all these constructions are still running, although perhaps not in their former manner. Not all peoples have the gift of the northern European peoples for self-abnegating administration. Most peoples tend to express themselves more by administering and maintaining structures of exchange and control.

The point of this postcolonial preamble is not to deny that there are differences in mentalities or in modes of thought. Indeed, there are, and we should be interested in them. But on the other hand, we should always be wary of the imperial impulse—the possibility that any interest in mentalities is betrayed by a *petitio principi*, a preexistent interest in maintaining and justifying a structure of privileges. It is perfectly natural to seek to maintain privileges, but this is not the purpose of anthropology, which seeks some simple knowledge of the species which surpasses our impressive capacity for self-interested and self-contained activity.

This caution is by no means overdrawn. I remember when I administered the Segall, Campbell, Herskovits visual illusions protocol in a Fang village in Gabon.[1] Now I had a good rapport in that village. I carried a local name. I came as a bachelor and later captured a wife, a North European wife at that, and brought her to the village—a palpable strengthening of the lineage. But that was a difficult protocol to administer. On the one hand I seemed to be getting a lot of extraneous answers, and on the other hand several of the younger villagers seemed mistrustful. It was during the De Gaulle Referendum, and politics was a strong interest among the young. For whom was I doing the protocol? they wanted to know. And what reason did I have for wanting to know such things? Admittedly those kinds of questions and the "laboratory" type conditions required of the test administration were much different from my customary participant-observer and notes and queries role. That role was more fitted to the reason I had given for being in the village, that is, to do a history of the Fang way of life and to make it known to "esi merika," the land of the Americans. The protocol was a harder-headed social science, to use terms from the hard-soft continuum which is a favorite metaphor in academic life. Some of the villagers sensed it as such, although most admittedly took such things as the Sander parallelogram and the Müller-Lyer illusion as just a peculiar kind of riddling popular with Europeans.

I had to admit, if not to my interlocutors, at least to myself, that the harder-headed social science was more highly regarded in my country than the softer kind I usually practiced. In part this was because the culture of science prefers hard data to soft data, but also in part because that harder data was more useful to those hard-headed people who sought, if not to maintain a world system of privileges, at least to engage in competent tough-minded administration of world order. It is of interest, incidentally, to note that the most fruitful and well-funded psychological testing, that of the Rockefeller ethnographic psychology team, has found a congenial field laboratory in Liberia, a country whose administration is

quite interested in maintaining a well-ordered system of inherited privileges. I have no doubt that it is quite coincidental as far as the Rockefeller
team is concerned. These days one does social and psychological science
where one can.

The difficult questions raised by my young informants must be an-
swered. We have some obligations when, as Geertz (1973) says, we plague
subtle people with obtuse questions. Why, really, are those who sponsor
that research really interested in sponsoring it? Is disinterested inquiry as
widespread as we would like it to be? Fang respondents were not so
optimistic and trusting as I was about the scientific neutrality of the
protocol.

The Rockefeller ethnographic psychology team under Michael Cole
and Sylvia Scribner has been conducting studies of the impact of literacy
on rural Liberians. These are valuable studies concerning memory, the
ability to recall, pattern recognition, and perception.[2] They have also
been attempting to get hard data on that perennial bugaboo, logical
thought process. This they have been doing by administering a series of
protocols which employ that old reasoning device: the syllogism. Here are
some examples from West African and Mexican protocols.

> All people who own huts pay hut tax.
> Boima does not pay a hut tax.
> Does Boima own a hut?

> So that Jose can carry corn from his farm to
>   the town he needs a cart and a horse.
> He has the horse but he doesn't have the cart.
> Can Jose carry his corn from his farm?

The results of administering the syllogisms support a number of gener-
alizations: (1) in all cultures populations designated as "traditional" have a
just somewhat better than chance solution rate; (2) within each culture
there is a large discrepancy in performance between schooled and non-
schooled; (3) within schooling there is little between-culture variation in
performance—grade in school, rather than society, is most determinate of
performance.[3] The results seem to be that schools teach you to solve
syllogisms. They are a particular genre, a kind of lore, as it were, typical of
that milieu. If you haven't been to school you won't be clued in on the
need to suspend disbelief in order to accept the propositions. You have to
be schooled to accept Boima's or Jose's hypothetical plight as real. You also
have to be schooled to the fact that you don't have to search elsewhere for

a solution to such questions. The answer to the question posed in the syllogism is found in the syllogism itself; it is self-contained.

Now what is most interesting, it seems to me, are the ways in which traditional rural peoples go wrong, that is, fall into logical errors in respect to conjunction, disjunction, and implication. When responding to these syllogisms, rural peoples, since they aren't schooled enough in the self-sufficiency of the syllogism itself, most often introduce new personal evidence. This is not surprising. Sylvia Scribner gives many examples of the way informants question the facts: "We don't carry corn in carts." "We don't pay hut taxes here!" In other cases they are stimulated into elaborate personal accounts recalling experiences relevant to the subject matter of the question, though not to the requirements of the syllogism.

What seems to occur is that these rural uneducated subjects tend to ignore the arbitrarily imposed relations among the elements in the problem and the rules of criterion implied. They tend to "go beyond the information given" and give consideration to the context in which the question is posed, such as the colonial context of domination and subordination evoked by my younger Fang visual illusion informants or the cultural context of the question—corn is not carried in carts, and not all huts are taxed. They creatively introduce personal experiences and use these academic riddles as an opportunity for edifying commentary on life in general. Or they simply introduce new evidence. Once you take the premises of the new evidence into account, the reasoning of these people turns out to be quite logical. Scribner calls this kind of reasoning "empiric" explanation as opposed to the theoretic or "schooled" explanation of syllogistic argument. Rather than fulfill a formal task, the respondent seeks concrete examples and particular correlative circumstances. Informants either reject the information given or verify it by imputing new evidence.

Lancy, who has worked with the Cole-Scribner ethnographic psychology team and encountered the same problem (the tendency of rural nonwesterners to ignore the rules involved and to answer in terms of setting and personal involvements) points out that responses to the syllogisms are like a certain kind of riddle solving found among Kpelle. There is no single right answer to these riddles. Rather, as the riddle is posed to a group, the right answer is the one among many offered that seems most illuminating, resourceful, and convincing as determined by consensus and circumstance.[4] This emphasis on edification as a criterion for "rightness" is found in Kpelle jurisprudence as well. The successful litigant is the one who can make the most resourceful and edifying argument. The argument is not simply the application of a set of legal rules, but involves taking a problem situation as a personal opportunity to explore the context of the problem and its relevant precedents. Application of a perceived rule is not nearly so important as is availing oneself of the opportunity of a puzzlement—those latent possibilities for the expression of a verbal and intellectual skills found in any riddle. The well-schooled are much more anxious about right answers and develop heuristics, formulas for rule applications, to obtain them.

There are various kinds of riddles, but on balance, I think it is a mistake to see riddles as simply an exercise in the application of academic rules. It is certainly a mistake to say that "a riddle is always closer to an academic test than to creative research" as Köngas Maranda (1971:296) has argued. Indeed it is the main point of this paper that such puzzlements as riddles have creative—or at least constructive—and edifying consequences in the more traditional non-schooled societies.

Images and Answers

Just the same, Köngas Maranda's work on riddles is some of the most interesting we have, and it is important to recall the main points of her analyses. Köngas Maranda's work is important because she shows that the riddle is really an enigmatic metaphor that follows the logical structure of metaphors and metonyms. Like all tropes, a riddle is the statement of a relation between or within sets (or domains of objects). Like lively poetic metaphor in contrast to dead or unprovoking metaphor, a riddle offers a fresh point of view. Köngas Maranda, in fact, contradicts her notion that riddles are not creative: "it causes us to see connections between things that we had not previously perceived." In a Durkheimian manner Köngas Maranda suggests that the final referent of riddles is to some basic aspect of human behavior—a kind of language in which a group speaks of its most basic social action—the union of man and woman. This may be why so many riddles, incidentally, deal with sexual innuendo. In any event, riddles perform a union or conjunction of separated entities on the cognitive level that on the physical level is one of the species' primary preoccupations. Riddles therefore necessarily consist of two parts which are to be conjoined—the riddle image and the answer. These must be analyzed together, though a tendency in riddle analysis has been to concentrate on the image itself.

This conjunction of image and answer in the riddle follows the old Aristotelian definition of an analogy. Analogy exists whenever there are four terms such that the relation between the second and the first is similar to that between the fourth and the third.

$$A/B \quad \text{as} \quad C/D$$

Now any kind of reasoning by tropes—by analogy—rests on two kinds of connection between phenomena: similarity (the metaphoric relation) and contiguity (the metonymic relation). In terms of this Aristotelian formula the similarity relationship runs across sets and the contiguity relation within sets:

This is better written since we are dealing within sets and across sets relations, A/a as C/c, where A is the human body and C is, let us say, the ocean. In metaphor we are given the analogy by being given both sides of the equation. The arm, a, is to the human body as an extended inlet, c, is to the ocean, hence the arm of the ocean. In a riddle, however, we are only given one side of the equation, say the body side, and we have to discover the other side. Perhaps we are given only the body side and have to discover the other natural object or manufactured object side. Let me send the reader on a riddle-provoked ramble of discovery.

> Riddle a diddle, unravel my riddle:
> "Long legs, sharp thighs, no neck, big eyes."

This riddle gives you the body or natural side, but you must busy yourself to discover the cultural side.[5]

Now all analogies—and riddles are analogies par excellence—have the capacity to establish or suggest connections between experiences within domains and between domains. They are cognitively integrating as it were, and in that way they are edifying. This is basically what I mean by edification: the cognitive construction by suggestion of a larger integration of things, a larger whole. Whereas we customarily discriminate and separate between animate and inanimate objects or draw contrasts between nature and culture, these puzzling predications suggest similarities between, in this case, the human body and a pair of scissors.

Now the very act of suggesting these similarities and noting these contiguities is edifying because the equation between the two sets of experience rests on the fact that both can be shown to belong to a set greater than the two original sets in analogous comparison. Köngas Maranda calls this greater set a *superset;* Keith Basso calls it paradigmatic integration; I have been calling this transcendence.[6] In the case of our riddle, the equation between leggy people and scissors suggests the transcendent superset which we may call the set or domain of articulated things. Though part of the pleasure in metaphor rests in its suggestion of a relation between things thought to be separate if not opposite, at the same time the metaphor or the riddle-metaphor builds a bridge across the abyss of separated, discriminated experience. Jakobson (1960) has argued that before there can be a sense of similarity there must be a sense of contiguity. This is true within sets brought into analogous relation—for we must be clear about the relationship of parts within domains before we can suggest similarities between domains. At the same time, out of the sense of similarities is produced a transcendent overarching sense of contiguity. This transformation of contiguities into similarities and similarities into contiguities is fundamentally edifying. And it is what Lévi-Strauss (1966) means when he speaks with (mysterious) edifying puzzlement about the transformation of metaphors into metonyms and vice versa.

In any event, I would argue, in contrast to Köngas Maranda, that it is this edification of a more integrated worldview that is the prime and typical function of this puzzlement. It is not primarily the well-situated discovery and application of rules done in order to find the right answers. Köngas Maranda tends to understand riddles too much in terms of the intellectual efforts of Western school days. There are, it is true, riddling situations in which these puzzles would qualify as what she calls "true riddles." They demand a scanning of the riddle images (or image) for the coded message, i.e., the relevant metonymic relation, in order to discover the right answer, i.e., that relation in another domain. My experience in African riddling situations, however, suggests a prevalence of what she calls the "monk's riddles": riddles that either have a rote answer which one repeats like a catechism or riddles in which there are felt to be a plurality of possible answers and in which the object is creative resourcefulness in providing an answer. Or they are riddles in which no answer is expected from the riddler. The edification is implicit. The audience is left to ponder for itself the mysterious connections between things which are established or implied by the riddles. The riddles here constitute an ambiguous stimulus for creative and constructive responses. They are not instruments designed to provoke the detection and application of certain rules.

This kind of reasoning by the puzzle of analogy is a mode of thought congenial to the older and more wholistic societies because it is serviceable to members of these societies, returning them to "a sense of the whole" of which they are a part and in which they are ideally to be incorporated. Such reasoning recurrently takes place in these societies. Analysis into parts is not really so important in these societies as is the periodic construction or reconstruction of the whole. The whole is what is truly edifying, and its reconstruction is a purpose which puzzlement can subtly serve.

Cosmogony by Puzzlement

I have seen this kind of reasoning in an African religious movement: Bwiti among the Fang of western equatorial Africa. This is a movement that is providentially trying to return the membership to the whole world in which the ancestors lived and from which the colonial situation has separated them. I became aware of that objective because of a recurrent dictum used by one of the leaders of a main branch of Bwiti, Ekang Engono of Kongouleu. He frequently said "the world is one thing but the witches try to isolate men from each other so they can eat them!" By what are called "likenesses" in Fang this leader sought to knit the world together—to cosmogonize. I should like to examine some of the ways by which this edification proceeds by looking at what the people of Bwiti, the Banzi, call Engono's "miraculous words." Various devices are employed in his sermons, these "subtle words."[7] For example, though the sermons or evangiles are neither didactic nor expository—they seem spontaneous and free-associative in the extreme—they can obtain a kind of integrity by "playing on roots." Thus, the root *yen*, "to see," is bound into different morphemes several different times in an evangile. For example, in a sermon of only five minutes in length we find the root *yen* coming up four different times bound into different words. The word play is, basically, between *yena*, "mirror," and *Eyene*, "he who sees." *Eyene* is the word for the savior figure of this religion, but he is also seen as a mirror who reflects the actions of mankind and whose nature mankind ought to reflect. One other key term in this brief sermon plays with the root: *enyenge*, a deep forest pool in which one sees one's reflection. It is Bwiti belief that not only do men and women see their own faces reflected in these pools, but the sky and the sky deities are also reflected in them. There is in the congregation, in any case, an expectancy gratified by the reiteration of these roots. That reiteration is one source of the sermon's integrity.

In order to get the flavor of these puzzling sermons, I will comment upon selected paragraphs from one of them. More than simply providing for its own integrity by playing on roots and recurrent elemental images, these sermons are designed to suggest an integrity in the religious world in which Bwiti seek to dwell:

1. This thing which I recount is no longer. Zame made us first out upon the savannah. And it was he that pierced and prepared our way through the giant adzap tree. And it was he that began to make it possible to make things of the forest. For Fang are of the forest.

2. Humankind shows four miracles. First he leaves the ground and comes to the foot. And he leaves there and comes to the calf. Then he leaves there and comes to the knee. Then he leaves there and is perched upon whence he came. On the shoulders he is put into the balance for the first time.

3. One fans in vain the cadaver in this earth of our birth. The first bird began to fly in the savannah. The night Cain slew Abel the people built the village of Melen. And after that they never turned back. What we Banzie call *Elodi Tsenge*, Fang call rainbow, and Europeans call *arc-en-ciel*. It was raised over the people. Then they passed through the adzap tree. Then they used the forest to construct things. That was the time of the Oban invasion from the north, the Oban of Olu Menyege.

4. The land of humankind was formed and it is a drop of blood. And that drop grew big and round until the white of the egg was complete and prepared, covering two egg sacks within: the white sack and the black sack. That is the ball of birth and of the earth.

5. Now Fang say that "the star is suspended there high up above." The fruit of the adzap tree is suspended up there high in the adzap. What is found suspended there between these things? Why, it is the raindrop. And that raindrop is the congregation—the group of Banzie.

6. The first food of mankind was the sugar cane, therefore the child takes and presses in his mouth the sweet fruit of the breast. It was Ndong Zame of legend who took up the wheedling ways of children. We are children of the rainbow because we are made of clay.

9. Eboga says: "Mopasama beba, mopasema beba ndembe." That means twins—twins over and over again without change. And that is sister and brother. And that is wife and husband, and that is child and mother. But still one dies alone and one is sick alone.

11. Nyingwan Mebege she is the oil palm. Zame ye Mebege he is the otunga tree. And he died and it is the same as the story of the widow of the forest who conceived on the day her husband died. And she conceived on the day her husband died. And she gave birth in the spreading roots of the adzap tree. They were the first stool. And the adzap we know dries up and dies when sorcerers climb into its branches. And we Fang began at the adzap but we set out quickly from under the adzap tree. Then Zame sat upon the stool and gave his child Eyene Zame. That stool is the otunga and it is also a cross. Adzap-mboga is the road of death. And the first stool, the adzap, was the door to death.

17. The ligaments of the small green bird who cries like boiling water they tie together the earth. Woman has the pierced adzap tree below. Man holds the adzap tree up above. And thus is life tied together. Zame makes life with two materials: the drumming stick is the male. The drum is the female.

As will be seen (the sermons themselves are not explained to the congregation), the interpretation of these midnight sermons requires reference to experiences otherwise acquired in Fang culture. As in a riddle, the images of these sermons send us elsewhere to obtain our answers. They are rich in images which must, however, be contextualized by extension into various domains of Fang culture. The interpretive task is, therefore, to move back and forth between text and context. And while this must always be the case with any interpretation of a text, there is here a much greater obligation to contextualize in order to find meaning due to the lack of expository or didactic aids. There is edification—an emergent sense of a larger meaningful whole—in being so obliged to seek for meaning in the cultural context. Such puzzling sermons, by condensing in one unitary presentation many diverse domains of Fang cultural experience, suggest in that experience an integrity, a relatedness, that Fang in recent years have been at risk of losing. At the same time, by forcing contextualization on the auditor, the cultural experience he is obliged to extend his interpretation to and consult is revitalized. This relating of the parts and revitalizing of the whole of a cultural context is cosmogony of an important kind.

These sermons are examples of what Vygotsky (1962) has called "thinking in complex." The sequence of images—the body images, the forest images, the vital liquids images, the suspended things images, the food images—put forth are not dominated by any overall conceived and stated purpose or by any dominant image. The materials presented cluster around a complex—a sequence of organizing images. These recur, but none is prevailingly nuclear. New materials from various domains of Fang experience are introduced on the basis of association by similarity or contiguity, contrast, or complementarity with this sequence. But then again, abruptly, new elements with all their alternatives are allowed to enter the thought process and raise new thematic preoccupations—and to suggest new possible nuclei of attention. By any standard of administered intellectuality, such sermons seem diffuse and spontaneous in the extreme.

And yet as the sermonizer promises, they "tie together" what brotherly enmity and witchcraft has torn asunder. By a sequence of "likenesses" he shows that the world, fallen into devilish particularities, is really one thing. For the sequence of images is in no way directly or explicitly linked, yet it does not seem especially disjointed to the membership. Nor does it seem to be the product of a mad or drugged mind. The sequences are riddles, puzzles, that force the membership to answers that suggest an overarching order and a relatedness to the diversity of the cosmos. Approached with the cultural knowledge the membership possesses they both condense and integrate that knowledge as they revitalize it. And the sequence of images link together various domains and levels of cultural experience. A cosmological integrity is suggested if not made explicit.

For example, taking any image, we can, even in this sermon segment, follow its transformations into various domains, thereby associating them. In the shorter sermon—not quoted here—to which we have referred in regards to playing on roots we find "the bag of waters" (abum menzim) of birth associated with the forest pool of creation (enyenge abiale bot), associated to the great river crossed in Fang migration (oswi ye okua), associated to the cosmic sea of the origin of all things (mang). A sense of reverberation and relatedness between levels and domains of Fang interest and experience is obtained. In circling around one image other attributes of that image embedded in other domains of experience are suggested. Out of our own puzzlement we are extended to larger integrities in wider contexts.

Syllogisms of Association

Extension, condensation, and revitalization are all products of this kind of puzzlement. But what is brought together is more a stimulated thought—a stimulated contextualization—in the auditor than explicit reasoning by the sermonizer. These sermons give their auditors cosmologic ideas even when these auditors don't understand them. The sermonizer himself reasons primarily by playing on roots and by playing on elemental images, by making these elements emerge in different domains and at different levels. His use of analogy is not purely random.

There is here, then, a kind of "reasoning together" of things which is important to the integrity of the sermon experience. We should recognize it for what it is, particularly in light of the academic testing by syllogism to which African subjects have been submitted. We may call this a reasoning by syllogisms of association. It is a kind of reckoning with an argument of images, as it were, which suggests a reconciliation of parts. More particularly, it represents a reconciliation of the social subjects of that thought: men and women, the living and the dead, men and the gods. These subjects are both problematic, inchoate, within themselves—What is a man? Who are the gods?—and they are problematic in their relationship to each other.

As far as the inchoate condition of the subjects themselves, Bwiti regularly, fulfilling its role as a religion, predicates a more concrete and manageable identity upon the believers. That is, metaphors and metonyms are brought to bear upon them personally. In the sermon cited, for example, it is said of Fang that "they are forest," and the identification of the members of Bwiti with trees or with the forest is recurrent and basic. It is what we might expect of a religion in the equatorial regions. Another inchoate subject of concern is life itself. What is life? The sermon offers the metaphor: "life is sugar cane," that is, it comes in sections, and if approached section by section it can be consumed with sweet satisfaction.

More interesting, however, are the sequences of "syllogism-like" predications in which two subjects are related to a middle or common image which is lost in the process of the "argument" leaving the two subjects in a situation of identity, equation, or reconciliation. Thus in paragraph 17 of the sermon cited, women are first equated with the adzap tree below and men with the adzap tree above. By eliminating the common term, the prevalent image, men and women are reconciled. This reconciliation of the sexes is one of the main objects of Bwiti.

The same kind of identification or reconciliation of focal religious subjects is accomplished in paragraph 9 where twins are used as the common term. We are told in brief compass that brothers and sisters are twins, and wives and husbands are twins, and mothers and children are twins. By dropping the mediating image, the central term, all three pairs are equated—as, indeed, they are equated in the archetypal stages of creation in Bwiti mythology.

Often these syllogisms involve complementarity of relationship. We have seen this in the equation of men and women to the adzap tree: men above, women below. In paragraph 17, this is seen in the equation of man to the drumstick and woman to the drum. This follows the Aristotelian formula

> man is to drumstick as woman is to drum
> drum is to drumstick as man is to woman.

Here we see the way that a contiguity is transformed into a similarity and is then translated back into a continguity or a reconciliation between male and female. For it is not enough to note the metaphor. The spiritual intelligence bound up in the metaphor is that men and women can make music together.

> drum : drumstick :: man : woman
> they make music together.

We see here, incidentally, an important kind of edification bound up in these puzzling analogies. Orderliness, the structure, perceived in one domain of experience, that of music instruments, is used to inform and structure—edify is the term I prefer—an orderliness in another more inchoate domain of experience, in this case, the domain of social and sexual relationships.

Finally we see in the sermon sequences of associations in which the social subjects of Bwiti undergo transformations of identity. They gain in the process a polyvalence and, at the same time, an equation with other social subjects. For example, in paragraph 11 we begin with an association of Zame to the Otunga tree. He is subsequently associated to the stool of birth, the cross, and finally the adzap tree in that sequence. Subsequently, as we have seen, man and woman are associated to the adzap tree and thus to Zame. We have the following syllogism of association.

$$Zame = otunga = stool = cross = adzap$$
$$man = woman = adzap$$
$$Zame = man \ \& \ woman$$

By this sequence Zame is found in every man and woman—a reconciliation which is a major and frequently stated purpose of Bwiti. It is a reconciliation that is not accomplished by direct statement but indirectly by a sequence of metaphoric predications. In the end all these mediating subordinate images of the transformation-reconciliation drop away, leaving the desired edifying equation.

Conclusion: Images of Edification to our Eyes

The very title of this presentation with its mellifluous latinate sesquipedalian intimations of mysterious intelligence—and possible revelation—exemplifies in one sense the mode of thought we have been exploring. In another sense—that of the imageless abstract quality of such terms—it is just what this mode of thought is not. For what we have before us is iconic thought primarily producing and working with images more or less visual and concrete in effect. It is not abstract or symbolic thought in Bruner's (1964) sense and the information it communicates is not coded in rules to be abstracted and applied. It is the nature of iconic thought to have much more of a personal component and also to excite contextualization. We may venture that this is because images arise out of personal experience and excite personal experience in their decoding. And images are, we may also venture, a part of larger contexts and lead the mind out to these larger contexts.

Thus, where it might have been expected of this author that he would stick to his last and develop for a modern science-oriented audience the abstract principles by which edification and puzzlement operate, we find him to be also an iconoclast embarking on his discussion by first contextualizing it into the colonial situation. And why? Because this specific problem of edification reminds me of a personal experience I had administering a narrow-context impersonal intellectual test in Africa. I was suddenly assaulted by a group of young men who sought out the ultimate context for those innocent exercises in visual illusion. They were asking me in effect: "These puzzles you are putting to us, they are a part of what larger whole?" I had, frankly, sticking to my last, given very little thought to that larger whole.

In a compartmentalized society like our own we are very able to compartmentalize our intellectual exercises. We are well schooled to heuristics—to looking for rules and applying them in limited and apparently self-contained contexts. That's intelligence for you! But more traditional societies with pretensions to cosmogony, and most traditional societies have that pretension, are more totalistic. Intelligence is a matter of relating to the context, in developing it, revitalizing it. Hence, it is an intelligence that employs images to a high degree in actual or suggested analogic relation. It plays upon similarities in experience, and in that play it suggests or requires answers that suggest overarching contiguities—cosmologies, totalities which encompass, absorb, and defeat particularities. All this is rarely done in a direct and explicit manner. "By indirections find directions out."

As well schooled as we all are in the modern specialized compartmentalized societies, we tend to misread in a schoolmasterish way the masters of iconic thought. We look for a limited set of applicable rules, or we are simply puzzled, and we fail to see how these masters edify by puzzlement. Our inclination is to deprive puzzles of their mystery—that's science for you—and thus we fail to see how the masters mysteriously suggest an overarching order—how they give concrete identity to inchoate subjects, how they reconcile these subjects. It is hard for us to tolerate ambiguities of this kind, let alone understand their function.

In the end, of course, the error is to suggest too great a difference between this very traditional and modern thought. That was long ago discovered by Lévy-Bruhl (1975) when he looked around and discovered towards the end of his life that there were quantities of prelogical thought going on all around him in French life. And so if we look around in academia, we will find quantities of edification by puzzlement. A great lot of it is found among the structuralists themselves who have so creatively put us on to traditional thought. As Edmund Leach said of Lévi-Strauss: "He gives me ideas even when I don't understand him." For many of Lévi-Strauss' readers, that's a lot of the time. But we all recognize that his work is full of delectable images.

Notes

1. See the section on the Fang in Marshall H. Segall, Donald T. Campbell, and M. J. Herskovits (1976).
2. The team has brought forth a series of publications on this topic. The first findings are summarized in Cole and Scribner (1973). The team has recently dispersed and left Rockefeller.
3. The use of these syllogisms and the results are reported in Scribner (1977).
4. This observation is taken from a xeroxed paper David Lancy circulated at an African Studies convention. The paper was among my many papers lost on a voyage to Europe aboard the S. S. Stefan Batory in October 1977, thrown overboard as it appears. At the time of rewriting this article, 1978, Lancy, who worked in Liberia with the Cole-Scribner team, was in New Guinea. I regret the lack of reference.

5. We might argue, with Lévi-Strauss in mind, that the riddle is the primordial culture-nature transformer.

6. Compare Keith Basso (1976) and chapter 3.

7. For a discussion of these devices, see J. W. Fernandez (1966).

Bibliography

BASSO, KEITH

1976 "Wise Words of the Western Apache." In *Meaning in Anthropology*, edited by Keith Basso and Henry Selby, pp. 93–122. Albuquerque: University of New Mexico Press.

BRUNER, JEROME S.

1964 "The Course of Cognitive Growth." *American Psychologist* 19:1–15.

COLE, MICHAEL, AND SCRIBNER, SYLVIA.

1973 *Culture and Thought*. New York: John Wiley.

FERNANDEZ, JAMES W.

1966 "Unbelievably Subtle Words: Representation and Integration in the Sermons of an African Reformative Cult." *Journal of the History of Religions* 6:43–69.

GEERTZ, CLIFFORD

1973 *The Interpretation of Cultures; Select Essays*. New York: Basic Books.

JAKOBSON, ROMAN

1960 "Linguistics and Poetics." In *Style in Language*, edited by Thomas A. Sebeok, pp. 355–73. Cambridge: M. I. T. Press (Technology Press of M. I. T.).

KÖNGAS MARANDA, ELLIE

1971 "The Logic of Riddles." In *Structural Analysis of Oral Tradition*, edited by Ellie Köngas Maranda and Pierre Maranda, pp. 189–232. Philadelphia: University of Pennsylvania Press.

LÉVI-STRAUSS, CLAUDE

1966 *The Savage Mind*. Chicago: University of Chicago Press.

LÉVY-BRUHL, LUCIEN

1975 *The Notebooks on Primitive Mentality*. Translated by Peter Riviere. New York: Harper and Row.

SCRIBNER, SYLVIA

Forthcoming "Modes of Thinking and Ways of Speaking: Culture and Logic Reconsidered." In *Discourse Production and Comprehension*, edited by R. O. Freedle. Hillsdale, N.J.: Ablex.

SEGALL, MARSHALL H., CAMPBELL, DONALD T., AND HERSKOVITS, M. J.

1966 *The Influence of Culture on Visual Perception*. Indianapolis: Bobbs-Merrill.

VYGOTSKY, L.

1962 *Thought and Language*. Cambridge: M. I. T. Press.

8

THE EXPERIENCE OF RETURNING TO THE WHOLE

Culture . . . taken in its widest ethnographic
sense is that complex whole which includes
knowledge, belief, art, morals, law, custom,
and any other capabilities and habits acquired
by man as a member of society.
                E. B. Tylor, *Primitive Culture*

Metonym celebrates the parts of experience
while the more eloquent metaphors refer back
to the whole for significance.
C. Lévi–Strauss, *The Raw and the Cooked*

The essential problem for contemprary thought
is to discover the meaning of wholes.
        Louis Dumont, *Homo Hierarchicus*

A Room Full of Mirrors

In this chapter I should like to bring materials taken from work with
revitalization movements in Africa to bear upon this "essential problem
for contemporary thought"—the discovery of the meaning of wholes. This
is a contemporary problem because of the atomization and economic
individualization of modern life, because of our harried existences trying
to manage an overload of information and, as a consequence, the appeal of
lowest common denominators and utilitarian general-purpose currencies
that generalize shared experience at a very reduced and impoverished
level of reality. We are better understood, it has been said, as "dividuals,"
rather than "individuals," negotiating multiple and often incompatible
memberships in separate self-contained associations.[1] The ideological
promotion of our individuality, the defense of our freedom for self-actu-

alization, stands in compensatory contrast to the dividedness of our commitments.

All this makes us agnostic when any whole is suggested. The plenitude of any overarching entity is regarded as illusory—medieval—something achieved by Kabbalistic or Thomistic conceits that have little to do with our daily ongoing efforts at competent management and pragmatic adaptation to the succession of abruptly changing circumstances. It stands in contrast to the affliction, in Durkheimian terms, of our endless profanity.

If we are unable in our present particulate existence to believe in or be persuaded by the whole, we are yet prepared to recognize the possibilities of its achievement in other times and other cultures. Indeed there is an old orthodoxy in anthropology, Durkheimian in tone and argument, which sees this matter in evolutionary terms—which sees human consciousness and powers of mind as evolving from synthetic to analytic capacities—as evolving from an easy and dynamic access to mystical participation in the presence of collective representations to the present state of sedate individuation in the presence of predominantly personal symbols.

Ernst Cassirer is a recent thinker who articulated this orthodoxy most persuasively, and his views, as the founding philospher of symbolic forms, should be all the more interesting to a contemporary symbolic anthropology which is persuaded, like Cassirer, by the constitutive power of symbols. Cassirer, picking up on observations present in the work of Durkheim and, more polemically, in the work of Lévy-Bruhl, discusses the "consanguinity of all things" which prevails as the fundamental presupposition of mythical thought in the mythopoeic societies. "Life," he tells us, "is not divided into classes and subclasses. It is felt as an unbroken continuous whole which does not admit of clear-cut and trenchant distinctions. Limits between different spheres are not insurmountable barriers. They are fluent and fluctuating . . . by a sudden metamorphosis everything can be turned into everything. If there is any characteristic and outstanding feature of the mythical world, any law," he tells us, "it is this 'law of metamorphosis'."[2]

There is an ambiguity in Cassirer, as there often is in those who address themselves to this old orthodoxy, as to whether we are dealing with rule-bound thought whose laws we can discover or whether it is simply the play of emotion . . . a sympathetic process. "Myth and primitive religion," we are told, "are by no means entirely incoherent, they are not bereft of sense or reason." But their coherence depends much more upon unity of feeling than upon logical rules.[3] Cassirer, to be sure, does not want this ambiguity to lead to an identification of his ideas with those of Lévy-Bruhl. And, on the facing page of this argument, he gives instances of the powers of observation and discrimination, vis-à-vis the natural world, characteristic of primitive man. "All this is scarcely in keeping with the assumption that the primitive mind by its very nature and essences is undifferentiated or confused . . . a prelogical or mystical mind."[4] Cassirer, we all know, would have been much better served here by more explicit reference to the Durkheimian argument and particularly to the Durkheim and Mauss study, *Primitive Classification*.[5]

But we are not concerned here with the long debate over the discrimination of parts in the primal and archaic mind; Lévi-Strauss's discussion of the intellectual impulse in totemism has laid that issue pretty well to rest. We are concerned, rather, with the relatively easy access to the whole which is characteristic of that mind. What interests one here, to use Cassirer's terms, are the principles of consanguinity and metamorphosis which are essential to the access to the whole and which make it, in effect and by virtue of symbolic statement, greater than the sum of its parts. This is an interest, in brief, in the mechanisms which lead to the conviction of wholeness.

We should not pretend that the excess meaning of symbolic wholes has not been explored since Durkheim's day or that "consanguinity of thought" or metamorphosis have been since neglected. It is just this relation of consanguinity, understood in the broadest sense, to metamorphosis (or transformation) that Lévi-Strauss has recurrently explored. Still, seminal thought is not always fully clarified thought and Lévi-Strauss's discussion of what he calls the "totalizing savage mind" is often complex and difficult of decipherment. As an example, consider the "roomful of mirrors" he offers to us as an "aide pensée" in thinking about the knowledge of totality achieved by the "savage mind":

> The object [of savage thought] is to grasp the world as both a synchronic and diachronic totality, and the knowledge it draws therefrom is like that afforded of a room by mirrors fixed on opposite walls which reflect each other (as well as objects in the intervening spaces) although without being strictly parallel. A multitude of images forms simultaneously, none exactly like any other—none furnishing more than a partial knowledge—but the group is characterized by invariant properties expressing a truth.[6]

The truth expressed is that of the whole. But is is a very "complex whole" indeed . . . one that is expressed for Lévi-Strauss in an interreflecting congeries of "imagenes mundi" as he calls them—or, as I would like to call it, by an argument of images.[7]

Tuning In to the Music of Social Spheres: The Experience of Relatedness

Cassirer's phrase, "the consanguinity of things," reminds us that "the whole," whatever else it may be, is a state of relatedness—a kind of conviviality in experience. Societies so largely adversarial as the modern ones are, by nature, alienated from the possibilities of such overarching conviviality and neglect the fundamental problem of relatedness—which is, one might argue, the central problem of the whole. But revitalization movements of the kind we wish to consider here—and perhaps all religions—*are* fundamentally interested in restoring the relatedness of things.

It is frequently enough argued in the anthropological literature that our social animality, that is to say, our empathetic (or antipathetic) species preoccupations with matters of domination and subordination, inclusion and exclusion, sympathy or empathy—which is further to say, our preoccupation with the restricted codes of our solidarity in interaction—must be the points of departure for any study of any institution or more elaborated code. We fool ourselves, in this view, if we posit the construction of these institutions on utilitarian and material needs, on cupidity in the appropriation of surplus value, or on an aesthetic or idealistic drive. Fundamentally, in this view, what men and women are doing in life is taking expressive and rhetorical action against or in the service of these preoccupations. As Justice Douglas—in the Holmesian tradition—used to argue about the law, it is a magnificent edifice based, however, not upon the lofty search for truth but upon an endlessly fertile rationalization of some quite simple and self-interested predilections. Those who have, without mentioning Durkheim, fastened on matters of relatedness as elemental are many. Bateson has pointed up the existential preoccupations about relatedness in animals and human animals.[8] Cooley founded his sociology on the "face to face" situation.[9] For Malinowski the "context of situation," that is to say, prevailing solidarities and divisiveness, preceded and underlay communicative acts which, in important measure, evoked these situations even if they did not refer to them directly.[10] For Sartre "le regard"—looking at and being looked at—was the point de répere of all social life.[11] And for Shutz, whom we have mainly in mind here, it was the "mutual tuning-in relationship" that was antecedent to all communication.[12] And he was, incidentally, pessimistic about our ability to illuminate these inchoate matters. "All communication," he tells us, "presupposes the existence of some kind of social interaction [he means the mutual tuning-in relation] which though it is an indispensable condition of all possible communication does not enter the communicative process and is not capable of being grasped by it."[13] Schutz consequently turned to music—to the non-verbal—to understand this "tuning-in."

Schutz's view that these elemental matters of relatedness are not capable of being grasped by the communicative process requires some qualification, I believe: first, in respect to the way it may privilege the needs elemental to social interaction and second, in respect to the view of language implied. We remember, first, that Malinowski's attempt to identify basic needs and thus found basic and secondary social institutions upon them was effectively countered by Dorothy Lee[14] who showed how needs themselves were a reality subject to cultural shaping. (A recent work in the same vein is that of Sahlins who shows how the empirical world of individuals posited by utilitarians and materialists as a reality upon which to found institutions of production and exchange is itself a creation of bourgeois culture.[15]) We cannot privilege the preoccupation with relatedness from cultural shaping, though we cannot exclude it from the founding moments in our study of institutions either.

Of greater interest is the view of language implied in Schutz, for it points to, though it does not sufficiently describe, a view taken in this paper that a narrowly grammatical view of language is insufficient. In order to understand the tuning-in occurring in social situations, we have to go beyond what is manifestly contained in the language events themselves, for these will tell us only so much about the emotions of relatedness which underlie the communication and the images evoked by it. They will tell us only so much about the general knowledge—virtually encyclopedic knowledge, from the point of view of formal linguistic analysis—that accompanies ongoing interaction and which is essential to the meaning of the language situation. The ethnography of a social situation requires, as we now well recognize in anthropology, that we go much beyond the language information given. Giving primacy to the imagination, I would like to refer to this ongoing interaction as "the argument of images" that lies behind and accompanies behavior. Some of these images have their source in language but many of them do not. The relatively accessory nature of the grammatical system itself is well expressed by the linguist Einar Haugen:

> It is at least the experience of this writer that many ideas do come in extralinguistic form, as images, patterns, relationships, flashes of illumination. That they are extralinguistic does not mean that language is not involved . . . but most of the meanings we wish to convey are not conveyed by the grammar at all. If my shepherd comes running to tell me that a wolf has eaten my sheep, there are three basic facts to be conveyed and for these I need a common vocabulary: "wolf," "eat," "sheep." A statement NP (actor)— V (action)—NP_2 (goal) is merely an empty schema into which he can, if he has the time, fit the words. But he need only cry "wolf" . . . I therefore contend that the grammatical system as such has a minimal connection with any formulation of ideas whatever.[16]

We all recognize that in lexicon alone powerful images may repose and that the sincere cry of "wolf" or "fire" can have powerful tuning-in consequences. We teach our children accordingly. But we also assiduously—and often with an established sense of propriety—teach our children grammar. We might better teach them about the argument of images which lie behind and accompany such established things as grammar. And if we teach them grammar, it should be the grammar by which these images are conjoined and transformed. That is to say, to recall Cassirer, we should teach them about the consanguinity that can be seen to prevail among classifications and the metamorphosis in social life attendant upon the discovery of that consanguinity. For it is in that process that proprieties—that is, the sense of acceptable relatedness—are established.

How then are we to proceed in an academic paper of this kind when we must go—as anthropologists are required to do—so far beyond the information linguistically given? Schutz argued that the experience of the "we"—the foundation of all possible communication—could only emerge from extended mutual "tuning-in" together, of the primordial kind we get through long mutual involvement at the perceptual level—hearing, seeing, touching, tasting—in primary groups, families, ethnic groups, fraternal or sororal associations, etc. If we don't have these things to begin with, we have to somehow recreate them by an argument of images of some kind in which primary perceptions are evoked. Of course, in many academic papers (unlike this one—and mathematics is the best example, though this will occur with any discipline that employs meta-languages and has high-level theory) the virtually imageless manipulation of abstract concepts can be sufficient. But in most human situations, particularly when we are trying to demonstrate how wholes are constructed, we must in some way pictorialize our topic, visualizing as we can the context of situation of the several religious movements whose reconstructive play of tropes we wish to consider.* We are obliged to deepen our participation with the help of "imagenes mundi."

What I should now like to do is, at once, verbally visualize aspects of these religious movements which relate to the return to the whole and supplement this verbal visualization with slides in which we can, perceptually, directly inspect manifestations of some of the organizing images which are at play in ritual performance. The auditor/observer may wish to speculate on the way these two modes of communication convey information about the relation of parts to wholes, microcosms to macrocosms, inner things to outer things, centers to peripheries, upper things to lower things, time-present to time-past.

Picture if you will, good reader, a new community of largely wattle-and-daub thatched buildings set upon the semiarid plain and amid the dry forest of the southern Volta region of Ghana. This is New Tadzewu, a religious community of the Apostle's Revelation Society of Ghana. In the center of this community is the three-story Prophet's house containing on the first and second floors the school, meeting rooms, and the archives. Close by is a long, low shed containing the administrative headquarters. On the long porch is a row of blackboards containing the Prophet's most recent dreams and revelations. And in the very center of this community is the church, very like any village church of Western Europe. We see as we walk around this community several things. Its boundaries are well demarcated and it is subdivided into quarters named after the tribes of Israel. We also see that the officials of this religion are dressed in spotless white uniforms with red piping. In our walk we hear and we see many groups, particularly school classes, marching to and from within to drumbeats and bugle call. During a day's time these groups marching to and fro will have "knit together," as it were, the whole community. Members of this society see themselves most fundamentally as the tribes of Israel and as Christian soldiers—spiritual soldiers ever watchful for the appearance of the devilish apparitions without.

---

*One shouldn't ignore that there are differences among us. Some of us are visualizers more readily convinced when we are shown a picture. Others of us are verbalizers anxious to be given by formal processes of argument powerful concepts necessary and sufficient to the logic of our own theoretical vocabulary.

Next and moving east on the Guinea Coast to Togo and Dahomey, picture, if you please, a wide white sand beach under a brilliant sun and next to the dark blue sea. Here under a cluster of three palm trees is a group of members of Christianism Celeste in their resplendent white and gold uniforms, kneeling around a deep hole dug in the sand at the bottom of which a small trace of ocean water has seeped up. Close by are bottles of holy water and fruit which will be poured and placed in the hole as an offering. After this, the Bible will be read and prayers will be said. The hole will be filled in with the whitest sand and the members, then covering themselves with the whitest sheets will, lying on their backs, go to sleep around the hole. The divine force of the heavens which they worship and the sea and earth which they have just propitiated will now ebb and flow back and forth through them without disturbance and with purificatory and healing power. When we return to their sacred precincts behind raffia walls inland on the outskirts of Cotonou, we see other people lying out upon the ground on mats with a lighted candle burning at their heads and pineapples and other fruit around the candle. These Celestial Christians see themselves as conduits between sea, earth, and sky. They are healed and rendered whole when they experience themselves as pure and perfect conduits who do not in any idiosyncratic way impede the flow of these overarching and underarching forces in their endless circulation.

Next, let us picture the thick equatorial forest of Gabon, Western Equatorial Africa, and a long narrow village with two lines of huts facing each other. Some time ago the clearing was slashed out of the forest, which is starting once again to lean back over the village. At one end of the village, close by the forest, is the chapel of the Bwiti religion. At precisely 3:00 P.M., when the sun is still beating down on the dusty courtyard, a phalanx of the membership, in rows of three abreast, in a series of entrances, dances from far out on the peripheries of the courtyard into the center of the chapel. They are dressed in red and white flowing uniforms—white on the pure upper half of the body and red on the impure and passionate lower half. Men and women are dressed exactly alike, with two exceptions. The leader—The Parrot's Egg, The Great Hunter as he is called—of the chapel is dressed all in red, and the guardian of the chapel and the player of the harp are dressed all in white. The leader dressed in red—for it is he who takes away the sins of the members—dances on the left side of the phalanx, the female side. The guardian of the chapel dressed in white—for it is he who maintains the purity of the night— dances on the right side, the male side. This sidedness is repeated over and over again in the all-night ceremonies; there is a male side of the chapel and a female side, a men's secret chamber and a women's secret chamber. And a totality of worship can only be obtained by dancing on both sides of the chapel and by counterdancing men on the female side and women on the male side. We must also know that the chapel is visualized as a body, a sacred body which can only be brought into being—embodied as it were—by the totality of these entrance and exit dances. The exercise of the orifices of this microcosmic chapel, the interactive celebration of its parts, its sidedness, altogether creates the religious macrocosm.

We have to picture the vertical dimension as well as the two horizontal dimensions. This is seen in the red-barked adzap tree, the loftiest tree of the equatorial forest in a grove not far behind the chapel. This tree is the route of the ancestors, and they proceed to and from between the above and the below. This route and this tree are represented by the central pillar, a central pillar laden with symbolic meaning thick with sculpted representations whose full reading—a reading of all available associations—would lead out virtually to the Bwiti universe. During the night dances, members frequently touch this pillar for it keeps them in contact with the below and the above as their entrance dances and counterdances keep them in contact with the other two dimensions of their quality space. Exactly at midnight just outside the chapel the members gather in a long line, each holding a candle. Slowly, led by the cult harp, they dance in file out into the thick forest along precut paths. They are soon swallowed up and all we can see and hear is an occasional glimmer of a candle, a floating chord from the harp. Later they return and, proceeding just within the entrance and beside the central pillar, they begin fifty strong to wind a tighter circle until all members are pulled together and the candles held above their heads form one large dancing flame. This is *nlem mvore*, oneheartedness, one of their main images of the wholeness of their communion—an experience otherwise achieved by the dancers as they dance together into one whole village and forest, microcosm and macrocosm. Worship ends with a final circle just before the sun rises. And then members gather in a thatched pavilion in a state of high euphoria and conviviality for a morning meal of manioc.

Finally, let us move to the seaside savannah and the semiurban zones of Natal, Southeast Africa. This is Zululand although in the city, Durban, the Zulu have no permanent permission to reside. Yet on Sunday afternoon, gazing out upon the vacant spaces of that city, unbuilt upon or abandoned, we see countless small groups of Zionists set up their blue and white flags, whipping in the constant Indian Ocean breeze, beside dusty circles worn deep in the grass. The main spiritual force these Zionists seek to evoke is the Holy Spirit, Umoya Oyingwele, or Holy Wind, and they evoke it by running breathlessly for long periods around in these circles. If they are pure, they are eventually drawn into the center of the circle for final purification and incorporation with that powerful wind; but if they are impure, they are cast out of the circle into the peripheries often in a state of possession. They must be purified before they begin running in the circle again. Eventually with any luck they will return as in previous weeks to the center of the circle. The whole worship arena is an image of the Zulu kraal. Here, too, as in West Africa members periodically go to the beaches for baptism in the crashing surf of this active ocean. Far out into the ocean they go—every year some drown—for complete immersion. For the ocean is the home of the Holy Wind and those immersed in it become, like those drawn into the circle, at one with this holy agency. After the immersion the group gathers on the shore in the image of the Impi, the Zulu regiments of yore. Chanting and stomping on the beach in the pincers movement characteristic of the Impi, they surround the specially sick members of the congregation. They fix them at the center of this military encirclement so that the leader may lay his hands upon them—in the name of the community and with special power—the powers of the multitude of purified eyes focused upon the afflicted one in the shadows.

The Mix of Elementary Postulates

The elementary thought, *elementargedanken,* notion despite some feeling that it, like the notion of mystical participation, is nineteenth century in locus persists in various forms in the anthropological literature whether as themes (that is to say, "underlying dynamic affirmations") or as "motifs," the basic units of folklore, or as "basic premises," "cultural axioms," or "existential postulates." In a more formal vein with both Lévi-Strauss "mythemes" and folklore models in mind, Dundes advances the "motifeme" as the basic unit. Subsequently and more relaxedly, he refers to folk ideas—such things as the idea of linearity, the idea of circularity,

the idea (Dundes prefers that to image) of limited good—as the basic units
or building blocks of worldview.[17] And most recently Witherspoon has
argued in connection with his study of the Navaho universe that "all
cultures are constructed from and based upon a single metaphysical
premise which is axiomatic, unexplainable, and unprovable."[18]

Such elementary postulations are characteristically out of reach to
ethnographic interview, but I would argue further that the search for
elementargedanken, if not misplaced concreteness, inadequately assesses
the experience of coherence and wholeness, which is an experience both
horizontal and hierarchical, peripheral and central, interior and exte-
rior—an experience of affinity and consanguinity, as it were. At the least
this kind of inquiry assigns to deep thought processes—or those thought
processes having to do with relatedness—an ideational explicitness and
clarity they do not possess. Participants may be within the reach of such
ideas but not their grasp. Such things are inchoate. From the anthropological perspective, the search for elementary ideas risks being a schoolmasterish kind of inquiry if it presumes that such formulations are causal
or controlling. In fact, they are emergent and consequent to a stimulating
thickness in experience—to primordial forms of postulating and participation in which by subsequent abstraction supposed elementary ideas can
be discovered to be embedded—but mostly by men of thought. The men
of action in the revitalization movements with which I worked under the
pressure of my inquiry or the problematics of their situation resurrected
from the depths of their experience prototypical images persuasive to
their well-being or apt for satisfying performance. Of course, the search
for *elementargedanken* is understandable because the primary problem if
we are to understand any kind of formal or structural study is to "find
operational units which can be manipulated and on which logical operations can be performed."[19] Since most well-schooled individuals in the
modern world are intensively taught to perform operations on things—to
be competent, that is—it is understandable that we are driven to search
for elementary ideas. But as Durkheim has shown, it is arguable, and
particularly if we are concerned as we are here with experience, that ideas
are always emergent. We squeeze them out of embeddedness—out of
participation—out of a relatedness of men and women. They do not have
experientially the primacy we seek to give them. To make a much longer
argument short,[20] because we have other purposes here, the elementary
forms in my view are, in experiential terms, first the personal pronouns
which point at the unities of our experience, and second the sign-images

(metaphors and other tropes) that are predicated upon them in order to give them actionable identity. These predications in their variety are the elementary postulates which formulate and stimulate experience.

In respect to the religious movements we have been looking at it is easy to recognize certain recurrent tropes—mostly metaphors but sometimes metonyms—which, since tropes are not only asserted they can be performed, satisfyingly organize considerable activity in the particular religious community. Here are the particular predications and the performative consequences:

Metaphoric Predications	*Performative Consequences*
For the Apostle's Revelation Society:	
We are the tribes of Israel.	Each group by manifesting its particularity shows that it is part of a whole chosen people.
We are Christian soldiers.	By marching to and fro we militate against devilish forces without and devilish disorder within.
For Christianism Celeste:	
We are the conduits between sea, earth and sky.	By living purely and in tranquility we will not disturb the forces which flow through us.
For Equatorial Bwiti:	
We are people of the forest threshold.	By gathering the forest around us and by ceremonially making our way out into the forest we can be reborn.
We are lost hunters of the forest.	
We are one heart.	We separated individuals can recapture our family identity.
For Zulu Zionism:	
I am the bull who crashes in the kraal. We are the regiments of the holy wind. We are the cattle of the Lord.	By moving faster and faster in tighter and tighter circles we can recapture our inner purity and the security of supernatural tutelage.

Earlier on in my thinking about the place of tropes in religious revitalization, I tended like Witherspoon—though I was specifically influenced by Stephen Pepper's *World Hypothesis*[21]—to argue for ultimate organizing metaphors. It will be remembered that in Pepper's view there are four basic philosophical worldviews each of which has one underlying hypothesis or metaphor which it is working out: these are the metaphors of "formism," "organicism," "mechanism," and "contextualism." Pepper argued for the instability, dynamism, and eventual collapse of any system that mixed metaphors.[22] More recently I have re-examined that presupposition and the search it implied as being overly philosophic in inspiration. The underlying unity found in religious culture cannot satisfactorily be expressed in any one metaphor. Religious movements, if not any act of cultural revitalization and returning to the whole, always mix metaphors and it is the dynamic interplay of these metaphors that is most interesting and consequential and which gives the impression of coherence—of the return to the whole. We turn now to this play of tropes—this grammar if by grammar we mean a series of predications upon pronouns whose constituents are in both syntagmatic and paradigmatic relation.

The Play of Tropes

In considering how metaphors are mixed in revitalization or, better yet, how tropes are mixed because metonymy is present, as well as on occasion irony, we begin to make music. Or at least we begin to see the music in our subject. And it is complex polyphonic music, the score of which can be difficult to follow in public presentation if one is not used to sight-reading this kind of music. Here also we are moving from simply "tuning in"—referring back to Schutz's use of the musical metaphor to get at the fundamentals of relatedness—to something more symphonic: the symbolic symphony, if you will, which returns to the whole.

Now there are as many kinds of polyphonic compositions as there are varieties in the play of tropes. Lévi-Strauss in the *Mythologiques* develops the possibilities of this variety with characteristic verve and resourcefulness as he begins *The Raw and the Cooked*[23] with an overture and conducts the reader through Arias, Recitatives, Variations, Interludes, and the Coda of Bororo Song, presents a "Good Manners Sonata," a "Caitatu Rondo," a "Fugue of the Five Senses," an "Oppossum Cantata," "Well-Tempered Astronomy," "Toccata and Fugue of the Pleiades and the Rainbow," and finally a "Rustic Symphony in Three Movements including a Bird Chorus"—a symbolic symphony indeed.

But here we are not interested in such variety or in such adventurous use of the musical metaphor but rather in the usefulness of music and more specifically orchestral performance as a metaphor for ritual sequence and the conviction of totality.[24] In its way this is profoundly a structural question but let me alert the reader to two differences of approach. First, while most structural analyses regard myth or ritual as being generated primarily to solve a culture's problematic and unwelcome contradictions of a cognitive, sociological, or technological kind—it is a method intent on setting up and solving such contradictions—we will regard them, or at least we will regard our revitalization rituals, as having two intentions: first, the intention to give definition to the inchoate, and second, the intention to return to the whole. More than this, we have a different sense of how the permutational dynamics of expressive statements are to be understood. This difference arises out of narrative-oriented analysis, on the one hand, in which the syntax of the narrative looms large—the structuralist method has been primarily interested in myths or other narrative texts—and a domain-oriented analysis, on the other, in which paradigmatic shifts in domain of interest are primary and, in the end, taken to be (experienced as) wholly convincing.

The "sight reading" for this subject rests on the very old but so often not well understood distinction (it is basic, in my view, to any anthropology) between associative relations of contiguity and associative relations of similarity. This is essentially the Frazerian distinction between contagious and sympathetic magic, that mix of manipulations that together move the whole realm of the unseen. And it is essentially what is involved in the distinction between consanguinal and affinal relations, that mix of relations that together constitute the whole kinship system. Pertinent phrasings are those of Jakobson and De Saussure. Jakobson clarifies for us the way that metaphor is an assertion of an association based on similarity of relations, and metonymy an assertion based on contiguity of relation.[25] De Saussure means much the same thing in distinguishing between paradigmatic and syntagmatic relations in language communication,[26] though the language-oriented understanding of similarity-contiguity relations to some degree inhibits our understanding as far as ritual sequences are concerned, which are arguments of images and not fully syntactical arguments in the linguistic sense.

In music the same distinction is afoot in the contrast between harmony and melody. Melody is the sequential contiguity of notes while harmony is the paradigmatic association of different instruments or voices playing with their respective pitchs and registers. In symphonic music we are familiar with different instruments, while they may have been all along in background accompaniment, being brought into focus as the melody progresses and even with shifts in key to suit these instruments. This is, although in musical terms, similar to what happens in similarity-contiguity relations. We can choose or are forced to see what is contiguous in our ongoing experience from another perspective, in other terms, in another key. A contiguous or syntagmatic sequence can be by paradigmatic permutation transformed into another mode of expression and vice versa. This metamorphosis, this transformative interaction, of syntax and paradigm, metaphor and metonym, is fundamentally what is at play as parts are related to wholes, universalizations to particularizations—and it is in sum wholly convincing.

It may be useful to remind ourselves of the Lévi-Straussian analysis of these matters.[27] It addresses itself to sequential and paradigmatic arrangements of myths—a narrative-oriented analysis. The method takes the contiguous narrative and first breaks it up into a sequence of episodes. These episodes are then arranged in such a way—into a paradigm—so as to reveal the unwelcome contradictions being wrestled with and the transformation of these contradictions being effected. This is the paradigmatic permutation that underlies the myth.[28]

The particular approach I would take to the symphonic play of associations assumes that the nether regions of the mind, whatever structures it may have for organizing subsequent expression, are a repository of images of former socio-historical experiences actively lived through or vividly described. Such an approach contrasts with the usual structural approach in which the nether regions are "always empty" or at least "alien to mental images"[29]—merely there to impose structural laws upon inarticulated elements which originate elsewhere. These images in their nether repository carry positive or negative signs according as the experiences associated with them were positive or negative, gratifying or deceiving, and they can be brought forward and predicated upon the subjects of religious experience and become the basis of ritual performance. We have attempted to see pictorialized here some of these enacted images: the

---

*Lévi-Strauss produced a quasi-, or perhaps only pseudo-, algebraic formula to describe it involving Proppian functions.[27] It has subsequently been an algebraic bone of contention, to say the least. The Marandas offer an interpretation—really a considerable reinterpretation—which involves a mediating personage or type who brings about a transformation in the revealed contradiction.[28] Crumrine and Macklin have applied the Maranda interpretation to Mexican folk religious narratives and, in their paradigmatic rearrangement, discover the unwelcome contradiction to be that of death in the midst of life. Of relevance to our interest here in revitalization is the transformation wrought by a prophetic mediator who sacrifices his vitality to restore life to society.[29]

image of the Zulu kraal or the Zulu impi, the image of the threshold tree of the Fang religious forest, the image of the tribes of Israel in organically harmonious production, the image of Christian soldiers, the image of religious men and women mediating, interceding, between earth, sky, and water All these images in either autochthonous or creatively synthetized and synchronized form are brought forward and, as ritual metaphors or metonyms, made the basis of ritual performance. Practically any of these revitalization rituals will be seen to be acting out a number of these images at various levels of attention.[30]

The consequences of the production and, often, the acting out of these images is cosmological, that is to say, it returns to the whole in at least three ways: by iteration, by the discovery of replication, and by the creation of novel semantic categories of wide classification. And here it is important to keep in mind that this is a domain-oriented approach. For each of these images derives from or is a pictorialization of a domain of experience—the domain of forest life, the domain of domestic life, of military affairs, of supernatural relations. Acting out these images restores vitality if only in expressive form to that domain of activity—a domain which has fallen into disrepute or questionable participation because of such transitional afflictions associated with revitalization movements as status deprivation, material exploitation, cultural deprecation, etc. The performance of these images revitalizes a domain of experience and participation. The performance of a sequence of images revitalizes, in effect and by simple iteration, a universe of domains, an acceptable cosmology of participation, a compelling whole.

To understand the second sense in which the acting out of these images is cosmological, we have to understand something more about the way in which images are associated analogically and the concept formation that goes on in this association. And here we return, as well, to the interplay of melody and harmony, which is to say the interplay of similarity and contiguity. Sometimes the association of images in ritual performance is that of continuous analogy: A:B::B:C::C:D, etc.—men are to trees as trees are to the forest as forest is to the world. But more often what we find is the production of a sequence of domains of performance by discontinuous analogy: A:B::C:D. Here the relational structure—the contiguities—existing in one domain of experience suggests by analogy the relational structure existing in another domain of experience: man's relation to his clan is as the tree's relation to the forest; or the heart is to the body as the center of the circle is to the circle, as the cattle kraal is to the Zulu homestead. In the play of discontinous analogies in ritual, what occurs is that in the performing of the contiguous experiences of one domain a sense of resonance or relation by analogy arises with some part or related parts of the contiguous structures of another domain. This produces first a shift from one domain of performance to another and second a sense of the coherence between domains—coherence by reason of analogous relational structures. In brief, the Order of Things in one domain comes to be perceived as somehow similar to the Order of Things in another. We use the expression "order of things" to remind us of Foucault's book by the same name[31]—his historical archaeology in which he demonstrates at successive levels of historical time similar synchronic structures of ordering—epistemes—in the varous domains of culture. It is the falling apart of these relational structures of ordering—these "structural replications"[32] in different domains—that produces the epistemological crisis which is one of the chief motives for attempts at revitalization by returning to the whole.

The third way the play of tropes returns us to the whole is through the "commanding image," as Herbert Read calls it[33] or the novel superordinate semantic category, as Basso calls it.[34] This commanding category is brought about by metaphoric predication of images upon the inchoate subjects of our interest—such predications as we have been speaking about. Metaphor, as we know, is the statement of an association between things that are normally categorized in separate domains of experience. This association cannot be based on designative or literal defining features but rather on figurative or connotative features which the two things have in common. Connotatively there is something elephant-like about Frank and something Frank-like about an elephant—they are both ponderous, deliberate, and unforgiving—although literally they belong in different domains. But when we make these associations on ostensibly connotative grounds we also create, as Basso has shown,[35] a superordinate semantic category to which both the animal, elephant, and the human, Frank, belong. This is a category characterized by the designative features living being, warm-blooded earth dweller, etc.

One way—it is not the only way—to show the creation by metaphoric predication of a superordinate semantic category is by reference to a lexical hierarchy, or semantic tree (Fig. 1), where the referents of, to take the leader of one of our movements, prophet and parrot, become members of the same domain at a very superordinate node of the hierarchy. The concept formed by metaphoric predication is always more inclusive

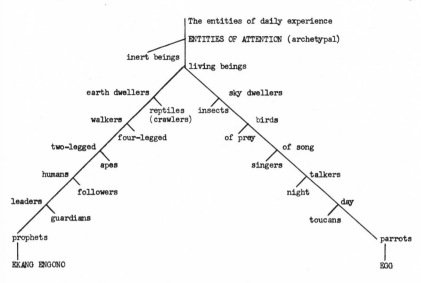

FIG. 1.   The Prophet as Parrot's Egg (Bwiti Religion)

than either of the categories involved in the predication. Metaphoric
predication produces exceptionally wide classification and "symbolically
coerces into a unitary conceptual framework"[36] that whose designation
was previously quite separated in our experience. The experience is of the
collapse of separation into relatedness. It is, as it is called, the "shock of
recognizing" a wider integrity of things. It is the recognition of a greater
whole. Metaphoric predication, this central form of the argument of
images, thus in its very nature impels a return to the whole—or at least
some whole significantly greater than the parts, elephants and hominids,
parrots and prophets, which enter into the predication.

I would like to emphasize again that this wider classification is emergent and not underlying in any behavioral sense. What we have from the
behavioral view is the experience of the separation (or at least the variety)
of domains into which we have classified experience and, at once, certain
similarities connotatively speaking, that exist between the members of
separated domains. There is a state of tension in our experience. Because
of the inadequacies of literal language—its constricted view of experience
and the lexical gaps characteristic of it—we turn to metaphoric predication. The shock of recognition arises because, in making these predications, we suddenly become aware of a wider classification of things which
was heretofore only implicit—embedded in experience. Particularly in
times of stress—where literal routines break down and where we are

constrained by false or moribund categories—do we turn to figurative language and the argument of images for a wider and more transcendent view of things. These are the times with which ritual and revitalization are most associated. It is important to recognize how the play of tropes and the metaphoric language characteristic of these times of stress by their very nature return us to the whole.

To take up our musical metaphor again, the shift from domain to domain is like the shift from instrument to instrument in orchestral performance, each in their domain following the basic melody—the overall order of things in that culture—but each adding the different properties, the complementary qualities of their domain of expression. No instrument and no domain can "make music" alone but performing together they create a vital—or revitalized—cosmological harmony out of iteration, replication, and wide classification.

Simple and Complex Wholes

We have been speaking about the conviction of wholeness obtained by the play of tropes—obtained, that is to say, by a complex transformative system of figurative predications upon inchoate entities. The overall effect of these predications is to give these entities a plentitude of experience they could not otherwise achieve. We have been speaking, in short, about a "complex whole" or, at least, a whole complexly achieved. We may wish to contrast this whole with the simple whole of the "communitas" experience discussed by Turner in his elaboration of the "liminality" phase of the rites of passage.[37] Communitas, we remember, in Turner's illuminating discussion is that "irrefragable genuineness of mutality,"[38] that undifferentiated experience of communion, equality, poverty, openness to the other; that recognition of the "essential and generic human bond" that periodically occurs as an anti-structural reaction to the hierarchical, differentiated and invidious relations of the structured everyday world. Turner contrasts the simplicity of communitas with the complexity of the status system[39] in the structured world of everyday life. Communitas is an experience spontaneous and elementally existential.

However the final experiences of wholeness are to be compared, and Turner only in passing considers the "wholeness" in communitas,[40] in this paper we have regarded the experience not as spontaneous or as instant and oceanic but as more elaborately achieved in an argument of images.

In such an argument, we have a productive tension between differentiated domains on the one hand and their collapse into wide classification on the other. It may very well be that there are two kinds of wholes to which we return—simple and complex. Or it may be that Turner is approaching the communitas experience at a different point of its appearance. Or it may be that the communitas argument in dichotomizing the structure from the anti-structure experience makes apparently spontaneous and not sufficiently emergent what is processually achieved in experience by complex argument.[41] Indeed, at several points in his discussion Turner recognizes the terms in which the argument for communitas must be cast—that is to say, in an argument of images. This is true of his own argument about communitas:

> Along with others who have considered the conception of communitas, I find myself forced to have recourse to metaphor and analogy.[42]

And it is true of the great figures such as St. Francis of Assisi who have argued for communitas to their followers:

> Francis is like many other founders of communitas-like groups . . . his thought was always immediate, personal and concrete. Ideas appeared to him as images. A sequence of thought for him . . . consists of leaping from one picture to the next.[43]

Indeed, Turner resists any notion that communitas is merely instinctual. It involves consciousness and volition. It is, he says, quoting Blake, "an intellectual thing."[44] Insofar as this is true, communitas is to be understood as a complex whole. In any event the "intellectual thing" in the return to the whole is what we have been seeking to illuminate here.

Symbolic Strategies

> Wholeness, holiness and adaptiveness are closely related if not, indeed, one and the same thing.
>
> Roy Rappaport, *Sanctity, Lies and Evolution*

Until recently the very phrase *symbolic strategies* would have seemed a contradiction in terms, for symbolic matters were seen as mainly expressive and adjustive—epiphenomenal. But this has changed. The presence of symbolic constraints has been shown for common sense[45] and practical reason.[46] The neo-Marxists in their effort to give us a more adequate grasp of the superstructure/infrastructure interaction deprecate the old "vulgar materialism"[47] with its exclusion of the symbolic and make common cause with the neo-structuralists[48] who arise out of the most symbolic of traditions. Even in such a preserve of positivism as medicine the importance of the placebo effect—symbolic healing, surely—is being re-emphasized.[49]

When we think of symbolic strategies, we must often think of the use of symbols to manipulate persons and groups and most often for deceitful self-serving purposes. We are surrounded by an advertising that seeks to symbolically associate questionable products, whether cigarettes or oversized cars, with desirable milieus of activity or belonging. And we have lived through catastrophic periods of history in which torchlit stadiums and Wagnerian symbolism were used to animate a sophisticated people to primitive deeds. In a later period in our own country authentic symbols of the frontier were used to animate a far-off and irrelevant war. We are aware of flag-waving and pseudo-patriotism of all kinds in which symbols are used to dominate and deceive.

But what about the ritual complex of symbols—these symbolic symphonies we have been talking about? Rappaport's *Pigs for the Ancestors* and subsequent studies influenced by it have been revelatory here in tying ritual activity directly into systems maintenance. Flow charts[50] drawn up on the basis of Rappaport's data integrate symbolic representations and ritual activities into the ecological model where they play their important part in preventing the Tsembaga system from passing beyond thresholds of carrying capacity and into a consequent production-population collapse. Thus there is a whole set of activities involved in or generated by ritual which are adaptive for that society in its milieu—strategic in the most crucial sense.

But it is not really this action or systems adjustment aspect of ritual that we have been concerned with here. Rather it has been the cosmological aspect—the reconstruction, or at least the intimation—of wholes accomplished by our symbolic symphonies. Could this reconstruction be strategic as well—or at least strategic in the adaptive sense? Our epigraph quote from Rappaport would imply that it is and that, in fact, wholeness and adaptation are in significant relation.

In the separated (though really mutually nurturant) cells of our modern organic (to use the Durkheimian metaphor) forms of solidarity, the individual reality looms very large and the study of strategy tends to be the study of "the manipulative ploys of individuals" rationally elaborating stratagems and enjoying spoils.[51] And such an approach is even more persuasive for anyone imbued with a market mentality. Returning to the whole seems, as we have said, somehow beyond our reach, something that pertains to societies characterized by mechanical forms of solidarity, by strong feelings of consanguinity and affinity, and by real possibilities of mystical participation. And this would appear to be so. At the same time it is we moderns who feel ourselves faced with the "tragedy of the commons" and who argue for holistic healing and for the "whole earth." And there are those who despair that analytic reason alone is sufficient to temper the ambitions of separated men so that they may subordinate themselves to such common interests. And those who are impressed with the reality of common interests tend to find just as illusory the self-sufficiency and autonomy ascribed to our individuality. Rappaport, whose touchstone is adaptation and consequently survival, is one who is impressed by these issues. He argues that the "ultimate corrective operation inheres in systems as wholes" and that, in effect, the ultimate strategy may be that of returning to the whole:

> Although humans are metabolically separate from one another, and although consciousness is individual, humans are not self-sufficient and their autonomy is relative and slight. They are parts of larger systems upon which their continued existence is contingent. But the wholeness, if not indeed the very existence, of those systems may be beyond the grasp of their ordinary consciousness. Although conscious reason is incomplete, the mode of understanding encouraged by liturgy may make up for some of its deficiencies. Participation in rituals may enlarge the awareness of those participating in them, providing them with understandings of perfectly natural aspects of the social and physical world that may elude unaided reason.[52]

When we read a passage like this, we may be inclined to take it as religious statement. And inasmuch as Rappaport began his field research nominalistically in counting the flow of kilo-calories, there has been a tendency to see signs of a conversion here. But in what way, really, is Rappaport's system allegiance any different from the system allegiance of those of us who, say, study symbolism as a cultural system? Is the cultural system we affirm more graspable to ordinary consciousness—more accessible to unaided reason—than the system which Rappaport affirms? Perhaps it is, and certainly in this paper we have been trying to give a graspable account of the mechanisms by which revitalization movements return to the whole. But it may well be that we have only succeeded in giving a partial account—have only pointed at the whole but have not really grasped the nature of it, not to speak of the experience of it. And it may be that the whole is never fully graspable. It is *there,* implied in our symbolic activity. But it is inchoate. So that when we say "cultural system," we are making a symbolic and not a scientific statement.

In any event allegiance to system is a characteristic of almost all anthropology and most of social science. Our discipline began, after all, as our first epigraph indicates, with the affirmation of a "complex whole" to whose study we were dedicated. Of course, there have been periods of seeing culture as a thing of shreds and patches—periods of concentrating on isolated traits and their diffusion. But the overall strategy of most anthropology is to take the students' too individuated awareness and demonstrate system to him—in some sense to return him or her to the whole. And this is often to revitalize him.

With that concept in mind, we should re-emphasize finally that the play of tropes we have been speaking about here are those of "revitalization movements"—movements which have a special and more open opportunity for creative ritualization, for a relatively unfettered argument and performance of images than is characteristic of most human situations, committed as they are to well-worn routines and the inertia of institutions. These movements are strategic in a special sense. Anthony Wallace, who coined the phrase and identified the phenomena, clearly puts their strategy in terms of system allegiance:

> A revitalization movement is defined as a deliberate, organized, conscious effort by members of a society to construct a more satisfying culture. Revitalization is thus, from a cultural standpoint, a special kind of culture change phenomenon: the persons involved in the process of revitalization must perceive their culture, or some major areas of it, as a system (whether accurately or not); they must feel that this cultural system is unsatisfactory; and they must innovate not merely discrete items but a new cultural system, specifying new relationships as well as, in some cases, new traits.[53]

Also it must be clear that these movements arise from, and their strategies derive from, deeper prototypical levels of awareness than is characteristic of the daily routine and the everyday life we know in the space-time object world out there—the mastered world, that is, to which strategic understandings normally apply. Revitalization movements are responses to the hyper- and hypo-arousal associated with the collapse of accustomed masteries and the frustration of received strategies once applicable within and between the various domains of that object world. In such situations of epistemological crisis dreams, visions, and deathlike excursions occupy an incipient and central part as they rise from the depths of experience with old or newly rehabilitated images with which to reclassify and reintegrate a world in which the pronouns can once again confidently move with the fullest sense of the consanguinities of their context and with the fullest sense of their powers of transformation into something more—something more whole—than they are.

Our argument here has been that in these, during masterful times, forgotten depths of our experience there is always a plenitude of entities which we can retrieve and with which we can construct an imaginatively integrated set of scenarios for satisfying performance. Such retrieval and such construction is the ultimate and recurrent strategy of the human experience. It is the experience of returning to the depths—that room full of mirrors in which we can see ourselves—in order to return to the whole.

Notes

This is a revised version of a paper given at the Anthropology section of the New York Academy of Sciences on May 19, 1980, and entitled "Symbolic Symphonics and Symbolic Strategies: The Reconstructive Play of Tropes in Culture Revitalization."

Acknowledgments: I have profited from comments made on this paper in the several places I have delivered it: at the New York Academy, at Princeton, at the University of Rochester and at Indiana. I would thank particularly Warren d'Azevedo, Charles and Bonnie Bird, Hildred Geertz, William Green, Grace Harris, Michael Herzfeld, Ivan Karp, James Spencer, and Aram Yengoyan.

1. This distinction has been made for a much different culture however. See McKim Marriot and Ronald B. Inden, "Caste Systems," *Encyclopaedia Britannica, Macropaedia* (1974) 3.1966, pp. 441–47.

2. Ernst Cassirer, *An Essay on Man* (New York: Doubleday Anchor, 1944/1960), p. 108.

3. Ibid., p. 108.

4. Ibid., p. 109.

5. E. Durkheim and M. Mauss, *Primitive Classification* (Chicago, 1963).

6. C. Lévi-Strauss, *The Savage Mind* (Chicago: University of Chicago Press, 1966), p. 263.

7. J. W. Fernandez, "African Religious Movements," in *Annual Reviews in Anthropology* (1978):195–234 and also in *The Dark at the Bottom of the Stairs* (A Hoijer Lecture for 1980. UCLA, May 1, 1980).

8. G. Bateson, "Problems in Cetacean and Other Mammalian Communication," in *Steps Towards an Ecology of Mind* (New York: Ballantine, 1972), pp. 364–78.

9. C. H. Cooley, *Social Organization* (New York, 1909).

10. B. Malinowski, "The Problem of Meaning in Primitive Languages," in *The Meaning of Meaning* by C. K. Ogden and I. A. Richards (London: International Library, 1923), pp. 451–510.

11. J. P. Sartre, *Search for a Method* (New York, 1963).

12. A. Schutz, "Making Music Together: A Study in Social Relationship, *Social Research*, vol. 18, no. 1 (1951), pp. 76–97.

13. Ibid., p. 84.

14. D. Lee, "Are Basic Needs Ultimate," *Journal of Abnormal and Social Psychology*, vol. 43 (1948), pp. 391–95.

15. M. Sahlins, *Culture and Practical Reason* (Chicago: University of Chicago Press, 1976).

16. E. Haugen, *Linguistic Relatively: Myths and Methods* Paper no. 1871, Ninth International Congress of Anthropological and Ethnological Sciences, Chicago, August, 1973, p. 11.

17. A. Dundes, "Folk Ideas as Units of Worldview," *Journal of American Folklore* 84:93–103.

18. G. Witherspoon, *Language and Art in the Navaho Universe* (Ann Arbor: University of Michigan Press, 1977), p. 5.

19. See Chapter 7.

20. This theory is laid out more fully in Chapter 2.

21. S. Pepper, *World Hypothesis* (Berkeley: University of California Press, 1942).

22. Ibid., p. 107.

23. C. Lévi-Strauss, *The Raw and the Cooked* (New York: Harper, 1969).

24. The usefulness of this metaphor is pointed up in E. Leach, *Culture and Communication* (New York: Cambridge University Press, 1976), chap. 9.

25. T. Jakobson, "Two Aspects of Language and Two types of Aphasic Disturbances," in *Fundamentals of Language* (The Hague: Mouton, 1956).

26. F. de Saussure, *Course in General Linguistics* (New York: McGraw Hill, 1966).

27. C. Lévi-Strauss, "The Structural Study of Myth," in *Journal of American Folklore* 78:428–44.

28. P. and E. K. Maranda, *Structural Models in Folklore and Transformational Essays* (The Hague: Mouton, 1971).

29. R. Crumrine and B. J. Macklin, Sacred Ritual versus the Unconscious: "The Efficacy of Symbols and Structure in North Mexican Folk Saint's Cults," in *The Unconscious in Culture*, ed. Ino Rossi (New York: Dutton, 1974), pp. 179–97.

30. I have pictured the acting out of these images in "The Performance of Ritual Metaphors" in *The Social Use of Metaphor*, eds. J. D. Sapir and C. Crocker (Philadelphia: University of Pennsylvania Press, 1977), pp. 100–131.

31. M. Foucault, *The Order of Things: An Archaeology of the Human Sciences* (New York: Pantheon, 1970).

32. See E. Vogt, "Structural and Conceptual Replications in Zinacantan Culture," *American Anthropologist* 67 (1965):342–53.

33. H. Read, *English Prose Style* (London: G. Bell and Sons, 1951).

34. K. Basso, "Wise Words of the Western Apache," in *Meaning in An-*

thropology, eds. K. Basso and H. Selby (Albuquerque: University of New Mexico Press, 1976), pp. 93–121.

35. Ibid., pp. 98–111.

36. Ibid., p. 103.

37. V. Turner, "Liminality and Communitas," in *The Ritual Process* (Chicago: Aldine, 1969), chap. 3.

38. Ibid., p. 137.

39. Ibid., p. 107.

40. Ibid., p. 127. "For communitas has an existential quality; it involves the whole man in his relation to other whole men."

41. In this regard see also the observations of T. Turner in an article addressing the problem of hierarchical and transcendent transformations. "Transformation, Hierarchy and Transcendence: A Reformation of Van Gennep's Model of the Structure of Rites of Passage," in *Secular Ritual*, eds. S. F. Moore and B. Myerhoff (Amsterdam: Van Gorcum), pp. 53–70. Particularly relevant is footnote 6— "I use V. Turner's term 'anti-structure' in quotation marks because the basic interpretation of liminal rites put forward in this paper is that they are an integral part of *processes of structuring*, and as such are no less 'structural' than the lower-level classificatory structures of relations they mediate. The notion of 'anti-structure' conceived as a level of being alien to 'structure' and set over against it as it were in binary opposition, has no foundation in the model presented here, and appears to stem rather from an equation of the notion of 'structure' with what I have called the *lower levels* of structure, i.e., static classificatory matrices of relations."

42. Op. cit., p. 127.

43. Op. cit., p. 141.

44. Op. cit., p. 188.

45. C. Geertz, "Common Sense as a Cultural System," *Antioch Review* 33:5– 26.

46. M. Sahlins, op. cit.

47. J. Friedman, "Marxism, Structuralism and Vulgar Materialism," *Man* 93:444–69.

48. K. Hastrup, "The Post-Structuralist Position of Social Anthropology," *The Yearbook of Symbolic Anthropology*, ed. E. Schwimmer (London, 1978), pp. 123– 48.

49. D. Moerman, "Anthropology of Symbolic Healing," *Current Anthropology*, vol. 20, no. 1 (1979).

50. S. B. Shantzi and W. W. Berens, "Population Control Mechanisms in a Primitive Agricultural Society," in *Toward Global Equilibrium*, ed. D. D. Meadows (Cambridge: Wright Allen, 1973), pp. 257–83.

51. F. G. Bailey, *Stratagems and Spoils: A Social Anthropology of Politics* (Oxford, 1969).

52. R. Rappaport, "Sanctity and Lies in Evolution," in *Ecology, Meaning and Religion* (Richmond: North Atlantic Books, 1979), pp. 236–37.

53. A. F. C. Wallace, "Revitalization Movements," *American Anthropologist* 63 (1956):264–81, p. 265.

9

THE DARK AT THE BOTTOM OF THE STAIRS

THE INCHOATE IN SYMBOLIC INQUIRY AND SOME STRATEGIES FOR COPING WITH IT

Wish I was a Kellogg's Cornflake
Floatin' in my bowl takin' movies,
Relaxin' awhile, livin' in style,
Talkin' to a raisin who 'casionn'ly plays L.A.,
Casually glancing at his toupee.
Wish I was an English muffin
'Bout to make the most out of a toaster.
I'd ease myself down,
Comin' up brown.
I prefer boysenberry
More than any ordinary jam.
I'm a "Citizens for Boysenberry Jam" fan.
Ah, South California.
If I become a first lieutenant
Would you put my photo on your piano?
To Maryjane—
Best wishes, Martin.
(Old Roger draft-dodger
Leavin' by the basement door),
Everybody knows what he's
Tippy-toeing down there for.

Simon & Garfunkel,
"Punky's Dilemma"

But underground nothing ran straight.
All the tunnels curved, split, rejoined,
branched, interlaced, looped, traced
elaborate routes that ended where they
began for there was no beginning and
no end, for there was nowhere to get
to. There was no center, no heart to
the maze.

Ursula Kroeber LeGuin,
The Tombs of Atuan

I hope the reader will forgive me the abundance of epigraphs[1]—perhaps a surfeit—that accompany my argument but they are necessary because, as Freud would tell us, our subject, the inchoate in human experience, is "over-determined." I have been arguing for some years, in respect to symbolic analyses, that the inchoate is categorical and irreducible in human affairs—an uncharted and imperfectly chartable hinterland to thought and feeling which nevertheless exerts its plenipotentiary attractions and repulsions upon us, impelling us to those recurrent but ultimately unsatisfying predications of objects upon subjects, and vice versa—which is characteristic of our humanity. But the subject matter of our existence in all its numinosity is, in actual fact, inchoate, neither black nor white but gray matter, as it is said.

Naturally I have been under some pressure about this notion of the inchoate, however privileged and irreducible I have tried to make it. Critics of my position have taken the centrality of this term as an instance of my incomprehensibility or obscurantism. But the fault is not mine. As far as symbolic processes are concerned, it is in the nature of the mind itself. Still and perhaps, something more might be said about the inchoate than I have managed to say. So I will try here to say something more without pretending to say anything final or definitive.

I should also say something about my method of composition here. Of course, I want to say something more about the inchoate so I must organize my materials to that end. But I also wish to be true to my subject matter and get at what it actually means to me. It means first of all a set of images—and I ought to confess here that I tend to be at incipient moments of thought a visualizer rather than a verbalizer. The inchoate is for me first of all the dark at the bottom of the stairs, and after its being that, whatever that is, it is all the other images and contexts that are swung into association with that central and organizing image to cast light upon it—and which are part of its polysemy and overdetermined quality. The epigraphs that appear here suggest some of these contexts.

I would go on to argue, moreover, that this method of argument—an argument of images really—is typical of symbolic problem-solving generally. It is this that verbalizers, of which our academies are full, tend to overlook. One has a problem of action or explanation in life. One doesn't always have to put a label upon it as, for example, the problem of the inchoate. An image is generated by pictorializing the problem. This image can be satisfying in and of itself. For a picture solves a problem for an essentially visual animal like *Homo sapiens* to whom "seeing is believing." Or a picture can lead out by association to other contexts and other pictures. Or an image can be acted out. We do it all the time. In any event, this paper begins in images which have led to other images. As explanation and argument it is an acting of images. When you created a problem for me by asking me, a Midwesterner more or less, rooted on the East Coast, to fly clear across the country to South California to talk to you about symbolism, I responded pretty much as most of my informants in various revitalization movements responded when I plagued them with problems of symbolic understanding.

1

> All we see is the living room where
> the action takes place. There is a
> flight of stairs at the far left . . .
> at the top the upstairs hallway.
> During the daytime scenes this small
> area is in semi-darkness and at night
> it is black . . . we are conscious of this
> area throughout the play as though it
> holds some possible threat to the characters.
>
> > William Inge,
> > *The Dark at the Top of the Stairs*
>
> The two skulls my dear friend Carl
> Gustaf, what do you make of them?
>
> > Freud to Jung

I hope the reader will permit a glancing reference to my cultural roots here—Henry County, Spoon River, western Illinois—for the images we generate to solve problems are always, in part, a function of our primordial experiences and the cultural ecology of our upbringing. Because of its resonance with that locale and the family romances characteristic of it, William Inge's play of the late 1950s, *The Dark at the Top of the Stairs*, was very powerful for me. It must have been mainly in my mind here. The house and the small Oklahoma town described in this play are very familiar. In my town, in my house I knew about the dark at the top of the stairs.

But what I knew and still know is rather different from what William Inge knows or at least what his various characters know. The dark has a significantly different meaning for each character according to their sex and age (I hope the reader will forgive me for passing over a central and powerful statement in the play about small town anti-semitism and color consciousness). For Reenie, the painfully shy 16-year-old just coming out of her chrysalis, the dark is the sheltering comfort of her microcosm, her own bed and bedroom removed from the glare of the drawing room downstairs and motherly pressures toward social engagement as well as male stares and male assessments of her developing charms. For the 12-year-old Sonny, his mother's favorite, already drawing-room wise, the dark is that "someth'n awful," an imagined monster of his infant years projected into the uncertainties of the future—once and future dreads. For the parents, Cora and her rough-mannered traveling salesman husband, Ruben, the dark—and this is surely sensed by their children—is their connubial situation, the pleasures and the domestic politics, the dominations and the subordinations of lovemaking in a marriage "by sex redeemed." In the final scene Ruben, celebrating his homecoming, calls to his wife from the top of the stairs. Only his bare feet can be seen by the light from the drawing room lamps.

I take time to detail this scenario not only because, as I was warned, I had picked a bad title for Californians who, living in ranch houses, are going to have little experience of stairs—but because I want to make clear that we are, as is characteristic of symbols, in the presence of polysemy. Within this play the dark condenses within itself past and future, comfort and threat, connubiality and virginity, loneliness and intensification, self-realization and the subordination of the sexual bond.

The more familiar symbol is the dark at the bottom of the stairs. Successful writers employ it with frequency. It appears appropriately enough in Agatha Christie's last and posthumous novel, *Sleeping Murder* (1976), as it does in Ursula Kroeber LeGuin's *The Tombs of Atuan* (1975), an anthropological science fiction in which the characters struggle against a sterile devotion to the dark labyrinth and black undertomb of an ancient religion. In these books the dark at the bottom of the stairs is both symbol and the actual scene of action showing us that subtle connection always present in symbolic analysis between the representative and the performative—between the syntagmatic of the scenario and the paradigmatics of our understanding—between models of and models for.

For the student of human nature, the most compelling instance of that dark to which we are turned is Jung's famous dream which he recounted to Freud on the seven-week 1909 voyage to America for the Clark University visit. During that period, in the spirit of master and disciple, they were recounting each other's dreams for the benefit of mutual analysis. Already Jung was noting a defensiveness in the master in free associating to his (Freud's) own dreams—an unwillingness to risk his authority and a tendency to place that authority above the truth. At the same time Freud in Jung's view seemed to be inordinately drawn to certain elements in Jung's dreams that had to do with death wishes possibly held towards the master himself. Here is an abbreviated form of the dream which we might otherwise remark was of central importance to Jung in developing his later ideas of the "collective unconscious."

> This was the dream. I was in a house I did not know, which had two stories. It was "my house." I found myself in the upper story, where there was a kind of salon furnished with fine old pieces in rococo style. On the walls hung a number of precious old paintings. I wondered that this should be my house, and thought, "Not bad." But then it occurred to me that I did not know what the lower floor looked like. Descending the stairs, I reached the ground floor. There everything was much older, and I realized that this part of the house must date from about the fifteenth or sixteenth century. The furnishings were medieval; the floors were of red brick. Everywhere it was rather dark. I went from one room to another, thinking, "Now I really must explore the whole house." I came upon a heavy door, and opened it. Beyond it, I discovered a stone stairway that led down into the cellar. Descending again, I found myself in a beautifully vaulted room which looked exceedingly ancient. Examining the walls, I discovered layers of brick among the ordinary stone blocks, and chips of brick in the mortar. As soon as I saw this I knew that the walls dated from Roman times. My interest by now was intense. I looked more closely at the floor. It was of stone slabs, and in one of these I discovered a ring. When I pulled it, the stone slab lifted, and again I saw a stairway of narrow stone steps leading down into the depths. These, too, I descended, and entered a low cave cut into the rock. Thick dust lay on the floor, and in the dust were scattered bones and broken pottery, like remains of a primitive culture. I discovered two human skulls, obviously very old and half disintegrated. Then I awoke. [Jung 1963:182–3.]

Freud's response to this elaborated dream was to query Jung repeatedly about the two skulls. "What did I think about them. And whose were they?" For Jung, the dream led primarily into deeper and deeper levels of the paleo-unconscious rather than out to the residue of contemporary relationships. It led to the world of primitive man within him. "I saw from this that (Freud) was completely helpless in dealing with certain kinds of dreams and had to take refuge in his doctrine (and his fantasies of father murder). It was up to me to find the *real* meaning of the dream." So Jung lied to Freud to put him at ease—or so he thought.

What was the *real* meaning of the dream? Freudians and Jungians have been locked in primal struggle ever since. This point is that the dream has at the least several meanings. And the "real" meaning is that interpretation which is apt and useful—manageable—for a given situation. For Freud, subjected as he was to the uncertainties of his relation to his assertive younger colleague, the motivated interpretation had to do with death wishes and parricide. That was most useful in helping him to deal with an uncertain and pressing personal situation. For Jung, whose mind was steeped in his own historical and prehistorical training, an interpretation that organized that superabundant content was most strategic—and only mildly parricidal in its reshaping of Freud's view of the unconscious. (After all, Jung was only a "little bit pregnant" with his system at the time.)

In the interpretation of complex symbolic matters we are inevitably in the presence of the motivating principle of strategic or pragmatic understanding. Symbols are themselves generated out of a need, whether, if one wishes, a life wish or a death wish. And there is no integration of them that is not also situational and strategic. To suppose that there is a true or real interpretation that surpasses situatedness and the preoccupations of a given participant or interpretant is the first strategy by which the inchoate has been approached. We may call it the adversarial strategy or the zero-sum strategy which presumes that there are identifiable winners and losers in symbolic analysis—the right analysis and the wrong analysis, a real analysis and an illusory one. Such strategists by eloquence or sheer brass may enjoy temporary parricidal or fratricidal victories but in the long run the scenario shifts and circumstances alter cases. In symbolic analysis the abhorrence of the excluded middle, inherited from Aristotelian logic is misleading if not misplaced. What we learn from Freud and Jung, perhaps, is the wisdom of both perspectives, the fact of "both/and" and the temporality and situatedness of either/or. What strikes us as real or right is what is apt and edifying for a given epoch or situation. Judgment in symbolic analysis is less empirical than moral.

2

The Prince of Paris has
Lost His Hat and Some Say

> This and Some Say That and
> I Say Number Five, Number
> Five to the Foot!
> Who Sir Me Sir?
> Yes Sir You Sir!
> No Sir Not I Sir!
> Then Who Sir?
> Number 1 Sir
> Ahh, Number 1 to the Foot.
>
> Midwestern children's game

There's a bit of a trick, isn't there, in what we have just put forth?

For while we have cut ourselves off from any Archimedean point that would give us ultimate and uncontestable epistemological purchase on the symbolic world, we still hold onto the possibility of edifying, and perhaps privileged, interpretation of the symbolic—for a certain time and place, of course. Indeed, we *have to* privilege that interpretation because we need it amidst the inevitable shiftiness of human social life. Role theory has long taught us that even within the confines of the domestic unit—and even within happy families, let alone unhappy ones and ones, like so many in present-day America, undergoing challenging changes in sex roles—there is role ambiguity and role conflict as between being a mother and/or a wife, a son and/or a brother. Primal scenes are the working out of these ambiguities amidst the added urgency of biological impulse. It is just these kinds of shifts of family role and social status as between daughter and prospective mate, mother and connubial partner that our play *The Dark at the Top of the Stairs* most intentfully explores. The yearly cycle and the life-cycle rites of passage and of intensification show us the celebration of the ambiguities of identity and the shape-shiftings from status to status. And of course when the institutional structures of civilization preëmpt the primacy of the family we have the added Antigonian ambiguities and discontents as beween filial and civic responsibility; as between nurturant fatherhood or attentive husbandhood and a respected and authoritative professional life; and as between being a homebody and a helpmeet or a pert business associate. Life is inchoate in that sense and requires of us all that we be shape-shifters. And a great deal of symbolic material is generated out of that incessant requirement and addressed to it, presenting to our imaginations our condition in some graspable form so that we might somehow better deal with it, understand our moral responsibilities in the face of it.

This shape-shifting or shiftiness (see Fernandez 1975:652–4)—just to be mischievous—in the human equation arises from not only our multiple and often conflicting roles, domestic and civic, nor the ephemeralness of our physiological states in life cycles and natural cycles. It also rests upon the cardinal role of duplicity, as Jakobson (n.d.) calls it, in language and the use of language—the incessant interplay of message and code, narrated event and speech event. There is a particular class of grammatical units of which the personal pronouns are examples, *par excellence*, in which message and code are particularly intertwined. Jakobson called these "shifters." As the word "I" shifts from speaker to speaker, its referent shifts completely for it is part of the message that is not only conventional but is tied in with the speech event, the code itself. The "I", like any personal pronoun, is in subjective and existential relation with the speech event at the same time that it is an objective and conventional part of the message. Shifters thus are a part of the linguistic code which make a particular comment upon the message in which they are contained and are particularly forceful examples of the duplicity of which Jakobson speaks. The duplicity and shiftiness contained in the personal pronouns— their subjective-objective or indexical-symbolic quality—is what makes them difficult for children to learn. Something of the uncertainty, even anxiety, they provoke is contained in this rapid-fire and accusatory children's game, with its quick interplay of subjective and objective pronouns and, under pressure, its quick and quite human transference of blame, which we have used as an epigraph in this section of our argument.

From the shape-shifting required of us in ongoing social life and from the duplicity of our language, there arises then this recurrent dilemma, impending disorder, moral uncertainty—the inchoate in its social and linguistic form. Now a common strategy for dealing with this phrasing of the inchoate is to presume that these productions conceal a set of normative principles or rules for behavior which the participant can detect and which will act to defeat ambiguity and steer him through the seas of social uncertainty to social trustworthiness and predictability. We can call it the didactive strategy which studies symbolic action for the rules contained in it. Of course some symbolic productions are plainly didactive, hortatory, ethically normative in this way. But a commandment-oriented people like Judeo-Christians, and also a people so committed to wiring diagrams, rulebooks, and flowcharts as we are, should be cautious here. Most symbolic productions are not only normative or are not really normative in this way. Surely not the most interesting ones. Most symbolic productions act more to excite the moral imagination than to alert it to its duty—arousing participants to a contemplation and greater tolerance of the centrality of ambiguity, paradox, and dilemma in the human condition. As much auguries of ambiguity as templates of conduct, they "edify, we might say, by puzzlement," stimulating us to trustworthy solidarities by showing us the potential disorder in our social and intellectual natures—reconfirming us in our commitment to accustomed material gratifications. Of course, the situation is volatile and our moral imagination can be so stimulated as to seek for new, and often revolutionary, solidarities heretofore unrealized.

Surely this is the lesson in the widespread trickster figure—the shape-shifter *par excellence*—whose extravagant and irrepressible actions are hardly models for any acceptable everyday behavior; but whose outrageous qualities excite our imaginations to the apprehension of something existential in the human condition—something that continually confronts us and is in us and lies behind and below the niceties of a well-structured social life. The trickster is the "type" symbolic figure, fleshing out the contrarieties which lie in the inchoate. He is exceptional in delineation, to be sure. Still, he or she is simply the more striking instance of the complex possibilities that symbolic statements so often ask us to imagine.

Recently in the literature, a number of us have been raising the question of anthropology's relation to the moral imagination. On the one hand we have wondered whether those who, like Victor Turner, perform dramatistic analyses of human behavior do not in laying out social dramas, invest that behavior with a moral structure that in all actuality—the humdrum mini-max situations of everyday life—it does not possess (see Fernandez 1975a). This moralistic impulse comes particularly to the fore in Turner's recent work on martyrdom and pilgrimage, where social dramas turn into the "via crucis" and where we find the subjects of inquiry taking up the martyr's role—submitting themselves to a preordained scenario of dramatic denouement. One wonders whether these dramas are more in the author and his own moral imagination, perhaps stimulated by a lifetime of saints' legends, than in the materials themselves. Important as it may be for the survival of culture that the recounters of legends, the tellers of tales, and the crafters of plays provide such dramatic antidotes to our inveterate self-interest, one asks whether the exercises of such moral imagination in self and its excitement in others is the particular challenge of anthropological science.

There are those who answer, resoundingly, Yes! And indeed one must agree with Clifford Geertz (1977) that anthropology has a particular power to exercise the moral imagination as we, by arresting narratives of other's lifeways, bring pressure to bear upon our own, showing alternate ways of working out human dilemmas and creating a renewed sense of the potentialities of our humanity. Particularly in the highly civilized societies—and I use the term only to refer to those societies with a high degree of overt and compulsive emphasis on organization and order and with correspondingly powerful tendencies toward one dimensionality and the lowest common denominator—are anthropological accounts a necessary antidote, though perhaps only a palliative, to the constriction of the human spirit. If there are some anthropologists who feel in our calling the impulse to moving narration and the dramatic craft, there is sufficient narrow-minded and self-interested temporizing mediocrity in modern life to justify such exercises of the moral imagination.

But the point, really, is that whatever set and scenario we construct on the main floor of our experience, there remain at the bottom of the stairs such dilemmas and ambiguities of social and personal life, such shape-shifting, as to offer no permanent resolution good for all seasons. Symbolic productions speak to that inchoate condition, at once providing us with images which we can perform so as to act our way through those intense moments in life (the sacred ones—in which dilemmas, ambiguities, and problems ultimately unresolvable threaten to overwhelm us); while at the same time they expand our awareness and temper our intolerance for such incongruities and incompatibilities. We are of course in this Western World, creators of a masterful culture which would put such disorder as is suggested here out upon the peripheries of life or seek to extirpate it whenever we find it rising up out of the basement. But I think that Tom Beidleman is just right, in a recent discussion relating the trickster to the moral imagination, in insisting upon the centrality of ambiguity and uncertainty (see Beidleman 1980). It is our tendency to see the trickster as a fraud, a social cheat, an outcast. The more often, and perhaps in the more perceptive cultures, he stands not in some far off closet but at the very center—dancing and pranking, wisecracking at the very top of the stairs.

3

A society is similar to a house, divided into
rooms and corridors. The more a society
resembles our own form of civilization the

> thinner are its partitions and the more open
> are its doors of communication.
>
> Van Gennep,
> *The Rites of Passage*

The moral imagination is one thing; the scientific imagination is quite another. Of course, the two can be confused. Science can be a sacred cow. But it is one thing to be confronted with our existential condition in all its complexity, paradox, and ambiguity. It is another thing to seek models as simple and clear and as isomorphic with the reality as possible. The moral imagination is full of rhetorical intent and seeks to excite persons and groups. The scientific imagination seeks to represent reality in such a way as to better manipulate things as well as to predict the course of their development. The probing and disclosing of essential structures in as parsimonious a way as possible is the main objective of the scientific imagination. One might go on to say that the moral imagination mainly promotes our humility while the scientific imagination excites our sense of power, were it not that we find so many humble scientists and arrogant moralists.

As an instance of the scientific imagination probing the structure of realities, I remember a conversation with the late Hadley Cantril, an eminent social psychologist and, I might add, personally anything but arrogant. Professor Cantril was proposing to take his self-anchoring scale to Africa. He asked me, ingenuously, about the Africans' acquaintance with ladders as well as about their orientation toward them. As will be remembered, the self-anchoring scale seeks to get at attitudes towards past, present, and future by having informants find themselves on a ladder. Where are you now? Where were you? Where will you be? The bottom of the ladder is taken as the worst conceivable way of life and the top the best.

I could only be helpful by pointing out that in two closely related branches of the same Fang religious movement in Africa there was dark, as it were, both at the bottom and at the top of the ladder. The New Life branch dug a grave pit behind the altar down into whose obscurity the membership descended in order to commune with the ancestors and obtain "the Word." The dark at the bottom of the ladder! In another branch, Dissoumba, a small dark chamber was constructed at the apex of the roof. The sacred Ngombi chestharp was kept in that chamber gathering the power of the ancestors and the great gods who hovered at the apex of the chapel. A ladder was put up to it before the all-night rituals and the harp was passed down to the harpist on the floor of the chapel. The dark at the top of the ladder.

It would be pretty hard to anticipate, I counseled, where a given African culture would locate the dark end of the ladder. It would be a harder thing yet to determine just what was meant by the dark and how it could be related to the good life and to past, present, and future. "From darkness we come and to darkness we will return" seemed to me a fair summary of much Bwiti belief.

My answer to Cantril was essentially what we have come to know as a structuralist answer: The concreteness of existential meaning is subordinated to underlying structures for it is not the concrete referent of our terms that is interesting—it is the relationship between them. It is not so important what the ends of the ladder mean; it is the fact that the ends of the ladder and the ladder itself constitute a system of understanding—ladders are good to think with and stairs, too, I suppose. There can hardly be a better structuralist symbol, in fact. The ladder has polarity, a satisfying binary quality. It has mediation. And best of all it has what structuralist studies rarely have—measurement along an equally divided continuum.

The structural strategy in symbolic inquiry, we can be brief about it, has the effect of draining symbols of much of their content—vitiating the plenitude of their resonances, the suggestive tension of their overdetermination. It is a strategy that makes, for example, out of all the superabundance of associations contained in the trickster figure a mere mediator, an operator rather than human existence personified. In some respects the structuralist strategy in the face of the symbolic is familiar to us. It is the logico-deductive strategy of Western man and modern science even though, in other respects as we see below, it does not follow through to state clearly the causes and conditions of its object of inquiry. It is a strategy, Lévi-Strauss tells us in *Tristes Tropiques* (1955), that by an "effort of understanding destroys the object of its attention." This phrase can have several meanings, but because of the penchant in structuralism to reduce existential complexities to their essence it may be justly accused of an "evasion of realities," of alienation and inauthenticity.[2] On the other hand it has been frequently criticized for its free and easy way with ethnographic data and for creative misinterpretation in laying out structures of opposition and transformation (see Thomas, Kronenfeld and Kronenfeld 1976).

This is hardly the place to give the structuralist strategy its due. It *is* worth reiterating that such a method vitiates the rich and overdetermined surface texture of symbolic activity and always risks beguiling its practitioners into a false consciousness of their unimpeachable objectivity and of their great parsimony and power. And yet the structuralist attention to Aristotelian analogy—summed up in the famous if confounding formula of mediation and transformation, $f_x(a):f_y(b)::f_x(b):f_{a-1}(y)$—teaches us something important about symbolic thought and about the inchoate from which it arises. It teaches that symbolic activity and hence symbolic inquiry is essentially the relating of domains of experience and the study of the relational equivalence of the arrangement of entities in these domains. We confront the inchoate in another way here in recognizing that in respect to symbols, we do not understand things in and of themselves. Symbolic understanding is understanding that is obtained by extension of our attention to something else which is more familiar.

This is not to say very much, perhaps, because what else do we mean by the phrase "to symbolize" than to let something stand for something else. (I should add here that I have had a long-standing objection to the symbol concept as at once so unitary and polysemic itself as not to reveal satisfactorily those processes by which, in objectified thought, more familiar and concrete objects are related to inchoate subjects—processes by which domains are related to each.) And yet, since empiricism would hold to the view that we understand most clearly that which we observe most directly, it is worth pointing out that structuralism teaches that we understand not by exclusive intense and unflinching attention to the subject of interest but by allowing for the eye to wander, searching out an interaction of this subject in other domains of experience. Lévi-Strauss's series, *Mythologiques,* would offer very feeble understanding if it focused on one or several myths only. It is by bringing into play many different myths so that their relational structures can interact that our understanding is enhanced.

I do not wish to necessarily profess adherence to the abstract principles and mental categories, the unwelcome contradictions such as being both born of one and of two or being of both nature and culture, that Lévi-Strauss adduces as the real referents of the objectified thought, the concrete things conglomerated by bricolage, that he studies. By the lights of my own field experience there is a jump in the production of these principles which makes me uneasy about them. One worries that they are more a product of Western academic preoccupations and categories than of the local thought in which they are embedded.

But I do wish to adhere to the structural strategy of understanding its materials by indirections—by recognizing that some domains of experience are more familiar and some more inchoate, the latter often the ones most focal to our interest. Symbolic thought brings the one to bear on the other. And even if we cannot readily differentiate between inchoate and familiar domains of experience, the central place of analogic thought and relational understanding in the structural approach—its strategic employ of the devices of the savage mind in studying the products of the savage mind, which is to say allowing oneself to be "thought of" by the materials themselves—gives it particular depth of penetration where symbolic constructions are concerned. This strategy brings us particularly close to those forms of explanation—proverbial wisdom we might call it—which are much more widespread in the world and surely in the anthropological data than the canons of discursive reasoning would lead us to believe. (This general point has been made succinctly by J. Maquet, 1974.) It is, as well, a strategy that points us towards the way that culture coheres: by the resonance between the relational structures of different domains of experience.

Our epigraph from Van Gennep now gives this part of our argument away—at least as far as our discipline is concerned. For we recognize how prevalent the house metaphor has been in our professional formulations—in our attempts to convincingly understand the inchoate experience of change and passage through the life cycle. The more directly we look at social life, perhaps, the more we are impelled to see it in other terms. We have familiarized our subject by bringing to bear one of the most familiar domains of experience—houselife—and in that, we have created a central and recurrent image of our social thought. It is not the only familiar domain to which we have turned to make our subject matter more satisfyingly intelligible. The game metaphor—social life is a game and we are all familiar with games—has long been beguiling. The drama metaphor—social life is a drama and we are all familiar with dramas and with being dramatic—has as long been compelling. And now we have the text metaphor—and what could be more familiar and persuasive to a text building animal like the academic one—which promises because of the moribund quality of the other metaphors perhaps—which is to say, the decline of the shock of recognition contained in them through overuse—to restore to us now a finally adequate explanation, justifying, indeed compelling, a new campaign of inquiry. We will bend the inchoate to our purposes at last.

4

I must be getting somewhere near the center
of the earth."

(Alice speculating as she is falling down the
    rabbit hole.)

The objectified thought or the objective correlatives of social science inquiry propel us away from the center of gravity of our particular argument here—an argument whose principal ideas we have been teasing out of their embeddedness in the dark at the bottom of the stairs. Let us return once more to our particular "fascinans."[3]

Recently we have been working among mountain cattle-keepers in northern Spain. These people, like many of the cattle-keeping countrymen of Europe, characteristically live above the stable. (It's a marvelous energy-saving arrangement, by the way.) The dark at the bottom of the stairs is the stable itself—and it is dark even at midday for the stable door is small and usually closed and there is but one small nether window. It is a hermetic environment heavy with the acrid odor of animals and animal wastes barely sweetened by the smell of hay. It is not only animal wastes. Until quite recent "improvements" in village life, the stable was used by humans as well.

For the urban visitor with little appreciation for animals or for the ultimate good uses of manure, the atmosphere is daunting. But for the villagers it is redolent with much, if not all, that is most meaningful to them. Or how else could it be that a villager could fling wide the stable door and turn to the visitor with the exclamation: "Ye un paraiso verda!" (It's a paradise, isn't it!). All the visitor can make out in the obscurity is the white muzzles of six or seven cows turned with vague curiosity toward the light which is itself reflected in a row of large, patient, luminescent eyes.

Even more at night does the stable become a part of family life. The family is attentive to the signs rising from the dark below: the shifting of weight, the rubbing of a flank against a post, the signs of the laborious bedding down, an unexpected bovine cough or eructation, and even the sound of a new calf suckling. One senses that the family is about as attentive to these nether regions as they are to their own visceral processes—quite without considering that their own visceral processes eventuate in the stable. A house without a ruminating, rumbling, wheezing shifting stable is a moribund house and, in fact, during the day or during the summer months when the cows are out or up upon the steep meadows the house is only half a house, its peristalsis suspended and the life of the inhabitants projected out upon the streets and plazas and up upon the high meadows.

The reader will now see what I am about here and what this mountain housing has made us aware of: that if for Van Gennep society can be a house (or whose basement, however, we empiricists have to constantly remind ourselves), so for many peoples the body can be a house and the dark at the bottom of the stairs can assume visceral cloacal genitive functions. (I am sure we were all vaguely aware of this even without the case of these countrymen.) These are the functions from which we, in all our urbanity, avert our eyes. But the countryman, a more natural man, looks directly at them seeing in them the sources of his well-being, the fertility of his fields, the marketable wealth of his patrimony, the very replica and repository of his vitality. The manger—we can understand it if we try—is his salvation and his paradise.

In symbolic inquiry the body and its multitudinous processes must be always present though just how it is present, for reasons of our impulse toward aversion and repression, we are never quite certain. Such things are most often deeply embedded and cloaked over with a seemly obscurity. Periodically throughout his career Kenneth Burke, who has so often played the devil's advocate to the literary sensibility and the literary establishment, has sought to whip off that cloak and discover evidence in even the most heroic, the most noble, and the most exalted texts of what he calls the cathartic functions or the Demonic Trinity: the three purgative outlets of the *parties honteuses* (see Burke 1966). The hidden sources of this cathartic imagery give it its power, he argues, and putting one's finger upon it is always ticklish, often tedious, and occasionally intolerable. Indeed, we have learned from the early years of Freudian interpretation where everything was turned into Phallic symbols just how tedious such interpretation could be.

But I do not want our possible perturbations over such interpretations to deflect us from that dark arena of our interest where thought emerges from non-thought—where ideas arise out of that embedded condition in which we so often find them in anthropological work. For anthropologists, exegesis is the exception not the rule in contrast with life in the academies where ideas grow on trees, are in the air, and are trodden underfoot. As academics we tend too much to take ideas for granted as if they were always there—there before us as, in fact, they are in the synopticons of the literary tradition. Symbolic inquiry recognizes how embedded ideas are in images and objects—among these the body—and how poorly understood are the procedures by which ideas are appropriately squeezed from their embedded condition. That is part of the inchoateness of our inquiry. We have already expressed misgivings here about the abstract ideas which Lévi-Strauss finds to be the referents of the concrete thought he examines, and I have elsewhere worried about the imposition of "imageless ideas" in anthropological inquiry (Fernandez 1978). I worried that a great deal of what we were researching was already defined or presented to us in cognitive terms before the research began, and that our field materials were being fitted pseudo-conceptually to our preconceptions. We could be surer of our authenticity if we would anchor ourselves in local images— and that may be perhaps the main strategy for dealing with the inchoate.

Still, the relationship between symbols, images, and ideas is difficult. No one should pretend otherwise. Take the central symbol of these village stables: the cow. I wish I could easily say what the idea or ideas of the cow are to these villagers who are so fascinated by them. As an ethnographer, one is tempted to paraphrase Tennyson: "Bovid in the stable stall, If I could understand what you are, I would understand the universe and all." There are words, of course, to attach to cows—plenty of them. And there are images of cows that one can elicit. But village "thinking" about the cow goes on largely embedded at a deeper level where bodily states of contentment and discontent, desire or satiety, extension and distention are experienced in relation to the cow. They know the cow much more that way than in relation to the emergent cognitive apparatus employed in the object world. That is to say that what Langer (1951) has described as the "symbolic transformation of experience" takes place at a very deep and obscure (one almost slips and says obscene) level having to do with bodily states presented in that symbolism. This profound organismic organization, if it is an organization, is characteristic of, in Langer's terms, presentational symbolism. It is a symbolism which achieves an ordering of experience a stage earlier—we would say here, a floor deeper—than discursive thought. Discursive thought may be applied to that symbolism as a system of ideas, but it cannot be as deeply associated with it. And unless such thought itself emerges out of that deeper organization, it risks not being associated with it at all—pseudo-conceptualization, as it were. The strategy for coping with these difficulties, the strategy of pseudo-conceptualization by ready-made interpretation, was convincingly rejected by Freud almost from the first part of his argument in *The Interpretation of Dreams* (1955). Let the dreams themselves be fully heard and told and seen before we begin our analysis.

But in respect to the matters we are seeking here to bring out, Jung may be the better guide. Jung (1959) frequently argued that ideas emerge into mental form from physiological remoteness and out of "undifferentiated totalities"—by which Jung meant the condensation characteristic of the symbol. He wrote that "symbols of the self arise in the depths of the body and they express its materiality as much as the structure of the perceiving consciousness." One does not have to accept Jung's notion of the archetype nor of the archaic unconscious to recognize the importance of this view. The psychologist D. W. Harding in a perceptive treatment of "The Hinterland of Thought," finds Jung's views of these deep processes valuable with the exception of his notion that the image archetype itself arises from the remote depths of the body. What Harding says of the horse symbol is apposite to these villagers' attachment to cows:

> For instance some sense of surging animal vitality and its huge potential power may arise in any of us and may emerge into conscious experience from below, in the way that the experience of hunger emerges out of bodily processes. As it comes towards "symbolic transformation" the most appropriate image to hand may be, or may have been for many centuries past, the horse; and the horse may then serve as the symbol of a very complex mass of inarticulate potential experience, including a sense of the delight, the danger, the power, the vulnerability, the wildness and the manageableness of animal vitality. But although the meaning of the symbol may have come towards definition out of the remotenesses of the whole psychosomatic person, the image—the horse—seems most likely to have entered by way of the sensory surfaces, especially the eye. [Harding 1960:21.]

Just so. The image of the cow—which, of course, has a different set of valences than the horse—comes to the villagers as it does not come to the urban dweller, out of their daily experience. But presented there, it is taken down to be associated with the deepest physiological awareness of repletion, evacuation, nurturance, and satiety. Above all, the cow is a symbol of satiety.

These matters are so inchoate that one despairs of getting one's ideas about them correctly put. The more we focus upon them the more they recede before us and the more we are driven elsewhere to other domains for such clarification as lies in metaphor and the argument of images. Harding recognizes this problem. And he has produced a notable master metaphor in which to embed his ideas. We may quote it as a useful contrast to the master metaphor we have been arguing here:

> We are still obliged to use similes and metaphors in describing these things, and I think the metaphor of distance as well as depth is needed. We stand at the harbour of our mind and watch flotillas of ideas far out at sea coming up over the horizon, already in formation of a sort; and though we can reorder them to a great extent on their closer approach, we cannot disregard the organization they had before they came in sight. They are all submarines, partly under water the whole time and capable of submerging entirely at any point and being lost to sight until analytic techniques undo the repression. But it constitutes a fundamental difference whether an idea is out of mind because it has been forced to dive or because it has not yet come up over the horizon. Sometimes repressed ideas may be close in-shore. . . . Others may be both under water and at a great distance; they find expression in some sorts of dreaming. . . . And in creative work great numbers of ideas, more or less organized, are simply out of sight beyond the horizon and can be brought into view only through the redispositions we make amongst the in-shore mental shipping that we *can* see and control. [Harding 1960:19–20.]

Would we not without such similes fall, like Alice, irremediably to the very center of our experience where we would have no perspective whatsoever? It is that fear of falling into the abyss that perhaps more than anything else energizes the analogies that are the first step in our climb toward cognition and our emergence into the realm of ideas. In the face of the inchoate, the first strategy is the argument of images. We cope by such versimilitude, even if only by wishing that in a situation of profound dilemma we were, to refer back to our epigraph, a Kellogg's cornflake floating in a bowl taking movies, relaxing awhile, living in style. Reflecting on that image will give us plenty of ideas about the normless situation of the student generation during the Vietnam War.

5

La vida es sueño.
Calderon de la Barca

In some respects this paper—this argument of images—in its rhetorical quality has the air of an epistle to the South Californians seeking to excite their moral imaginations, to bring about some conversion in them. It's a normal impulse experienced by Bible Belters in Elysian climes. But we are not untrue to our subject because symbolic activity is mostly rhetorical, seeking to convert self and others to other notions of things. And symbolic constructions are worlds in which it is hoped the converted can live, if only for an imaginary moment. Any inquiry into symbols must recognize the conversion and conviction that lies in them—they move us in quality space. The particular quality space we have been exploring here by means of a sequence of symbols is a dark environment, close and heavily charged. The claims of the object world prevent extensive sojourns but it would be a mistake to ignore the particular coalescences taking place there however obscure—or its everpresence.

Elsewhere in my particular approach to symbolism—I prefer the technical term sign-image—I have sought to, by a discursive effort, distinguish signal activity from symbolic activity, social consensus from cultural consensus. I have sought to follow through the harmonic permutations of syntax and paradigm. I have argued that metaphor-metonymic progressions have a predictability within cultures—and that they are culture-specific. This has all been mainfloor analysis. It's a different thing to turn to things subterranean—where one must turn perforce to the argument of images.

Now an objectionable thing occurs—at least to a pragmatic, civic-minded people—when we turn our attention to the dark at the bottom of the stairs. It begins to claim a primacy, exert an exclusive and indulgent fascination. We sense that it risks turning the world upside down. And here the play by that master dramatist of the *Siglo de Oro*, Calderon, comes to mind. *La vida es sueño* is a play that espouses that tendency present in the Mediterranean world since Plato's cave, and surely pervasive in Iberian eschatological thought, to devalue the things of this world as imperfect and confused and transient—like a dream. In its somber and more philosophic moments, it is the tragic view of life.

Science is not only pragmatic and civic-minded—it is also, essentially, robustly optimistic. The consequences of its activity may be tragic but its cast of mind is surely not. Such a cast of mind is bound to be uncomfortable in the presence of such deep fascinations as we have been exploring here. What is the good of such explorations? What responsibility to the management of the social order and the preparation of a brighter future is present in it? One remembers those insinuating phrases in that piece of Vietnam popular culture we introduced to begin with, "Punky's Dilemma"—a song like so many songs of the period about the larger civic responsibility, about the social order, and about the light at the end of the tunnel:

> Old Roger draft-dodger
> Leavin' by the basement door,
> Everybody knows what he's
> Tippy-toeing down there for.

And yet Calderon's play—all his plays—if not about social order is surely about social solidarity, about collective responsibility, and about the limitation of personal visions. But Calderon's cast of mind, and this is, perhaps, a predominant strain in the Spanish mentality since the Golden Age and the collapse of the empire, can place no great confidence in devotion to the material and social advantages of life—to the pragmatics. For Calderon the only guide is renunciation of personal advantage. So the tragic view of life envisions a basis for social order and enduring solidarity—even if it is that of the "last best hope" variety. It is enough, perhaps, to stimulate moral imaginations with the comparative possibilities for social solidarity and social order contained in a tragic, world-renouncing, darkness-obsessed view on the one hand and an optimistic, strategic-minded, world-embracing view on the other. But it cannot, at least for an anthropologist, be assumed out of hand that a preoccupation with the dark at the bottom of the stairs negates *everything* we hold most dear!

In the end here I am myself too much committed to the pragmatic optimism of my generation—to the sunny side of the Bible Belt—to leave a reader pondering the tragic path to social order and conviviality, leave her or him with only a stimulated moral imagination or an indignant one as the case may be. There is an additional and very practical reason why the inchoate should interest us. It is, very simply, the matrix of those revitalized images which enable cultures to regroup themselves and live on a bit. Perhaps because of our commitments to the tenor of normal life we tend to be preoccupied in the social sciences with the more or less smooth coordinations of signal behaviors, with commonsense understandings, and with the strategic management of the object world. We hold the inchoate in abeyance. But we anthropologists above all, because we have seen it so many times, know how quickly a society can be precipitated into anomie, the normal state of daily life in the world out there brought to a halt. It is then that the central nervous system, which has been held in abeyance in the normal routine, reasserts its reality and men and women return to deeper levels of experience to find images and symbols to live with, and live by (see Fischer 1971). At any rate, for an anthropologist like myself who has spent his life studying revitalization movements, the importance of these deeper levels in the generation of revitalized culture is undeniable. Most of the movements I studied in Africa began in an extended dream or vision. In a very real sense "su cultura es sueño."

And perhaps it is not only the culture of revitalization movements. Perhaps the method we must follow to understand the coherence of any culture in the most comprehensive sense is little different from the method employed by Freud in understanding the coherence of dreams: identification of elements, tracing their overdetermination out to their superabundant associations, and finally synthesizing underlying themes (see Foulkes 1978). Or why would one of the most stimulating collections of recent years (Geertz 1973) be named so precisely after the master's work: *The Interpretation* (not of dreams but) *of Cultures?*

Postscript

In lively discussion at the UCLA Department after this paper was read, I was pressed to be more specific and didactic. A problem with the argument of images, of course, is that ideas—the currency of academic life—are often embedded and not explicit. Academic auditors want, quite naturally, useful—that is, negotiable—results. Let me therefore be explicit here about (1) the definition of the inchoate and (2) the strategies for coping with it.

By the inchoate we mean the underlying (psychophysiological) and overlying (sociocultural) sense of entity (entirely of being or wholeness) which we reach for to express (by predication) and act out (by performance) but can never grasp. Hence frustration is constant and predication is recurrent. The wholeness of the inchoate is complicated and obscured by such dilemmas, paradoxes, and ambiguities as (a) the duplicity of language, (b) role conflict in social life, (c) the idiosyncrasies of experience and its interpretation, etc.

As regards the difference between the inchoate and the unconscious, it should be said that the former term seeks to be a concept pointing at the systematic intersection of the sociocultural and the psychophysiological. It is a concept that seeks to suggest the ultimate undefinability of this sociocultural-personal wholeness, but it is a concept which locates in that ultimate undefinability the "fascinans" that is the impulse to recurrent predication and performance.

It follows that there are certain strategies for coping with the inchoate, at once undefinable *and* impulsive: (a) we should not begin with imageless inquiry but we should consider first the images predicated upon the inchoate and in which a culture's idea system is embedded; (b) we should recognize the polyvalence—overdetermination—of that which issues from the inchoate and the centrality of ambiguity; (c) we should recognize the temporal quality of any interpretation—its idiosyncrasy of time, place, and person; (d) we should recognize the relational quality of such coherence analogic reason is able to assign to the inchoate and the indirection of such intelligence, which always confirms itself in other domains. There are, as this paper has argued, several strategies to be avoided: the adversarial strategy, the essentialist strategy, and the direct-inspection strategy.

Anthropological colleagues were kind enough to provide me with their associations to the "Dark" image. The readiness of their response and its diversity proves the resonance of the image in our culture and its multivocality. Here is a sampling:

"The dark was my father's incompetence—or at least that sump pump that he could never fix," or "It's me lying in bed and worrying that some door on the first floor was open to the burglars of our family well-being," or "It was illicit adolescent love-making with an ear tuned to family stirrings above," or "To me it's all these neighbors' children who had disappeared and might be in our basement, our skeletons, as well as any others," or "It once was for me musty barely growing things or preserved things—roots, apples, potatoes, comestibles—in the cellar, but now it's a rumpus room or a music room or a washer-dryer and a humming heater—not very dark at all."

Acknowledgments

Thanks to Hildred Geertz and Buck Schieffelin for prodding me to concentrate my attention on the "inchoate." To Nancy Schwartz special thanks for, once again, bringing her frame of reference to bear on a particular problem with such fertility. And to various colleagues—professional privilege prohibits me from naming them—who have free-associated so readily to the "Dark at the Bottom of the Stairs."

Notes

This paper was delivered as one of the annual Hoijer Lectures at the University of California, Los Angeles, in the early spring of 1980. The sea-change involved in flying from still wintry New Jersey to "South California" no doubt influenced the style of argument here. I am grateful to the Department of Anthropology at UCLA and particularly to its chairman, Jacques Maquet, for the invitation and the hospitality.

1. Both are very apt for our argument here: "Punky's Dilemma" is in my view one of the "deepest songs" of the Vietnam War generation; the other is also suggestive of where the anthropological patrimony might lead.

2. Diamond points up the inconsistency in the "presumably highly symbolic categories of structuralism and the reductionism inherent in its explanatory principle" (1974:302). It is the reduction of the symbolic to the banal symbolic function.

3. One has in mind Rudolf Otto's discussion of the core mystery of life— unfathomable, paradoxical, and antinomic—which he treats both as a "mysterium tremendum," that is to say, an object of awesome contemplation, and as a "fascinans," something which impels man to do something about it. I hope it's clear that we treat the inchoate here as a "fascinans," *not* as a "mysterium tremendum" (see Otto 1923).

References

BEIDELMAN, THOMAS O.
   1980   The Moral Imagination of the Kaguru: Some Thoughts on Tricksters. *American Ethnologist,* 7(1):27–42.
BURKE, KENNETH
   1966   Mind, Body and the Unconscious; The Thinking of the Body; and *Somnia Ad Urinandum*. In *Language in Symbolic Action:* essays on life, literature, and method. Berkeley: University of California Press, pp. 63–80, 308–343, 344–358.
CHRISTIE, AGATHA
   1976   *Sleeping Murder.* New York: Bantam.
DIAMOND, STANLEY
   1974   The Myth of Structuralism. In *The Unconscious in Culture,* ed. by Ino Rossi. New York: Dutton, pp. 292–335.
FERNANDEZ, JAMES W.
   1975   On the Concept of the Symbol. *Current Anthropology,* 16(4):652–654.
   1975a On Reading the Sacred into the Profane: The Dramatic Fallacy in the Work of Victor Turner. *Journal for the Scientific Study of Religion,* 14:191–197.
   1978   Imageless Ideas in African Inquiry. Paper read at SSRC-ACLS Conference on Cultural Transformations in Africa, January 1978, at the Smithsonian Conference Center, Maryland.
FISCHER, R.
   1971   A Cartography of the Ecstatic and Meditative States. *Science,* 174:897–904.

FOULKES, DAVID
1978   *A Grammar of Dreams.* New York: Basic Books.
FREUD, SIGMUND
1955   *The Interpretation of Dreams.* Orig. 1900. New York: Basic Books.
GEERTZ, CLIFFORD
1973   *The Interpretation of Cultures.* New York: Basic Books.
1977   Found in Translation: On the Social History of the Moral Imagination.
       The Georgia Review, 31:788–810.
HARDING, D. W.
1960   The Hinterland of Thought. In *Metaphor and Symbol,* ed. by L. C.
       Knights and Basil Cottle. London: Butterworths, pp. 10–23.
INGE, WILLIAM
1958   *The Dark at the Top of the Stairs.* New York: Random House.
JAKOBSON, ROMAN
n.d.   Shifters, verbal categories and the Russian verb. In *Russian language
       project,* Cambridge, pp. 1–14.
JUNG, C. G.
1959   *The Archetypes and the Collective Unconscious.* Trans. by R. F. C. Hill.
       New York: Pantheon.
1963   *Memories, Dreams, and Reflections.* London: Collins.
LANGER, SUSANNE
1951   *Philosophy in a New Key.* London: Secker.
LEGUIN, URSULA KROEBER
1975   *The Tombs of Atuan.* New York: Bantam.
LÉVI-STRAUSS, CLAUDE
1955   *Tristes Tropiques.* Paris: Plon.
MARQUET, JACQUES
1974   Isomorphism and Symbolism as "Explanations" in the Analysis of Myths.
       In *The Unconscious in Culture,* ed. by Ino Rossi. New York: Dutton,
       pp. 107–122.
OTTO, RUDOLF
1923   *The Idea of the Holy.* London: Oxford University Press.
THOMAS, L. L., J. Z. KRONENFELD, AND D. B. KRONENFELD
1976   Asdiwal Crumbles: A Critique of Lévi-Straussian Myth Analysis. *American Ethnologist,* 3(1):147–174.

10

MOVING UP IN THE WORLD
TRANSCENDENCE IN SYMBOLIC
ANTHROPOLOGY

The Multitude Within—The One Without

When I was very young in the Spoon River country of northwestern Illinois—what sophisticated easterners and H. L. Mencken called the Bible Belt—we used to recite a rhyme with our hands . . . you all will know it. "Here is the church, here is the steeple, open the doors and see all the people!" For some reason I used to think of the head when we popped our thumb-doors open and not of a church. I thought that the human head if we could pop it open would prove to be full of people. I still think so. That was long before I had read Edgar Lee Masters's *Spoon River Anthology* or Ralph Waldo Emerson's set of essays on *Representative Men*. For Masters our mind is a graveyard poignantly planted with the shades of all the people we have known and who have remained in or emigrated from the communities of our lives. Though I come from Masters's country I prefer Emerson's view that our mind is a perpetual "multilogue" in vivid or at least revivified communion with all the significant others we have known. Emerson treated his inner life in dramatic terms. "Turning inward I am my own comedy and tragedy," he said. He felt that if he could keep that multilogue going some of those transcendental truths, that overarching unity, of which he had a priori intelligence—uncertain as it often enough was—could be revealed. Out of multitude, singularity.

Emerson, though he was projected transcendentally beyond them,[1]

This chapter is reprinted with permission from *Stanford Literature Review* 1, no. 2 (Saratoga, Calif.: Anma Libri, 1984).

was part of a movement which gave what James Agee in praising "famous men" called "weight" to the incidental personal presences of life.[2] It is that "weight" and voice" which must lie at the heart of anthropological endeavor. To paraphrase the quantifiers' Humean maxim: "Take up your ethnography! If there is therein no weight of personal presence—no voices heard—cast it aside for it is mere self-serving methodology and inert to the moral imagination."

This paper is a kind of multilogue—though not a very dramatic one—between some representative characters I have known directly as an anthropologist or indirectly through texts which I have found for complex reasons attractive. My characters—I use the possessive because it is I who brought them together—are Emerson, an African hunter named Ekang Engono, and a Spanish mountain herdsman named Santos Bandera. It is appropriate I begin with Emerson because he was something of an "eminence" of my youth. I attended Ralph Waldo Emerson Grade School as a child. Of course there are many other representative characters in this paper—important accessories to the argument.[3] Can anything coherent possibly emerge from such a multitude? I think so. I think that considered together they can help us see some transcendent principles involved in human behavior. Taken together they can help us transcend certain confining and confounding categories of cultural analysis.

It also ought to be said that our heads are not only full of people but also full of our own prior texts with which any new text such as this is in interaction. Two texts of my own are particularly relevant here: a paper I wrote on "The Mission of Metaphor in Expressive Culture" and a critique I did of a review of the work of Leslie White,[4] an early though rather hesitant user of the symbol concept in anthropology. I hope that this present text can illuminate further some of the points made about "transcendence" in those earlier efforts.

"Practical Idealism" and Symbolic Anthropology

> A foolish consistency is the hobgoblin of petty
> ethnography.

Let me begin with a contradiction, possibly an unwelcome one and perhaps of the kind which Lévi-Strauss argues to energize cultural activity in its expressive aspect. In part it will energize this paper. It might better be called an inescapable paradox of our procedure in the study of man. Very simply there is no self-consistent, no non-self-contradictory method in this study insofar as we pretend to give an adequate account—render intelligible—human experience in culture. Such an account will always be both and rather than either/or. It will be, for example, in the given case both personal and impersonal, explicit and implicit, synthetic and analytic, materialist and idealist, structural and processual, practical and spiritual, descriptive and formal, and, to use the terms that most interest us here, both empirical and transcendent. It will not be all of these things at once but it will always be some of these things together.

One would not argue for an indiscriminate Whitmanesque mix of these perspectives in our work. Rather one argues for an interactive tension between them—the kind of tension that energizes symbolic activity and is productive of insight in the reader. This kind of interactive tension is best produced where there is a clear understanding of the essential differences between the paradoxical options appropriate to a given cultural analysis. The challenge to ethnographic style—though it is not simply a matter of style alone—is to grasp the differences of approach at play and to negotiate them fruitfully and systematically. One doesn't argue against system, only against a foolish consistency in system.

The challenge is to develop contrasting but interdigitating perspectives in treating our materials without having the one collapse into, be absorbed by, or become a mere reflex of the other. The challenge is the maintenance of that double angle, that stereoscopy which is the source and best guarantee of depth in human understanding as it is of depth in human vision. I do not argue that the sequence of neat bipolar sets we have given necessarily and self-sufficiently summarizes the varieties of interactive tension that may be present in our ethnographic accounts. I argue only that the nature of the phenomenon under scrutiny and our inescapable involvement with it require that we transcend any given perspective. Anthropologists—paladins of the comparative method *par excellence*—are fond of arguing that we do not understand any culture in and of itself, only by comparison. So only by transcending a given perspective on human behavior do we understand it—and through it our materials. Perhaps we understand this very well already in anthropology in our stubborn insistence on placing a paradoxical procedure, participant observation, at the very heart of our method?

The either/or mentality is, for many good and quite logical reasons, an ingrained one in the academy. There is a certain innate interest in taking, if only, as we say, "for the sake of argument," consistent and hence combative positions and fighting it out upon the parapets. Just the same, in recent decades in the human sciences we find arguments being made for just such interactive approaches as we argue for here—arguments being made for "subjective behaviorism,"[5] for example, or for a biological axiology[6] or for a cognitive symbology.[7] And in general terms our argument is similar to that put forth by phenomenologists in their requirement that we recurrently "wrench ourselves away" from a taken-for-granted, mundane perspective in order to reflect upon it and reinvest it with "primordial strangeness."[8] The necessary interplay of opposed perspectives is essential as well to dialectical method. Our argument is manifestly not a new one. It simply affirms that symbolic anthropology is an interactive, self-transcending approach—a kind of, to use Ralph Waldo Emerson's turn of paradoxical phrase, "practical idealism."

Enraptured Yankees

> Nature is the incarnation of a thought and turns to a thought again as ice becomes water and gas. The world is mind precipitated and that volatile essence is forever escaping again into the state of the free thought.
>
> Essay on *Nature*

Putting it that way and evoking Emerson, the enraptured Yankee, as one of his biographies labels him, gives us a much older reference for the interactive approach. Hardheaded, well-grounded, and astutely strategic people like Yankees could become enraptured in the presence of natural symbols pregnant with transcendent emotions. To be a transcendentalist was to transcend over and over again the received and customary categories of early nineteenth-century existence.

The Sage of Concord may not immediately appeal to us. There seems to be something altogether too sternly romantic there, expressed in a rather too ponderous, if not pontificating, prose.[9] Yet if there ever was a participant observer, it was Ralph Waldo Emerson, an intense participant in the experiences of his everyday world. He had great capacity as a realist—for seeing and saying exactly how things were in nature and society. And this was widely admired in him. But his was, of course, a "mystical participation" as the Durkheimians and particularly Lévy-Bruhl came to call it among the primitives. For he was constantly alert and receptive to the inrushes of emotional conviction—emotional conviction of an overarching order—that this participation brought him. He was constantly alert to emanations from the oversoul—the voices of other realms—in mundane things—"fire or rain or a bucket or a shovel or dead sticks could do new duty as an exponent of some general truth."[10] Readily convinced, he was easily carried away to transcendental observation. Lévy-Bruhl, in respect to prelogicality, might have avoided a long, painful denouement of his otherwise valuable investigations of "primitive thought" had he taken Emerson as one of his *naturvolker*. It would have been quite legitimate.

We should not be, however, so put off by the mystical element in his participation as to think that it has nothing to say to us—or at least to us in symbolic anthropology. For though in some respects it might be argued that Emerson lived in a world different from our own—worked through a different episteme, as Foucault has taught us to call it[11]—in one respect, at least, his world, the post-Kantian world, in its emphasis upon the constitutive power of mind,[12] the shaping power of pure reason, is the same as ours. It is the same as ours in its insistence that certain dictates of common sense such as produce hardheaded realism, astute materialisms, calculating utilitarianisms, or complacent unitarianisms (to mention the particular commonsense religion Emerson was in struggle with) do not sufficiently speak to the constitutive power in human experience . . . the power of mind over matter, of culture over practical reason.

Emerson and the transcendentalists were interested in transcending the commonsense commitments of the popular and professional philosophies of his time. So today is symbolic anthropology. Emerson was interested in the problem of the subject-object relation. So—if only to transcend it—is symbolic anthropology. And Emerson was interested in symbol. As he said, "There is a joy in perceiving the representative or symbolic character of a fact, which no bare fact or event can ever have. We learn nothing rightly until we learn the symbolical character of life."[13]

There is also a comparison to be made between what Emerson and the transcendentalists were reacting to in their time and what symbolic anthropologists are reacting to in ours. In both cases the reaction is to what might be called a popular Newtonianism—a clockwork, overly mechanistic, determined view of man's place in nature and society, a view of the human as overly much an effect caught up in an "iron cage" of causes with limited options—strategic and otherwise—to create meanings. It is a view that neglects the human power to shape universes within which to live, that neglects the contradictions, inconsistencies, ambiguities, and strains within and between systems which sooner or later require of some men and women that they be causes and not only effects, creators of categories and not only creatures of them.

Two Representative Men: A Hunter and a Herder

> There was a tone in his preaching that
> awakened all elevating associations.
>   J. R. Lowell on Emerson

Though Emerson has left us a great deal of luxuriant text to go by, we cannot know him as the anthropologist always wishes to know his subjects—in the fullness and weight of their personal presence, in close attendance upon the unfolding of their life histories. Let me therefore ground this discussion in a way that is comfortable to me as an anthropologist by referring to two "enraptured" personalities known to me who appear in two quite separated cultural traditions: the Northwest Bantu tradition of the Fang of the western equatorial forests of Africa and the Western European Atlantic fringe (cum Alpine) tradition as found in the Cantabrian Mountains (Peaks of Europe) of northern Spain. So much cultural time and real space separates these two personalities that it would be easy to show their incomparability. Yet sitting in their reflected presence one finds figurative processes at work which identify them. In psychological parlance these seem alienated individuals—and they are perceived by some of their fellows as sociopathic. These men eschewed normal social intercourse. They frequently railed against the qualities of the social life of their times. They wandered lonely in the forests or the mountain heights in transcendent communions, keeping to themselves yet returning to society infallibly at intense ritual or ceremonial moments to communicate their visions. These communications were received by their fellows with particular attention in the expectation of emergent understanding. Many of these communications were memorable and became general knowledge in the auditors' subculture.

I have discussed some of the texts of these personalities elsewhere[14] and will limit myself here to the briefest reference to these texts. I want to contextualize their texts in part, but I will be mainly interested in the arguments they put forth—the argument of images, as we are calling it— which give us insight into constitutive understanding, the kind of understanding, Kantian in inspiration but surely Emersonian as well, which since the work of Ernst Cassirer and Susanne Langer has been central to the symbolic approach. The symbolic emphasis on the constitutive contrasts—since we have evoked psychological parlance—with a certain psychological understanding and its emphasis upon diagnostic, classificatory, categorizing operations. We are not here so much interested in putting our two representative men in their place—categorizing them—as in understanding how their arguments transcend categories, awakening certain kinds of emergent conviction in auditors by, as it were, the use of elevating associations. As Emerson observed, there is "a great parallax in human nature best ascertained in observing it from different states of mind."[15]

Our lonely hunter of the equatorial forest, Ekang Engono, is the chapel leader of a religious movement, Bwiti, in the Gabon Republic. His height and stately bearing, his eloquence when he is moved to speak, his wisdom in judging the disputes brought to him by the membership, in short, his prophetic manner, make him a charismatic leader. But for much of the week he wanders alone as a hunter in the deep equatorial forest. On Fridays or early on Saturdays he returns from these long sojourns to prepare for and be present at the all-night ceremonies of Saturday and Sunday morning. But even here he maintains, as he can, his isolation, periodically resting hidden out of view in a semisomnolent state in the grave pit during the all-night rites. At midnight, in particular, he or his assistant speaking in his name rises to present the "miraculous words" that have come to him in the grave pit. These words—actually a sequence of aptly associated images—are followed with awestruck attention by the membership.

In the morning, after the all-night ceremonies have concluded at 6 A.M., and in the euphoria of an arduous task happily completed, the prophetic hunter sits moot on the disputes within his membership, restoring conviviality in those still resistant to its achievement in the ceremonies. It is a conviviality more easily reestablished because it is achieved in the afterglow of the ancestors' presence. It is a main purpose of the all-night ceremonies to attract the ancestors, abandoned through the efforts of missionary evangelization, back into the presence of their descendants. The ancestors leave the chapel at first light but enough of their presence remains to maintain euphoria well into the coming day.

Not so long after the ceremonies are finished and if there are not other chapel matters to detain him, Ekang Engono returns to the forest to his life as a hunter. This hunter's life, he tells us, removes him from that constant strife of village life which has produced the conflicts he has just sat in judgment upon. How could he, if he is to sit in judgment upon them, participate in that life himself? The hunter's life is best for him. The deep forest maintains his purity. It also keeps him in the closest relation with the ancestors, whose abodes are in the watercourses of the deep forest.

Our second representative of a transcendent lifestyle was a gifted village versifier, Santos Bandera, who gradually withdrew himself from village life, taking more and more to wandering in short-range transhumant husbandry from cabaña to cabaña in the mountain heights. In these long, lonely, lofty itinerations he mulled over his verses and then, at festival periods, patronal feasts, or calendrical holy days, returned to the villages below to recite them. Many of these poems constitute memorable images remembered after his death.

For both men, the lonely lifeways they pursued were not exceptional to their cultures' ranges of lifestyles. Fang combine hunting with tropical agriculture and all men hunt to some degree, though few with such concentration as Ekang Engono. In all Cantabrian Mountain villages all families engage in cattle keeping and agriculture. And all families or their representatives must herd their cattle in the common pastures of the high peaks. But no villager stayed as long in the peaks as Santos Bandera, and none was so independent of his relatives. For both cultures these pursuits of hunting and herding are regarded as freeing their participants from the strains of village life. Fang men look forward to hunting to free themselves from the clamor of the village and the demands of their wives, and Cantabrian cattle keepers look forward to life in the cabañas in the summer pastures to free themselves of intrafamily tensions in the villages. So both cultures offer these possibilities for the transcendence of the give and take, the rancorous rub, of village life. But our two representative men have taken advantage of these possibilities to an extraordinary degree—and in doing so they have, like the possessed or the ecstatic in worldly cultures, placed themselves (or have been thrust) beyond and above those interactions of the subject-object world held to be practical and normal.

Transcending the Subject-Object World

Within man is the soul of the whole; the wise
silence, to which every part and particle is

> equally related, the eternal *One*. The act of
> seeing and the thing seen, the seer and the
> spectacle, the subject and the object are one.
>
> "The Over Soul"

In a self-possessed, pragmatic, and industriously efficacious culture like our own, possessive and ecstatic experiences seem bizarre and bootless states of mind, at best irrelevant. Yet anthropologists know how widespread they are in cultures and how there is a potential for them even within pragmatic cultures. We have only to remember the recent years of our own youth culture. Emerson, who had a very tranquil and self-possessed turn of mind, was yet possessed by the possibility of elevating the mind through "the high functions of the intellect" to the ecstatic apprehension of the oversoul. (The lofty metaphors of height were recurrent as he argued toward this apprehension.) Emerson had the hard if not impossible task of finding common ground between two opposing realities: the Great Reality of Spirit and the undeniable reality of individual and evolving nature. He could not deny his natural individualism. And he could not deny the oversoul into which it must inevitably collapse. Thus was he driven by these contradictions to his final theory of the identity of subject and object "in a substance older and deeper than either mind or matter."[16]

Because this ultimate identity sorely tested his expository powers—its ineffable quality better addressed, as he intimated, by a "wise silence"—Emerson turned to the symbol as the only instrument of mind capable of teaching us that apprehension and embodying the contrarieties involved. He was constantly searching for symbols of the oversoul though often enough they turned out to be earnest abstractions like "The One," "All-dissolving Unity," "Great First Cause"—symbolic intellectual offsprings that only a transcendentalist could love.[17] More interesting to us now, I believe, and more illuminating, is the problem of the interaction and the transcendence of the subject-object relation. One useful way to approach possession and ecstasy is to see these phenomena in terms of the transformation and collapse of the subject-object relation—in the case of possession the appropriation of the subject by a significant other, a significant object; in the case of ecstasy the appropriation by the subject of an object significantly other than itself. There are two different vectors involved when we speak of possession on the one hand and ecstasy on the other, different vectors or tendencies as between the subject and the object. In both cases it is transcendent interaction. In possession we predicate the significant other upon ourselves. The transcendent is embodied. In ecstasy just the opposite occurs and we are predicated upon *it* . . . *we approximate it.*

I refer here to what I believe must be a central concept in our study of human behavior insofar as we wish to understand how self, society, and culture are constituted. This is the concept of predication. Human nature is a constant process of predication of subjects upon objects, in this view, and vice versa.[18] This begins in the infant as the primordial self learns to know of itself as subject to others' actions and to think of itself thus as an object to others. It also learns of the differing relations that it, as subject, has to the object world whether persons or things—the ways it can predicate itself upon them. Some of these developments are approached in Piaget's notion of "decentering"[19]—a notion that enables us, also, to think of Emerson's identification of subject and object as a kind of recentering or egocentrism.

We learn in life to construct a more or less workable model of life in here, in the self, and life out there in container space and chronological time. Customarily our maturity and practicality is judged by how well we learn the limited boundaries of the self, how well we learn to give credence to the constancies of the routine, practical, everyday world, how well we learn to avoid transcendent attractions that rearrange and even collapse the normal subject-object relations of the workaday world. Common sense and practicality wish to preserve these routine commonsense working relationships between subject and object. Alas, there is built into the predicative process itself an impulse toward transcendence. We are inevitably aroused from routine subject-object relations.

Fischer argues that these recurrent arousals are of two kinds: ecstatic and meditative.[20] He gives us a model, in fact, that helps us grasp Emersonian "identity." Fischer makes a distinction between the deep subcortical "self" and the competent "I," controlling and managing its affairs, operating effectively in the normal subject-object world. Ecstatic or meditative arousal acts to return to the self. The space-time constancies learned by the "I" contract and vanish as perception-behaviour becomes increasingly dependent upon the subcortical stratum and hence increasingly self-referential. There is an increasing paralysis, loss of freedom, in the objective world. There is produced that inability so characteristic of the mystic to experience the subject-object dichotomy of the daily routine in the physical dimension. Fischer refers, very appropriately for us here, to Behannen's account of the yogi experience.[21] At the peak of the meditative experience the yogi can "see" objects but the objects have no "predicative properties," no "compelling content." The loss of predicative properties, one supposes, would be the equivalent of Emersonian "identity."

We have no good evidence of these kinds of arousal in Emerson such as we have in the case of Coleridge and Carlyle, Emerson's congeners in Anglo-German idealism. Coleridge's heavy drug use undoubtedly aroused him in this way and Carlyle's enraptured experience of the "everlasting yes" qualifies as this kind of arousal. Emerson as he himself admitted was a distant, chilly person incapable perhaps of reaching with his subcortical self what his intellect grasped. He could not march personally to the supercategorical imperative he so clearly heard.

Though we speak here of the transcendence of the subject-object relation, it is in the interaction of that contrasting relation that we are primarily interested. For we argue here the inescapable necessity of interaction and transaction in human experience between categorically separated entities. We symbolic anthropologists, since we are not transcendentalists, are not really interested in identity but rather in the interactive tensions and transformations between the plurality of subjects and objects—and kinds of subjects and kinds of objects—involved in social predication. Transcendence and identity are achieved in that transaction but it is on the transaction itself that we should concentrate our attention.

The Flow of Features in the Argument of Images

> The possibility of interpretation lies in the
> identity of the observer with the observed.
>
> "Representative Men"

Emerson, Coleridge, Carlyle are lofty and high-flying references for the usual anthropology and made the more difficult by the complexity and sophistication of their writings. We prefer the enlightenment to be found in the lives of humbler folk, less affected by the complexities of the written word and the burdens of accumulated texts—the written tradition in which it is enmeshed. Let us return to our herder and our hunter and look more closely at what they were reacting to and what they were trying to achieve. Very simply, they were reacting to the subjectively demeaning force of the utterances and idiom of village life—the debasing and vitiating urgings and persuasions that were characteristic of that life.

In the case of Santos the Herder, debasement was the primary motive. Like many another Cantabrian villager with a gift for spontaneous verse, Santos the Herder for many years of his life dealt ably in the jousting of that verse, a verse largely devoted to putting up and putting down of fellow villagers—mostly putting down. This is a verse* which makes natural use of what lies at hand and is well understood: things found in stables, stableyard and fountain plaza, in meadows, streams, and mountain pastures.[22] It is a very physical poetry seeking objective correlatives to social situations in cows, donkeys, goats, manure, lice, and chickens and in physical defects—goiter, baldness, and lameness. It is a poetry that is very much a part of the irritating rub of the social life of the village and it contributes in its physicality to the vitalization of that life. But the manipulation of the verse is mostly devoted to putting down rather than putting up. It is most often derogatory, derisive, or plainly abusive. Apparently, and this is the case with Santos, the constant jousting of the verse, the jocular hostility characteristic of it as well as its endless deprecatory physicality, is tiring. Older village versifiers frequently enough tire of it if they do not, like our herder Santos, retire from the village itself to more metaphysical perspectives. Here is an example of that exchange— part of a jocular hostile exchange between two villagers one of whom had been called "bald as a pig's fanny."

Sepas tu ignorante,	Take heed, ignorant one,
Faltoso de entendimiento,	Lacking in understanding
Este calvo muy honrado	This honorable bald one
Ye de buenos sentimientos!	Has very good judgment!
Mientras tu con melena	While you with your mane
Paez un burro penco.	Appear a raw-boned burro.
Quien sabe en tu pellaje,	Who knows of your pelt,

---

*See the study of some of these same poems lent to quite a different purpose in Chapter 3.

Cuan habitantes habra dentro?	How many inhabitants within?
Correte por alli peludo	Run along, hairy one,
Con melena de carnero.	With your ram's mane.
Vete y dile a tu amo	Go and tell your master
Que te lleve al asadero.	To carry you off to roasting.

What Santos has moved away from and attempted to transcend is a poetry of bold mockery of fellow countryfolk, at best, and in part of the genre a poetry of *campanillismo*—celebration of place—where the village or the parish locality is celebrated usually by invidious comparison to another place.[23] Thus this folk poetry is a poetry of persons and places. The argument the poems make is argument by analogy in which the subjects of the verse are put up but mostly put down by their association, by similarities or contiguities, to estimable or reprehensible qualities inherent in the objects—so often barnyard objects taken up and predicated upon them.

Whatever reasons may account for Santos's alienation from this topical verse and from his village, at the least we may identify in him a sense of surfeit and insufficiency in this argument and particularly as regards (1) the mockery and settlement of scores that the verse is mainly devoted to, and (2) the physicality of practically all images introduced in the argument, which is to say the reduction of village culture to brute nature, and (3) perhaps a sense of insufficiency as regards the argument itself—the elliptical progression of unexamined associations by which persons or parts of persons are identified, moved about in quality, included or excluded. The identification process is too reductive.

Whatever the constellation of causes, the poet's later poems are mainly lofty and contemplative, and, instead of employing the everyday and the very familiar to move persons and places around in the quality space of everyday life, seek for and invite the auditor to conceive of an Archimedean, metaphysical point beyond the self-serving village hurlyburly, the unexamined and too easily identified round of life. They are even a denial of place. Here is one of his best remembered poems, "An Eternal Passport," cast from this lofty Archimedean point. The passport reference comes from Santos's much earlier experience as emigrant to Cuba, an experience shared by many villagers. In metaphysicality these poems are, perhaps, reductive, too, although in a different way—the way of transcendence.

Adios mundo engañador	Goodbye world of deception
de ti me estoy despidendo,	To you I am bidding farewell
los años me lo permiten	The years permit it of me
yo la culpa no la tengo.	The fault is not mine.
Adios mundo engañador,	Goodbye world of deception,
que triste fin a la postre!	What a sad end for the conclusion!
una larga supultura	A long interment
y un eterno pasaporte.	And a passport to eternity.

There is an apparent paradox in our charismatic African personality, Ekang the Hunter. For if his lifestyle is as lonely, as apparently alienated, as that of our mountain troubadour, at the same time he warns against the loneliness (by which he means, I think, the competitive individualism) of modern life along the highways of colonial commerce in which witches have isolated man from man and men from their ancestors and men from their milieu in order the better to attack and eat them. But not only are men and women lonely, they are lost. They have lost what he calls the Path of Birth and Death. He announces that it is his task to knot together again, to show the relation of things—for the world, he says (not so differently from Emerson), is really one thing. And he wishes to show men and women the way. His method in his miraculous midnight words is to work with "likenesses" *(efonan)* and string them together in such a way as to show that all things can be associated with one another. For, to abstract very simply from one of his midnight sermons, a man is like a tree and a tree is like a path and a path is like a stream and a stream is like the course of human life and the course of human life is nothing more or less than what men and women are—altogether, to tie this particular sermon back together in typical tautological fashion, trees that grow upward, paths that move outward, and streams that flow onward. Thus is the world tied together and men and women returned to a directionality in their lives, for all things can be shown to resonate with one another by an argument of images strung together by plausible associations—images which expand and contract, which reoccur thematically with various parts of themselves coupling with other images. The progression of images is altogether edifying. One has only to read a typical passage of these sermons to capture the thick resonance of imagery which creates the overall impression, at least for an auditor privy to the culture and its customary associations. Here is a passage in which intelligent spirit is being identified with tobacco smoke:

> The clay of our flesh collapses and the spirit comes forth arriving in rapid waves of wind. And the wind of bright light is brighter than the light of the mirror. And it passes away forever. The hot tobacco we smoke brings reflections [thoughts] upon that light . . . it becomes hot and takes fire and it endures forever. These reflections [thoughts] arise, climb up as the smoke. They become hot. They take fire. They endure forever.

This charismatic if elliptical sermonizer excoriates the modern condition of lonely and lost villagers abandoned by or abandoning their ancestors with witches preying upon them, and justifies his own loneliness as a hunter on the basis that it is no loneliness at all, for unlike the "lonely crowd" of village life, as a hunter he is in the constant presence of the ancestor spirits whose village of the dead lies in the deep forest and whose miraculous messages he reproduces in his communications. Moreover, as an alert hunter he is in close attendance upon the natural surround, detecting the "likenesses" that all the natural objects display and storing his detections for future sermons. Unlike the Cantabrian village versifiers to whom Santos was reacting, Ekang uses analogies to build up rather than tear down. Thus he finds himself in his hunting and embodies part of the world of the dead and a resonating part of the interwoven equatorial forest. In the same way perhaps—though we have no specific commentary from him on the point—our high-mountain herding troubadour would argue that his isolation is more closely accompanied by spiritual presences with intelligence of overarching order than anything that could be achieved in village life. The contemplative life brings him closer to completion than can be achieved amidst the jocular hostilities and the invidious versification of the give-and-take of village life.

Both our prophetic hunter and our metaphysical herder have achieved a transcendent perspective, although that transcendence is addressed in different terms and has different vectors. Ekang the Hunter is said to have died many times in his forest sojourns, coming to know the dead better than the living. For Santos, villagers more often employed a vocabulary of quasi-psychological categorization. While finding power in his verses they tended to see him as alienated, disturbed *(chiflado)* "not fully functioning in village life" *(mal adaptado)*. Nevertheless both these folk descriptions of our transcendent characters exactly miss the dynamics of transcendence involved. For the village impulse to categorize Santos misses his desire to escape local categories—to deny them. And the assigning of Ekang the Hunter to the category of the dead—although an assignment differently interpretable than in Western culture—misses the life, the vitality he was seeking to restore to, and the change of category he was seeking to effect in, equatorial life.

To get a better grasp of the dynamics of transcendence in these two representative men, we might now usefully transcend the particularities of our description and apply semantic concepts to the subject-object relationships and the predicative acts involved.[24] This is especially the case when we are dealing with the argument of images where predications are figurative and violate ordinary selection rules for the relating of subject and objects and where metaphors and metonyms are brought to bear upon uncertain—inchoate—subjects. We have before us a poem where the passage between life and death is predicated to be ironically a customs transaction between separate sovereignties. And we have before us a sermon passage where hot tobacco smoke is predicated upon the intelligent spirit enmeshed in the degenerating clay of our corporeal selves. In these figurative predications we have presented for interpretation, then, the interaction between a subject and a predicate, either a verb or a verb and a predicate object.

Figurative predication is anomalous in the sense that it violates normal rules of predication; semantic features characteristic of the subject are incompatible with features found in the predicate—death is a passport and spirit is tobacco smoke—and we must decide how to interpret the relationship between these features and whether the features characteristic of the object are to be transferred to the subject or vice versa. When we are told that spirit is hot tobacco smoke or death is a passport we have to decide whether something is being said primarily about spirit or about hot tobacco smoke, about death or about frontier transactions, that is to say, about emigration—or about both of these at the same time. These are questions of conjunctive or interactive reading. And there is directionality to this reading: there is an interactive reading that moves toward the subject and another that moves toward the object—toward the predicate. Thus we may read the predication "Death is a permanent passport" in the subjective direction as death is a guaranteed passage to an alien territory. Or we may read it in the predicate direction as emigration is a kind of cultural death. We may read "Spirit is hot smoke" in the subject direction as spirit is warming, stimulating, and diaphanous, or in the predicate direction as tobacco smoke is animating.

In the conjunctive or interactive interpretation, though there is directionality in reading, the subject and predicate remain in interaction.[25] But there is also a possible reading that suppresses that interaction—which suppresses what is in effect an enriching sense of interaction between the various categories of experience. This is called semantic displacement or deletion—a kind of semantic reductionism. Emigration is read simply as death, or spirit as simply something diaphanous that floats above. No doubt it was the tendency toward displacement in village verse—the tendency to displace humanity with animal nature—that repelled Santos. And it was just this loss of the capacity to villagers to interassociate the various categories or domains of experience—their isolation in categories—that provoked in Ekang his efforts to convince villagers that all things were one thing.

Relevant to Ekang's efforts there is a final interpretive possibility. We have to decide whether the anomalousness in the predication—the incompatibility of features—asks of us that we generalize in the semantic hierarchy, attempting to find the least general feature or set of features which dominates the incompatible features and is therefore consistent with both. Death and emigration are passages into foreign territory. This is called a disjunctive or generalized reading. It is a kind of semantic induction in which the main emphasis lies in finding a level of semantic reading in which incompatible or anomalous features become consistent. In some consistent sense death and emigration are passages of frontiers and spirit and tobacco smoke are essences that float upward. We may also call this a transcendent reading and it is a reading characteristically encouraged by our hunter and our herder as it is by Emerson. The transcendence they promote in important part is achieved in their mode or argument and in the reading they characteristically require of their listeners. For both men ask of their auditors—they are no different in this than the transcendentalists—to conceive of a different world in which to live—a world pointed to by their anomalous poetic assertions—and a world that would, coming into conception, make their anomalous assertions true.

If both of our representative men ask us to conceive a different world, nevertheless, the constructions to be put upon the conception are quite different. Santos is reacting to the displacement and reduction characteristic of village poetic combat. It is a displacement and reduction that produces a village world of turbulent physicality and animality. "*Somos* (or '*sois*') *animales, bestias!*" is a frequent exclamatory self-judgment. Such debasements, in which Santos once skillfully participated, drove him, one surmises, to his solitary herding and his search for transcendence.

In the heights he sought not to reduce village life to its animal equivalents—its lowest common denominator—but rather by temporal and spatial images of quietude and eternity to generalize village life to its highest spiritual enumerator. These poems were laden with pathos and argued for the inconsequence of village life, converting its vitalities into mortality, its lively temporality into eternity. Reacting to the reductive displacement in village verse, Santos's method remained the same. By the predication of images of the eternal upon the temporal of village life, the mortal upon the vital, quietude upon turbulence, he displaced the vital features of village life. Instead of a lively and conjunctive interaction we have alienation of self and understanding auditor from the turbulent assertions of village life. It is an effective form of transcendence, although in the end devitalizing.

The construction which the equatorial hunter and sermonizer offers to his coreligionaries is of a different order. He edifies in a different way and he "revitalizes." First of all, his sermons are such a flow of elliptical images, each of which resonates with every other, that the net effect is conjunctively persuasive. The incompatible features of distinct natural images from different domains of experience are brought together in such a way as to be interactively illuminating. By appealing to likeness he means to suggest that nothing is isolated; all things are connected and mutually resonant. He argues for a persuasive conjunction of the features of experience and saves thereby the isolated and the lost from a feeling of isolation and the mortality contained in it.

But periodically Ekang asks of his listeners that they constitute meaning beyond and above the conjunction and mere interaction of things. He asks that they constitute by disjunction a higher-level apprehension that all interresonating things are really to be seen as one thing. All these resonating but distinct images can be discovered to have at some higher-level conceptualization a consistent set of features dominating their mutually incompatible features. Thus he argues that all these resonating things are really one transcendent overarching all-encompassing thing under the control of a set of transcendent powers—the ancestors primarily and behind them the Great Gods. His followers are thus revitalized not only in their sense of the overarching power from which that coherence flows.

Our hunter and our herder by different methods—devitalization and revitalization—and along different vectors constitute a better world for those who would be their followers. Their lonely ways, we see, are part of their method for they remove them from the debasement or vitiation of the ongoing social life of their time and place.

Returning now to our epigraph from this section of our discussion, we may ask in what sense we can identify with these men we observe and whose work we seek to interpret. After all, each of them asks that we conceive a world much different from the pragmatic one we presently occupy. Willing as we may be—to use the Coleridgian phrase (Coleridge himself was faced with the inertia of commitment to category)—to "suspend disbelief," it is difficult for us, given our mechanistic world view and commitment to categorical thinking—such commitment as is characteristic of much social science thinking. For the men we consider here, like all transcendentalists, ask that we collapse and transcend categories. They ask that we take categories as means to some larger sense of entity and not as the endpoints of economic or political order.

It is also the case that their world to begin with—out there on the fringes of the Western empirium (our world system)—is so different from our own that for that reason also we have difficulty in identifying with their impulse towards transcendence. For that reason alone our recurrent evocation of Emerson is useful to our understanding of them. It helps us lodge them in our own tradition even though Emerson himself, it must be admitted, is difficult for many to empathize with.

The first answer to the problem of identifying with those observed in different cultures—and the first task of interpretation—lies in the anthropological effort at descriptive integration—giving, as the fruit of our participation and this task, the descriptive grounds and the particularities necessary for subjective identification. In this way we can transcend our ethnocentric preoccupations, suspend disbelief, and obtain a certain empathy with the objects of our inquiry. We may approximate, thereby, the kind of identity of empathizing subject and observed object that Emerson envisioned. When we have thus transcended ourselves the second task of interpretation awaits us—a second act of transcendence. For interpretation *is* transcendence. This is the attempt to transcend the cultures brought into comparison in some universal vocabulary of understanding pertinent to both—by the nature of the case, a vocabulary analytic and formal. In this paper and in response to this second interpretive task we have argued for the transcendent understanding contained in a semantic vocabulary: an understanding of the panhuman processes by which subject and object are identified by processes of feature transfer. By understanding how objects are related to subjects in predication and vice versa, we not only learn about the necessary subjectivity of experience, we also learn how antecedent subjectivity can be objectified. Understanding subject-object predications can give, in its way then, a second transcendent understanding and an enduring basis for "identifying" with the observed.

Conclusion: Categorical Imperatives

> The first thing we have to say respecting what
> are called *new views* here in New England, at
> the present time, is that they are not new, but
> the very oldest of thoughts cast into the mould
> of these new times.
>
> *The Transcendentalist*

It is now time to come to a conclusion—to take our representative men, our interdigitated personalities, fold them and our hands together like the priesthood and silently point to the sky. One way of stating my point, perhaps, is that since the Kantian defense of the powers of pure reason over against practical reason and over against Lockian empiricism many of us congregate in the same church—the church, it may be called, of categorical understanding or constitutive understanding, however we might phrase it. Unlike most churches, of course, it is not a church with closed doors but one that can periodically "pop open" its doors allowing its members to reconstitute themselves. By categorical understanding I mean (there is a long history of philosophical debate over this term) understanding of the predicative processes by which (1) social subjects are assigned qualities, quantities, relations, substances, conditions, etc., (2) features can be transferred between subjects and objects, and (3) categories can be transcended in order to achieve ultimate and pervasive being, oneness or goodness. This paper has largely been devoted to this latter problem. Though this way of looking at category is not precisely the Kantian way it, like Kant, gives full play to the constitutive powers of mind and can even offer a categorical imperative based on a recognition of the human imperative to transcend confining categories: "Assign categories to others only insofar as you would be willing to have such categories applied to yourself!"[26] This is an imperative at least as difficult of realization in the practical world as the Kantian one—but no less worthy of contemplation!

Such an imperative—while no doubt frustrating to much social science[27]—would seem to me to promote the most reflective kind of inquiry into human behavior in its own terms and would seem to be at the very center of a truly symbolic account of that behavior. And this is to say in other terms that any consistent and self-sufficient account of that behavior conducted without what Emerson called parallax or phenomenologists call "reflective shifting" or what we have argued here to be progressive transcendent interpretation produces by its very nature constricting categories. At the heart of these "new views" of ours in symbolic anthropology, we see then, are some very old thoughts on categories cast into the mold of our times—the times of the organization man, the categorized man, the performance-tested man, living in the control society.

It may be our tendency to think that, in addressing this issue of transcendence, we are addressing micro-matters or epiphenomenal matter of very personal matters of the play of mind in its immediate circumstances. Nothing could be further from the truth. The transcendental impulse, the search for a new and reconstituted whole, lies at the heart of revitalization—it energizes most of the major social movements of human history.[28] The recurrent vision of the possible transcendence of bad times is a vision basic in social upheaval.

We have ignored these large-scale matters here as we have also ignored many kinds of transcendence—or perspectives on transcendence—because of our preoccupation with our three main problems: (1) the problem of the possible kinds of transcendence (devitalizing and revitalizing were identified here), (2) the problem of the transcendence implicit (or imminent) in symbolic activity, and (3) the role of transcendence in the anthropological tasks of descriptive integration and in choosing relevant modes of construal in the interpretation of culture. We have thus had to ignore such problems as the relation between transcendence and transformation, as for example in the contrast between the transformation obtained in "rites of passage" and the transcendence obtained in rites of intensification. We have also ignored the related problem of the anti-structural or countercultural element in transcendence—the search for, or achievement of, a distinctly nonhierarchical or nonstructural "communitas."[29]

Transcendence is, *par excellence,* the problem of symbolic anthropology because the symbol, like any of the figurative correspondences to which it can be reduced[30] cannot be processed in everyday, routine rational ways but necessarily evokes associations that surpass the immediate situation[31]—that in some way carry us beyond, above, before, behind, that immediate situation. This is, to be sure, the Durkheimian point about collective representations: Men and women situated in their own individual bodies and preoccupied with personal individual interests and impulses could yet through collective representations transcend such intimate involvements and recognize collective obligation and collective sentiment.

If we think back now on our title here, we recognize that it is a mischievous one for the moving up it suggests is not the transcendental movement we have been discussing but rather movement within the system—and more particularly the American system. It is movement—or rather mobility—of the kind that conforms to the clockwork, mechanistic view of man, that view so ingrained in the dominant American value system—the dominant pragmatic world view. This mechanistic causation predicated upon human nature, we are all aware, displaces the complex features of that nature and yields a machinelike nature ticking away. Tinkering with a nature so constituted, we are too naively inspired with the possibility of perfection. But while, no doubt, a certain kind of perfection can be reached within categories or a system of categories, human creative capacities of displacement, conjunction, and disjunction of features are such that no final—nontranscendable—perfection will ever be found within any set of categories. We are too inchoate to begin with and too mischievous in our predications to end with. And that is all that, practically, this paper is ideally about . . .

Notes

The central section of this paper was given at the 1979 meetings of the American Anthropological Association in a session organized by James Peacock and Theodore Schwartz on "Psychological and Symbolic Approaches in Anthropology" and carried the title "Psychic Alienation and Semantic Transcendence: On Constitutive Understanding." The present version of the paper was read before a December 1981 colloquium at the Center for Art and Symbolic Studies, University of Pennsylvania. Barbara Hernstein Smith extended the invitation. The two horns of the argument received, inevitably, different emphases in these two quite different contexts, the one much more science-oriented, the other much more humanistic. I believe the center of the argument held, however.

1. No doubt Emerson's congener Wordsworth and his disciple Whitman gave more weight to the "incidental personal presences of life" than Emerson, who had too much austerity to him to experience that strong empathy characteristic of the Romantics with everyday men and women. Nevertheless there was an everyday alertness in Emerson as well.

2. James Agee and Walker Evans, *Let Us Now Praise Famous Men* (Boston: Houghton Mifflin, 1941), p. 12.

3. These include Emile Durkheim, Claude Lévi-Strauss, Leslie White, and Samuel Levin.

4. See Chapter 2 in this volume and "On the Concept of the Symbol," *Current Anthropology* 16, no. 4 (1975):652–54.

5. G. A. Miller, E. Galenter, and K. Pribram, *Plans and the Structure of Behavior* (New York: Holt, 1960).

6. Derrick Freeman, "Human Nature and Culture" in *Man and the New Biology* (Canberra: ANU Press, 1970), pp. 50–75.

7. Cf. "Symbolism and Cognition," A Special Issue of the *American Ethnologist* 8, no. 3 (August 1981).

8. For a perceptive discussion of this "wrenching away and phenomenological search for strangeness," see Maurice Natanson, "Phenomenology as a Rigorous Science," *International Philosophical Quarterly*, 7, no. 1 (March 1967), 5–20.

9. This is Kenneth Burke's term—introduced in his discussion of Emersonian transcendence (Burke 1966:187). Burke finds in pontification the essential transcendent act—bridge building. "That's what transcendence is, the building of a terministic bridge wherein one realm is transcended by being viewed in terms of a realm beyond it." Alden Becker (n.d.:6) applies this term to Emerson's sentence-focused prose. Emerson was, Becker points out, an innovator at the level of the sentence—a level at which the brisk modern reader does not expect such extraordinary investment of attention as Emerson gave it. Emerson thus "slows us way down" and we tend to find him ponderous . . . pontificating.

10. *The Journals of Ralph Waldo Emerson*, vol. 9 (Boston: Houghton Mifflin, 1914), pp. 277–78.

11. In *The Order of Things: The Archaeology of the Human Sciences* (1970).

12. An interpretation of Kant that makes his emphasis upon the constitutive power of mind central to subsequent philosophy is that of Langer, *Philosophy in a New Key* (1951). The dauntingly mystical term "transcendental idealism" is more mundanely seen as, simply, the argument that that which we know is conditioned by factors in our cognitive apparatus and if we are to get at "things in themselves," it is not to appearances but rather to our cognitive apparatus and the culture in which it is embedded that we must repair.

13. For an illuminating selection of Emerson's writings on symbol, see chapter three, "A Thread Runs Through All Things" in Alfred Kazin and Daniel Aaron, *Emerson: A Modern Anthology* (Boston: Houghton Mifflin, 1958), pp. 102–60.

14. See Chapters 3 and 4 particularly.

15. From the essay "Representative Men" in *Essays and Poems,* selected and edited by G. F. Maine (London and Glasgow: Collins, 1954), p. 314.

16. See the discussion of this aspect of Emerson's philosophy in H. D. Gray, *Emerson: A Statement of New England Transcendentalism as Expressed in the Philosophy of Its Chief Exponent* (Palo Alto: Stanford University Press, 1917). See particularly chapter five, "The Identity of Subject and Object."

17. In the constant struggle within Emerson between idealism and materialism or realism and nominalism (see his essay "Nominalist and Realist") the compelling essence to be found in General Ideas proved overpowering to him very often.

18. The subject-object distinction is certainly problematic insofar as it is conceived of in mind-body terms and is cast, to quote the beginning of Marshall Sahlins's eloquent argument against it, "in terms of the endemic Western antinomy of a worldless subject confronting a thoughtless object: ineradicable opposition of mind and matter, between the poles of which 2,500 years of philosophy has succeeded in plausibly drawing the line of reality at every conceivable position" (1976:x). For any truly effective cultural argument about or against, the primacy and reality of practical activity—whether this primacy is Marxist or not—must eradicate the mind-body antinomy in any of its terms (the same is true for any argument about the healing [physiologic] efficacy of symbols [Moerman 1979]). But our purpose here is to show precisely how subject and object *are* interactive and mutually influential—how subjective thought constitutes the objective world and the objective world gives identity to subjective thought. While the whole program of breaking all propositions down into subjects and predicates may have come under telling criticism in philosophy, the pointing up of subject-object interaction remains a relevant task and, in my view, is part of that criticism.

19. If we introduce here—as relevant to the notion of transcendence—Piaget's Copernican view of the ontogeny of reasoning processes in children—the transcendent shift from egocentrism to a decentered perspective—it is pertinent also to refer to the views of the "other" psychology, psychoanalysis. Transcendence, there, would be that escape from a constricting, categorizing superego and a turbulent and misbegotten "id" offered by the distancing and self-objectifying processes of abreaction—processes in which, to use Ricoeur's term, in *Freud and Philosophy* (1970), the regressive is transcended and turned into the progressive. See also G. Obeyesekere's Morgan Lectures, *Psychoanalytic Anthropology and Some Problems of Interpretation* (MS) for a discussion of regression-progression in psychosymbolization. See particularly chapter one, "After Medusa's Hair: Progression and Regression in Personal Symbols." The point is that if cognitive growth is transcendent in one sense, psychic healing is in another.

20. Roland Fischer, "A Cartography of the Ecstatic and Meditative States," *Science* 174 (26 November 1971):879–904.

21. Ibid., p. 901.

22. These "barnyard correlatives" and their argumentative effect are discussed more fully in Chapter 4.

23. Santos's verse is discussed in Chapters 3 and 4.

24. The best recent summary and innovative formalization of the subject-predicate interactions involved in anomalous (metaphoric) predications is that of Samuel Levin, *The Semantics of Metaphor* (Baltimore: Johns Hopkins Press, 1977). See particularly chapter 3, "Modes of Construal."

25. The interactive view of metaphor is most persuasively put forth in Max Black, *Models and Metaphors* (Ithaca: Cornell University Press, 1962).

One cannot pretend that all that is occurring in the generation and predication of tropes—that which makes them relevant and that which is implied by them (matters of relevance and implication)—is explained by identifying semantic movement of this rather mechanical kind—disjunction, conjunction, displacement. For example, the most complex problems of metaphor having to do with transformative sets of predications such as underlie the analyses of Claude Lévi-Strauss are not addressed by this semantic theory (as I have argued elsewhere, in a review of *The Semantics of Metaphor* [*Language and Society* 8, no. 2 (1979):281–84]). One must argue, however, that the mechanics of this argument are a useful way to break down and transcend an epistemic subject-object dichotomy.

26. Or perhaps "only insofar as you allow for their transcendence of these categories.".

27. Not to anthropology, however, whose task it is, in my view, in its cross-cultural accounts to amplify categories and to show the possibility of other categorizations of experience than the ones we are accustomed to. A remark by Emerson is apt to anthropology's skepticism about categories: "A classification or nomenclature used by the scholar only as a memorandum of his last lesson in the laws of nature and confessedly a makeshift, a bivouac for a night, and implying a march and a conquest tomorrow—becomes through indolence a barrack and a prison, in which the man sits down immovably, and wishes to detain others" (*Complete Works*, vol. 7, pp. 22–23).

28. This is a point fully made in a special issue of *Daedalus* devoted to transcendence (Vol. 104 [Spring 1975]). See also G. F. Willey, "Mesoamerican Civilization and the Idea of the Transcendent," *Antiquity* 4, no. 2 (1976):205–15.

29. These problems of transformation, transcendence and the structure of "communitas" are discussed in T. Turner, "Transformation, Hierarchy and Transcendence: A Reformulation of Van Gennep's Model of the Structure of Rites de Passage" in *Secular Ritual*, ed. S. Moore and B. Meyerhoff (Ithaca: Cornell, 1978), pp. 53–70.

30. See the argument for underlying correspondences in symbolism in "Analysis of Ritual: Metaphoric Correspondences as the Elementary Forms," *Science* 182 (28 December 1973):1366–67.

31. For the capacity of the symbol to evoke extra situational references see J. W. Fernandez, "Symbolic Consensus in a Fang Reformative Cult," *American Anthropologist* 67(4):902–27, particularly p. 922 where it is pointed out that whereas the signal is "immediate, dependent, imbedded in the existential situation of coexistence and coordinated interaction, (the symbol) is autonomous with super-added meanings forever pulling the culture carrier's attention beyond his immediate situation to the larger implications of his action—creating self-awareness." Dan Sperber has given a clear and useful account of the differences between rational and symbolic processing of experience and the necessary evocativeness of the latter. "Is Symbolic Thought Pre-rational?" in *Symbol as Sense*, ed. M. L. Foster and S. H. Brandes (New York: Academic Press, 1980), pp. 25–44.

11

CONVIVIAL (AND IRONIC) ATTITUDES

A NORTHERN SPANISH KAYAK FESTIVAL IN ITS HISTORICAL MOMENT

Just as in the case with respect to persons in whom the reasoning power is absent, the figurative imagination of crowds is very powerful, very active and very susceptible to being keenly impressed. . . . A crowd thinks in images and the image itself immediately calls in a series of other images having no logical connection with the first. . . .

Gustave Le Bon, *The Crowd*

The progress of human enlightenment can go no further than in picturing people not as vicious but as mistaken. When you add that people are necessarily mistaken, that all people are exposed to situations in which they must act as fools, that every insight contains its own special kind of blindness, you complete the comic circle returning again to the lesson of humility. . . .

Kenneth Burke, *Attitudes towards History*

The focus of discussion in this chapter is an international kayak festival and race held in the seaside mountains of northern Spain, and particularly the folklore parade *(desfile folklórico)* held just before the race. The paper is motivated by enduring Durkheimian interests in the "laws of collective ideation" and in the problem of the creation of moral order in community.

264

But this paper also bears relevance to the work of two thinkers of inescapable concern to students of the human condition: Kenneth Burke, and particularly his concern with viable *Attitudes towards History* (1937), and Ivan Illich (1975), and his repeated attention to the problem of conviviality in the "technological iron cage" of modern society.

The race takes place from Arriondas to Ribadesella in the Province of Asturias, northern Spain, and the parade takes place in Arriondas. In this parade, to borrow and rephrase W. L. Warner's (1961) observation on a similar American event, the citizens of Arriondas and Asturias collectively state what they do not really believe themselves to be and thus leave open what they can become. Locating the parade within a simple typology of northern Spanish street events, I also attempt to locate its historical position. The most instructive comparison for this time and place— immediate postauthoritarian democratic Spain—is with the military parade. Rather than the military "instruments of violence," we might say, the folklore parade displays "instruments of conviviality." But the parade is also a powerful counterstatement to the exaltation of national culture. The consequence of such playfulness is a potentiality for a wider collectivity of human relations.

Knowledge from work in the behavioral sciences on collective behavior and crowd formation is employed to understand the phases of the festival. But fundamentally, it is a theory of the role of figurative predication in behavior—the play of tropes—that is explanatory and helps us to account for the "convivial attitudes" of this kayak festival. The basic trope considered here is "reflexive irony"; and we must think about its place in historical process. This mix in the inquiry leads to a theory of "transcendent humanization" in behavior. The play of tropes is shown, essentially, to be the play of collective mental processes of classification and collection. In briefest formulation, this paper deals with the relation between collective ideation and historical processes of human enlightenment.

An Obstreperous Individual

On the first Saturday of August 1982, I once again participated in the folklore parade that preceded the Fifty-first Annual International Kayak Race from Arriondas to the sea and the seaport town of Ribadesella.[1] I later observed the race from the special fluvial train that accompanies the racers along the west side of the river. And later yet I participated in the seaside afternoon and evening festivities in Ribadesella that follow the race. I should say that this year, as opposed to previous years, I observed the parade more than participated in it. Because of a friendship of some years with the incumbent socialist mayor of Arriondas, I was invited onto the reviewing stand along with the mayor and other friends, as well as some of the assemblymen *(concejales)* and their friends. Not all of the *concejales* were on the reviewing stand—some because of differences with the mayor and his party and others because they were not so inclined. Those on the stand were thus raised above the crowd which the parade always attracts and which is often so numerous as to intermingle with the paraders and even to interfere with the progress of the parade. It is often difficult to distinguish the parade from the crowd that engulfs it.

We were not raised so far as to escape, early on before the parade really got started, the loudly delivered and, for the most part, humorously received observations of an obstreperous and slightly tipsy individual on the other side of the street. A young man in his late 20s, he began by calling out, "Mr. Mayor, Mr. Mayor. You of the opposition side there. [He meant both of the opposition party and the opposite side of the street.] What are you doing up in the stand placing yourself up above the people. Aren't you the party of horizontal democracy? What is this outmoded 'verticalism' [*verticalismo*] you practice there? Come down! Come down into the street with the rest of us!"

These and other similar observations continued to be shouted until the parade began in earnest, although the man's remarks were increasingly dampened by the rain, which is a frequent accompaniment of the fiestas and *romerías* of the Cantabrian slope of northern Spain. Disappointingly, the rain became more intense as the parade proceeded. And this obstreperous young man was, like practically all the young people and despite the justness of his remarks, without an umbrella—the indispensable accoutrement of Asturian life. Those of us in the reviewing stand were amply provided with umbrellas. The mayor, it ought to be said, stood the entire time without an umbrella and, furthermore, was bareheaded, a populist gesture that was perhaps not lost on the crowd.

Before an account of the parade itself is given, let us consider for a moment the humor involved in the remarks directed at the *tribuna* from the other side of the street. The humor played on several anomalies. First, there was the incongruity of having a reviewing stand at all for a folklore parade. The various floats and musical and dance groups had only the vaguest sense of passing in review. And the review process itself—a highly

disciplined presentation to a select and judgmental group of authorities—
which is integral and, indeed, the focus of the military parade, was largely
absent. No prizes were to be awarded, at least not from the reviewing
stand. More humorous, though, were the ideological issues. The previous
authoritarian regime, in their "national socialism," argued for (and sought
to impose) a "democracy" characterized by a syndicate organization of
vertical communication between the ruling elite and its followers. This
worked only by coercion, particularly in Asturias, a province with marked
egalitarian values and a large working class of miners and metalworkers.
During the Franco years, these workers maintained surreptitious "horizontal" unions and *verticalismo* was the subject of ironic commentary, if
not derision, by such elements of Asturian society as were present in large
numbers in this parade (e.g., smallholders, workers, small-town merchants and tradesmen, and members of the rural bureaucracy). That the
socialist mayor and assemblymen of his party—a party whose politics
were those of egalitarianism—should raise themselves above their countrymen on a reviewing stand, a structure on which, in any event, the
former regime was much more at home—was clearly apt for humorous
commentary.

Another issue ripe for irony, at least at the time of the parade, arose
from the fact that the socialist party (meaning here the PSOE—Partido
Socialista Obrero Español) seemed to be clinging to the opposition role
despite its manifest strength in many provinces, and surely in Asturias.
This continuing preference for "opposition" was a source of humor. Given
the many economic difficulties with which Spain was confronted in the
transitional years, coupled with the continuing presence of Francoist
elements in the state bureaucracy and the army and other "forces of
order," the party seemed to be strategically postponing its accession to
power and settling into a more comfortable permanent opposition. This
source of ironic commentary, however, was to be eliminated soon with the
convincing electoral success and accession to power of the Socialists in the
national elections of November 1982.

One has difficulty, in any event, imagining this kind of mocking commentary taking place in front of a municipal body during the Franco
period, even though the use of Carneval and the carnival atmosphere to
mock political authority has august ancestry in Spain and Europe.[2] Such
commentary simply would be unimaginable as an intrusion into the
military parades that were the favorite events of the former regime. Even
folklore parades in that period were provided with large contingents of

civil guards *(Guardia Civil)* and national police, not to mention local municipal police. And their presence was always quite evident. There were still many of these "forces of order" present on this Saturday in August 1982, but they kept much more in the background. The socialist mayor and his colleagues may have agreed to appear on a reviewing stand, yet they did not go so far as to surround themselves, as in the Franco days, with the "forces of order." They were willing to suffer the "indignities" of an "obstreperous individual" and an "unruly crowd"!

Ironic Incongruities of Situation

While one cannot easily imagine an "obstreperous individual" openly shouting out ironic and mocking observations to the authorities at public functions during the Franco period, irony was the main covert weapon against oppressive authoritarian situations of domination and subordination. As in contemporary Poland, ironic commentary in the form of jokes about the disparities between official pronouncements and pretentions and the actual state of affairs was extensive. One consequence of the democratic transition is, as we see, the opening up of public life to such heretofore more circumspect observations. But in any event, irony has the advantage, since it speaks by opposites and depends on a rather moot sense of incongruity, of not directly confronting authority. Authorities can tolerate ironies as relatively mild challenges to their hegemony and control of the means of violence. Ironies just work away in the rotten hulls of authoritarian repression—they do not attempt to seize the cannons on the deck.

By irony I mean any of a variety of standard rhetorical devices by which something is asserted in such a way that we understand just the opposite or at least something clearly different from what is asserted. Ironic awareness is essentially the awareness of incongruity. By dramatic irony I mean an incongruity between what is asserted in any form of discourse and the actual developing state of affairs. For example, the "obstreperous individual" was pointing out the incongruity between socialist rhetoric and the actual "verticalism" being acquiesced to by the mayor and his *concejales.* Such incongruities are inevitable and inescapable in human social and political life, and no laudable commitment to sincerity and authenticity in that life should allow us to forget their abundance. Incongruities are more present in some social and political situations than in others, however. Here it should be recognized that the years following the forty years of the Franco regime are transitional in the evolution of Spanish political life and hence are full of ironies apt for humorous interpolation. That is, they are full of incongruities in which people are saying one thing or being told one thing but are aware that they are living another. Thus the irony of a situation of apparent new freedom and new hopes and new options while the "forces of order" of the former regime are still in place—the army, the civil guard, the national police, the state and provincial bureaucracy. Their continuing presence in the Spanish situation makes the rhetoric of democratic freedom and equality sound dramatically ironic and incongruous with the actual state of affairs.

Whatever ironies are a part of these transitional times in a much larger sense, there is an incongruity and a dramatic irony in Spanish history bound up in Spanish decline. The developing situation, beginning in the late 16th century, of loss of empire and increasing economic and political disorganization and impoverishment at home, the increasing falling out of contact with the science, technology, and industry of the rest of Western Europe, stands in ironic contrast with and reveals the inappropriateness of the continuing rhetoric of empire and Spanish universality. The bold posturing of successive military regimes—the *triunfalismo,* as the Spanish ironically call it—is simply belied by the empirical situation. This seems to have been sensed already by Cervantes in Quixote's ironic commentary on the adventurous promise of picaresque tradition. There is a deep irony in Spanish history itself, in the development of a state of affairs—drastic decline—the very opposite of what was to be expected of an empire. It is my experience that these historical ironies are not lost on the Spanish, at least not on the Asturians. Provincial literature is abundant in "humorous histories." In more austere parts of Spain, these ironies may give rise to the pessimistic and ultimately "eschatological dignity" of a "tragic sense of life." This is not the case in the province, except perhaps in the very highest echelons of the Asturian intelligentsia. Asturians readily see the irony in their situation, as this *desfile folklórico* shows. The ironies are not only those of an obstreperous individual.

A Joyful if Rainsoaked Procession

This particular kayak race has gained such renown in the province[3]—indeed, it is well known nationally and internationally, and points gained there qualify racers for the annual international championships—that this Saturday in August attracts people from all over the province and much of northern Spain. They begin arriving the day before the event. On Friday evening and well into the next morning Arriondas is alive with roaming groups of young people, with street dancing and street music. Often, the crowds that attend the parade and the subsequent race have had very little sleep the night before. This adds a readiness to participate as well as a certain indiscipline and intermingling that makes it difficult to bring the parade off with any precision. The "obstreperous individual" on the opposite sidewalk showed all the signs of all-night revelry.

Participation in the parade is invited from anyone who takes an interest in it. International kayak teams and their representatives are especially invited. Since the race begins just after the parade, very few foreign visitors participate as the crews and their support teams are busy preparing the start. Also, the foreign teams are puzzled as how to take the parade. Is it a serious review and authentic presentation of self? Or is there something essentially frivolous about it? In any event, only an English, an Australian, and a Dutch group paraded in 1982. Indeed, the sincere demeanor of these groups did seem out of place amidst the cavorting multitude. Perennial elements in the parade are folklore groups from various parts of the province, all similarly dressed in their black, red, and white traditional costumes. They are most often young people in their late teens and early twenties led by two elderly men playing the bagpipe and drum. Periodically, these groups stop to form a circle and dance. There were eight groups from various parts of the province in the 1982 parade. Since these folklore groups are ubiquitous at practically any celebration—*romerías,* patronal fiestas and holy days, fairs and *certamenes* (e.g., *ferias de muestra)*—they are not as interesting a challenge to explanation as the other less traditional and more calculatingly composed and presented elements in the parade. That is, these classic folkdance groups make their obviously important contribution to the definition of situation, and definition of provincial identity, but they are not subject to a very complex reading. Essentially, their presence signals the folklore situation and demarks the phases of its progress, but they are not part of the play of tropes.

Most interesting is the attempt on the part of the organizers of the parade[4] to present a kind of historical overview of the province. The word went out to various kayak groups and booster organizations *(peñas)* of the vicinity that such was the intention. But specific assignments were not made and it was left to these various groups to communicate among themselves. William Lloyd Warner's (1961) study of the parade of town and state history in the bicentennial celebration of Yankee City (New-buryport), Massachusetts, is relevant here. As Warner (1961:89–159) points out, "the town fathers of Yankee City decided that the successive floats of their parade should develop their history . . . the Aboriginal Indians and the Forest Primeval, the Coming of the White Man, the settling of the town, the Revolutionary War etc. . . . ." In this way the leading citizens, and especially the Protestants, sought to legitimate their past and to state collectively what they thought themselves to be. Nothing so well organized and intentional was ever worked out in Arriondas. No deep study of local history accompanied by distinguished lectures was made. No attempt was made to assign the various historical events to specific groups. It was simply suggested to the various groups that histor-ical motifs were in order. The result, naturally, was desultory. But the chief differences between the two events is the utter seriousness with which the town fathers and citizens of Yankee City sought to portray their history through the parade. The only irony, and that was inadvertent and existed largely in the eyes of Warner and his readers, was the initial assignment to the local Jewish community of the Benedict Arnold float. In Arriondas, by contrast, every historical presentation was designed to make ironic commentary, to make light of that history by interpreting it within a framework of comic portrayal of some of its main elements.

Thus, the only float—it came along after a bagpipe, drum, and dance group and the alternates for a number of provincial kayak teams—was a wagon drawn by a tractor. It held some 15 or 20 men, all dressed in cavemen skins and carrying the red and yellow plastic billy clubs common to Carneval, as well as some rough-hewn hand axes. A very large papier-mâché hand ax covered with tin foil towered over the wagon. Although this float was labeled España, to set it off from the foreign groups that were to precede it (but did not), it carried Asturian flags and was intended as the first entry in the historical series representing the Stone Age ancestors of the Asturians. It was an ancestry amply confirmed by the paleolithic sites and considerable cave art actually present in the province. The seaside town of Ribadesella, in fact, possesses one of the finest examples of paleolithic polychrome art of Franco-Cantabrian Europe.[5] Note the em-phasis on mock weaponry in this float, in playful relation to the real instruments of violence of the military parade. The *porras* (plastic billy clubs) were not only in the possession of the men on this float but had been widely distributed among the young people marching in the parade. As the marchers danced along they beat tattoos on each other in time to the music and occasionally "menaced" bystanders in the crowd who had lined up on each side of the street. The cavemen with their mock weapons were so calculatedly brutish as to make obvious the ironic contrast with any serious image of paleolithic Asturian forebears.

Following the Stone Age float were members of the Ribadesella canoe club—*Unión las Piraguas*—dressed in roman togas and led by a monarchical figure in a tin crown. From time to time they knelt before and around him as he delivered a peroration praising Asturias, its people, and its climate while the "famous" Asturian rain poured down. This group was obviously a conflated representation of Roman and Visigothic history and the eventual conquest of Rome, as well of the Romans in Asturias, by the Visigoths. They were accompanied by musicians playing instruments made of stovepipes, water hoses, and plastic toilet pipes and by a considerable number of young people flailing around with their *porras*. The Visigothic king and his Roman court were followed by a kayak team carrying paddles and dressed as pirates. One sensed that they were out of place because after them appeared a group dressed as Arabs and immediately after them was a group of capitalists in black suits with stovepipe hats scattering play money—in thousand-dollar denominations—to the crowd. The Arabs harassed the Romans and the Visigoths with large clubs and were themselves engulfed by the capitalists and the swirling green stuff they scattered around. Subsequently, the pirates fell back to mingle with a kazoo band whose instruments also were made of plastic plumber's piping. This band, from the port city of Gijon, were inveterate participants in events of this kind. They traveled many weekends a year to participate in such events wherever they were held. Their worldliness gave them some sense of superiority over the other groups, and they did not hesitate to take center stage and monopolize the space in front of the reviewing stand until asked to move on by a sign from the mayor.

After this, the historical representations ceased. Various kayak teams then passed by, and finally, at the very end of the parade and preceded by a sports team from Avilles dressed as Neptune's minions with trident spears mounted on their paddles, came the Giants and Bigheads. The tiny Bigheads marched around under the feet of the Giants, presented in provincial costume as the traditional countryman and countrywoman, Pin and Tielva. The final units of the parade were composed of other sports groups, including the three foreign representatives mentioned earlier.

Because of the rain, the bagpipe drum and dance team assigned to bring up the rear had tired of waiting and had joined the procession much earlier on. So without any final marker the parade really faded off with a very large crowd of people tailing after it. No one, at least on the reviewing stand, was quite sure whether the parade was really over or whether there were several more groups to come. By the time the decision had been made that it was over, the street was so crowded that the mayor and his assembly, even with the aid of the municipal police, had difficulty making their way the several blocks to their reserved platform at the river's edge. When they arrived, the kayak race had already started—an ironic outcome of their supposed supervisory role, something the "obstreperous individual," had he been present, would have been sure to note. The irony also would not have been lost on sympathizers of the former authoritarian regime. Had the mayor made use of the civil guard, he would have arrived on time.

The Phases of a Festival of Two Towns and a River

Although the main focus is on the "folklore parade," something further must be said about the events of the day in order to understand the festivities in their entirety. After the start of the kayak race, the town empties and as many people as can by car and autocar, by the fluvial train, by biking or hitchhiking, follow the kayaks the 25 kilometers or so of their strenuous passage to the sea. For most of this distance the Sella River winds through the steep canyons of the coastal range and is flanked by the railroad and the highway. The race is usually over by 1:30 P.M.—all racers who are going to arrive (that is, who have not foundered) doing so in two and a half hours.[6] At that time the *romerías* begin. I use this term in the most general sense to mean a convivial gathering in an extramural, necessarily outdoor milieu, although all the stages of the classic Asturian *romería* (see Fernandez and Fernandez 1976)—in particular, the religious functions—are not present. For families from the origin town of Arriondas, and for their relatives and friends, the race is followed by a *romería*-type picnic on a riverside meadow on the outskirts of Ribadesella. Many clusters of extended family groups, each gathered around their food and drink, are spread around the meadow more or less oriented toward a platform next to the willows by the river where a string of performers of the Asturian bagpipe, the deepsong, and the dialect country-bumpkin monologues all appear. Their performances may be followed by general singing and dancing. This *romería* is very much an Asturian affair and few of the multitude of strangers in attendance participate here. It is a time of provincial and local conviviality.

In the streets of Ribadesella it is another matter. Here, all the other visitors gather—those from distant parts of the province, from other provinces, and from other countries. All of the thousand or so kayakers, with their team associates, are gathered here. The various teams congregate and technique and technology are compared, perhaps a kayak is traded or sold, and T-shirts are exchanged. Shortly, multinational groupings of young people begin to make the rounds of the tents set up on the wharfs purveying *calamares, gambas a la plancha,* fried *chorizo, churros,* and all the other *tapas* Spain is known for. Ever-present and a challenge that is laughingly engaged in by the foreigners is the drinking of Asturian hard cider. It must be poured from its bottle, while held high over the head, into a large glass held at the knee. There is always a great crowd at this urban *romería* added to late in the afternoon by those who join it from the other *romerías*. And if things go well—if the rain stops, for example, as it did in 1982—it goes on until late into the evening or into the early morning hours. The various provincial and national groups lose some of their awkward sense of difference and carouse together, feeling themselves, perhaps, part of a greater human whole.

If we now consider the festivities in their entirety, we note that there are phases of participation and observation, intensification and dispersion, in the crowd's experience. These are the phases of foregathering, of the parade itself, of the kayak race, of the *romerías*, and of the aftergathering. The foregathering—of the evening and morning before the parade and race—and the aftergathering—after the *romerías*—are phases of relatively unorganized conviviality in which the different identifiable groups—familial, provincial, and national, are of slight importance. One promenades about, and full participation is possible simply on the basis of attendance and membership in the crowd. In the parade there is separation between the performers and the observing crowd, but this is not tightly controlled and some of the crowd is regularly inspired into full participation in the parade. In the race there is, necessarily, full separation, and the crowd become merely observers of the event. At the same time they are, each and every man and woman, each and every family, engaged in their own race to keep up with the kayaks and make their way through the crowd to the seaport city. Indeed, after the conviviality of the foregathering and the parade, there is a pell-mell, everyone-for-oneself atmosphere. The crowd undergoes a separation phase. Finally, it is gathered together again, first in the *romerías*—in which the separateness of family units and sports teams and groups is still featured—but more assuredly in the subsequent aftergathering.

This festival, more complex than the usual rite of passage, is also unusual, perhaps, because it is not the festival of one locality and one community. It moves from one town to another and thus escapes the sociocentrism, the community focus, of traditional Spanish festival. It is really the festival of two towns linked by a river. It is also, in its way, a provincial, an interprovincial, and, indeed, an international festival. It is equally a composite of several varieties of street life.

The Varieties of Street Life

It is useful to briefly review the three genres of street life in this northern Spanish province so as to more adequately frame this "folklore parade" and grasp the contexts that, in part, give it its meaning. I make a simple distinction between orientation toward images of the self and orientation toward images of the significant other for in the shift from self-interest to other-interest lies the fundamental creation of moral order. We note that the festival shows a mix of all these genres.

Paseo (Promenade)

Every evening after 7:30, and on Sunday afternoons after 4:00, the streets of Asturian towns, except in the smallest hamlets, and except during rainy weather, fill with the *paseo*. The *paseo* is a social promenade, and primary to it is the presentation of self—along with a secondary interest, complementary to the first, in observing *(fisgando)* "significant others" of the town. One might say that one purpose of the *paseo* is to make the self over into a significant other. Many parts of the kayak festival have a *paseo* feeling.

"The Procession"

The images one sees presented in the *paseo* are largely the images of self that individuals and families want to make public, putting their best foot forward. The religious procession is also an occasion for self-presentation, but the attention is given over here to the religious images being transported—the image of the significant other than can define the self is of dominant importance. With the greatest sincerity there is the presentation of group belief and group identity. It is the religious icons—those images of saintly devotion, of human weakness and betrayal; of suffering and crucifixion; of sorrow, hope, and exaltation; of maternal love; of saintly martyrdom and saintly equanimity—from which the townspeople learn both about themselves—the potentialities of their most authentic humanity—and about the ultimate circumstances and values of life as embodied in these imaged others who are the ultimate referents of their identity. In the kayak festival parade there is a progression of images of significant historical others. But ironic rather than sincere presentation is the norm.

Parades (*desfiles*)

The events focused on here make us aware of two kinds of parade: the military parade, the normal unmarked category; and the folklore parade, the marked category to be understood within the frame of the military parade. Military parades have been a pronounced presence in Spanish national life not only because of the imperial past but because of the succession of military regimes that have appropriated and exercised power since the mid-19th century. These regimes have sought to consolidate and manifest their power by frequent displays of the instruments of violence . Military parades are largely the parades of provincial and national capitals—very large cities where large numbers of troops and weapons are quartered and can be marshaled.

With present democratization, military parades are on the decline. But it is still necessary to read the *desfile folklórico* in the context of the military parade and as standing in meaningful contrast with it. In both cases of procession and parade the self is caught up in the greater whole attracted by the display of the significant other. The spectator is re-impressed, constrained, and loyally reconverted to expected allegiances by that display. Parades and processions are, I argue, moments of both constraint and conversion in the presence of the significant other, though there is much more constraint in the former and conversion in the latter;

there is also more imposed sincerity in the latter and voluntary sincerity in the former.

There are other kinds of street activity that have characterized northern Spanish life. There have been many spontaneous and disgruntled crowds in the history of Asturias, such as those that have appeared regularly in the mining zones of Asturias since the turn of the century. These crowds—an example is the one that gave rise to the miners' revolution of October 1934—have a high potential for concerted and destructive action. Because of the potential volatility of such crowds in Spanish history, indeed in European history (Rude 1981), successive regimes have been uncomfortable about crowds of any kind, including festival crowds. They have always sought to send among these crowds the "forces of order" to make sure that the crowds do not suddenly change the framework of their being, shifting from playful representations to serious protestations, from desultory and self-interested milling about to concerted action. Bateson (1974) discusses with instructive subtlety the ever-presence of the possible shift from the "this is play" frame to the "is this play?" frame in the life of human groups. The "forces of order" are present in large numbers, paradoxically to guarantee continuing playfulness. In the festival before us—the summer crowd of 1982—there was, first of all, very little if any latent disgruntlement or resistance to the "willing suspension of disbelief" which might shift the festivities into something much more serious and challenging, so far as the authorities were concerned. Second, the ironies were too patent in this curious and playful mix of *paseo*, procession, and parade.

The Festival Crowd: Its Composition and Dynamic

One takes away from this festival day of the descent of the Sella a memorable impression of the crowd. Total participation in 1982 was estimated at well over a hundred thousand people. The town of Arriondas was crowded, as was the town of Ribadesella after it. The fluvial train was packed and the highway to the sea was congested with cars, buses, bikes, and hitchhikers. Even the river was crowded with kayaks (some 700 kayaks and 1050 kayakers participated in 1982). Indeed, as more and more competitors show up for this race over the years, the start of the race has become increasingly cumbersome and disadvantageous for those kayak teams who draw low numbers and must start hundreds of yards upstream. There has been, in recent years, a great melee of kayaks at the start of the race, and many founder. At the same time, in order to be successful in the minds of the organizers and participants, not to mention the dozens of itinerant vendors and tent merchants, the festival must attract a crowd. The fact of the crowd is an obviously important, and memorable, part of the experience. Everyone loves the crowd on this occasion, just as they love the parade as a sign of the success of the proceedings.

We have only to remember Albert Einstein's profound mistrust of parades and the crowds they enchant to recognize how problematic the phenomenon is—and not only for authoritarian regimes who suspect its volatility. On the one hand, from the Durkheimian (1965) point of view, a crowd is a crucible that, working through the law of large numbers, guarantees that kind of intensification of social experience in which the moral order and community ideals often embodied in images of significant others can be revivified, in which egocentrism can be restrained in favor of altruism, and in which the obligatory can be made the desirable. Einstein, on the other hand, had good reason for his mistrust of the "altruism" inspired by the parade and motivated by the crowd. And, quite beside the bigotry parades and crowds inspire, the martial spirit and the particular kind of "mindlessness" characteristic of parades and enthusiastic crowds are very far removed from the cerebral and inner-sanctum atmosphere in which a theory of relativity could be worked out. Still, the crowd "mind" has long been postulated and its working has intrigued its students since Gustave Le Bon (1920[1895]), the pioneer in this study, as the general epigraph of this paper indicates.

Before addressing the question raised by Le Bon, one that is central to our interest here—the way in which the collective mind works—it is instructive to consider several other implications of his work having to do with the broader historical context in which the *desfile folklorico* appears, for profound questions of "attitudes toward history" are before us. Up to this point in the discussion, the *desfile folklórico* is framed mainly within the context of the Spanish military parade. If we take note of Le Bon's conservative preoccupations and realize the influence of his own thought on the "forces of order," we find even more reason for regarding the military parade as the relevant ground from which to consider the folklore parade. Also, while Le Bon tended to, with one exception, generalize about all crowds, subsequent work has sought to differentiate between the types of crowds. The exception to Le Bon's lumping of all kinds of crowds together sprang from his ideas on race. He distinguished crowds according to the "national soul" of the nationality composing them. Thus he distinguished sharply between a Latin and an Anglo-Saxon crowd: "Crowds are everywhere distinguished by feminine characteristics [he meant that they were volatile, willful, and changeably fickle] but Latin crowds are the most feminine of all. Whoever trusts in them may attain a lofty destiny with the certainty of being soon precipitated" (Le Bon 1920: 96).

It should be remembered that the most avid readers of Le Bon's work and the quickest to exploit this new knowledge of crowd behavior were the military minds of his time. In particular, the French General Staff studied this new discipline of collective psychology in an effort to raise the level of commitment and the esprit de corps of French troops in the face of the highly disciplined and self-abnegating German armies (Nye 1975). Le Bon's "collective psychology of the crowd" promised knowledge of the phenomenon useful to those who would motivate and/or control large congregations of people. On the positive side, from the military perspective, such knowledge could be used more effectively to animate troops (and public spectators) to higher levels of commitment in nationalistic enterprises and foreign wars. Parades, with all their glamorous and romantic display, surely had that result. On the negative side, at a time in history when, as a consequence of the industrial revolution, class-conscious crowds were having an increasingly turbulent effect on orderly government, the military charged also with maintaining internal order could profit from this new knowledge of crowd psychology. In any event, the emerging totalitarian—mostly military—regimes of the twentieth century have been quick to appopriate this knowledge for their authoritarian purposes. Military parades with their somber, cold-spirited display of these "instruments of violence," which it is the state's legitimate right to employ, are effective means for the control of the crowds they attract.

To say that because these processions of folk images in the *desfile folklórico* are called parades brings them into meaningful contrast with military parades is to make, in its way, a historical statement about the interaction of varieties of contemporary experiences. It is to say that a part of the meaning of the *desfile folklórico* derives from its play on the resonance, in the minds of the participants, with the military parade.[7] Indeed, the use of the term *desfile* for this folklore procession is very much a twentieth-century usage, one of the authoritarian era dating from the 1920s dictatorship of Primo de Rivera and confirmed in the unilateral encouragement of folklore by the Franco regime.[8]

But there is another term in the phrase which has historical dimension—and that is the term "folklore." This is, as is well known, a nine-teenth-century term invented to conceptualize popular culture at a time when nation building and centralization of administration acted to pe-ripheralize local popular culture. This centralization both threatened popular culture and, as well, created an awareness of it by contrast to emerging national culture. Involved, then, in the contrast between the *desfile folklórico* and the *desfile militar* is also the contrast between local provincial culture and national culture. This contrast in levels of cultural allegiance contained in the term *desfile folklórico* itself is actually seen in the rows of small paper flags hanging above the parade route. The blue and white provincial flag hangs side by side with the red and yellow national flag.

A folklore procession is, by definition, a show of local culture and a manifestation of local identity, just as a military parade is a parade of national culture and national identity (in Spain, for many decades it was a parade by a nationalist party dominated by the military). The military parade is a parade of the "instruments of violence" of which the nation-state enjoys sole possession and legitimate use (Weber 1958), just as a folklore parade is a parade of the instruments of conviviality. Weber asks in his discussion of the state, defined as a relation of men dominating men supported by the means of legitimate violence, "If the state is to exist the dominated must obey the authority claimed by the powers that be. When and why do men obey? Upon what inner justification and upon what external means does this domination rest?" (1958: 79).[9] The use of the military parade is one of these means. The question of inner justification, a propos, is a more subtle question and one more Durkheimian than Weberian in import. It is a question that mainly concerns us here.

The *desfile folklórico* appears very much, then, in the historical context of "nationalist centralization" and provincial peripheralization—in the context of the creation of national culture. It stands as a playful coun-terstatement to these historical developments. If we ask, rephrasing Weber, What inner justification does it have? Toward what end is it directed? the obvious answer is that its inner justification lies in its resistance to domination by the center and in its reestablishment of the claims of local culture. But in this parade the answer is more complicated. For not only does it, on the one hand, stand as a counterstatement to the nationalization of culture in favor of provincial and local culture, but on the other hand, it stands as a counterstatement to both local and national culture in favor of international culture.

Crowd Formation

If there is an international counterstatement in this kayak festival and race it is in part because the composition of the crowd is international. Although the actual number of foreigners present in the various phases is never above 3000 to 5000, or 5 percent of the total,[10] they give a flavor to the crowd, constrain the representations presented to it, and are thus inescapably a part of its thinking about itself. We might call this crowd "postindustrial," keeping in mind Rude's (1981: chapter 4) distinction between preindustrial and industrial crowds. It is certainly not simply a preindustrial crowd—a crowd such as the "menu people" who participated in the French Revolution: tenant farmers, rural smallholders, landless laborers, rural and urban craftsmen and journeymen, small shopkeepers, peddlers, artisans, students, clerks, and servants. Nor is it a proletarian industrial crowd of factory or mine workers more or less of the locality where they gather. The Arriondas-Ribadesella crowd is international and postindustrial. It is a crowd that gathers very much as the consequence of mass transportation and relaxed provincial and national frontiers. It is a crowd made possible by trains, motorcars, automobiles, and even airplanes. Only because of such modernity could this diverse multitude congregate in these small provincial towns whose resources are greatly taxed by their presence. Even though many of the images out of which the *desfile folklórico* is composed are found in carnival processions of earlier centuries—the Giants and the Bigheads, for example, or the obstreperous young people armed with plastic billy clubs (formerly, inflated pig bladders), or the floats representing diverse topical tableaux— the sheer numbers who participate in and observe these proceedings and performances are very much a twentieth-century phenomenon, and in Spain a late twentieth-century one at that. A law of large numbers and a law of diversity in large numbers rule in this *desfile* that did not rule in the genres of street life antecedent to it.

If we look at the composition of the crowd in local, provincial and extraprovincial terms, some distinctions are in order. There are, for example, elements of all three crowds present. There are rural smallholders, clerks, servants, craftsmen, small shopkeepers, and beggars. Because of the relatively high wages of Asturian miners and metalworkers and their relative prosperity of the late 1970s, many of these people are present with their cars and their families. Particularly in evidence are those individuals associated with the various kayak clubs from industrial cities such as Aviles or Sama de Langreo, which are working class in origin. We also see many of the middle classes: bureaucrats, owners of small businesses, businessmen, and professional people such as doctors and lawyers. In short, it is a crowd of great diversity. It is true, withal, that it is predominantly a "young peoples" crowd, the average age of the participants being not over 30. There are, above all, many students of *instituto* and university age, perhaps 50 percent.

Because of the history of class conflict in Asturias, something more should be said about the presence of the class dynamic in the crowd and at the parade. The early industrialization of Asturias, by Spanish standards, led to the formation of a working class of miners and metalworkers who periodically gathered in disgruntled crowds. This was a phenomenon of the late nineteenth century onward, and it is a constant preoccupation to authorities whether of the right or the left. Indeed, such preoccupation has a basis in fact, for the miners' revolution of October 1934—the first Socialist revolution in Spain—virtually rose out of the decision of a crowd of long-disgruntled miners gathered to protest working conditions and salaries, to march on the provincial capital of Oviedo, and to take over the government.[11] This uprising was suppressed bloodily by the military. Throughout the Franco years, particularly in the last two decades of the regime, miners gathered in large crowds, seemingly spontaneously, to protest work conditions and wages and to mark the deaths of fellow miners in mine accidents. These disgruntled gatherings of the working classes were a significant worry to the Franco regime, particularly because of the infiltration in the last decades of the regime of socialist and communist organizers from France. As a consequence, there were as many constraints on public events and as heavy a presence of the "forces of order" in whatever gathering in Asturias as in any province.

In the democratic period, crowd events were no longer under authoritarian constraints and the "forces of order" kept a low profile. Their manifest presence, their silent bodying forth of the potential of state-legitimated violence, was a technique of control of the authoritarian government hardly compatible with democratic aspirations and rhetoric. Nevertheless, on the side streets in Arriondas, in national police and civil guard vans, they were waiting for any spontaneous disorder or unruliness in the crowd that might be a threat to property, to the orderliness of civic life, or to provincial or state institutions.

Gilmore (1975), in an article on the contribution to working-class unity made by pre-Lenten Carneval in a *campiña* agro-town of southern Spain

(Andalusia), shows that the main participants are lower-class agricultural laborers *(jornaleros)* or smallholders. The ritualized intraclass aggressions that take place in Andalusia Carneval—present to a mild extent in the *desfile folklórico*—serve cathartically to bind these lower classes more tightly together against the upper classes *(señoritos)*, who in any event absent themselves from Carneval lest they be the direct objects of aggression. Their absence confirms both the class system and Carneval as a lower-class festival. Similarly, the wealthy class in the Asturian towns of Arriondas and Ribadesella do not participate directly in the *desfile* or mingle with the crowd, although they do observe the race and attend the *romería* picnic down at the sea. There are nonetheless some important differences between the class system of southern Spain, with its privileged elite of large landowners contrasting with a large class of landless laborers, and the class system of northern Spain and particularly of Asturias. In Asturias we find, as a context of a festival of this kind, a "minifundia" system whereby practically all countrymen are landholders. The very large landholders—the Asturian "aristocracy," based mostly on bought titles of the late nineteenth century—have their holdings in very dispersed parcels. These large landholders, perhaps several dozen in the province, live in the capital city or in Madrid and are hardly known locally except through their administrators *(mayordomos)*. Class antagonism based on very marked differences in landholding is thus neither a significant provincial dynamic nor an Asturian town dynamic in the twentieth century.

The predominant dynamic of class is that between the mining and metallurgy working classes, on the one hand, and the mine and factory owners and managers, and the administrators, managerial staff, and bureaucrats in their service, on the other. This dynamic, which was at the base of much crowd disgruntlement in the late nineteenth and early twentieth centuries, was considerably transformed during the Franco years by the nationalization of most of the mines and factories. The antagonism was thus directed away from local or provincial personages— known representatives of their class—toward the national corporate state. In recent years, the "multinational manipulators" of the Spanish middle class and its corporations have become one of the main objects of antagonism. In the 1982 parade this antagonism was jocularly represented in the personages of the black-suited, black-hatted capitalists *(los multinacionalistas)* who danced around scattering handfuls of thousand-dollar "bills." This was the only representation, frivolous to be sure, of class antagonism in the parade. There was, in short, little land-based local class antagonism to begin with, and the composition of the parade was otherwise too diverse to admit a generalized middle-class proletarian antagonism. The parade was understood as an Asturian parade—and more than that, as an international parade.

Given the diversity and size of the crowd, questions arise as to the dynamics of crowd formation, the way that, to use the vocabulary of the theory of collective behavior (Milgram and Toch 1969), an unformed aggregate of individuals and small family units is formed into a crowd defined as a collective phenomenon oriented around joint stimuli and whose members respond to each other in an interactive way.

As the theory of crowd dynamics well recognizes, the convergence of such numbers of diverse outsiders, many with different languages, creates a special turbulence and poses a special difficulty for crowd formation. In the "foregathering phase" there is much milling about in the streets, with small knots of people in multiple foci ringed about many different points of attraction. The parade provides the first joint stimulus for this entire collectivity, although there are still many people confined to the side streets who are unable to watch and to participate in the performance, and there are many others who prefer to assure their viewing position for the start of the race at the riverside. The parade is thus essential to the dynamic of crowd formation in that it provides a common stimulus that the crowd can observe and with which its members can interact. Even more fundamental to crowd formation, however, is the race itself, the central common stimulus of the day, even though the nature of the race over so many downriver miles puts the crowd through a strenuous pell-mell experience of accompaniment. When the crowd gathers again in the seaside port town of Ribadesella, they have all had not only their experience of trying to keep up with the race but their common interest and commentary about the conduct of the race and the winners. This "forms" the crowd in a way that carries over into the *romerías*. It persists in the "aftergathering" in which, once again, the former crowd begins to disperse into small groups milling about scattered points of attraction, finally returning to an aggregate of individuals and family and friendship groups beginning to think about their departure.

Commanding Images and the Elementary Play of Tropes

In one of the most systematic, and in that sense satisfying, theories of collective behavior, Smelser (1963) introduces what is in my view the

unsatisfactory notion of "generalized belief"—the set of ideas or ide-
ologies that emerge (and, indeed, must emerge for proper crowd "formation") to define the crowd's objectives. Assuming we know what belief
means, Smelser's notion is unsatisfactory because it overestimates the
consensual situation prevailing in the crowd at the cultural level of belief
(see Fernandez 1965). It thus ignores the diversity of "faces in the crowd"
that emerges even to historians working only with documents when they
inquire into crowd composition and crowd belief (Rude 1981:chapter 5).
Not only do the subtleties of consensus pose a challenge to the notion of
"generalized belief," there is also the problem of the processes of collective mentation—the kind of information processing that goes on in the
crowd. It is my view, and here I am in agreement with Le Bon, that the
crowd's thinking mainly takes place through an "argument of images." The
set of images presented to all or most members of the crowd plays a
powerful role in the coalescence of these members and in the transformation in feeling, tone, and attitude set which they experience and which
have been widely observed in crowd activity.

Lang and Lang (1968:556) account for the rise of collective action on the
basis of a failure of commanding and centralizing images.

> Problematic situations [those that give rise to collective behavior] are defined
> here as those in which participants lack adequate guides to conduct. When-
> ever imagery that is conventionally accepted or officially sanctioned fails to
> take account of or runs counter to deeply felt sentiments or common percep-
> tions of reality people create currents of agitation by whose actions they are
> stirred from the planes along which they normally move and remain agitated
> until they settle back again into a pattern resistant to further change. What
> takes place during the interlude is *elementary* collective problem solving
> rather than structured social action.

It is just this elementary collective problem solving that is involved in the
argument of images.

Although I think the kayak festival crowd can be understood as undergoing "formation" in terms of image loss and image gain, the more obvious
case is the crowd of miners that forms in Asturian mining valleys the day
after an accidental death in the mines of one or more of their comrades.
Such a gathering is at the time of the funeral. The crowd mills about at
first in an agitated state, but it is quiet and not turbulent. The miners seek
to show their solidarity and fraternity with the lost miner(s). Usually,
funeral services are going on in the church for the families involved, but
the great majority of the miners gathered do not enter because they are
anti-clerical or irreligious and cannot satisfactorily coalesce around that set

of images. When the coffin exits from the church to be carried to the grave on the shoulders of fellow miners, then one can *feel* the coalescence of the crowd around these images of ultimate circumstances. The entire crowd becomes oriented around these images and, as one, follows these coffins to their grave. The coalescence of the crowd is such that this is an apt time for directed agitation and crowd organization—the lesson of Antony at Caesar's grave. The coffins, the yawning grave, and the burial are powerful images with which to make an argument.

There are no images in the kayak festival parade before us that are as compelling—as coalescing and authentic—as a comrade's coffin being borne along to the grave. The racers in their kayaks, paddling furiously as they are carried along to the sea, and the images of the funeral procession are similarly authentic; so, too, are the victors, raised on the shoulders of their comrades or stepping onto the awards platform as very live heroes, and the dead heroes of Asturian mining accidents, in coffins carried on their comrades' shoulders. But the intensity is much different.

Still, the emphasis here should rather be on the authenticity of these images and not on the intensity. Like religious icons, all these icons are authentic because, following the dictionary sense of the word, they are not open to challenge; they are worthy of acceptance because they are not contradicted by evidence; they conform to fact or reality. There is nothing playful or ironic in either the coffin or the kayak racer. No double vision is involved; no suspension of disbelief is required in observing or participating in these activities; no incongruity is being addressed. What the crowd sees is what it gets from life—what life is in the end all about: a matter of being dominated or subordinated, of winning or losing, of living or dying. Since what the crowd feels it is getting from life may be incongruous with its images of itself, these images of victory or defeat, life or death, can be used, if the crowd takes itself seriously, to animate it to excited collective behavior in favor of its perceived interests and desired images. Burial ceremonies are not the only occasions for motivating crowds. The results of athletic contests often lead to disgruntlement and destructive crowd action despite the supposedly playful character of the events. What started out as a statement, "This is play!" to recall Bateson again, is rapidly transformed because of the disagreeable consequences of the play into the statement, "This is not play!" because this is unfair and an affront to our dignity and images of ourself.

This disgruntled transformation of a playful crowd into an authentically destructive crowd has never happened in the Arriondas-Ribadesella kayak race. Playfulness is always maintained, and not just by the "forces of order." Among the most important reasons for this, I believe, is the ironic presentation of the Spanish and Asturian self that occurs in the parade. The parade takes mock arms against taking oneself and one's situation seriously. It makes a playful counterstatement to the "sincerities" of the military parade, though in no sense is it a direct mockery of those parades. It is a parade in which the citizens of Arriondas and all of Asturias, in contrast to the serious presentations of self by the citizens of Warner's Yankee City, tell themselves not what they are but, ironically, what they are supposed to be. The parade makes a playful counterstatement and takes an ironic attitude toward the serious pretensions of Asturian history.

With this point in mind, let us recall just how the parade does this. The historical tableaux and groups of historical personages, for example, all burlesque the ancestral Asturians: the grubby prehistoric aboriginals, the pretentious Visigoths, the subservient Romans, the shifty-eyed Moors. And bringing up the rear, after all of these playful images of self, come the Asturian giant couple, Pin and Tielva, with the frolicsome Bigheads at their knees. How should we interpret these most commanding images? If one thinks that these Giants, because of their towering size, are exalted and celebratory images of Asturian country identity, that they are icons to be taken as seriously, somehow, as the religious icons of patronal processions, then one overlooks the incongruities involved. Not only are their physiognomies virtually those of simpletons—representations writ very large of the well-known country bumpkin, the *tonto Asturiano*—but their swaying dance through the streets is more ungainly than stately. They are awkward giants—*gigantes torpes*. Periodically, their occasional mock embracing of each other, their stateliness subverted by public display of visceral impulse, is another incongruity. Altogether these Giants are anomalous and have to be read in ironic terms.

Brandes (1980) has given us a notable study of the Giants' and Bigheads' parades in Andalusia, analyzing the psychological seriousness underlying the playfulness. In the Andalusian parade the regal, stately Giants represent at once both parental figures and the upper classes dominant over the Bigheads, who represent at once impulsive children and the impulsive lower classes. The parade plays out and confirms both class and generational relations. The Asturian Giants and Bigheads, I believe, must be otherwise understood, for they are commanding images that playfully mock the image of Asturian traditional rural identity. The seriousness that underlies their playfulness is the seriousness of the Asturian self-image, undercut at once by its impulses (the Bigheads) and magnified and burlesqued. These final figures in the parade are symbolic types[12] in the sense that they stand for that traditional rurality that undergirds Asturian identity. They are allegorical types[13] in the sense that they play out the bumptiousness (or bumpkinness), the "mistakenness," that is implicit in this type.

If one is persuaded, as I think we must be, to read these folklore parade images in playful counterstatement to the solemn icons loftily displayed and carried along in religious processions, one must also recognize that these images have simply replaced carnival images in this function. In previous centuries, of course, it was the carnival processions that stood in contrast to religious processions, for the pieties and projections of sacred commitment and secular order bound up in religious processions found their meaningful counterstatement in carnival processions, with their impieties and representations of misrule and disorder. The folklore parade is a kind of carnival, then, freed from confinement to a single time of year—the pre-Lenten period. It is a carnival that contextualizes and to some degree undercuts the seriousness and authenticity of the ensuing competition.

Commanding Images and a Theory of Transcendent Humanization

We cannot pretend that all members of the festival crowd understand in the same way the images paraded before them in the *desfile folklórico*, or even that all members of the crowd can be present at the parade to understand it. What can be argued is that though these images are particularly Asturian or Spanish, there are enough elements in them of broader, even universal, communicability to make them comprehensible to extraprovincials and foreigners alike.[14] It can also be argued that the ironic overtone of the parade presentation is widely understood and is part of the uncertainty foreigners have about participation. And it is certainly arguable that the parade is instrumental in setting for Asturians a convivial tone to their festivities and in facilitating an inclusive rather than an exclusive and discriminating—and invidious—interaction in the crowd. This was done in 1982 by playfully bringing into ironic perspective the commanding images of the Asturian past and present.

At the risk of considerable simplification, it can be argued that crowd formation really has two fundamental dynamics: the achievement and celebration of exclusiveness, which is to say the crowd's employ of the classificatory and specifying impulse in human mental activity, and the celebration of inclusiveness, which is to say the employ of the collection-oriented (collectivist) and genericizing impulse distinctive in human mental activity.[15] In the former, wholes are discriminated into parts by attention to features; and in the latter, relational matters become dominant and parts are amalgamated into wholes. The latter is the best strategy for a truly convivial and noninvidious festival. One of the ways that it is accomplished is to take the various specifics of a whole identity—the Spanish-Asturian one, in this case—and present them ironically, suggesting another possible whole than the one that has been specified and on which irony has given us a new perspective. In the particular dynamics of the Asturian parade, it might be said that this new whole is given to us in those towering and hence truly commanding images, the giant Asturian couple, who follow after all else and, in a way, sum up all the ironic particularities that have gone before. But this "commanding" couple is presented in such a way as to undercut and mock itself. Pretending to overwhelm the spectator, they come to be seen for what they are: giants with feet of clay . . . that is, very human feet! They suggest an even more transcendent perspective, an ever larger, more human whole from which these successively larger ironic perspectives are taken. What I suggest here is the humanity of irony, or at least the humanity that lies in ironic detachment from the self—in reflexive irony, as it were. Of course, irony can be sharp, satirical, and disdainful. But the sense of incongruity in which irony reposes—the sense of human "mistakenness"—need not be invidious and painful.

There are many theories of Carneval and of the playful misrule and disorder that prevails in impious carnivallike processions—theories of catharsis, theories of class formation and political organization and protest, theories of psychic integration. But the theory I advance here is simply a theory of "transcendent humanization," an experience evoked by Carneval and surely present in the *desfile folklórico*. This theory rests on a theory of figurative predication of social identity, which argues simply that the inchoateness of the human condition requires that we recurrently escape literal-mindedness and, making use of the various rhetorical devices, recurrently predicate figurative identities upon ourselves. We inescapably turn to *tropes*. In these predications we significantly transform ourselves and escape the stultifying routinizations of our structured existence—in the modern world, our existence in the "iron cage" of organizational and bureaucratic responsibility. The point is that we recurrently transcend these routines and commitments and we do that in a variety of ways. We can exalt ourselves by practicing a kind of verticalism (to recall the shouts of the obstreperous individual); that is, we can separate ourselves out by various processes of competition and struggle and establish our primacy and uniqueness. We can become heroes or, failing that, we can celebrate heroes and identify with them (the transcendence taking place in the kayak race itself). Or, we can turn to the leveling, the horizontal, trope of irony and point up—celebrate, as it were—the incongruities and the recurrent "mistakenness" in the human situation, and in ourselves. Rather than taking the images of one's self and society seriously and trying to make such sober images stick both to self and to other, we can suspend belief in ourselves (I am more inclined to twist the Coleridgian phrase and say that we can finally and voluntarily accede to the gnawing disbelief in ourselves) and celebrate incongruities. We can recognize our "mistakes" for what they are—recurrent in the human condition. This accession is what the folklore parade is about—an ironic leveling of the pretentious images of the Asturian historic identity. And it is a leveling that, at the same time, suggests the potentiality for a greater festival inclusiveness.

Thus, this "irony" has important humanizing consequences for the continuing playfulness of this international kayak festival. Of course, one could argue as a general principle that in the human equation it is easier for unknowns or casual acquaintances to relate to each other in a relaxed way when they show that they are not taking themselves too seriously, when they are not pretending to their virtues but recognizing their foibles and their vices, when they are displaying the contrarieties of their humanity. This recognition sets the tone for their carnival interaction and is certainly the consequence of the *desfile folklórico* of Arriondas.

I further argue that a theory of play necessarily involves a theory of transcendent humanization. Such an argument is lodged in a theory of tropes. It is not enough to identify simply the "this is play" frame and to say that it is recurrent in human and protohuman activity. It is important to recognize that play is a predication of nonliteral, or inauthentic, identities on the players, and in that sense play is always a play of tropes. (Of course, that play may suddenly be taken quite seriously and literally, and thus transform the play frame.) To really understand play we must understand the play of tropes and the transcendence involved in that play.

The trope that interests us here is irony—the ultimate trope, really—

which emerges from the recognition of the dramatic incongruities in the human situation. To point out these incongruities by ironic commentary is to suggest their transcendence, to suggest the passing beyond the necessarily pretentious claims of our roles in particular social organizations and institutions.[16] A truly persistent playful and joyful festival, one must argue, will be based on a vision of our ultimate humanness in this sense. The *desfile folklórico* helps very much to achieve this for the kayak festival of the two towns and a river. In doing so, in creating reflexive images of incongruity in which the crowd can find some unpretentious bemusement, the *desfile folklórico* creates a relaxed atmosphere of celebration that will withstand the competitive pressures exerted on both racers and the hurrying spectators by the race itself and its necessarily hierarchical, zero-sum result. The ironic comments with which I began, then, set a certain playful tone for the festival as a horizontal celebration of common humanity. And it is a celebration of that humanity which makes a convivial collection of Le Bon's (1920) two great European classes of human (Anglo-Saxon and Latin) "races."

It is true that I use a very broad definition of irony here. I want to resist such narrow definitions as superciliousness, invidiousness, disdainfulness, with which we often associate ironic attitudes, because I want to see irony for what it essentially is: one of the tropes. That is, one of the devices we have for dealing with the perception of differences and of incongruity— one of the devices other than the ordinary logical devices of conceptualization. In truth, the kind of self-conscious reflexive irony before us is generally felt to be a modern attitude. Recall that Nietzsche, who blamed irony on Plato and the Platonic sense of the incongruity between the ephemera of everyday experience and the reality of the pure and enduring forms, felt irony to be, like romanticism, a pusillanimous attitude. He had in mind the idealism and informed irony of liberal humanism. He wished to eradicate such attitudes in favor of robust comedy and heroic tragedy.

Nietzsche's alternating "frolicking in the images of comedy and tragedy" may have been appealing in the late and sedate nineteenth century. But in this twentieth century of total war, and particularly of the Spanish Civil War and the subsequent "heroic crusade" rhetoric of Francoism, it is hard to conceive of a comedy that could possibly alternate with such manifest tragedy. We are forced back, as I think these Asturian townsmen and countrymen are, to the ironic awareness, the quixotic awareness, of the differences between what men and women—at least Iberian men and women—are and what they pretend to be. I see nothing pusillanimous in such recognition. I see, and I think this is what the folklore parade shows us, the basis for transcendent humanization.

This parade is essentially to be situated in Asturian and Spanish history and suggests, to recall Kenneth Burke (1937), a humanizing set of attitudes toward that history. But in its implicit ironic comment on military parades, on the one hand, and on "international competition," on the other, it also situates itself in world history. Indeed, it situates itself in the most contemporary world history struggling to find terms of order for the mischievousness of competition and for the burdensome threat of self-willed tools of destruction. This parade suggests an appropriate framework for both the acceptance of that history in its long-term engagements and a rejection of that history in its short-term hysterias.

Notes

Acknowledgments. The ethnography on which this paper is based was undertaken as part of the Princeton University-University of Madrid Anthropology Project supported by the Spanish-North American Joint Committee. I am indebted to the committee for their support. I thank my colleagues at the 1983 AES Symposium on "Text, Play, and Story," and particularly Alton Becker, Edward M. Bruner, Roberto DaMatta, Bruce Kapferer, Smadar Lavie, and Emiko Ohnuki-Tierney. David Kertzer has asked good questions about the context and content of the kayak festival, not all of which I have been able to answer here. Celina Canteli de Pando provided valuable supplementary ethnographic information, and Honorio Valesco Maillo commented on the *desfile folklórico* from the vantage point of his wide knowledge of Spanish folklore. I am grateful to the Center for Advanced Study in Behavioral Sciences for its facilities and support during my fellowship year, 1982–83.

1. I have attended this kayak festival for a number of years. It is one of the best known of the summer fiestas in Asturias. There is considerable variation in the content of the *desfile folklórico* from year to year, although the generally playful tone is constant. The phases of the festival remain the same also.

2. The literature on this topic is extensive, but see the pioneering piece by Natalie Z. Davis (1971).

3. The race was first organized in 1930 by Dionesio de la Huerta of the further upriver town of Infiesto. He still holds honorary leadership of the event. Before and after the Spanish Civil War, the race was a competition between towns in Asturias and did not become truly international until the late 1950s.

4. The parade is organized in only a very general way by a committee composed of the two mayors of Arriondas and Ribadesella and their assistants, and by representatives of the national and provincial kayak federations.

5. This is the recently discovered cave of Tito Bustillo.

6. On this Saturday in 1982 the two-man kayak team (K2) winners, a Basque team, paddled the course in 1 hour, 11 minutes, 30 seconds. The record (set in

1980) is held by the Spanish Olympic team of Misione (Galicia) and Menendez (Asturias) in 1 hour, 10 minutes, 47 seconds. In 1982 the first foreign team, from Portugal, placed seventh. Generally, over the years, the North Europeans have done much better, and particularly the English, Danes, and Dutch have been frequent winners. The American Olympic team did much better in 1982 women's and K1 events.

7. The resonant interaction of carnival and military parades as two kinds of national ritual that compose a total ritual statement in Latin cultures has been examined by Roberto DaMatta (1978).

8. It is well known that authoritarian regimes make use of "folklore" to celebrate national identities, on the one hand, and to allow for the relatively innocuous expression of regional identities, on the other. The term *desfile* in relation to folklore, besides being a 20th-century usage, has in other parts of Spain mainly been used for brotherhood and religious society *(cofradia)* parades, for parades made up of floats (a basic meaning in Asturias), for parades of masked personages representing various stereotyped groups, and for parades of ethnic celebration such as the Moros and Cristianos parades (Honorio Velasco, personal communication). In other words, the term seems to be used where nonreligious or quasi-religious solidarity groups are involved (sodalities).

9. Weber (1958:79) defines the state: "We have to say that a state is a human commodity that (successfully) claims the monopoly of the legitimate use of physical force within a given territory. The state is considered the sole source of the right to use violence."

10. Foreign participation in the canoe race itself was much higher: 20 percent of the total, or about 200 kayakers.

11. As Shubert (1982) points out, there were long-standing reasons for the deep mistrust of the Asturian miners by both the Republican government and their own mine unions. Still, the uprising was unpredictable and spontaneous and not desired by the union structure itself.

12. This is a term introduced into the literature by Handelman and Kapferer (1980) to focus our attention on the social tendency to concentrate norms in selected personae.

13. This is a term introduced by Smadar Lavie (1983) to capture those standardized melodramatic events in a culture, in which symbolic types may well participate to be sure, that communicate a "metamessage" about the general social structure and essential norms.

14. Needham (1978) has recently advanced an archetypal theory of images in behavior in which he identifies the various elements that, for example, go into the making of the image of the witch. These elements, if not universal, are found in many cultures but are synthesized in particular cultures in particular ways. Not all the elements are synthesized in any one culture at any one time, but enough elements are present to enable cross-cultural understanding.

15. In previous work (Chapter 2.) I analyze the play of tropes in terms of the interplay (transformative predication) of metaphor and metonym in relation to inchoate social subjects. Leach (1976) should be consulted for a statement—curiously ironic—of the logic of this interplay. Always involved in this interplay are the two logics of classification and collection. The trope of irony points us more to this underlying logic than do discussions of metaphors and metonyms, and that is why this logic is featured here. See Markman (1981) for a psychologist's summary of this classification-collection interplay in children's concept information.

16. It is Victor Turner's (1969) work on *communitas* that constitutes the basic statement in anthropology on the periodic—liminal—escape in human experience from the constraints, separations, and distantiations of normative social structure. The emphasis here is on seeing that process in terms of the logical transcendence of categories and not of the collapse of categories.

References

BATESON, G.
  1974   A Theory of Play and Fantasy. *In* Steps to an Ecology of Mind, pp. 177–193. San Francisco: Chandler.
BRANDES, S.
  1980   Giants and Big-Heads. *In* Metaphors of Masculinity, pp. 17–36. Philadelphia: University of Pennsylvania Press.
BURKE, KENNETH
  1937   Attitudes towards History. New York: The New Republic.
DAMATTA, R.
  1978   Constraint and License: A Preliminary Study of Two Brazilian National Rituals. *In* Secular Ritual. S. F. Moore and B. Myerhoff, eds. pp. 244–264. Ithaca: Cornell University Press.
DAVIS, NATALIE Z.
  1971   The Reasons of Misrule: Youth Groups and Charivaris in Sixteenth Century France. Past and Present 50:41–75.
DURKHEIM, E.
  1965   The Elementary Forms of the Religious Life. New York: Collier.
FERNANDEZ, J. W.
  1965   Symbolic Consensus in a Fang Reformative Cult. American Anthropologist 67:902–927.
FERNANDEZ, J. W., and R. L. FERNANDEZ
  1976   El Escenario de la Romería Asturiana. *In* Expresiones Actuales de la Cultura del Pueblo. C. Lison, ed. pp. 230–261. Madrid.
GILMORE, D. D.
  1975   "Carneval" in Fuenmayer: Class Conflict and Social Cohesion in an Andalusian Town. Journal of Anthropological Research 31:331–349.
HANDLEMAN, DON, and BRUCE KAPFERER
  1980   Symbolic Types, Mediation and the Transformation of Ritual Context: Sinhalese Demons and Tewa Clowns. Semiotica 30 (½): 41–71.
ILLICH, IVAN
  1975   Tools of Conviviality. New York: Macmillan.
LANG, KURT, and GLADYS ENGEL LANG
  1968   Collective Behavior. *In* The Encyclopedia of the Social Sciences, Vol. 3. David Sills, ed. pp. 556–564.
LAVIE, SMADAR
  1983   "The Madwoman": Spontaneous Theater and Social Inconsistencies among the Mzeina Bedouin of the Sinai. Ms. Files of the author.
LEACH, E.
  1976   Culture and Communication: The Logic by Which Symbols Are Connected. New York: Cambridge University Press.

LE BON, GUSTAVE
  1920
  [1895] The Crowd: A Study of the Popular Mind. New York.
MARKMAN, E.
  1981 Two Different Principles of Conceptual Organization. *In* Advances in Developmental Psychology, Vol. 1. Michael E. Lamb and Ann L. Brown, eds. pp. 199–235. Hillsdale, N.J.: L. Erlbaum.
MILGRAM, S. and H. TOCH
  1969 Collective Behavior: Crowds and Social Movements. *In* The Handbook of Social Psychology, Vol. 4. Gardner Lindzey and Elliot Aronson, eds., pp. 507–610. Reading, PA: Addison Wesley.
NEEDHAM, R.
  1978 Primordial Characters. Charlottesville: University of Virginia Press.
NYE, R.
  1975 The Origins of Crowd Psychology: Gustave Le Bon and the Crisis of Mass Democracy in the Third Republic. New York: Sage.
RUDE, GEORGE
  1981 The Crowd in History: 1730–1848. London: Lawrence and Wishout.
SHUBERT, A.
  1982 Revolution in Self-Defense: The Radicalization of the Asturian Coal-Miners, 1921–34. Social History 7(3):265–282.
SMELSER, NEIL J.
  1963 Theory of Collective Behavior. New York: Free Press.
TURNER, VICTOR
  1969 The Ritual Process. Chicago: Aldine.
WARNER, W. L.
  1961 The Protestants Legitimate Their Past. *In* The Family of God. pp. 89–154. New Haven: Yale University Press.
WEBER, MAX
  1958 Politics as a Vocation. *In* From Max Weber: Essays in Sociology. H. Gerth and C. Wright Mills, eds. pp. 77–128. New York: Oxford University Press.

INDEX

abstract categories, 47
acculturation, 24
adaptation, 209
"affecting presence," 8
"alienation," language of, 151
allegorical types, 288
Alverson, H., 66
ambiguity, 15, 78, 83, 152, 189–90, 221–22, 224, 235, 244; centrality of, 222, 236; dimension of, 78
ambiguity, evocative, 76
analogy, 7, 177, 183; argument by, 251; energizing of, 232
analysis: narrative-oriented, 202
analytic capacities, 189
animal: as mirrors, 165; domains of, 92; games, 32, 34; human attributes of, 32–33; metaphor, 34; play, 34; predicates, 32; master of, 35
aptness, 19, 22, 58, 132, 135, 141, 267–68; as corporeal quality, 135; in metaphor, 19, 130; in metaphors of analysis, 137; in speech contexts, 141; of association, 116
aptness of association, 117, 119
archetype, 231
argument, ix, xi; expanded, xi; figurative, x; formal, x–xi; imagistic, xv
argument of images, 152, 192, 201, 207, 232, 235, 244, 249, 253, 285
Aristotelian formula, 183
Aristotle, xi
Armstrong, R. P., xvi, 28
arousal, 162, 211; in ritual, 59; two kinds of, 248–49
Asch, S. E., 6
association, 54, 116, 124; aptness of, 116–20; between mining and sexuality, 121; between place and person, 113; by contiguity, 43; by similarity, 43; dominant, 50; interplay of, 44; latent factors involved in, 5; metonymic, 91; of womenfolk with locality, 115; principles of, 52; problem of,

54; role of mediation in, 5; sentiments of, 118; sexual, 118; similarity and contiguity by, 126; structure of, 60; syntagmatic and paradigmatic, 44; synthetic, 52; systems of, 52
associational processes, 31
associationist theory, 44
Asturian: deepsong, 90, 103, 114; language, 131; lexicon, 132
attitudes toward history, 278
Avello, M., 156

Babcock, B., 168
Basso, K., xvi, 101, 178
Bateson, G., 191, 277
Beidelman, T. O., xvi
"being there," xi–xii
Benedict, R., xv, 164
Bernstein, B., 109
bilateral symmetry, principle of, 162
"bilectualism," 146–47
biological axiology, 242
Bird, C. and B., 211
Black, M., 29
Blanco, J., 155
Boas, F., ix, 28, 32
body image, 75
Boulding, K., 60
boundaries, maintenance of, 149
Bruner, E. M., 292
Burke, K., xv, 8, 29, 229
Bwiti, 17, 18, 179

Cabezas, J., 122
Campbell, D., 174, 186
Canteli de Pando, C., 292
Cantril, H., 224
Cassirer, C., 245
Cassirer, E., 189, 190, 192
Catedra, M., 100
categorical imperative, 259
categorical thinking, commitment to, 257

296

JAMES W. FERNANDEZ is Professor of Anthropology at the University of Chicago
and former Chairman of Anthropology at Princeton University. His book *Bwiti: An
Ethnography of the Religious Imagination in Africa* won the Herskovits Award of
the African Studies Association in 1982.